MEANING AND CONTEXT IN
THE THANKSGIVING HYMNS

Society of Biblical Literature

Early Judaism and Its Literature

Rodney A. Werline, Editor

Number 42

MEANING AND CONTEXT IN
THE THANKSGIVING HYMNS

LINGUISTIC AND RHETORICAL PERSPECTIVES
ON A COLLECTION OF PRAYERS FROM QUMRAN

by

Trine B. Hasselbalch

SBL Press

Atlanta

Copyright © 2015 by SBL Press

Library of Congress Cataloging-in-Publication Data

Hasselbalch, Trine, author.
    Meaning and context in the thanksgiving hymns : linguistic and rhetorical perspec-
tives on a collection of prayers from Qumran / Trine Bjørnung Hasselbalch.
        p. cm. — (Society of Biblical Literature. Early Judaism and its literature ; 42)
    Includes bibliographical references and index.
    Summary: "This book challenges the consensus that the Hodayot consist of leader
hymns and community hymns respectively, and it breaks with the habit of interpreting each hymn as expressing basically either leadership issues or ordinary community
member issues. Instead it argues that all of the compositions in 1QHodayot^a were
perceived by their owners to express the sentiments of a worshiping community at
large, and that the members of this community saw themselves as holding a mediating
position in the agency of God. This way, the Hodayot express a theology according
to which God acts in the world through the members of this particular community,
and the collection of 1QHodayot^a seems to reflect an emergent socio-religious pattern which is different from that of the book of Psalms. The book engages in an array
of methods, most prominently from the field of sociolinguistics, in an attempt to find
more sophisticated ways to approach the relationship between the Dead Sea scrolls,
in this case the Hodayot, and their socio-historical contexts"— Provided by publisher
    ISBN 978-1-62837-054-6 (paper binding : alk. paper) — ISBN 978-1-62837-055-3
(electronic format) — ISBN 978-1-62837-056-0 (hardcover binding : alk. paper)
    1. Thanksgiving Psalms. 2. Hymns, Hebrew—History and criticism. 3. Dead Sea
scrolls. 4. Qumran community. I. Title.
    BM488.T5H38 2015
    296.1'55—dc23   2014036282

Printed on acid-free, recycled paper conforming to
ANSI/NISO Z39.48-1992 (R1997) and ISO 9706:1994
standards for paper permanence.

For Jan, Liva, and Sara

CONTENTS

Acknowledgments

This book is the revised version of my 2011 Ph.D. thesis from the University of Copenhagen. I want to thank a number of people and organizations that over the years have contributed to its completion. First of all, I want to express my gratitude to my supervisor Bodil Ejrnæs, who eagerly encouraged me to go ahead and apply for a Ph.D. scholarship in the first place. Second, thanks to the Faculty of Theology at the University of Copenhagen for giving me the opportunity to get started. Apart from Bodil, I have had the pleasure of being supervised by Jesper Høgenhaven and Niels Peter Lemche in Copenhagen. Each in their own way, they have guided me well at different points in the process of the Ph.D. work.

I had the opportunity to spend a semester in Manchester and enjoy fruitful master classes and discussions with George Brooke. The project took a decisive turn during this stay, and I am much obliged to George Brooke for this, and also to Todd Klutz, who introduced me to sociolinguistics. The visit to Manchester would not have been possible without generous grants from the following institutions: the Carlsberg Foundation, the Oticon Foundation, Julie von Müllen's memorial trust, Johannes Pedersen's memorial trust, the University of Copenhagen Fund for Theological Students and Graduates, and Nørregaard's Travel Fellowship.

On my Ph.D. committee were Eibert Tigchelaar (Leuven), Jutta Jokiranta (Helsinki), and Søren Holst (Copenhagen). I want to thank them for meticulously reading and commenting on my thesis and thus getting me a decisive step further. I want to thank Judith Newman, the now former editor of this series, for accepting my manuscript for peer review. Warm thanks go to the two peers who anonymously worked their way through the manuscript and gave me some very encouraging and valuable advice. Finally, I am grateful for the patience of my editor, Rodney Werline, and for all that he has done to enhance my work. Birthe Hasselbalch has done a great job revising the English, and any English problems left at this point are completely my own responsibility.

Many people have enriched my working process—and my life—during the years of work. Some are people that I know well, whereas others were inspiring, albeit brief, acquaintances. I am grateful for all of them, but will mention only a few, such as my colleagues at the Department for Biblical Exegesis in Copenhagen, whose company I have much enjoyed through the years. Very special thanks go to Pernille Carstens and my colleagues at the Centre for Bible and Cultural Memory: they were wonderfully supportive, and the Centre has provided the best conceivable environment for my work. I also want to thank everyone engaged in the Nordic Network in Qumran Studies; this fellowship, too, has been immensely valuable, as I trust it will be in the future.

I warmly thank my parents, Tor and Anne Bjørnung, for their enduring support and encouragement. Finally, my husband, Jan Hasselbalch, has my endless gratitude for his unfailing support and for his unbelievable patience from the very beginning to the very end.

Abbreviations

ASOR	American Schools of Oriental Research
BA	*Biblical Archaeologist*
BASOR	*Bulletin of the American Schools of Oriental Research*
CTJ	*Calvin Theological Journal*
DJD	Discoveries in the Judaean Desert
DSD	*Dead Sea Discoveries*
DSSR	*The Dead Sea Scrolls Reader*. Edited by D. W. Parry and E. Tov. Leiden: Brill, 2004–2005.
DSSSE	*Dead Sea Scrolls: Study Edition*. Edited by F. García Martínez and E. J. C. Tigchelaar. Leiden: Brill, 1997–1998.
DTT	*Dansk teologisk tidsskrift*
ETL	*Ephemerides theologicae lovanienses*
JBL	*Journal of Biblical Literature*
JJS	*Journal of Jewish Studies*
JNSL	*Journal of Northwest Semitic Languages*
JQR	*Jewish Quarterly Review*
JSOT	*Journal for the Study of the Old Testament*
JSP	*Journal for the Study of the Pseudepigrapha*
HS	*Hebrew Studies*
HTR	*Harvard Theological Review*
NovT	*Novum Testamentum*
RB	*Revue biblique*
RevQ	*Revue de Qumran*
SBFLA	*Studii biblici Franciscani liber annus*
ZAW	*Zeitschrift für die alttestamentliche Wissenschaft*

1
Introduction

It can be tempting for a Dead Sea Scrolls scholar working on ancient texts on the basis of damaged manuscripts to complain about the missing parts and think it is they that prevent her from fully understanding a text. It is tempting to surmise things about the contents of a missing line, thinking it might be the clue to wonderful new insights, and it is frustrating not to know for sure. One is aware that something is missing and cautious not to ignore this.

However, it is not only in the handling of material that caution is called for. Also when everything originally written in a manuscript is still in its place, the text carries knowledge that is not explicitly stated. This has to do with how texts are related to their literary, physical, situational, social and cultural environments, both at the time of composition and in later usage. The issue is how texts do, or do not, express a number of contextual factors. It is most pertinent to Dead Sea Scrolls studies since so many efforts have been made to read the Dead Sea Scrolls as sources to the life and history of the Dead Sea community. Yet, the theoretical and methodological assumptions behind scholarly identifications of sociohistorical contextual factors are often implicit and unclear. For obvious reasons, we are less aware of that which is simply not stated than of clearly missing bits of parchments, letters and words in a manuscript.

This fundamental problem underlies the present work on 1QHodayot[a], a collection of prayer texts from Qumran. Greater attention to this general problem in close textual analyses may lead to conclusions about this prayer collection's place in the life of the Dead Sea community, indeed about the community itself and its theology, that differ significantly from most current interpretations. The aim is not to prove earlier interpretations wrong, or to prove this particular interpretation correct. Rather, by applying theories that properly address the relationship between discourse

and context I want to show that alternative readings are viable. Others will
have to judge if these readings are also preferable, and I hope this book can
contribute to reconsiderations of the methods used in linguistic and literary analyses of the Dead Sea Scrolls.

1.1. The Composite Nature of 1QHodayot[a]

1QHodayot[a] is a collection of thanksgiving hymns or prayers. The collection belongs with a group of documents designated Hodayot, literally
"thanksgivings," due to the reiterated formula, "I thank you, Lord," at the
beginning of several compositions. Sukenik introduced this designation
in the very first edition of the text in 1948, and it has continued to be used
ever since. [1] 1QHodayot[a] was found as early as 1947 in the first cave of
Dead Sea Scrolls discovered near Khirbet Qumran. From an early point
of research the scrolls were thought to belong to a religious community
settled there, and because 1QHodayot[a] was among the first manuscript
findings, it has had its share of influence on how we perceive the historical
and social realities behind the production of the Dead Sea Scrolls. It has
been pointed out by Moshe Bernstein that 1QHodayot[a] and other large
documents found at an early stage in the scholarly history of the Dead Sea
Scrolls have exerted an unduly large influence on our understanding of
the Dead Sea community simply because the rich and variegated Cave 4
materials were found and published much later.[2]

---

1. 1QHodayot[a] consists of nineteen to twenty-four thanksgiving hymns distributed on twenty-eight columns of text. The *editio princeps* is Eleazar Sukenik, *The
Dead Sea Scrolls of the Hebrew University* (1955), which was published in Hebrew
(אוצר המגילות הגנוזות שבידי האוניברסיטה העברית) in 1954. Smaller parts of
the scroll were published in his מגילות גנוזות. מתוך גניזה שנמצאה במדבר יהודה
in 1948 and (with a few more comments on the contents) in 1950. A new edition
by Eileen Schuller and Hartmut Stegemann has been published quite recently:
Qumran Cave 1.III: 1QHodayot[a] with Incorporation of 1QHodayot[b] and 4QHodayot[a–f]
(DJD XL). Stegemann, who had spent years improving Sukenik's reconstruction,
passed away, and Schuller completed the work. Smaller and generally more damaged
Hodayot documents have been found—1QH[b] (1Q35); 4QH[a–f] (4Q427–4Q432). Different orders of hymns are seen in them. I use the designation Hodayot when speaking of 1QHodayot[a], which is the object of analysis here, as well as of all the texts considered to be of the same genre.
2. Bernstein, "Introductory Formulas," 30. See also Schuller, "Prayer, Hymnic,
and Liturgical Texts," 155.

On the other hand, our notions about the Dead Sea community have also left their stamp on our interpretations of this collection of hymns, and I believe they have to some extent been influenced by dubious scholarly images of the underlying social reality. To be more precise, according to general consensus the compositions are divided into two main categories: "teacher hymns" or "leader hymns" on the one hand, and "community hymns" on the other. In 1960, Günter Morawe and Svend Holm-Nielsen both published dissertations in which, independently of each other, they divided the collection into two main types of compositions. Morawe distinguished one group, which he named thanksgiving songs (*Danklieder*), from the remainder, called hymnic songs of confession (*hymnischen Bekenntnislieder*). His distinction was based on the inclusion in the former group of the speaker's accounts of how he had suffered at first, but had eventually experienced salvation. These accounts were lacking in the latter group.[3] Holm-Nielsen made his division on the basis of differences both in form and in content. The one category, called by him psalms of thanksgiving, concentrated on the "surrounding world" of the community, whereas the other, called hymns, concentrated on the "conditions of the community" itself.[4] As it happens, Morawe and Holm-Nielsen's categories largely correspond to each other, and they have been adopted by subsequent scholarship roughly as they were outlined by these two scholars.[5]

The two categories have come to mirror a fundamental scholarly perception of the social realities behind the collection of hymns. As early as 1950, Eleazar Sukenik suggested that this collection of anonymous compositions in its entirety had been composed by the Teacher of Righteousness, the founding leader described in other Dead Sea Scrolls (CD I 4–11; 1QpHab I 17–II 10; VII 4–5; 4Q173 1 4; 2 2).[6] It was later suggested by

3. Morawe, *Aufbau und Abgrenzung*, 108–13; 135–38. The book, published in 1960, is a slightly shortened but otherwise unaltered version of his dissertation, which was defended in 1957 (ibid., 5).

4. Holm-Nielsen, *Hodayot*, 320. This dissertation was both defended and published in 1960, and it contains no references to the work of Morawe.

5. See Douglas, "The Teacher Hymn Hypothesis Revisited," 245, for an outline of how Holm-Nielsen, Morawe, Jeremias, Becker and Kuhn demarcate the categories of compositions.

6. Sukenik, מגילות גנוזות (1950), 32. See also idem, אוצר המגילות הגנוזות שבידי האוניברסיטה העברית, 34, and the English edition, *The Dead Sea Scrolls of the Hebrew University*, 39; Dupont-Sommer, *Le livre des hymnes*, 10–12 ; Delcor, *Les hymnes de Qumrân*, 22–23.

Gert Jeremias that the Teacher of Righteousness was the author of only a part of the compositions, the part categorized by him as individual thanks-giving hymns (*individuelle Danklieder*).[7] Heinz-Wolfgang Kuhn proposed that the Hodayot should be seen as Teacher Hymns, hymns composed by the Teacher of Righteousness, and Community Hymns, respectively.[8] Others doubted that the Teacher of Righteousness had authored any of the compositions,[9] and Philip Davies argued that the Teacher of Righteous-ness was not the actual but the implied author.[10] The Teacher of Righteous-ness's real or implied authorship continues to be argued or asserted by scholars, and so does the idea that the bifurcation of the collection mirrors the different social roles of their speakers.[11] Those who have reservations about this position tend not to reject the possibility that the Teacher of Righteousness could have been the author, but they find the arguments methodologically unsound.[12] The issue of the Teacher's authorship seems to be of secondary importance to these scholars: matters of theology take priority, and perhaps this explains why designations like "Teacher/Leader/ Individual Hymns" and "Community/Collective Hymns" are still widely used—perhaps out of habit.

Carol Newsom is also critical of the idea that a subset of the hymns came from the hand of just one prominent leader. She explains the dif-

7. Jeremias, *Der Lehrer*, 168–77. With few exceptions, this group corresponds to Holm-Nielsen's psalms of thanksgiving and Morawe's thanksgiving songs. Jeremias operates not with two but three categories of compositions: hymns, psalms, and thanksgiving songs. Ibid. 170.

8. Kuhn, *Enderwartung*, 24–25.

9. Mansoor, *The Thanksgiving Hymns*, 45; Licht, *Thanksgiving Scroll*, 25–26; Holm-Nielsen, *Hodayot*, 118–19. Holm-Nielsen did not find the question of authorship par-ticularly relevant. On the contrary, he found the contrast between individualistic and collective ways of understanding the speaking voice artificial: "Es ist zu gleicher Zeit 'individuell' und 'kollektiv', weil es den Einzelnen allein kraft seiner Zugehörigkeit zum Ganzen repräsentiert" ("'Ich' in den Hodajoth," 222).

10. Davies, *Behind the Essenes*, 88–90.

11. Michael Douglas has argued at length that a subset of the compositions was authored by the Teacher of Righteousness. See Douglas, "The Teacher Hymn Hypoth-esis Revisited," 247–57; "Power and Praise," 239–394. Others in favor of this position are Lange, *Weisheit und Prädestination*, 200–2; Tanzer, "The Sages at Qumran," 113, 116, 140; Charlesworth, "Jewish Hymns, Odes, and Prayers," 413–14.

12. See Holm-Nielsen, *Hodayot*, 327–28; Kittel, *The Hymns of Qumran*, 8–11; Davies, *Behind the Essenes*, 87–90; Callaway, *The History of the Qumran Community*, 190–96; Hughes, *Scriptural Allusions*, 15–16.

ference between the types of compositions not by their authorship, but rather by the rhetorical and identity-formative power they potentially had in their social context. She believes that the general leadership is represented by the speaker in the one group of compositions, the community members in the other. [13] Newsom's approach is intriguing because it opens up new questions about the *meaning* of the composite whole, which is also the focus of this book.

In any case, the status quo is that the dichotomy between leadership and ordinary membership is maintained in readings of 1QHodayot[a]. One subset of compositions continues to be seen as representing a form of community leadership. The remainder, on the other hand, are thought to express the sentiments of ordinary community members, and usually this goes without discussion. As an exception to the rule, Sarah Tanzer suggested as early as 1987 that "[t]he title, Hymns of the Community, seems to have been applied as a way of distinguishing these Hodayot from the very personal character found in the Hymns of the Teacher. Yet, it may not be the best way to characterize this group of twenty-five compositions."[14] She identified two subgroups of community hymns, the Deuteronomic Hodayot and the *Niedrigkeitsdoxologie* Hodayot, but with few exceptions these designations have not gained ground in subsequent scholarship.[15] In the following discussions, I shall refer to the two sets of compositions as the so-called Leader Hymns and the so-called Community Hymns, respectively.

Clearly, there is a literary basis for the bifurcation of 1QHodayot[a]. A conspicuous difference between the two groups of compositions is the introductory formulas. The so-called Leader Hymns consistently employ the formula "I thank you, Lord" (אודכה אדוני), whereas the so-called Community Hymns prefer "Blessed be you" (ברוך אתה אל / ברוך אתה אדוני).[16]

---

13. Newsom, *Self as Symbolic Space*, 287–300, argues that the institutional leadership of the Dead Sea society, and not one single leading figure, is the implied author of these hymns.

14. Tanzer, "The Sages at Qumran," 144. Harkins, "The Community Hymns Classification," 140–54, has recently argued that some of them, the so-called *maśkil* hymns, had circulated independently and might originate outside of the Dead Sea community.

15. Tanzer, "The Sages at Qumran," 144–54.

16. Stegemann, "The Number of Psalms in the 1QHodayot[a]," 222. Within the so-called Community Hymns the variant אודכה אלי occurs in 1QH[a] XIX 6 and possibly also in line 18. The latter example, which occurs a few millimeters from the left margin, is preceded by a small ink dot, and this leads most scholars to assume that

Also, the consistent use of the first-person singular in the so-called Leader Hymns is broken in the so-called Community Hymns.[17]

Already Jeremias held that the speaker of the so-called Leader Hymns must have been an individual, because he, unlike the speaker of the so-called Community Hymns, recounts his inner feelings.[18] Stegemann agreed that the speaker referred to personal experiences, but according to him, these were external events involving the speaker's enemies, which are mentioned by several names in the so-called Leader Hymns, but not in the Community Hymns.[19] Several scholars have pointed out that each set of compositions favors a particular vocabulary, and this tendency has been confirmed in recent years, for example, by Michael Douglas's identification of rare and idiosyncratic language usages in the so-called Leader Hymns.[20] Émile Puech acknowledges that there are differences between the groups of hymns, but still underscores their "unmistakable unity of style and vocabulary." In his view, the Teacher of Righteousness could have

---

אודכה אלי was preceded by a now lost word of transition (e.g., ואני); this would indicate that a new composition did not begin in line 18. See Schuller and Stegemann, 1QHodayot[a] (DJD XL), 242–3, 245–6.

17. 1QH[a] VII 12–20 consistently employs the first-person plural. The orthography of this composition deviates from the orthography of the compositions surrounding it, and this suggests that the hymn had been transmitted independently before its incorporation into 1QHodayot[a]. Angela Harkins also points to some other signs of a plural speaker in 1QHodayot[a]: a reference to a plural subject (אוזננו) in 1QH[a] VI 13; a list of groups of people that could be included in this subject in the following lines (13–15); a reference to the community (בשיחד צול אנשי סודי) 1QH[a] VI 29). Finally, the fragmentary composition(s) found in 1QH[a] XXV–XXVI (The Self-Glorification Hymn and the Hymn of the Righteous) does not preserve any occurrences of the first-person plural, but its parallel text in 4Q427 does, so there is a possibility that the Cave 1 text originally did too. See Harkins, "Observations on the Editorial Shaping of the So-Called Community Hymns," 246–47, 253–54.

18. Jeremias, Der Lehrer, 170.

19. "Diese durchweg im Ich-Stil formulierten 'Lehrerlieder' enthalten nun zahlreiche Aussagen über Gegner ihres Autors, die nicht einfach als allgemeine Klagen über die Bösheit seiner Umwelt zu berurteilen sind, sondern auch nach Art der Darstellung konkrete geschichtliche Bezüge haben müssen" (Stegemann, Die Entstehung der Qumrangemeinde. Bonn: Published privately, 1971, cited in Callaway, The History of the Qumran Community, 239 n. 18).

20. Douglas, "The Teacher Hymn Hypothesis Revisited," 247–56. Earlier analyses of differences in language usage are found in Jeremias, Der Lehrer, 173–76; Holm-Nielsen, Hodayot, 320–22.

been the author of all compositions, because he was probably able to vary his expression as needed.[21]

One can argue that the speaker in the so-called Leader Hymns depicts himself as someone who has special leadership duties toward other people.[22] As Kuhn already pointed out, the speaker's authority in this regard was rooted in certain revelatory qualities: in compositions where the speaker depicts himself as a mediator of revelatory knowledge he also distinguishes between himself and the community.[23] The so-called Community Hymns, on the other hand, use sapiential rather than apocalyptic language, as argued by Sarah Tanzer in her Ph.D. dissertation. Tanzer demonstrated that there is a strong presence of wisdom elements in the so-called Community Hymns, but hardly any in the so-called Leader Hymns. Such elements include themes like creation theology and determinism, the future reward of the righteous and the punishment of the wicked, expressions of low regard for humanity given in the form of *Niedrigkeitsdoxologien* and rhetorical questions.[24]

In his recent Ph.D. dissertation on religious epistemologies in the Dead Sea Scrolls, Shane Berg has confirmed Tanzer's conclusion regarding the so-called Community Hymns, and he has examined the character and function of the wisdom elements found there. He analyzes three works: the Tractate on the Two Spirits, 4QInstruction, and the Hodayot; and he concludes not only that the former two and the so-called Community Hymns are all sapi-

---

21. Puech, "Hodayot", 366.

22. In the so-called Community Hymns the speaker sometimes states that he will tell others about the glory and the wonders of God (1QH^a XVIII 16–17; 22–23; XIX 9). In the so-called Leader Hymns, however, the speaker in various claims about how he affects other people indicates that he has functions to fulfill vis-à-vis them. For instance, he describes himself as "a mocking song for transgressors" and "a banner for the elect of righteousness" (1QH^a X 13–15); "a snare to transgressors but healing to all who repent of transgressions, prudence for the simple, and a resolute purpose for the eager" (1QH^a X 10–11). God has made him "a father to the children of kindness and like a foster-father to the people of good omen" (1QH^a XV 23–24), but he faces difficulties when trying to address his disciples "in order to revive the spirit of those who stumble and to support the weary with a word" (1QH^a XVI 36–37). The translations are from Schuller and Stegemann, *1QHodayot^a* (DJD XL).

23. Kuhn, *Enderwartung*, 22. Kuhn remarks that where the speaker depicts himself as a mediator of revelatory knowledge, he also distinguishes between himself and the community.

24. For an overview, see Tanzer, "The Sages at Qumran," 55–56, 75–79.

ential, but also that they represent a particular development within wisdom literature. Unlike the view of earlier wisdom traditions, the wisdom of God according to these texts is not immanent and therefore is not available to everybody. Divine wisdom is available only to an elect group of people who receive it through spiritual revelation. Thus, Berg argues, the epistemological outlook of the so-called Community Hymns paves the way for a sectarian mentality where only a limited number of people have access to God's knowledge—and it is this knowledge that will enable them to live according to the will of God. Furthermore, Berg explores the epistemological outlook of the so-called Leader Hymns and finds that they have an apocalyptic outlook inspired by prophetic modes of revelation. This epistemology, too, undergirds a sectarian identity, but in a different way: it conveys divine knowledge only through exclusive revelation to a prophet-like mediator who may subsequently share his wisdom with a select group of like-minded people. Berg's definition of these epistemological outlooks is based on observations on the anthropology of each group of compositions and on analyses of their central concepts.[25] In this way Berg conveys convincing arguments for the bifurcation of 1QHodayot[a] according to literary criteria.[26] In sum, a variety of criteria have been identified over the years to justify a division between two main groups of hymns:

So-Called Teacher Hymns	So-Called Community Hymns
Personal and authoritative speaker	Universal speaker
Accounts of personal and historical experiences	References to general experiences

---

25. In order to emphasize man's lowly nature and his inability to achieve knowledge of his own accord, the so-called Community Hymns draw on the creation imagery of Gen 2, according to which man has been created from dust and earth. See Berg, "Religious Epistemologies," 161–95. The so-called Leader Hymns, on the other hand, rarely make such general claims about human nature, but focus instead on the speaker's suffering due to social and religious conflicts. Some of the central concepts investigated by Berg in the so-called Leader Hymns are what he labels "metaphors for revelation" in the field of teaching and instruction (שכל, ידע), concealing and revealing (סתר, חבה, גלה), building and construction (אמץ, כון), light and illumination (אור, יפע) (ibid., 213–28). In the so-called Community Hymns he looks into concepts which in this context are used to show man's ability to obtain knowledge of God's covenant and the ability to live up to God's will: "spirits" (רוחות), "understanding" (בינה), "wonder" (פלא) and "secrets" (רזים) (ibid., 173–99).

26. Ibid., 153–264.

Apocalyptic epistemology	Sapiential epistemology
Rare and idiosyncratic language	Stereotyped language
Consistent introductory formula	Varied introductory formulas
אודכה אדוני	ברוך אתה אל /ברוך אתה אדוני
Consistent use of the first-person singular	Occurrence of first-person plural

1.2. Social Implications of a Literary Bifurcation?

The well-founded literary division of 1QHodayot[a] tends to be interpreted under the influence of suppositions about the sociohistorical realities behind the texts. This is the case not least among scholars who identify the speaker of the so-called Leader Hymns as the Teacher of Righteousness, and I want to draw attention to a couple of examples.

Michael Douglas criticizes Jeremias, Becker, and Kuhn for having made this identification in an unjustified way, because they had not proved on literary grounds that only one author had written the so-called Leader Hymns.[27] His own interpretation, however, provides a significant example of the fault he criticizes in others. He puts forward the premise that one can legitimately begin to discuss the historical identity of the speaker of a group of compositions if and only if it has been "established by literary criticism" that they were written by only one person.[28] He then identifies variants of the phrase הגבירכה בי, occurring five times in cols. X–XIII (and only there), as the *signature phrase* of one individual.[29] Based on the signature phrase and occurrences of other idiosyncratic expressions in these and the following columns, Douglas argues that the compositions in cols. X–XVII were "substantially the work of a single author," and that col. IX was subsequently added as a sort of introduction to his work.[30] Douglas goes on to argue that the author of cols. X–XVII was the Teacher of Righ-

---

27. Douglas, "The Teacher Hymn Hypothesis Revisited," 247.

28. Ibid.

29. Ibid., 247–49. He argues that this phrase, not found in any of the biblical or pseudepigraphical texts, is unique; and, because it occurs several times in the Hodayot compositions under consideration, that it must be one particular individual's way of expressing himself.

30. Ibid., 256.

teousness.[31] At one stage this group of texts, labeled "The Teacher's Book," was incorporated into the collection we know as 1QHodayot[a].

Douglas's linguistic analysis is persuasive insofar as it points to a different authorship for this group of compositions compared to other compositions in 1QHodayot[a]. His claim that only one person could have been the author of the so-called Leader Hymns, however, is not entirely convincing. He sees these hymns as composed close to the events to which they refer: according to him, they were directed to authorities in Jerusalem in an effort to make them endorse the views of the Teacher of Righteousness, and not the views of his antagonists.[32]

One problem with this reading is that, in the spirit of Gert Jeremias, it presumes identity between the author and the speaker. A related problem is that it rests on the assumption that the compositions came into being as rhetorical actions intended to solve pressing communal matters. This, however, is not necessarily the case. First, the genre of prayer may not be the most suitable medium for such rhetorical action. Secondly, the idea of the compositions as rhetorical action composed in the wake of a single, concrete situation underrates their capacity for *reflecting* on ideas, or on events that were rather more remote. This is a question of experiential distance that has implications for the argument that there could be only one author: if the so-called Leader Hymns did not emerge directly from pressing, political events, but came into being over a longer lapse of time, they could very well have been written collectively by a group of like-minded people.

Shane Berg reaches similar conclusions as Douglas and contends that the literary bifurcation mirrors a sociohistorical group with a leader-

---

31. The reasons Douglas gives for this opinion are basically the following: The signature phrase and other distinct linguistic expressions show that the speaker identifies himself not as just any member, but as a revolutionary leader, as "the sifter who determines who pleases and who displeases God" (ibid.). Furthermore, the "Teacher's Book" clearly refers to the experience of being expelled, to a breach with opponents, and to an escalating crisis resulting in a final schism. Consequently, the compositions (which on these points resemble accounts about the Teacher of Righteousness) must relate to events taking place in the earliest stage of the community. Finally, Douglas repeats an argument made earlier by Jeremias: he claims that there could not have been room for two revolutionary leaders in the community simultaneously, and therefore that the author of the "Teacher's Book" must have been the Teacher of Righteousness (ibid., 258–64).

32. Ibid., 263.

ship (specified as the Teacher of Righteousness) and ordinary members. In spite of their lowly nature, community members would have received divine knowledge through the spirit of God and other spirits because this was God's will. The Teacher of Righteousness, on the other hand, would have received revelatory insights directly from God, like a prophet, and conveyed it to other community members.[33]

It is to Berg's credit that he reflects on the societal function of the two religious epistemologies. Yet his conclusion that 1QHodayot[a] with its two groups of compositions and two different epistemologies corresponds with a social bifurcation within the Dead Sea community is not wholly convincing due to an asymmetry between the two epistemologies. If God had indeed chosen to impart divine wisdom to a collective of Dead Sea community members, why would he need a Teacher of Righteousness to prophesy his messages to them?[34] I am not saying that the two epistemologies might not have worked together in some way in the Dead Sea community—apparently they did—but it is quite likely that they originated in different social contexts before they were adopted into the literary context of 1QHodayot[a]. In that case, it is hardly self-evident, as Berg implies, that the two groups of compositions must represent the perspective of a leader and that of his followers, respectively. On the contrary, it is possible that the two groups of compositions were juxtaposed because they were felt somehow to *overlap* and to express, each in their own way, a common core of ideas or experiences. Such a common core might be the sense of a "sectarian outlook" according to which access to divine knowledge is restricted, *in one way or another*, to those who are predestined from their creation to belong in the covenant with God.[35]

The problems that I have identified in the approaches of Douglas and Berg relate to an insufficient consideration of the genre of the Hodayot and, on a general level, of how discourse and texts relate to their social

---

33. Berg, "Religious Epistemologies," 239.

34. Berg asks the following in regard to the speaker of the so-called Leader Hymns: "Might not the hymnist simply be expressing in powerful terms the presence and activity of God that is available to any devoted disciple? The answer to this reasonable question is 'no.'… [T]he hymnist regards his experience of God to be unique. God is directly present to the hymnist and imparts revelation to him, but for others in the community such revelation is mediated to them by the hymnist. The Teacher's role is unique within the community" (ibid., 213). From this perspective, the epistemology of the so-called Community Hymns seems to be rather superfluous.

35. Ibid., 20.

and cultural contexts. How do we know that the literary dichotomy identified by numerous scholars in numerous ways mirrors a particular social dichotomy among the owners of the prayer collection at a particular point in time? Do we know exactly *how* the sociohistorical context of the Dead Sea community has put its imprint on this collection of prayers? This is fundamentally a question about how texts are related to their contexts. For this reason, it is also a question underlying the present work on the compositional meaning of the Hodayot. Theoretical aspects of the relationship between text and context preoccupy many linguists, but to my knowledge it is hardly discussed in Dead Sea Scrolls scholarship. Linguistic perspectives on this problem would be welcome, however, and some of them will be included in my analysis of 1QHodayot[a].

1.3. FUNDAMENTAL ASSUMPTIONS OF THIS STUDY

Before the specific research problem is introduced, I am going to outline some of the basic assumptions underlying this study. Some of these assumptions pertain broadly to the nature of the relationship between discourse and context while others pertain to issues of genre and function in relation to 1QHodayot[a] in particular. All of these issues bear on the important question of how the texts are related to their social contexts of production.[36]

---

36. The combination of "linguistic" and "rhetorical" perspectives in the title of this book also hints at the importance of considering connections that exist between a text and its context. Rhetorical needs and authorial intentions are one side of the coin, and they are often involved in discussions of the Hodayot; unintentional linguistic vestiges of the mental and communicative activity behind discourse are the other side of the coin, but they rarely come into play. Even if 1QHodayot[a] and other Hodayot compilations are well-planned literature, they contain linguistic choices that do not reflect conscious rhetorical needs related to specific rhetorical situations, yet still reveal aspects of their social contexts. Peter MacDonald touches upon the difference between linguistic, or discourse, analysis of texts and rhetorical analysis of genre: "In addition to having specific functions for linguistic devices, each discourse type (narrating, describing, teasing, dreaming, etc.) has a set of characteristic strategies that may be used to accomplish its global speech act…. This is familiar territory for those scholars versed in classical rhetoric. The difference is that, unlike the rhetoricians, who attempted to relate the forms of discourse to the intentions of the speaker, discourse analysts attempt to relate the patterns of discourse to the subconscious attitudes and psychological strategies that have given rise to them" ("Discourse Analysis and Biblical Interpretation," 164).

Assumption 1: The meaning of 1QHodayot[a] is situated not only in the extant words.

This is true of texts in general. Just as the meaning of oral discourse resides in the situation of speech, the meaning of a text is also context-dependent.[37] In the words of archaeologist Ian Hodder, meaning "does not reside in a text, but in the writing and reading of it."[38] This insight is especially important when we deal with composite works like 1QHodayot[a]: The redactor or compiler does not explain which criteria guided his inclusion of one text or another. We have to guess on the basis of our own textual analyses and our sparse knowledge of the contextual background.

Following John L. Austin, we can describe different levels of meaning in discourse in terms of *different ways of doing things with words*: Through the enunciation of words and phrases (locution) discourse participants produce statements, requests, orders, wishes, promises and other *speech acts* (illocution). These kinds of meaning are largely expressed directly in the words themselves, and in the grammatical and syntactical patterns used by the speaker or writer. In the course of a discourse, however, contextual factors like the discourse participants' motives and desires, their power relations, and their use of bodily gestures may invoke additional effects, such as persuasion, fear, comfort, or relief (perlocution). This is true especially of oral discourse, taking place between co-present interlocutors with first-hand knowledge of the situation of speech. Their immediate experience of the situation will influence their perception of that which

---

37. George Brooke thus aptly points to the situation that texts originating in worship do not convey the whole religious experience: "[T]he theological significance of prayer and worship can only ever be somewhat partial, since the texts that reflect such spiritual activities cannot in themselves convey the fullness of the religious experience, either corporate or individual, that they were intended to facilitate. That is not least because prayers and liturgies are not just reflections of intellectual activity, but find their complete significance only when they are recognised as part of a much wider context. Liturgical texts are the limited vehicles that help create the lived experiences that are enacted by the whole person or group as they put themselves before God, but they do not contain that whole ritual experience" ("Aspects of the Theological Significance of Prayer and Worship in the Qumran Scrolls," 36).

38. Hodder, "The Interpretation of Documents and Material Culture," 158. He draws upon the view of Jacques Derrida in *Writing and Difference* on the difference between oral and written discourse.

is enunciated, and it will invoke meanings that they could not deduce from the words and sentences alone.[39]

With Paul Ricoeur, texts can be described as discourse that has been fixed in writing. In the process of being written, some of the fundamental characteristics of (oral) discourse are lost. Like speech, the writing of texts takes place in social contexts, but written discourses do not convey as much contextual information to readers as oral discourses do to interlocutors. What we are left with in written discourse are mainly the ostensible referential contents *inscribed* in the form of words and sentences (the locutionary and illocutionary meaning); namely, discursive elements that can be expressed in grammatically and syntactically well-formed sentences. The perlocutionary meaning, on the other hand, does not easily get inscribed. Therefore, the written discourse is itself largely bereft of the context-dependent, uninscribed meaning that was nevertheless involved in the writing process.[40]

All of this this may seem commonplace. Nevertheless, when interpreting texts in relation to their assumed original contexts—and we do this to the Hodayot and other Dead Sea Scrolls literature all the time—we do well not to forget about the presence of uninscribed meaning. Moreover, the distinction between inscribed and uninscribed meanings is pertinent also when we interpret redacted or composite works like 1QHodayot[a] and try to explain their *reuse* of existing texts. Like writing processes, processes of quoting, alluding, redacting or juxtaposing existing texts are imbued with meanings that are not clearly inscribed in the final product.

To many readers, reading largely makes sense exactly because they are ignorant of some uninscribed meanings and instead add, or ascribe, new ones relative to the new situation of use—for example, their own goals and desires. From the perspective of usage, texts are comparable to material objects in the sense that they come to obtain new, evocative meanings in a community by being used in its common, social practices. Ian Hodder explains how texts not only carry their once-inscribed, linguistic meaning but are also imbued with new, however mute, meanings in new contexts of use.[41] Such new meanings may be very different from their enduring, inscribed messages, because:

---

39. Austin, *How to Do Things with Words*, esp. 98–107.
40. Ricoeur, "The Model of the Text," 189.
41. In his article, "The Interpretation of Documents and Material Culture," Hodder basically contrasts the linguistic, representational meaning of documents

[T]here is often a tension between the concrete nature of the written word, its enduring nature, and the continuous potential for rereading meanings in new contexts, undermining the authority of the word. Text and context are in a continual state of tension, each defining and redefining the other, saying and doing things differently through time.[42]

To Hodder this tension between inscribed and uninscribed meaning shows that texts share some qualities with material artifacts, such as utensils and memorial monuments: the artifacts are mute about their concrete meanings which can only be deduced from experience and their context of use. Similarly, texts carry muted, uninscribed meanings that can only be deduced from their contexts of production and use. In the same vein, the anthropologist Brigittine French argues that texts and artifacts are involved in similar semiotic processes because the social meaning of both changes from one context of use to another: "Although usually etched in stone, the meanings of official state memorial projects are not fixed. As a state's geopolitical commitments and military conflicts shift, so do the messages embedded in monuments and memorials."[43]

In sum, texts are similar to mute things in that they carry not only their explicit, inscribed meanings but also uninscribed meanings that change throughout their existence, from one context to another. If we want to hypothesize about the sociohistorical significance of a text at the time of its production or in any later context of use we need to be aware of this duality in meaning and perhaps seek alternative ways to explore that which is not immediately visible on the inscribed manuscript sheets.

Without doubt, the theoretical viewpoints presented above on the types of meaning involved in the production and use of texts must bear on how we understand the production of larger, composite works. The complete meaning of any single part of a complex, redacted work must have changed during its movement from one context of use to another. Theoretically, this situation has been described by linguists and anthropologists in terms of *entextualization*, which is the (re)use of existing pieces

---

with the nonlinguistic, evocative meaning of artifacts. Artifacts have not been created to produce meaning, but are intended for, and become meaningful through, their practical usages. Documents, on the other hand, are intended to be meaningful; their meanings are largely produced linguistically and work through symbolism. And yet, they too have evocative meanings. See especially pp. 156–64.

42. Ibid., 157.
43. French, "The Semiotics of Collective Memories," 342.

of discourse in new social and literary contexts. What is important about entextualization is that it has a *metadiscursive* dimension. The linguist Jan Blommaert describes it as a process of decontextualization and recontextualization that "adds a new *metadiscursive context* to the text."[44] The moment when a piece of text is inserted into another text—for example, through juxtaposition, allusion or rephrasing—it has de facto been recognized as something already existing and belonging in a different social, cultural, historical, or literary context, and peoples' awareness of such uninscribed meaning adds to the meaningfulness of texts. A text's original context of production fades away as it "is accompanied by a metadiscursive complex suggesting all kinds of things *about* the text (most prominently, the suggestion that the discourse is indeed a text)."[45] In other words, just as there is more meaning in the process of writing than that which becomes inscribed in the text, there is a surplus of meaning involved in processes of entextualization; for example, in a redacted or collected work. The implication of this is that composite works come into existence through discursive processes that are *larger* than the textual remains that we are left with. Thus, as implied by the title of a central work on entextualization, *Natural Histories of Discourse*, processes of entextualization should be investigated on the level of discourse, not text. [46]

In biblical and Dead Sea Scrolls studies, discussions about redactional processes usually revolve around *texts* and their development. It is texts that become the natural objects of investigation. Texts are, after all, what we have available. Furthermore, we tend to see these texts, as a matter of course, as natural expressions of the Jewish society in which they belonged. Problems arise if we assume that the texts express something like the essence of the beliefs and worldview of their owners. Thus, Michael Herzfeld, one of the contributors to *Natural Histories of Discourse*, terms such bias toward texts as a "decentering of discourse." According to him, the very idea of a "text" is an expression of essentialism, especially when we think of a text as something that has to be in a "correct version" (correct in relation to what?—every written text comes out of a social situation) because it assumes "a bounded semantic universe located outside the passage of time."[47]

---

44. Blommaert, "Text and Context," 187.
45. Ibid.
46. Michael Silverstein and Greg Urban, eds. *Natural Histories of Discourse*.
47. Herzfeld, "National Spirit or the Breath of Nature?," 279.

Every composition included in 1QHodayot[a] must have evoked ideas in the collector or redactor about its meaning apart from the literal, inscribed meaning. He must have had knowledge or assumptions about whose experiences the compositions related to, how they could be used, on which occasions and under which circumstances. He must have found that the compositions shared some of those social meanings, and this must have warranted his act of bringing them together into a single collection. It is hardly the case that compositions were included simply out of habit or as tokens of the community's past or conventions. Rather, they were familiar and reusable cultural expressions felt to pinpoint present situations or even foreshadow future worlds. Thus, if we want to make suggestions about how the work of 1QHodayot[a] may have made sense to its composers and ideal audience, we should consider both the enduring, inscribed meanings visible in the compositions, and the uninscribed, evocative meanings that they may have had in shifting contexts of production and use.

The juxtaposition of different compositions in 1QHodayot[a] carries mute vestiges of evocative meanings that the compositions once had. My suggestion is that, in the eyes of the redactor(s) or compiler(s), the compositions in various ways bespoke and evoked one and the same type of worshiper: someone seeing himself as belonging to the elite and taking some sort of leadership responsibility upon himself.

Assumption 2: The Hodayot are prayers and, therefore, remains of a profoundly social activity aiming to affect God.

There has been some controversy over the question of the function of the Hodayot—were they compositions intended for liturgical purposes or not? Apart from the occurrence of thanksgiving formulas, blessings, and doxologies, which could indicate a liturgical setting, signs of liturgical usage found in other hymnic compositions from Qumran are sparse in the Hodayot.[48] This is the reason for my reluctance to view the Hodayot as liturgical in the sense that they must have been recited or sung on

---

48. See, however, Puech's suggestion about five occurrences of dedications to the *maśkil* in 1QHodayot[a]. Puech assumes that each dedication stood at the beginning of a section, and that the collection was divided into five parts, like the book of Psalms: "These five 'rubrics' suggest grouping the Hymns of 1QHodayot[a] into five sets, which cannot help but be reminiscent of the ordering of the scroll of the 150 biblical Psalms into five small books. It is thus possible, and even likely, that the Hodayot Scroll, or at

specific occasions as part of the service of God. Bilhah Nitzan is probably correct to assume that the Hodayot were not liturgical according to her definition of liturgy as "[t]he service of God through prayer, conducted in the community in accordance with a fixed order and pattern."[49] However, the one alternative she offers—namely, that the Hodayot must have been "poetry of the individual"—is not satisfactory either. It rests on the unjustified assumption that only prayers conducted in accordance with a recognizable, fixed pattern could be part of social life. Even suggestions that the Hodayot were originally composed by individuals and were later used in collective settings to convey theological messages to the community are unsatisfactory. What such models and their categories provide are some restricted social situations to choose from, but they do not bring us nearer to an understanding of the significance of the Hodayot in the community.

Instead, the Hodayot can be seen more broadly as prayer compositions. With regard to form, I employ Judith Newman's rather elastic definition of prayer: "Prayer is address to God that is initiated by humans; it is not conversational in nature; and it includes address to God in the second person, although it can include third person description of God."[50] This definition excludes representations of dialogues between God and human beings in the narrative parts of the Hebrew Bible, as well as human speeches that are prompted by the initiative of God.[51] On the other hand, it includes both prose texts and poetic texts, independent compositions and compositions embedded in narratives and other genres, and it does not distinguish between texts that employ stereotypical phrases and texts that do not.

Newman seems to believe that this variety of prayers shares the same basic function—such an assumption would justify the inclusiveness of her definition—but she does not concretize such a general function of prayer. It is doubtful whether one can explain the function of a prayer adequately simply by determining the specific situation in which the prayer

least most of the Hymns, rather early on (about 100 BCE at the latest) had a liturgical purpose" ("Hodayot," 366–67).

49. Nitzan, *Qumran Prayer and Religious Poetry*, 64.

50. Newman, *Praying by the Book*, 6–7.

51. Ibid., 7. According to these criteria, the dialogues of Abraham with God in Gen 18 are not prayers because they are dialogic in character and are initiated by God. The same applies to Cain's complaint to God in Gen 4:13–14.

is used; the function of each and every prayer should be understood also on the basis of what prayers accomplish on the most general level. For this reason, I also employ the complementary, function-oriented definition of prayer given by the sociologist Marcel Mauss: "Prayer is a religious rite which is oral and bears directly on the sacred."[52] Because Mauss defines religious rites, the concept of which is included in his definition of prayer, as "efficacious, traditional actions which have a bearing on things that are called sacred,"[53] it becomes clear that he sees prayer as a kind of action. To pray is not only to pour out one's inner feelings and thoughts, but also to participate in a profoundly *social* activity.[54] This applies even when prayers are not uttered aloud or in a group, but take place in someone's mind, because "however freely one prays, one always observes the general principles of ritual simply by not violating those principles. Consciously or not, one conforms to certain norms and adopts an approved attitude. And it is with the language of ritual that the internal discourse is composed."[55]

Mauss's definition problematizes the notion that prayer develops from free, often individual usage into fixed, institutionalized practice. This is an idea that has been expressed most clearly by Bilhah Nitzan. According to her, psalms and prayers in the Hebrew Bible, even when occasionally they accompanied sacrifices, were "no more than a cultural expression of the individual and collective religious experience and of the natural need to pour out one's heart in supplication or in song of thanksgiving and praise."[56] Nitzan contrasts this sort of prayer with fixed prayer, which is evidenced in the Dead Sea Scrolls and involves the duty to perform prayers as a form of sacrificial cult, at fixed times, and according to fixed patterns.[57] Naturally, such distinctions between prayers according to their particular settings

---

52. Mauss, *On Prayer*, 57. The definition was worked out by Mauss in his unfinished dissertation on the subject of prayer. It was based on anthropological studies of religious practices among Australian Aborigines. Mauss intended to undertake a comprehensive study that was to include both primitive and highly developed, modern levels in the evolution of prayer. He failed to do so, but notice should be taken that his declared goal was to avoid a definition biased by modern, Western conceptions of prayer. See ibid., 27–30.

53. Ibid., 54.

54. Ibid., 33–37.

55. Ibid., 34.

56. Nitzan, *Qumran Prayer and Religious Poetry*, 38.

57. Ibid., 47–69.

Confuse officials study
∧ w/ reality
20   Meaning and Context in 1QHodayot[a]

and preconditions are important for studies of how prayer practices developed,[58] but they are less important for this study.

Because of their formal communicative situation, the Hodayot represent the discourse of human beings directed to God. This applies whether the compositions were performed publicly or in private, on specific occasions or randomly, and whether they were sung, spoken, or meditated upon. More importantly, the formal communicative situation, an obligatory feature of the genre of prayer and expressive of its purpose and meaning, is a constant factor in the Hodayot. It is repeated throughout the collection and reminds us of the fact that any rhetorical function that the Hodayot might have served must have been subordinate to the primary function: whichever practical, political, ideological, or other motivations lie behind their performance at different times in the life of the community, they would have to be in accordance with the fundamental function of prayer, which is in Mauss's words to "[cause] the god to act in a certain way."[59] Mauss concedes that prayers may have additional effects, and that they are often hoped to affect changes in the life of the praying persons and in their environment. Nevertheless, these additional effects are categorized as a "by-product," and are not the essential aspect of prayer.[60]

By way of an example, I want to illustrate the conflict between rhetorical approaches and the approach encouraged by the function-oriented definition of prayer utilized here. In her monograph, *The Self as Symbolic Space*, Carol Newsom analyzes identity construction in the Hodayot and in the Rule of the Community (Serekh ha-Yaḥad). She builds on the theoretical insights of Mikhail Bakhtin and his linguistic circles.[61] According to Bakhtin, each discourse type springs from a particular speech community (within a larger speech community) and gives voice to it, so to speak. Newsom is interested in the dialogical character of discourses in a society in the sense that the various discourses are in constant interaction with each other. Within this framework, Newsom explains how the Hodayot's

---

58. Aspects of the historical development of prayer have been treated by several scholars, including Baumgarten, "Sacrifice and Worship among the Jewish Sectarians," 153–54; Chazon, "Prayers from Qumran," 273–77; and Nitzan, *Qumran Prayer and Religious Poetry*, 40–45.

59. Mauss, *On Prayer*, 54. This is another way of expressing how, according to his definition, prayer "bears directly on the sacred."

60. Ibid., 56–57.

61. Newsom, *Self as Symbolic Space*, 6–12.

Rhetorical vs. functional
approach   approach

so-called Leader Hymns and the Rule of the Community each in their way represent the community leadership: the Rule exercises leadership authority whereas the Hodayot appeal to the continued loyalty of the community members by way of a masochistic self-representation.[62] These discourse types both provide symbolic representations of community identities, and they do it in complementary ways.

Newsom is right to allot complementary functions to the two genres, but she seems to put too much stress on the rhetorical function of the Hodayot. Seeing the so-called Leader Hymns as appeals from the leadership to community members, she reads them as rhetorical means to assert control over the community. The implication is that they were spoken from a relatively fixed position by someone who had identified a particular rhetorical situation—the threatening disloyalty of community members—with specific problems that needed to be solved on the social level. [63] The speaker then sought to resolve this situation through rhetorical persuasion of community members. I acknowledge that hodayot compositions may have functioned rhetorically in this way, but this function was hardly exhaustive.

— thanksgiving can also

A purely rhetorical (human) view of prayer texts is inexpedient if we *do this* grant that the primary function of prayer is to affect God and cause him to act. Admittedly, the speaker of the Hodayot gives thanks rather than supplication. Nevertheless, the relation of the praying person to God deserves to be taken into consideration, and we need to take care that rhetorical analyses relating to "down-to-earth" social situations do not come into conflict with this perspective. In so far as the speaker has a "situation" in mind when addressing God, it must involve an acknowledgment of God's will and the speaker's commitment to it. This means that the speaker cannot rely solely on his own judgment of the situation; he must remain open also to God's evaluation and response. This viewpoint informs my approach to the Hodayot in general, and receives special attention in chapter 3.

con als, be social

---

62. Ibid., 325–27.

63. According to the definition by Lloyd Bitzer ("The Rhetorical Situation," 5–6), a rhetorical situation is "a necessary condition of rhetorical discourse." It is a situation that "needs and invites discourse capable of participating with situation and thereby altering its reality." Correspondingly, discourse capable of meeting the demands of the situation is rhetorical discourse.

Assumption 3: The Hodayot constructs the speaker as an agent of God.

It is generally recognized that the Hodayot draw on psalms literature from the Bible.[64] References in the Hodayot to biblical psalms, however, do not usually consist of verbatim quotations. Therefore, it is difficult to establish when and if there is a direct relationship of dependency. John Elwolde, who has investigated possible Hodayot references to biblical psalms, suggests that the authors' use of the Psalms often took place unconsciously. He believes this reveals that the authors saw themselves as "living in the same world that the figures of the Bible lived in, to be, as it were, still living in the biblical period, and, therefore, open to divine revelation and inspired interpretation."[65] Even if there was such a deep and emotional dependence on the Psalms, however, the Hodayot deviate from them with regard to formal features, contents, and perspectives.[66] Carol Newsom gives a brilliant description of how the Hodayot carry an extra layer of reflection in their representation of agony and deliverance:

> The sectarian's formative moment is not that of crying out and being heard but one of recognition of his place in an already scripted drama. Even when the Hodayot use the drama of danger and deliverance, so familiar from the Psalms, it is not the deliverance per se but the insight into the true meaning of his experience that is what the speaker has to tell.[67]

Exactly because the Hodayot resemble the Psalms, it is significant when they deviate from the scriptural compositions, which represent a

---

64. See Hughes, *Scriptural Allusions*; Carmignac, "Les citations de l'Ancien Testament," 391; Holm-Nielsen, *Hodayot*, 307–309, 357–58 (a list of biblical psalms used in the Hodayot).

65. Elwolde "The Hodayot's Use of the Psalter," 80–81. Elwolde remarks that there are frequent divergences "for linguistic or literary reasons" from the biblical text as we know it from MT, and this also indicates that it was the meaning of the psalms, rather than the accurate reproduction of them, that concerned the authors of the Hodayot.

66. Formally, the Hodayot resemble biblical psalms, particularly the thanksgiving psalms, but they still deviate from this scriptural *Gattung*, for instance by their inclusion of elements from biblical psalms of complaint. See Kittel, *The Hymns of Qumran*, 1. With regard to contents, the speaker of the Hodayot is distinguished by expressing his gratitude for *knowledge* of God's redemptive actions, and not primarily for the redemptive acts themselves. See Nitzan, *Qumran Prayer and Religious Poetry*, 344 n. 60.

67. Newsom, *Self as Symbolic Space*, 208.

common Jewish heritage and tradition. Differences in the compositions can be seen as indications of a changing social context and of a developing ideology and self-perception. In some of the Hodayot, the speaker clearly displays himself as someone who plays an active part in God's salvation of other people:

> I became a snare to transgressors but healing to all who repent of transgression; prudence to the simple, and a resolute purpose for the eager. (1QH[a] XV 23–24)[68]

> Through me you have enlightened the face of the many and you have increased them without number. For you have let me know your wonderful secrets and in your wonderful council you have shown strength in me. (1QH[a] XII 28–29)[69]

> According to someone's [un]derstanding, let me draw him near; and according to the amount of his inheritance, let me love him. Let me not turn my face to the evil and not acknowledge an unrighteous, corruptible person. Let me not exchange your truth for riches or any of your judgments for a bribe. For according as [a ma]n [… let me lo]ve him, and according as you keep him at a distance, let me abhor him. And let me not bring into the council of [your tru]th [anyone] who has not taken account [of] your covenant. (1QH[a] VI 29–33)[70]

> Though you made the tongue strong in my mouth, unrestrained, yet it is not possible to lift up (my) voice or to make (my) disciples hear, in order to revive the spirit of those who stumble and to support the wary with a word. (1QH[a] XVI 36–37)

The self-representation of the speaker in these utterances is markedly different from that of the psalmist in any of the biblical psalms. In the book of Psalms, the psalmist's experience is generally that of being, or hoping to become, subject to God's redeeming actions; there he speaks of himself as of any human being and not as someone who has special functions or obligations. Admittedly, a couple of scriptural psalms have indications that

---

68. Unless other information is given, I use the translations of Carol Newsom in Schuller and Stegemann, *1QHodayot[a]* (DJD XL).

69. My translation. See chapter 5.

70. My translation. See chapter 3.

the psalmist might see himself as a role model or representative of others, but not in a particularly distinct or emphasized way.[71]

The innovative way of self-representation in 1QHodayot[a] is theologically significant. It implies that 1QHodayot[a] as a collection contains the idea that a praying person can conceive of himself as someone with an active role to play in the agency of God and not just as an object of it: when claiming to be a "healer" the speaker suggests that he is part of God's scheme to redeem those who repent. Likewise, by pointing to his own role in acts such as enlightening people and drawing them near, he shows himself as someone who contributes to the preservation of others in the covenant. Most of the time, this agency pattern is expressed in vaguer terms than the quoted examples. Yet, I aim to show by the end of this book that it is present and can be identified in other instances as well. In any case, the frequency is less important than the fact that it occurs at all. Perhaps the impression that the speaker was an agent of God was not so much an opinion that the authors particularly wanted to advance as it was a relevant experience or self-understanding that unavoidably put its imprint on some of these compositions.[72]

One could argue that the speaker's self-representation in the examples above simply sustains the notion that some of the hymns must have originated within the institutional community leadership. However, this explanation in itself does not show the real significance of these utterances.[73] When occurring in a context that must be expected to have had some sort of communal function, whether didactic, edifying, or liturgical, this agency pattern must be expected to have had an exemplary function. It unfolds a particular self-understanding that can be taken over by others through their identification with the voice uttering the compositions. To say the least, being an agent of God in this sense was hardly as exclusive an

---

71. Pss 69:7; 119:79.

72. Daniel K. Falk thus makes the important distinction between "ideology underlying and motivating the practice of prayer," on the one hand, and "ideology and theology that is communicated by prayers," on the other ("The Contribution of the Qumran Scrolls," n.p.). See also Collins, "Prayer and the Meaning of Ritual in the Dead Sea Scrolls," focusing on enacted versus propositional meaning. "The explicit theology expressed in prayers and treatises...provides context for the ritual action, but it does not necessarily exhaust its meaning or fully articulate its effectiveness" (84).

73. Of the examples quoted above, the first two are from the so-called Leader Hymns. The last quotation is from a hymn that is normally treated as a community hymn, an assumption that I question in chapter 3.

New agency pattern in Hodayot

experience as that of Moses, the one and only giver of the Torah. Whatever we make of the utterances above in relation to the history and social organization of the Dead Sea community, we must acknowledge that they have some theological implications: the God of the Hodayot is demonstrably someone who continues to ally himself with human partners; they become his representatives or agents among other human subjects. This argument applies whether the Hodayot were used by a small group of community members (for example, leading persons), or by the community at large.

This is not the place to explore the exact content and function of the speaker's place in the agency of God, but we can make some general observations. In all likelihood, the development and poetic expression of this new agency pattern in 1QHodayot[a] would have been perceived by covenanters as congruous with the community's deterministic worldview; perhaps they perceived biblical psalms to be incongruous with the idea that every person's place with either God or Belial was preordained. There was a tension in particular between determinism and petitionary prayers, typically involving the praying persons' expectations that their acts of repentance would restore their relationship with God and change their situation for the better.[74] As Esther Chazon has pointed out, there are a number of penitential elements in the Hodayot; declarations of God's justice are particularly frequent.[75] Petitions, however, are remarkably absent.[76] Instead of petitioning, the speaker repeatedly declares his knowledge and understanding of how things are (destined to be).[77] Due to his God-given knowledge and understanding, he is in a position to discern between those people who have been included in the covenant with God and those who

---

74. For a definition of petitionary prayer, see Werline, "Defining Penitential Prayer," xv. For discussions of the tensions between determinism and petition, see Knohl, "Between Voice and Silence," esp. 29–30; Schuller, "Petitionary Prayer," esp. 38–41 (focusing on the Hodayot) and 45; Arnold, "Repentance and the Qumran Covenant Ceremony," esp. 170–71.

75. Examples include: 1QH[a] IV 32; V 36; VI 26–27; VIII 26–27; IX 28–29; XII 31–32, 38–39, 41; XIX 10–11, 21; XX 22–23. See Chazon, "Tradition and Innovation."

76. The speaker refers to the act of petitioning or supplicating (e.g., 1QH[a] XVII 9–13; XIX 37; XX 7), but does not actually make petitions (cf. Ezra 9:10–15; Neh 9:32; Dan 9:15–19). The supplications of Ezra 9 and Neh 9 are in a way similar to the references in the Hodayot, as the speaker seems to reckon on the favor of God in spite of all the peoples' wrongdoing. For apocryphal examples, see Chazon, "Tradition and Innovation," 57.

77. See 1QH[a] IV 33–36; IX 9–11, 21–22.

have not. He seems to think he can even contribute to the inclusion of people in the covenant, or their exclusion from it, in accordance with their preordained destination.[78] This is how, I imagine, the ideal audience of 1QHodayot[a] may have conceived of itself. This particular collection of hymns would have sustained this way of thinking, as the reading or reciting of at least some of the compositions would involve the enactment of peoples' active participation in the agency of God.

Let me briefly summarize these basic assumptions, which bear on my analyses of individual compositions in the following chapters. First, with regard to the relationship of texts to their social contexts, we must be aware that not all meaning is grammaticalized and inscribed. Individual compositions and the collected work provide but glimpses of experienced realities and larger discourses that took place. Second, we need to consider that no prayer could function purely on the social plane as an instrument of social control; we must expect that the prayers were felt by praying persons to be adequate means to address and even manipulate God as well. In other words, those two perspectives must converge in the textual analyses. Third, the agency structures and the praying person's place in them have social and ideological implications. Indirectly they bear witness to real life experiences of being human, of belonging to a particular social group and setting, and of being related to God. The agency structures carry information that may not have been inscribed and put forward in clear propositions in every composition. They index additional, contextual meaning.

1.4. Research Problem

Over the years, scholars have provided insights into the literary character of 1QHodayot[a] that should encourage a renewed interest in the question of how the collection mirrors its social context. It has been realized that the collection is more complex than first assumed, and that the so-called Community Hymns are not simply a homogeneous group of compositions. Günter Morawe and, subsequently, Heinz-Wolfgang Kuhn showed that these hymns were marked by different themes and messages,[79] and

---

78. In this context, I understand "covenant" broadly and not as coincident with the Dead Sea community as a social and ideological unit.

79. Morawe gave seven criteria (*Gattungselemente*) for distinguishing the Hymnic Songs of Confession (*Aufbau und Abgrenzung*, 21–91 and 159–61). Kuhn restricted himself to three: *soteriological confessions* (always introduced by the formula ואני ידעתי כי

others have continued this work and shown that the group of so-called Community Hymns is far from homogenous.

Further, several scholars have pointed out compositions that for one reason or another defy classification. As mentioned above, Sarah Tanzer demonstrated that some of the Hodayot compositions have a strong presence of wisdom traits, whereas others have a fainter sapiential flavor.[80] Tanzer demonstrated that wisdom material dominates in the so-called Community Hymns, but is absent or limited in the so-called Leader Hymns (or Teacher Hymns, as she calls them).[81] However, she categorized six hymns, all among the so-called Leader Hymns, as *hybrid* compositions, arguing that each of these compositions includes some wisdom material typical of the so-called Community Hymns.[82] In all of these examples the wisdom material is more or less confined to one part of the composition and is not present throughout.[83] Therefore, it appears that the sapiential material has been added to the compositions at some point in time. The so-called Leader Hymns and the so-called Community Hymns are not homogeneous groups according to Tanzer, but each has its subcategories of compositions. Thus, the general picture emerging from Tanzer's study is that of a heterogeneous collection where individual compositions consisting of elements of differing origins have been brought together.

Subsequently, other scholars have pointed to ambiguous traits in some of the other compositions. In contrast to prior scholarly consensus, Newsom

---

or כי ואדעה, contrasting the situation of the speaker with that of the ungodly), *Niedrigkeitsdoxologien*, and *Elendsbetrachtungen* (*Enderwartung*, 26–29).

80. Tanzer, "The Sages at Qumran," 155–56. For an early highlighting of principal differences within the group of so-called Community Hymns (some generally resembling biblical songs of praise and others marked by the specific ideas of the Dead Sea community), see Holm-Nielsen, "'Ich' in den Hodajoth," 220–21.

81. See Tanzer, "The Sages at Qumran," 130–34, for a schematic outline of her findings.

82. These compositions are: 1QH[a] X 5–21 (X 3–19/*II 3–19*); XI 20–37 (XI 19–36/*III 19–36*); XII 6–XIII 6 (XII 5–XIII 4/*IV 4–V 4*); XIII 22–XV 9 (XIII 20–XV 5/*V 20–VII 5*); XV 37–XVI 4 (XV 34–XVI 3/*VII 34–VIII 3*); XVI 5–XVII 36 (XVI 4–XVII 36/*VIII 4–IX 36*). See page 40 below for an explanation of how I make references to columns and lines in 1QHodayot[a]. For a brief overview of the hybrid compositions, see Tanzer, "The Sages at Qumran," 139–40.

83. In contrast, the wisdom material in the so-called Community Hymns, although limited, tends to be spread throughout the compositions. See Tanzer, "The Sages at Qumran," 128–29.

interprets 1QH[a] VI 19–33 as a leader hymn, and she also addresses the ambiguities contained in some other compositions:

> If I am correct in attributing the hodayah in 1QH[a] 10:20–30 and 11:1–18 to the ordinary sectarian rather than the leader, then he, too, is represented as a solitary individual besieged by enemies and saved by God for the purposes of God's manifestation of glory. Certainly 1QH[a] 11:19–36, which is generally regarded as a hodayah of the community, represents the individual as redeemed from guilt and the eschatological judgment not by entry into the sect but by being placed with a heavenly community of rejoicing. The language throughout is highly personal and highly emotional. A heightened, dramatic, highly figured quality characterizes the experience.[84]

Newsom categorizes the two compositions, 1QH[a] X 22–32 (X 20–30) and XI 2–19 (XI 1–18), in ways other than what is customary. Her argument is basically that the apparently personal as well as emotional accounts of life experiences in the Hodayot are symbolic representations that "serve to create a standardized experience for all members of the community."[85] She perceives the last composition mentioned, XI 20–37 (XI 19–36), as a somewhat atypical community hymn because of its heightened language, but this does not seem to be a problem to her. Elsewhere, she points out that the ambiguity about the identity of the speaker is what "makes such a first-person singular prayer, creed, or pledge so powerful an instrument in the formation of subjectivity."[86] It can potentially lend voice to different persons and identity types within the community. In Newsom's treatment, then, the categories of leadership and community compositions are maintained, but due to the symbolic and elastic quality of the language used, they appear to be blurred—and less decisive for the way in which each composition is interpreted.

---

84. Newsom, *Self as Symbolic Space*, 296.

85. Ibid., 240. In connection with this argument, Newsom notes that most of the few explicit references to the community are found in the so-called Leader Hymns, and that community perspectives are generally not made visible in the so-called Community Hymns (ibid., 239).

86. Ibid., 201. Tanzer describes this particular hymn as a conglomerate consisting of parts from several source types. Yet, she interprets it as a leader hymn due to the choice of introductory formula and its placement within the block of so-called Leader Hymns (Tanzer, "The Sages at Qumran," 106–7, 126).

Julie Hughes finds that 1QH[a] XI 6–19 and 1QH[a] XI 20–37, due to their diversity in style and contents, can be categorized as neither leader (or teacher) hymns nor community hymns—categories that, in this case, she refers to as "inadequate." Instead, she suggests that the compositions be seen as a "sectarian 'class exercise' in poetic interpretation."[87] Moreover, because of how the composition 1QH[a] XVI 5–XVII 36 is saturated with scriptural language, she expresses doubts about the common classification of it as a leader hymn.[88] Such findings lead Hughes to conclude that the hymns in question and the Hodayot in general had "a variety of backgrounds."[89]

In several articles, Angela Kim Harkins explores the complexity of the so-called Community Hymns from a redaction-critical perspective.[90] Unlike Tanzer, she has had access to previously unpublished and partly overlapping Hodayot manuscripts from Cave 4.[91] In one of her earlier articles she approves of Puech's view that the Community Hymns may have had an independent existence as a collection of *maśkîl* hymns in five parts, analogous to the book of Psalms.[92] She also differentiates this material, noting that the *maśkîl* hymns in the columns neighboring the so-called Leader Hymns in 1QHodayot[a] contain some language typical of the literary productions of the Dead Sea community, while hymns that are located farther from the so-called Leader Hymns do not.[93] More recently she has suggested that the so-called Leader Hymns and the group of Community Hymns following it (the latter group referred to by Harkins as CH II) had circulated in tandem before they were juxtaposed to a different group of

---

87. Hughes, *Scriptural Allusions*, 233. See also pp. 206–7 and 228–30 for discussions of each of the hymns.

88. Ibid., 154, 170. This hymn is quite often described as a teacher hymn. Due especially to the heavy influence of Isa 40–66 on this hymn, Hughes sees it as an exegetical hymn, developing themes that would support a collective identity, rather than as an autobiographical composition. See especially pp. 167–73, unfolding the exegetical achievements, and the concluding remarks on p. 183. According to Tanzer, it is a hybrid and thus, in her opinion, to be placed among the Teacher Hymns.

89. Hughes, *Scriptural Allusions*, 233.

90. Harkins, "Observations on the Editorial Shaping"; "The Community Hymns Classification"; "A New Proposal for Thinking about 1QH[a]." Previously she has published under the name Angela Y. Kim: "Authorizing Interpretation" and "Signs of Editorial Shaping."

91. Harkins, "Observations on the Editorial Shaping," 233–56.

92. Puech, "Quelques aspects," 39–40.

93. Harkins, "The Community Hymns Classification," 153.

Community Hymns (referred to as CH I), which in 1QH^a is located before the so-called Leader Hymns. The former two groups share orthographic praxis as well as contents, specifically the idea that the speaker experiences communion with heavenly beings. With regard to both orthography and contents they differ from the latter group, which according to Harkins displays the speaker only in the context of human fellowships.[94]

I do not intend to discuss Harkins's suggestions here in any detail,[95] but only to stress how important it is to investigate the complexity and developmental aspects of the material in the way she does. The recognition of smaller units that occur in more than one manuscript and appear to have circulated in more than one literary or social setting is an important step away from the habit of unconsciously referring to the compositions *as if* they represent one of only two identity categories within a particular community at a particular time in history.[96] Instead of insisting that the composite character of 1QHodayot^a mirrors a social dichotomy in the Dead Sea community, Harkins explains it as the result of *redactional activity.* The heterogeneous collection may be the result of a wish to address various aspects of life in the community, perhaps to some didactic end.[97]

The observations of various scholars with regard to the complexity of 1QHodayot^a can be grouped together schematically like the table on page 31:

---

94. Harkins, "A New Proposal for Thinking about 1QH^a," 110–24.

95. The two analyses by Harkins do not seem compatible, but that is beside the point here.

96. Thus, Harkins questions the idea that the Community Hymns largely belonged to one particular community, and she indicates that 1QHodayot^a, as a sectarian document, may have inherited some of the hymns from outside of the sect. See "The Community Hymns Classification," 140–41.

97. Schuller likewise points to the variations in scope, length, contents, and order of the compositions that appear in the Hodayot from Cave 4. In addition, there are a number of often fragmentary "Hodayot-like" compositions that in several cases could be included in the Hodayot tradition. See Schuller, "The Classification *Hodayot* and *Hodayot*-Like." Furthermore, she notes the different handwritings, the dating of the various manuscripts, and the occurrence of a plural speaker. See "Prayer, Hymnic, and Liturgical Texts," 167–68.

	Feature	Argument	Implication
Tanzer	Wisdom language merged into non-wisdom compositions	Blending of originally distinct features	Compositions are redactional hybrids
Newsom	Apparently personal, first-person accounts in so-called community hymns	Symbolic expression of communal identity	Blurring of the categories
Hughes	Systematic use of scriptural language in so-called leader hymn	At variance with identification as leader-hymn	Category inadequate
Hughes	Diversity with regard to style and contents	No clear community leader or community member profile	Category inadequate
Harkins	Sectarian language in the so-called Community Hymns clustered around the so-called Leader Hymns	The Community Hymns were originally nonsectarian, but some of them seem to be influenced by sectarian language through redactional activity	Blurring of the categories
Harkins	Special affinities between so-called Leader Hymns and one group of so-called Community Hymns	Hymns not belonging in the group of so-called leadership hymns do not constitute a unity, either in form or in content.	Blurring of the categories

Clearly, these observations about hybridity, blurred categories, and redactional activity within the Leader Hymns and Community Hymns prompt us to avoid explanations that depend heavily upon a rigid bifurcation of the collection and on the notion that the different authors of the compositions must be the key to the social meaning of the compilation. As Angela Harkins has noticed, there are signs that the collection of 1QHodayot[a] "has been compiled in a purposeful way…, even though today it is not clear what the purpose was."[98]

In light of the seemingly dissolving literary dichotomy of 1QHodayot[a], it becomes difficult to abide by the traditional conception that the collection represents its social milieu as consisting of its rank and file members on the one hand, and its leadership on the other. Within that explanatory framework, it is possible to account for the juxtaposition of the so-called Leader Hymns and the Community Hymns and explain it as resulting from an authorization process where the more authoritative group of texts could lend some of its legitimacy to less reputable compositions.[99] However, the partition of 1QHodayot[a] into hymns of the leadership and hymns of the ordinary members can hardly explain the redactional merging of the different categories into hybrid compositions, as identified initially by Tanzer. Previous attempts at doing so tend to be overly rhetorical and instrumental in their focus. I suspect this is because they mostly resort to social categories and human affairs but ignore that, among the owners of the collection, the genre of prayer must also have functioned as organizer of the relationship between the human and the divine spheres—whatever social functions the prayer may have had.

For instance, Tanzer believes the compositions with strong wisdom elements served other purposes than the non-wisdom compositions, which are generally found among the so-called Leader Hymns. She states that the function of the former was didactic, whereas the function of the latter was to "build a sense of security for a persecuted individual or possibly persecuted community through an expansion of thanksgiving to,

---

98. Harkins, "Community Hymns Classification," 135.

99. One model has it that the authoritative compositions of the great leader, the Teacher of Righteousness, could lend some authority to the anonymous Community Hymns. See Kim, "Authorizing Interpretation," 31–32. Another model is that the so-called Community Hymns, which resemble other prayer literature of the time, could lend their natural legitimacy to the somewhat more anomalous compositions of the teacher.

and sometimes, confidence in, God."[100] Her explanation of the merging of wisdom material into some of the non-wisdom Teacher compositions takes its starting point in the observation that those hymns are generally quite concerned about the wicked people and their destiny, whereas the group of "righteous" are referred to only briefly. Then, according to Tanzer, a specific situation, "a possible split in the community, in which people are being seduced away from following the psalmist," may have necessitated a redactional intervention devoting more attention to the righteous followers of the psalmist, who were also the intended audience for the hymns.[101] Tanzer seems to think that these Teacher Hymns, originally the product of a leading individual facing persecution, were recontextualized into a broader community setting at a later stage and adapted by that community in order to meet threats of seduction by an opposing party within it.[102] So, all in all, as far as the redactional hybrids are concerned, her explanation points to a rhetorical situation prompting such redactional action.

This sort of rhetorical explanation has two shortcomings. First, as briefly mentioned above, it does not adequately explain the meaning of the genre. Whichever functions the different categories of prayers may have had on an interpersonal, social level of communication, it should not be forgotten that the genre of prayer does more than just solve rhetorical situations involving human beings. Therefore, the relationship between the praying persons and the deity, which is consistently reflected in the formal communicative situation, should also in some way be accounted for when we consider the meaning of juxtaposing different categories of compositions.

Second, when considering the purely social level, we must be aware that, whichever persons and social groups were originally behind each category of compositions, the texts would take on new meanings when juxtaposed to other categories of compositions in new literary settings. In their new literary and social contexts they could potentially mirror other social groups and categories of people. This is a matter of *entextualization*, and the implication of it is that scholarly notions and even basic knowledge of the authorship and social origin of groups of prayers are not sufficient to explain the meaning of the collection as such. The fact that 1QHodayot[a] is the result of redactional or compilatory arrangements—

100. Tanzer, "The Sages at Qumran," 78
101. Ibid., 113.
102. Ibid., 138–39.

and there is general agreement that this is the case—undermines the idea of a simple causal relation between the origin of individual compositions (or parts of compositions) and their meaning within the redactional whole. We must be open to the possibility that the various compositions were included in the collection because the evocations they triggered were fundamentally alike.

1.5. Approaches

Current theories about the social background of 1QHodayot[a] are unable to explain its heterogeneous character. Against this background, I would like to suggest a reading strategy that leaves our presumptions about the underlying social contexts aside for a while. In relation to traditional perceptions of the milieus behind the so-called Leader and Community Hymns, the hybrid character of some compositions may seem to pose a problem. As long as alternating literary traits (for example, between apocalyptic and sapiential outlooks) are thought to correlate with alternating speakers, it becomes difficult to explain why such disparate features have been merged within some of the compositions (and thus in the collection as a whole). This applies especially since 1QHodayot[a] lacks indications of a liturgical usage that could account for alternating speakers throughout a composition. Instead, I shall work on the assumption that in the eyes of the compilers the diverging compositions had *common denominators*— evocative or textually explicit—which rendered their fusion meaningful in some way. In other words, I choose to see hybridity as a *clue* rather than an obstacle to an understanding of 1QHodayot[a] as a whole.

Provisionally, common denominators can be sought in the genre and its formal features, which is something that runs through the whole of 1QHodayot[a] and most Hodayot prayers in general. A speaker, mostly in the singular, addresses God with thanksgiving and blessing.[103] Doing this, he acts out a particular role vis-à-vis God and his fellow community members. On one level, at least, the speaking "I" possesses a fundamental unity throughout the collection by virtue of the genre, the formal communicative situation, and the recurring introductory formulas.[104] In so far as single compositions are hybrids, this recurring speaker is a hybrid as well,

---

103. Kittel also remarks on "the consistent style of addressing God" (*The Hymns of Qumran*, 174).

104. Introductory formulas used within the so-called Leader Hymns contain the

hybridity not problem but clue

Frames hybrid speaker

and it is this hybrid speaker and the processes in which he participates that are going to be the object of investigation. This strategy will enable us to offer a meaningful explanation of 1QHodayot[a] as a collection—in spite of and *because of* the occurrence of "hybrid" compositions within it.

Methodologically, this is a multifaceted approach. It should be clear by now that I do not expect to be able to offer a comprehensive explanation of the logic behind this collection based solely on the information that is textually explicit or grammaticalized in the compositions. In all likelihood, some of the factors that guided the collectors of 1QHodayot[a] to include some compositions and leave others out were not, or only vaguely, expressed directly in the compositions. In some cases valuable information that has not been given in clear propositions may still be indexed in the texts. The ancient collectors may have taken such hints about the social significance of a composition because of their specific cultural and sociocontextual knowledge. To some extent, I believe, modern, attentive readers can also retrieve information that has not been put forward in clear propositions.

For instance, I have already suggested that the Hodayot reflect an agency hierarchy according to which God acts through someone—the speaker of these hymns—who becomes a mediator between God and other people. This agency hierarchy is quite easily spotted in some of the so-called Leader Hymns, but may also be present in a subtler manner or through evocation in other compositions, even if it has not been expressed directly. In some of the textual analyses to come, I will retrieve such information with the help of *transitivity analysis*, a tool developed within Systemic Functional Linguistics (SFL). This is an analytical approach undertaken on clauses, yet it is not grammatical analysis. It seeks to describe in some detail the processes that are expressed in clauses and thereby to characterize the logical subjects (and other participants) of those clauses.

This kind of analysis is exemplified at the end of chapter 2, where in a demonstration of SFL I show how the speaker in 1QH[a] X 22–32 repeatedly describes himself as "standing" and "walking": "from you comes my *steadfastness*"; "from you are my *steps*"; "my *standing* is due to your kindness." These propositions can easily be interpreted as expressions of how the speaker is completely dependent upon God's mercy. An analysis of

---

verb אודכה, as in אודכה אדוני, "I thank you, Lord." Otherwise, blessings containing the verb ברך are used (mostly ברוך אתה).

the circumstantial information, however, shows that his walking/stand-
ing denotes a quality that he possesses in three very different situations:
first, it is a secret quality, unnoticed by his adversaries; second, it occurs in
connection with his redemption by God; third, it occurs as God redeems
other people through the speaker. Thus, a close linguistic analysis shows
this special quality in the speaker both when he appears to be a passive
receiver, and when he plays an active part in the agency of God. The composition displays the speaker in different roles and situations and thus
exemplifies how the speaker of 1QHodayot[a] at large is multifaceted.

The goal in applying transitivity analysis, and occasionally other elements of SFL, is to investigate possible similarities between texts that, on
the grammaticalized surface, appear to express conflicting ideas. This is
a concrete way to account for the possibility of evocative meaning. By
way of transitivity analysis it is possible systematically to register nuances
in the clauses and propositions that are not self-evident or detectable
through ordinary grammatical or rhetorical analysis. Experiential and
ideational meanings that have not been stated directly are still indexed
in the choice of words and are available for analysis. Yet another SFL tool,
lexical strings, can help identify experiential and ideational meanings that
do not become apparent through investigations of the intended information structures of a text. These sociolinguistic tools are far from common
among Dead Sea Scrolls and biblical scholars—indeed, they are quite different from traditional, philological approaches and belong in a specialized field of their own. Accordingly, chapter 2 offers a short introduction
to Systemic Functional Linguistics—its premises and those of its analytical tools to be used here.

My approach to the meaning of 1QHodayot[a] is holistic; there is no
analytical method that on its own can explain the range and impact of
uninscribed and indexical meaning in a text. I therefore apply various
additional methods accordingly as I address different problems. These
methods are introduced in the chapters where I (first) use them, and in
the following I will mention them only briefly.

1.6. COMPOSITIONS ANALYZED IN THIS BOOK

Four Hodayot compositions, all of which can be characterized as hybrids
in one way or another, will be analyzed. Hybridity is not defined by fixed
criteria, and in what follows I abandon Tanzer's narrow, redaction-critical
definition according to which hybrids occurred when wisdom material

had been fused into otherwise non-wisdom compositions. The texts manifest hybridity in varying ways, and only one of the compositions, 1QH^a XII 6–XIII 6, is a hybrid according to Tanzer's definition. This composition, by general consensus a leader hymn, includes some wisdom passages of the kind that is so typical of the so-called Community Hymns. This "classic" hybrid will have our attention in chapter 5. Apart from this, I use the designation "hybrid" about compositions that *otherwise* appear to contradict the notion that the two main categories of compositions identified in 1QHodayot^a represent distinct social groups or types (leadership and membership, respectively) within the Dead Sea community.

In chapter 3, I analyze the text of 1QH^a VI 19–33, which is traditionally treated as a community hymn. More specifically, it has been argued that it was used ritually at initiation or confirmation ceremonies and expresses community members' creedal statements and pleas for acceptance into the community. The composition is a hybrid on the level of *expectancy* because, as Newsom argues and contrary to the usual expectations, it shows elements of leadership. Transitivity analysis is applied in this chapter and brings out aspects of leadership agency in the composition which has not yet been noticed by scholars. I also include a discussion of modality because this turns out to be a decisive factor in discussions of whether this hymn is spoken by a (prospective) member or a leader. Modality is difficult to assess in Hebrew and is rarely discussed in analyses of the Hodayot. The chapter therefore includes an excursus on modality. Finally, I engage with the performance theory of Jeffrey Alexander in yet another attempt to address the purpose of this composition. Alexander points out a number of criteria that must be fulfilled in order for a ritual or performance to be trustworthy and effective. On the basis of these criteria I question the idea that the composition was spoken by community members at initiation ceremonies.

Chapter 4 deals with two texts: 1QH^a XX 7–XXII 39 has much in common with the concluding hymn of 1QS, including the fact that the speakers of both compositions appear to see themselves as *maśkîlîm*. However, whereas scholars see the Hodayot composition as spoken by a community member, they mostly see the 1QS text as representative of the leadership. For lack of a better term, we describe this as hybridity on an intertextual level, because two similar-looking texts are interpreted as markedly different based on their appearance (entextualization) in two different works. Theoretically, the very similar features of the texts may have represented two distinct social identities within the Dead Sea community. This is questionable, however, and a comparison of the compositions suggests that they exhibit different aspects of one particular self-understanding, the identity of a *maśkîl*. Another prominent feature that the two compositions have in common is the fact that they include calendrical sections. It is reasonable to infer that in the context of 1QS, which explicitly gives instructions to the *maśkîl*, the calendrical section functioned to give instructions about the right times for prayers. This explanation may not be exhaustive, however, and in the context of the Hodayot such an instructional function seems somewhat out of place. I seek to demonstrate in both cases that the calendrical section is an integral part that adds to the meaning of the composition as a whole. In the case of the Hodayot text, it is difficult to outline the structure of the composition and the relationship between the parts because of the poor state of the manuscript. For this reason I include the SFL tool lexical strings in my analysis of the Hodayot text in order to bring out its coherence and thus establish the basis for a comprehensive analysis of the composition. Transitivity analysis is also central in this chapter.

The concept of "suture" developed in part by Émile Benveniste will have a part to play in the discussion in chapter 5 of 1QH^a XII 6–XIII 6, the hymn that fits Tanzer's classical definition of a hybrid. Suture is the process by which members of an audience come to identify themselves with elements in a text (or in a film or play). Thus, it is useful in investigations of how the Hodayot may have functioned to shape the self-understanding of their audience. Previously, Carol Newsom has applied the concept of suture in her analysis of 1QH^a XII 6–XIII 6. She believes it is a hymn through which the community leadership wanted to persuade its audience into loyalty. The audience of the hymn would perceive the speaking "I" as the voice of its own community leadership, and it would identify itself with a group which in the composition is designated "the many" and presented as followers of the speaker. Considering that this composition is a hybrid, things get more complicated, and I have found the concept of suture as employed by Newsom useful with a view to including considerations of hybridity in the discussion.

In chapter 6 I deal with a text that consists of two quite different looking compositions, the Self-Glorification Hymn and the Hymn of the Righteous. The text occurs in a fragmentary version in 1QH^a XXVI, and I work primarily with a better-preserved version in another Hodayot document, 4Q427. Because this text reveals attempts to knit together two distinct compositions—traditionally seen as spoken by a unique individual and a collective of worshipers, respectively—it has a sort of redactionally achieved hybridity. The two compositions also appear together in the apparently earlier, non-Hodayot manuscript 4Q491c, and it is intriguing to observe that efforts have been made in the Hodayot to integrate the two compositions more closely than in the 4Q491c version. In this chapter I leave SFL methods aside completely and focus on how and why the two compositions, and thus their speakers, have been joined by fusion.

In each chapter I pinpoint ideas and experiences surfacing in the texts while trying to detach my reading of them from common notions about their particular sociohistorical significance within the Dead Sea community. In most cases transitivity analysis is involved because this enables descriptions of the speaker and his roles in God's agency with minimal recourse to extratextual information. This process can be described as an attempt to decontextualize my readings, but eventually I do suggest some sort of social and contextual meaningfulness. What I try to avoid is the pitfall of *essentialist reading*, mentioned in section 1.3 ("Assumption 1"), where some compositions are thought to express the essence of a particular group of people while slightly different looking compositions are consequently thought to express the qualities of another, *essentially different*, group of people.

To those who used and composed Hodayot compositions, uninscribed and evocative knowledge added significantly to their meaning. This extratextual, communal knowledge influenced the work of those who composed or compiled 1QHodayot[a]. I have described this process on a general level in terms of entextualization. In chapter 7 I want to concretize this process and outline a scenario of how 1QHodayot[a] may have developed in its sociohistorical context, and of how it may have served to shape a particular self-understanding. I argue that the composers and owners of 1QHodayot[a] saw themselves as religious elites with special obligations to fulfill in the agency of God, and that all of the compositions, or rather, the whole compilation, could function to support this self-understanding among the users.

Focus shifts in chapter 7 from the texts to their owners and the cognitive processes underlying the work of collecting and compiling. Teun van Dijk, a specialist in text linguistics and discourse analysis, has developed a sociocognitive theory about how people process large amounts of knowledge in order to produce discourse that makes sense. They must be capable both of identifying knowledge relevant to the situation and of making inferences about the knowledge and other prerequisites of the address-ees. The theory implies that people sharing the same social knowledge can produce relevant discourse because of their competence to identify both knowledge that is already shared, and which may therefore remain implicit, and knowledge that must be introduced to the addressees during the discourse.[105] Van Dijk introduces the concepts of *context model* and *K-device* in order to describe these processes, and these concepts will also be used in chapter 7 to explain how different looking Hodayot composi-tions could in a complementary way express aspects of just one identity for a single group of people.

On the practical level, readers should be aware that references to 1QHodayot[a] follow the arrangement of columns and line numbers found in *Qumran Cave 1.III: 1QHodayot[a] with incorporation of 1QHodayot[b] and 4QHodayot [a–f]*, edited by Hartmut Stegemann and Eileen Schuller (Discov-eries in the Judaean Desert XL, Oxford: Clarendon Press, 2009).[106] When necessary or particularly helpful, the column and line numbers of *DSSSE* are included in parentheses. Likewise, the numbering from Sukenik's *editio princeps* is sometimes provided in italics. Thus, for example, 1QH[a] X 22 may be cited like this: 1QH[a] X 22 (X 20/*II 20*). Unless other information is given, translations from the Dead Sea Scrolls are my own. Translations of biblical texts are taken from the New Revised Standard Version.

---

105. Van Dijk calls this an epistemic community (*Discourse and Context*, 87–88).

106. See also Émile Puech, "Quelques aspects," 38–55; Hartmut Stegemann, "The Material Reconstruction of 1QHodayot," 272–84. The line numbering of Sukenik is used in *The Dead Sea Scrolls Study Edition* (*DSSSE*).

2
SPECIAL METHODOLOGICAL ISSUES

The various methods involved in this study have been introduced briefly in connection with an overview of the book chapters. Of these methods, Systemic Functional Linguistics (SFL) deserves special attention because it belongs to a specialized field of its own and is rarely seen in biblical and Dead Sea Scrolls studies. SFL has been developed by M. A. K. Halliday and others for the purpose of analyzing different kinds of meaning in discourse.[1] In this study, I am indebted in particular to linguist Suzanne Eggins's introduction to SFL, which is user-friendly and accessible to non-linguists.[2] SFL has been developed with respect to modern languages, primarily English, but is also occasionally employed with ancient texts, including the Bible.[3]

Two SFL tools in particular, *transitivity analysis* and *lexical strings*, will be applied in this study and need special attention because of the intricate rules one has to observe when using them. I have found in these tools the obvious advantage that they enhance the retrieval of (socio) linguistic information from texts that are poorly preserved in distorted manuscripts. If large parts of the lines are missing, the text's information structures are broken and it becomes difficult to analyze the argument.

---

1. Halliday, *An Introduction to Functional Grammar.*

2. Regarding the detailed descriptions of the distinct analytical processes, most references are indeed to Suzanne Eggins, *An Introduction to Systemic Functional Linguistics* (hereafter referred to simply as *Introduction*). This book offers comprehensive and practical guidance beyond the theoretical descriptions.

3. See, for example, Todd Klutz, *The Exorcism Stories in Luke-Acts: A Sociostylistic Reading.* I have found pages 15–81 particularly useful, because there the author provides a practical introduction and demonstration of how SFL can open up ancient texts. Silviu Tatu, *Verbal Sequence,* provides detailed, grammar-based interpretations of ancient Hebrew texts, but shows less interest in discussions of texts beyond clause level.

With the help of transitivity analysis and lexical strings, other kinds of data, which lead to core meanings within a text, can be retrieved from single clauses and phrases.

Another advantage, which is even more central to this study, is the fact that these tools offer a delicate set of categories that must be applied in the course of the analysis. This forces the interpreter to *describe* what goes on in a text with the use of these linguistic categories before he or she can go on to interpret the texts sociohistorically. Very often, expressions in the Hodayot are instantly described as typical either of the leadership or the communal religious experience through the use of words like "leader," "extraordinary," or "unique" on the one hand, and "collective" or "ordinary" on the other. These words betray more than anything else scholarly notions about the people who authored or employed the texts.

With the use of transitivity analysis, in particular, I want to show how a systematic approach to clause analysis in some of the compositions can bring out nuances that should be considered before we jump to conclusions about the sociohistorical implications.

After a presentation of SFL—general aspects of its theoretical basis and some of its methods, I shall present a test case on 1QH[a] X 22–32 (X 20–30/II 20–30) in order to demonstrate some aspects of transitivity analysis, which is the SFL tool used the most (in chapters 3–5) in this book.

2.1. Systemic Functional Linguistics: A Brief Introduction

Halliday's theory of language is sociologically (rather than psychologically) oriented. It investigates how language functions in society and seeks to find and describe traces of linguistic functions in oral and written discourse.[4] It develops the idea of anthropologist Branislaw Malinowski that language is context-dependent: each language is constantly evolving to meet specific needs and circumstances within a culture, and each utterance is shaped by the context of the situation in which it takes place. Also inherited from Malinowski is the idea that linguistic meaning is essentially *the function of language in context*.[5] In other words, language is not

---

4. See Kress, introduction to *Halliday: System and Function in Language*, vii. The following remarks about the historical background to Halliday's theory are also based on Kress's introduction to the book, pages vii–xxi.

5. See Malinowski, "The Problem of Meaning in Primitive Languages," and Malinowski, *The Language of Magic and Gardening*.

self-contained. It makes meaning only when used in a social situation. The linguist John R. Firth was important to Halliday's work because he, in a Malinowskian spirit, developed categories that could connect linguistic material to its cultural context, categories that served to formalize the connection between linguistic meaning and social function on different linguistic levels.[6] The grammarian Benjamin L. Whorf also set his imprint on Halliday, with his accentuation of how language is not only a product of social structures, but also contributes to the ordering of society through its deep, covert grammatical structures.[7]

The designation Systemic Functional Linguistics expresses something about how this method detects meaning-making in a text: The *functional* approach involves analyzing how signs on any textual level are sequenced to produce several types of meaning.[8] This involves a focus on grammatical structures, which are multifunctional. Halliday developed distinct labels and modes of analysis for identifying each kind of meaning within a textual unit,[9] as illustrated (but not explained) in this simple table:

Sentence:	*John*	*threw*	*the ball*
Grammar:	subject	finite	object
Mood:	MOOD		RESIDUE
Transitivity:	Actor	Process	Goal
Theme:	THEME	RHEME	

The *systemic* part, on the other hand, reflects a concern with the choices text producers are bound to make when producing discourse:[10] If someone wants to use a pronoun in English, for example, she will have to choose between the first, the second, and the third person. Furthermore,

---

6. See Firth, *Papers in Linguistics 1934–1951.*

7. See Whorf, *Language, Thought and Reality.*

8. Early writings by Halliday on this issue are found in his articles, "The Form of a Functional Grammar" and "Functions and Universals of Language," reproduced in Halliday, *Halliday: System and Function in Language,* 7–25, 26–31.

9. See section 2.2 on the three textual functions.

10. See Halliday, *Halliday: System and Function in Language,* 5, 91–98; Eggins, *Introduction,* 194–200.

singular or *plural* will have to be chosen, and finally *masculine, feminine* or *neuter*. Only these choices are possible within this particular system, and every system consists of a limited set of choices. The importance of system to linguistic analysis lies in its display of the meaning that is potentially available. One can ask why, in a specific clause, the imperative was chosen instead of the indicative, and the answer may point to aspects of the situational context that made the imperative a meaningful and appropriate choice.[11] Thus, SFL offers a system for identifying linguistic choices and their meaning—that is, their function in context—as they are realized within the structures of the text.

On the following pages I am going to highlight some central elements of SFL theory and introduce transitivity analysis and lexical strings—two SFL tools that I find particularly useful for the present work on the Hodayot.

2.2. The Three Textual Functions

According to Systemic Functional Linguistics, language produces three different kinds of meaning in any text. This can also be expressed in terms of language having three separate *functions* that can be analyzed. First, the *ideational* function of language is to realize the speaker's or writer's experience of the world. Second, the *interpersonal* function of language is to realize the social context in which a particular discourse was produced, including the partners involved in the act of communication. Third, the *textual* function is the realization of the discourse through the arrangement of textual elements on different levels, starting in principle with the phonological and phonetic elements, and moving on to the morphological level and to the levels of sentence, clause, clause complex, and genre. Simply put, the three functions can also be described in terms of *what* the text is about, *where* it belongs, and *how* it is realized.

In the following I shall give a brief outline of each of the textual functions, although only the ideational function plays a major role in my work on the Hodayot. The purpose is to do some justice to the theoretical complex behind the chosen methods and to give an idea of other paths within the theoretical framework that could prove fruitful in future analyses of the Hodayot or other Dead Sea texts.

---

11. Eggins, *Introduction*, 204–5.

One more general comment remains before I continue. SFL analysis is not an interpretive, but an *explanatory* activity. It tries to uncover, not what a text means, but *how* it means. This is not to say that insights about what the text means cannot be achieved during the process of analysis. On the contrary, Suzanne Eggins makes the bold claim that "in the very process of demonstrating *how* a text means, we are also in fact laying bare *what* a text means."[12] When using SFL methods in the analyses of Hodayot compositions, I take a roundabout way. To look into *how* the Hodayot produce meaning in this methodical way is to detach the interpretations of the texts from current notions about how they relate to their social contexts.

2.2.1. The Ideational Function: To Realize Experience of the World

Ideational meaning is expressed on two different levels in texts: On the level of the *clause* it is expressed through a selection of processes realized by verbs and participants in those processes. Each clause contains a verb that can be analyzed as a process of realizing a particular experience. Other elements in the clause are analyzed with regard to how they participate in the process. This is called transitivity analysis, and it is the single SFL method to be employed consistently throughout chapters 3–5.

On the level of the *clause complex* (defined as a sentence consisting of two or more clauses), ideational meaning is expressed through syntactical structures and projecting clauses, enabling the text producer to order ideas and experiences for the reader or listener to understand. The clause complex is a structure that reveals how experiences are connected logically by the speaker or writer, and it is also called the *logico-semantics* of the text.[13] The logico-semantics are "particularly sensitive to the contextual dimensions of genre and mode."[14] This means that variation in logico-semantics may reflect variation in contextual situations as well as their need for communication ("rhetorical situations"). This aspect will be touched upon occasionally because the clause complex structures in the Hodayot deviate from those of the biblical psalms in some respects, and this could be an indication of a different situation of use or of different communicative needs.

---

12. Ibid., 329.
13. Ibid., 256.
14. Ibid., 295.

2.2.2. Interpersonal Meaning: To Realize Social Context

Texts can be seen as dialogue in which people negotiate and argue about the truth. Such negotiating can be recognized through *Mood* analysis, explaining how grammatical structures enable this activity, and how clauses are used to "challenge, assert, agree, contradict, offer, refuse."[15] Additional choices detected in Mood analysis are the different ways of expressing *modality* and *modalization*. Modalization is the use of adjuncts expressing polarity (yes, no), probability (perhaps, probably), usuality (sometimes, usually), inclination (happily, reluctantly), and so forth. It provides information about the speaker of a text as it expresses "the implicit judgement of the speaker."[16]

Mood analysis will not be employed here, and neither will modalization, in any systematic way. Modality, however, is involved in the analysis of 1QH^a VI 19–33 in chapter three. Interpreters' realization of this composition's social context (covenant renewal) largely rests on their reading lines 30–32 in the indicative. But it is possible, and preferable, to analyze these lines as the expression of the speaker's wish to fulfil God's purpose, and this affects how one understands the social setting: instead of seeing the composition as spoken by (prospective) members wanting to have

---

15. Ibid., 144. When someone utters something in speech or writing, he is taking on one of two possible speech roles, the role of *giving* or that of *demanding*. In addition, he takes part in the *exchange of a commodity*, that of *information* or that of *goods and services*. Doing this, he can make one of four possible *moves* in the text: make a *statement*, ask a *question*, give an *offer*, or make a *demand*. All these moves can be made in a number of ways, depending, in part, on whether the speaker is making an initiating or a responding move. However, some grammatical structures are preferred to others in the making of such a move. For instance, if someone wants to give a command, he may want to express himself through an imperative and not a question. On the other hand, if he wants to urge someone, he may want to choose a question or, alternatively, make a statement that in the particular context will be perceived as such. "Oh, I am so hungry," uttered by a little girl in the kitchen, could easily be perceived as an urge for some of the candy lying in a bowl on the kitchen table.

16. Ibid., 174. Palmer describes modality similarly, saying it reveals the speaker's subjective attitude toward an event (*Mood and Modality* [1998], 16–17). Choices of structures to express interpersonal meaning can sometimes be atypical and therefore unexpected. These are then called *marked* choices. It is interesting to ask just when and why marked choices are made. According to Eggins, "It seems likely that the choice between a marked and unmarked structure will be influenced by contextual demands" (*Introduction*, 147).

their community membership confirmed, I suggest it is spoken by some-one who acknowledges having leadership responsibilities. He expresses his hope to fulfil his duties. Whether or not this makes him an institutional leader in the Dead Sea community is a different discussion.

Modality analysis of ancient Hebrew texts is a complicated matter. For this reason, the theoretical aspects pertaining to analysis of modality will be treated in an excursus on modality at the end of chapter 3.

2.2.3. Textual Function: To Realize the Text

To analyze the textual function is basically to analyze information struc-tures. The textual function is to highlight the element that makes the start-ing point for a discourse (Theme) or for its continuance (Rheme), and thus to organize clauses and paragraphs in the way that most effectively sup-ports the purposes of the text. The starting point for analysis is the clause, but the textual function can also be analyzed on higher levels.[17] Analysis of textual function in the Hodayot would be welcome. However, such analy-ses are dependent on prior, comprehensive mood and transitivity analysis, and I have not had the opportunity to apply this aspect of SFL in the pres-ent work.[18]

What is the purpose

---

17. Eggins, *Introduction*, 297–326.

18. In English, the analysis of textual function is rather mechanical. The moment one of the constituent categories of transitivity analysis has appeared in the clause, this element and the elements preceding it are defined as the Theme. The rest of the clause is the Rheme. Of the three functions of a text, the textual function must be analyzed last. This is because the textual meaning is dependent upon the choices of interpersonal and ideational meaning. The choices and the patterns of mood and transitivity realized in the clauses are the starting point for the making of textual meaning. "[T]he textual strand of meaning, while not adding new reality nor alter-ing interpersonal dimensions of the clause, is concerned with how the constituents of a clause or larger unit can be organized in different ways to achieve different pur-poses" (Eggins, *Introduction*, 298). To translate this method into Hebrew poetry is a complicated matter, not least because of its parallelistic structures involving reversed word order. For an interesting treatment of the balance between marked choices and poetical structure, which ought to be taken into consideration in a thorough analysis of Theme in the Hodayot, see Nicholas P. Lunn, *Word-Order Variation in Biblical Hebrew Poetry.*

2.2.4. Transitivity and the Realization of Experiential Meaning

In traditional grammars, transitivity is a grammatical category on the morpho-syntactical level and has to do with the valency patterns of verbs; for example, whether or not a verb is capable of taking a direct object. In SFL, however, transitivity is not a grammatical category. It is a way of describing how ideas are realized in a text; more specifically, how experiential meaning can be expressed on clause level. Transitivity analysis focuses on the verbal constituents of the clause as it investigates how experiential representation is realized in the text through a selection of *types of processes*. The finite verb in a clause will be evaluated by the systemic-functional linguist as the result of a particular selection of process types. Along with a chosen process type comes a set of participants realized in the clause by nominal elements. By choosing a particular verb for his discourse, a speaker or writer simultaneously chooses a particular process type and participants eligible for this particular process.[19]

Process	Participant(s) (list not exhaustive)
Material	Actor; Goal/Range
Mental	Senser; Phenomenon
Behavioral	Behaver; Behavior
Verbal	Sayer, Receiver; Verbiage
Existential	Existent
Relational	Carrier; Attribute/Token; Value
Causal	Agent; Actor

In the following outline of the different processes, some examples will be provided. Whenever possible, they are taken from the text of 1QH[a] X 22–32, which will be analyzed subsequently. Examples that are not from 1QH[a] X 22–32 will be marked by an asterisk. For the sake of simplicity, all examples are clauses in the indicative.

---

19. The following outline is an extract of the presentation of transitivity given by Eggins, *Introduction*, 206–53.

Material Processes   Doing

The material process is a process of *doing*. Only one participant is obligatory in a material process, the one that *does* something. This participant is called *Actor*[20] (or, occasionally, *Agent*).[21] If the finite is transitive (at the moment I am referring to the traditional grammatical category of transitivity, not the SFL term), there will be another participant, the element to which something is done. This participant is called *Goal*:

You	have protected	me
Actor	*Process: Material*	*Goal*

The referent constituting the Actor in a material process expressed in the active voice will remain the Actor if the clause is made into a passive:

I	have been protected	by you*
Goal	*Process: Material*	*Actor*

By looking at this passive construction, one will see that the Actor found through transitivity analysis does not coincide with the subject found through ordinary grammatical analysis. Actor and subject will often, but not always, label the same group of words. This is because the concepts subject and Actor belong to different modes of analysis and are used to describe different aspects of a clause. Likewise, the grammatical direct object is not identical to the Goal of a material process; again, we are talking about different categories. This is seen in clauses where the material process cannot be said to be *done to someone or something*. In these cases the Goal can be replaced by the participant called Range. Range is either a restatement or a continuation of the material process (as in: "They ran the race"), or an expression of the extension or "range" of the process (as in:

---

20. Please note that labels for participants in processes start with a capital letter; the purpose is to distinguish these categories from other uses of the same words on different analytical levels. For instance, when discussing agency on a more general level, but informed by transitivity analysis, we may want to distinguish between actor and Actor.

21. Sometimes the Actor (the one who *does* something) is also an Agent (someone who initiates something being done; see the causative relational processes below). See Eggins, *Introduction*, 224.

"They were playing football).[22] The Range does not have an autonomous existence (by itself), but only as part of the process.[23]

In addition to the process and the participants, different circumstances can be expressed through adverbial or prepositional phrases, not only in material processes but in all types of processes.[24]

You	have put	my soul	in the bundle of the living
Agent	*Process: Material*	*Goal*	*Circumstantial: location*

Mental Processes   *cognition* *affection* *perception*

Mental processes can be divided into three types involving cognition (verbs of thinking, knowing, understanding), affection (verbs of liking, fearing) or perception (verbs of seeing, hearing). There is no such thing as an intransitive mental process, and there will always be (at least) two participants: *Senser* and *Phenomenon*. The Senser must be a conscious human being (or an anthropomorphized nonhuman). There are *simple* Phenomena expressed by nominal phrases, and Phenomena of *acts* or *facts*, expressed by embedded clauses:

They	did not listen to	your words*
Senser	*Process: Mental*	*Phenomenon (simple)*

They	did not know	that my steps come from you
Senser	*Process: Mental*	*Phenomenon (fact)*

Behavioral Processes   *psychology*   *b/w*   *material + mental*

Behavioral processes are semantically halfway between material and mental processes. Behavioral processes are typically processes of physiological and psychological behavior. The majority of behavioral processes

---

22. Ibid., 218.

23. See Halliday, *An Introduction to Functional Grammar*, 134–37.

24. A whole range of circumstances are possible: circumstances of extent ("how long?"), location ("when?" "where?"), manner ("how?" "with what?"), cause ("why?" "what for?" "who?" "for whom?"), accompaniment ("with whom?"), matter ("what about?"), role ("what as?"). See Eggins, *Introduction*, 222–23.

have only one participant, the *Behaver*, and thus expresses "a form of doing that does not usually extend to another participant."[25] This Behaver is usually a conscious being (like the Senser in the mental process clause). If there is a second participant, it will be of the type Phenomenon or Range. A sign of the closeness to the mental process is the fact that the verbs in the two types of process clause may very well be synonymous ("look at" and "listen to" are behavioral processes, whereas "see" and "hear" are mental). However, in spite of all the similarities to the mental process, the behavioral process functions more like the *doing* of the material processes:[26]

They	do not believe	in me*
Behaver	*Process: Behavioral*	*Phenomenon*

The traitors	watch	them getting drunk at festivals*
Behaver	*Process: Behavioral*	*Phenomenon*

Verbal Processes   — Saying

Verbal processes are expressions of the verbal action *saying* and its many synonyms. Participants are *Sayer* (typically, but not necessarily, a conscious being), *Receiver*, and *Verbiage*, which is similar to Range in that it restates the verbal statement of the verbal process. The Verbiage, which is often nominalized, can also project a second clause of *quoting* or *reporting*:

They	told	a lie*
Sayer	*Process: Verbal*	*Verbiage*

I	said	that	they	had besieged	me*
Sayer	*Process: Verbal*	*Verbiage (quoting)*			
		Actor		*Process: Material*	*Goal*

---

25. Ibid., 233.

26. According to Eggins "the evidence of this is that the unmarked present tense for behaviourals is the present continous, as it is for materials" (ibid., 234). As the evidence rests on the use of verbal tense in English, this is an example of a rule that does not apply to Hebrew.

Existential Processes   ⌐ to be | existe

Existential processes have only one obligatory participant, the *Existent* (a phenomenon of any kind, often an event). In English the structure of existential processes involves the element "there" (because English sentences demand a subject) as in "there was/is something." "There" is left unanalyzed for transitivity, and in existential processes realized in Hebrew it is not an obligatory element. In Hebrew, existential clauses can be constructed as nominal clauses consisting of a subject with a prepositional phrase. They can also be constructed with a form of the verb היה or by use of יש and אין.[27]

There	is	no mediator*
	Process: Existential	*Existent*

Relational Processes

The category of relational processes covers a range of ways in which "being" could be realized. This group can be divided into basically two main subgroups: 1) the *attributive intensive*, the function of which is to say that "x is a member of the class a," and 2) the *identifying intensive* relational process, saying that "x serves to define the identity of y." The attributive intensive has two participants, the *Carrier* and the *Attribute* (an indefinite nominal group or adjective):

They	are	a congregation of Belial
Carrier	*Process:*	*Attribute*
	Attributive intensive	

The identifying intensive also has two participants, *Token* (the element being defined) and *Value* (the defining element):

The hymnist	acts as (defines himself as)	the mediator*
Token	*Process:*	*Value*
	Identifying intensive	

---

27. See Baasten, "Existential Clauses in Qumran Hebrew," 1–11; Baasten, "Nominal Clauses with Locative and Possessive Predicates in Qumran Hebrew," 25–52.

Other subtypes of the relational process are the *circumstantial, possessive,* and *causative* relationals. In the causative relational an *Agent* or *Attributor* causes a *Carrier* to be something or to have certain attributes:

You	Made	yourself	(become)	Great	through me
Agent	*Process: Causative*	*Carrier*	*(Process: Intensive)*	*Attribute*	*Circumstantial (Circumstance?)*

In Hebrew such a causative relational process will typically be expressed by a verb in the *hiphil*. [28]

For the purpose of demonstration I have provided the small tables above for each clause analyzed for transitivity. In the following chapters I will not be as explicit about the analytical process, but will simply state the Process and Participant types of each analyzed clause and concentrate on the implications for the transitivity of the text. Readers are encouraged to consult these pages as required.

Transitivity analysis has the obvious advantage that it can help retrieve information from distorted manuscripts where considerable parts of the texts are missing: Where only a half (or less) of the lines in a section are extant it is really impossible to reconstruct the information structures and analyze their logico-semantics—the ordering of experiences into meaningful sequences. To some degree, transitivity analysis may compensate for this by bringing attention to nuances in the clauses, or processes, that are extant in the manuscripts.

Through transitivity analysis it is possible to give refined descriptions of the processes referred to in a text and of participants involved in these processes. It is significant whether the speaking "I", when a grammatical subject, tends to occur as Actor, Behaver, or something else. Similarly, it is relevant to know which participant roles are ascribed to the addressee (God) and third parties referred to by the speaker. If participant patterns can be identified, this may also help us define the relationship between the parties—Speaker, God, and others—as they occur in the texts.

What we retrieve by using transitivity analysis is experiential meaning. This is not objective knowledge about actual experiences, events, or

---

28. As a matter of fact, material processes also may involve a participant Agent; only there Agent and Actor will be "mapped onto the same constituent," because the Actor (the one who *does* something) is often also the Agent (the one who *initiates* something being done). See Eggins, *Introduction*, 224.

activities that have taken place in history. Rather, it is information about
types of experiences that the authors knew of and considered relevant.
Through their work, the authors ascribed various kinds of experiences
and participant roles to God, the speaker (whomever he might represent)
and other people (such as fellow worshipers or opponents), and thus they
simultaneously interpreted and shaped their own socioreligious reality.

The sort of experiential meaning that we can retrieve by way of transitivity analysis is grammaticalized, inscribed meaning. Yet it may not
have been consciously inscribed by authors to the same degree as other
meanings that they may have wanted to share. Authors can make clear
propositions and they can sequence their texts meticulously in order to get
their message communicated (whether through adherence to or abolition
of genre conventions). It is doubtful, however, if they actually control the
sort of information that we can retrieve by way of transitivity analysis. This
is not information that has been fronted by the author, yet it betrays how
he imagines the figures appearing in his texts. One of my basic assumptions about 1QHodayot[a] is that it unfolds a divine-agency pattern in which
the speaker acts as a mediator.[29] This mediating role is fronted in some of
the so-called Leader Hymns, but in other compositions it is not. I suggest,
however, that it is fundamental to 1QHodayot[a] as a collection and that we
can catch glimpses of it here and there by way of transitivity analysis.

2.3. Text and Context

For a text to be meaningful, it must follow conventions to some degree
and live up to its reader's expectations. It must be *cohesive* and *coherent*,
because: "texts display continuity … with elements within their boundaries" and "with contexts within which they take place."[30] Cohesion is
the way the text itself is glued together by use of lexical compactness and
conjunctions, as well as through the use of clause complexes in order
to make logical sequences in the text. Coherence, on the other hand, is
the way in which continuity with the extratextual elements is realized in
the text. In SFL this is explained in terms of Genre and Register, which
will be accounted for below. First, however, I shall turn to one partic-

---

29. See introduction, section 1.3, "Assumption 3."
30. Eggins, *Introduction*, 85.

ular aspect of textual cohesiveness, lexical cohesion, which is realized through lexical strings.[31]

2.3.1. Lexical Cohesion: Lexical Strings

Through the choice of lexical items the producer of the text is able to present to the reader the reality with which he is concerned, or as Eggins puts it, "to relate the text consistently to its area of focus or its field."[32] Once a lexical item has been chosen, it actually points to a context from which the reader gets information about what to expect next. On the basis of such information, the reader is enabled to make judgments about the appropriateness of any textual information she is offered while reading or listening: Does the text live up to her expectations? Does it make sense? For instance, if the word "snare" occurs, words like "hunting" or "treason" may seem appropriate, while "florist" may not. By making lexical strings it is possible to identify themes in the text that may not have become apparent through the plain reading of it.

Lexical cohesiveness can be found through the identification of lexical strings in a text. The following couple of examples are from 1QHᵃ X 22–32,[33] which will shortly function as a test case. A lexical string consists of meaning-carrying words: noun, main verb, adverb, and adjective (but not preposition, pronoun, article, or auxiliary verb). Several lexical strings can be identified within a text, and a word can be part of more than one string. Longer strings are more significant than shorter strings.

Lexical string: Body/Being: (1) soul—the living—(2) *x* protect—sought *x* soul—(5) soul—(6) soul—(7) men—(11) *x* healing—consuming *x* trees—(12) *c* voice—(14) *c* heart—soul—(16) *c* feet—(17) soul—(19) *c* foot—(20) *x* bless

Lexical string: Standing/Walking: (4) steadfastness[34]—(5) *x* steps—(7) standing—(16) entangling *x* feet—(18) fell—(19) *x* foot *x* stood

---

31. Ibid., 42–47.

32. Ibid., 42.

33. Text and translation are printed in section 2.5. Note that numbers in the text refer to the number of the sentence, whereas clauses within the sentence will be numbered i, ii, iii, and so on. In my reproduction of 1QHᵃ X 22–32, I prioritize a division of the text into units suitable for linguistic analysis, rather than a division according to lines in the manuscript or a division into poetic units.

34. מעמד: lit., "standing."

There are rules for how to connect lexical items in such a string: Words can relate to each other taxonomically through *classification* or *composition*. Classification involves two or more lexical items that are *hyponyms of a superordinate* term. The main types are co-hyponomy (body/soul), class/subclass (movement/steps), contrast (blessing/curse), and similarity (man/being; heart/heart). Composition involves *meronomy* (two lexical items are related as a whole to one of its parts: body/heart) and co-meronomy (two lexical items are related because they are both part of a common whole: heart/foot). In addition to these taxonomy relationships, there are *expectancy* relationships between a verbal and a nominal element (the nominal expressing the *doer* or *action*). As implied by the terminology, this is a relationship of expectancy. Who could be expected to carry out a specific action mentioned in the text (*foot*/stand), or which participant would typically be affected by a particular action or process (hide/*traps*)?

In the lexical strings above, references are made to the number of the clause (not the number of the line in the manuscript). A relation of expectancy is indicated by an *x*, and a relation of composition is indicated by a *c*. Where nothing else is indicated, the relation is one of classification.

2.3.2. Genre: Exposition of Cultural Context

Put very briefly, according to SFL, genre is how we get things done. Jim Martin has put it this way: "Genre is a staged, goal-oriented, purposeful activity in which speakers engage as members of our culture."[35] A genre originates from and is closely tied to a specific type of social situation occurring within a culture. This applies whether it is a literary genre or a speech genre. It is habitualized, economical language usage, a language pattern that enables people to get things done in an effective manner. Genres save discourse participants from the trouble of inventing ways to deal with situations every time they occur.[36] A prayer is thus a habitualized way of worshiping God in a religious community. According to SFL the identity of a genre has three dimensions: (1) register configuration, (2) staged sche-

---

35. Martin, "Language, Register and Genre," 19. According to Martin, genre includes a variety of activity types, such as "making a dental appointment, buying vegetables, telling a story, writing an essay, applying for a job, writing a letter to the editor, inviting someone for dinner, and so on" (ibid.).

36. Eggins, *Introduction*, 56–58.

matic structure, and (3) realizational patterns. I shall deal with the latter two here, and with the register configuration in the following paragraph.

The *schematic structure* of the genre is "a way of getting from A to B in the way a given culture accomplishes whatever the genre in question is functioning to do in that culture."[37] Each stage in the schematic structure accomplishes something, has a function. So, when describing the schematic structure, functional rather than formal criteria are used to identify each step. One has to ask for the function of each step in relation to the others. When we classify the Hodayot as thanksgiving hymns, we do this on the basis of our knowledge of such a category in ancient Hebrew literature, supposing they may have served a function similar to that of the biblical thanksgiving hymns. The following typical steps can be identified in this biblical genre: Invitation to give thanks or praise to Yahweh; account of trouble and salvation; praises of Yahweh and acknowledgement of his saving work; offertory formula at the presentation of sacrifice; blessings of participants in the ceremony; exhortation.[38] This division of structural steps is informed by a form-critical approach; it is used as a means to approach the *Sitz im Leben* of psalms and prayers, and is thus largely made on the basis of functional criteria. For instance, the initial invitation to praise God reflects the overall purpose to give thanks to God; and, in addition, its function is to involve an audience of worshipers in this process. The account of trouble and salvation is the public flashback of a once-afflicted person who has by now experienced God's salvific acts. In the liturgical setting, the account functions as proof of God's act of salvation and provides the collective of worshipers with a concrete reason to thank him.

The schematic structures in the Hodayot do not necessarily coincide with those of the biblical psalms, and steps that on the surface seem familiar may not function in the same way in the text.[39] This is in part because genre and form-critical *Gattung* are not completely overlapping categories; the genre of prayer encompasses subcategories, such as those *Gattungen* in the biblical psalms that qualify as prayers. A distinct, possibly liturgical, and shared situational context type is probably the main reason for the relatively uniform schematic structures of these *Gattungen*. Likewise, one

---

37. These are the words of Jim Martin, cited in Eggins, *Introduction*, 59. The original source is Jim Martin, "Process and Text: Two Aspects of Semiosis," 251.

38. See Gerstenberger, *Psalms*, 15.

39. See the discussion of שבועה and נגש in section 3.2.2.

can explain the different schematic structures of the Hodayot and biblical thanksgiving psalms by the fact that their situational or social contexts differ. Both text corpora are prayers in the sense of habitualized ways of affecting God, but due to their otherwise different social, geographical, material, and ideological contexts, they accomplish this through different schematic structures.[40]

The *realizational pattern* is the concrete way in which each stage in the schematic structure is realized through lexical choices, mode, syntactical features, and so forth. It is through analysis of these aspects that one can "establish objective justification for claims about different stages."[41]

2.3.3 Register: Exposition of a Specific Situation

The register of a text is a function of its linguistic habitualization. SFL register theory describes how the particular, situational context of a text is reflected in the linguistic choices made by its producer. I have already mentioned some reservations as to the degree to which we can access the social context of the Hodayot through SFL methodologies. Nevertheless, below I shall touch upon one particular, useful element of register theory, *Mode*, "the role language is playing through interaction."[42]

---

40. See the modal analysis of 1QH[a] VI 30–33 in section 3.2 ("VI 28–32: *Commitment*," etc.), 3.2.3, and 3.2.4.

41. Eggins, *Introduction*, 65.

42. See Eggins, *Introduction*, 90. In register theory, linguistic choices are divided into three types—Mode, Tenor, and Field—according to the aspect of the situational context that they describe. Mode is by definition "the role language is playing through interaction," and elements of Mode are treated in this paragraph. In order to provide readers with a general idea about SFL register theory, I offer the following brief remarks on Tenor and Field. *Tenor* is about the interpersonal relations in a text and reflects a situation as formal or informal. If there is equality in power, frequent contact, and affective involvement between the interactants, then informal situations will typically occur. Unequal power relations, rare contact, and a low degree of affective involvement, on the other hand, tend to create formal situations. The interpersonal aspects of situations influence language use. Mood and modality look different in addresses between people who are socially equal, compared to when subordinate persons address superiors (ibid., 99–102). *Field* covers the topic or focus of a text, but also the way the topic is presented in terms of technicality. At one end of the scale, we find the very technical text aimed at specialists; that is, people with insider knowledge. It will typically have a deep taxonomy in the sense that the different areas of the field will be classified and subclassified into several layers. At the other end of the scale, there

It makes a difference whether language is spoken or written. In spoken language a considerable amount of information will only be comprehensible in the specific situation in which it is given. The grammar will often be flawed, the sentences incomplete. In a conversation it is possible to give immediate responses, and each utterance is an action within the ongoing social interaction. Written texts, on the other hand, are not as immediate and dynamic; they are planned, staged in a rhetorical manner. Polished feedback will be delayed or even unlikely (consider the possibilities of using email, a fax, newspaper articles, or a novel). Written texts tend to be lexically dense and grammatically correct, and tend to express reflection rather than action.

The function of language in a social situation can be described in terms of *experiential distance*, which is the distance existing between language and social processes. Does language function as action or as representation? This question can be illustrated as follows:[43]

Playing a game	*Commentating*	*Recounting experience*	*Constructing experience*
e.g., bridge	e.g., a match	e.g., news- paper report	e.g., (non)- fiction

←——————————————————————————————→

Language accompanying a social process
Language as ACTION

Language constituting a social process
Language as REFLECTION

Where could we place the Hodayot on this scale? Are the Hodayot compositions action or reflective representation? This is a highly relevant question, which is often ignored in scholarship on the Hodayot and the Dead Sea Scrolls.

It will suffice to give a tentative answer to this question, and to propose that the question itself be kept in mind in the course of textual analysis.

---

are common-sense texts that cover a field in a less specialized language and with a shallow taxonomy (ibid., 103–9).

43. The model is a reproduction from ibid., 91, which is based in turn on Jim Martin, "Language, Register and Genre," in *Children Writing: A Reader* (ed. F. Christie; Geelong, Vic.: Deakin University Press, 1984), 27.

Given the character of 1QHodayot[a] not only as *written*, but as written *and collected*, it should not be regarded as purely action. Regardless of their roles in other oral and literary settings, the compositions were incorporated into the collection for a reason. Due also to the lack of liturgical signs, it is reasonable to infer that the collectors had other criteria for juxtaposing these compositions. In spite of their different character, they were all perceived as fit representatives of someone or something of the meaning of this collection. This means that the *joining* of the so-called Leader and Community Hymns turned into a representation of something that was not identical to what any of the categories of compositions originally represented. It also means that the differences in authorship and origins of the categories are potentially irrelevant to the interpretation of 1QHodayot[a] as a collection.

2.4. The Merits of SFL for This Project

For the analysis to be undertaken in this study, the merit of SFL is its detailed, analytical apparatus for describing the different levels of linguistic functions. SFL provides us with a detailed, multifaceted set of tools to describe language and for asking, potentially, several questions concerning the texts simultaneously. I shall carry out SFL analysis mainly on a descriptive level. As outlined in the introduction, the perception of the sociohistorical context is misguided and need to be scrapped. Alternative descriptions are needed, descriptions that are less dependent on the notion that one group of compositions represents community leadership whereas the remainder represents ordinary community members. Only when this has been achieved will I attempt a recontextualization—this time with the help of the sociocognitive theory of Teun van Dijk.

But what about the central claim of SFL theorists that using SFL methods provides knowledge about the social context of a text? My answer to this is twofold. First, the purpose of using SFL here is different, because of the need first to *decontextualize* the Hodayot and free the reading of them from unjustified notions about their social contexts (leadership communication or communal worship). Second, SFL has received criticism on this point, and I shall deal briefly with a couple of accusations raised against it.

Generally, the critics are concerned about the danger of exaggerating the amount of knowledge we can get regarding the exact relationship between text and context. Criticism has been raised against SFL for approaching the social contexts of discourses mainly through analysis of the discourses themselves, and for not providing methodologies for analyzing institutions and other relevant, socially bound entities.[44] Particularly ethnographers working with contemporary communities insist that purely discourse-analytical approaches to context are insufficient. In Ben Rampton's words, "Contexts for communication should be investigated rather than assumed," and linguistic analyses provide only "a provisional view of the communicative affordances."[45] When dealing with ancient texts, however, our ability to investigate contexts by means other than texts is limited. There may be artifacts, but these are often even muter about their specific meanings than texts are, and the relationship between texts and artifacts may be difficult to determine. Nevertheless, this sort of criticism raised by researchers of language use in contemporary cultures reminds us that only to a limited extent can we reach social contexts through texts. It thus encourages us to be cautious in our contextualizing efforts.

Another critique raised against SFL is that it does not deal with mental aspects of communication. Kieran O'Halloran criticizes critical-discourse analysts and SFL analysts alike for exaggerating the role of semantico-syntactic structures and of readers' knowledge of grammatical structures for their mental representation of events described in texts. General knowledge of the world, he says, controls the perception of textual representations to a higher degree than these analysts allow.[46] Teun van Dijk insists that the social situations themselves do not influence people's production of discourse, but rather "the *definition, interpretation, representation or construction of participants* of their social situation."[47] Therefore,

---

44. Christo van der Merwe notes that the analytical categories of Halliday lack an empirical basis ("Some Recent Trends in Biblical Hebrew Linguistics," 12). Stef Slembrouck claims that in SFL "we do not find any traces of a stated need to engage with context separate from textual analysis" ("Discourse, Critique and Ethnography," 253).

45. Rampton, "Linguistic Ethnography," 235–38. The implication is that linguistic analysis cannot stand alone; *pragmatic* aspects of contexts, typically not made explicit in text and speech, are seen as indispensable for a genuine understanding of meaning-making in discourse. An important theoretical basis for such critique is the assumption that discourse is not simply the communication of ideas and messages, but is part of cultural *practice*. For a brief introduction to ethnographers' pragmatic approach to contextualization, see Alessandro Duranti, *Linguistic Anthropology*, 215–18.

46. O'Halloran, *Critical Discourse Analysis and Language Cognition*, 21–22, 162. Critical-discourse analysts often employ SFL categories for analyzing the relationship between text and social context. See also Fairclough, *Analysing Discourse*, 5–6.

47. Dijk, *Discourse and Context*, 119.

the social contexts themselves are not directly accessible through analysis of discourse. Contexts *as perceived by speakers and writers*, on the other hand, are.

When in chapter 3–5 I use SFL in the textual analyses, the aim is not primarily to display the social context behind the texts. SFL will be employed as a delicate tool in the effort to make the descriptions of the texts as independent as possible from customary scholarly notions about their social context. This task has a high priority, and the SFL analytical categories to which I shall turn shortly are suitable for the purpose.

The reservations about the degree to which we can grasp the social contexts behind texts on purely linguistic grounds must be taken into consideration. They have been developed by researchers who work together with contemporary language users, and who have access to additional knowledge and experience of these language users' communication. When dealing with discourses belonging to ancient peoples, we do not get the opportunity to participate in their communication and interaction like ethnographers dealing with their contemporaries. We, on the other hand, have to rely on the texts themselves, and on theories of how, for different reasons, texts might relate to their original social contexts. We must assume that some of the additional factors of communicative situations detectable in contemporary discourse must have been present also in ancient communities. We must take into account such factors (for example, the participants' gestures, their immediate or long-term aims and goals, their ideas about other participants, relevant tools that they had at their disposal) and assume that their presence would influence the meaning of a text in its original setting. For all practical purposes, this means that we must approach also the social context of the Hodayot with the awareness that the text forms part of a communicative activity, but does not by itself constitute it.

2.5. Test Case: Analysis of 1QH^a X 22–32

The purpose of this brief test case is primarily to demonstrate the use of SFL methods—especially transitivity analysis. Accordingly, it has not been shaped to form a part of the book's argument. Nevertheless, I want to direct attention to the fact that the speaker of this hymn holds two different positions in the agency of God. Mostly he appears to be an object of God's agency, but he is also a mediator of it to the benefit of other people.

For the sake of clarity I have organized the Hebrew text and its translation in the following way. Each sentence is numbered and given a line of
its own (1, 2, 3) The constituent clauses of the sentences have also been
numbered (i, ii, iii). Nonfinite Hebrew phrases functioning as circumstantial information are not treated as clauses, even if they appear as such in
the English translation.[48] The arrangement of the text does not reflect the
lines of text as found in the manuscript, nor does it in any way represent
poetic structure.

Hebrew Text of 1QHᵃ X 22–33

(1i) אודכה אדוני

(1ii) כי שמתה נפשי בצרור החיים

(2i) ותשוך בעדי מכול מוקשי שחת

(2ii) כ[י]א עריצים בקשו נפשי בתומכי בבריתכה

(3i) והמה סוד שוא ועדת בליעל

(4i) לא ידעו

(4ii) כיא מאתכה מעמדי

(5i) ובחסדיכה תושיע נפשי

(5ii) כיא מאתכה מצעדי

(5iii) והמה מאתכה[49]

(6i) גרו על נפשי בעבור הכבדכה במשפט רשעים

(7i) והגבירכה בי נגד בני אדם

(7ii) כיא בחסדכה עמדי

(8i) ואני אמרתי

(9i) חנו עלי גבורים

(10i) סבבום[50] בכל כלי מלחמותם

(11i) ויפרו חצים לאין מרפא ולהוב חנית כאש[51] אוכלת עצים

(12i) וכהמון מים רבים שאון קולם נפץ וזרם להשחית רבים

(13i) למזורות יבקעו אפעה ושוא בהתרוממם גליהם

---

48. For example, במוס לבי כמים / "when my heart melts like water" in (14i).

49. מאתכה (line 25 of the manuscript). The scribe has written *mem* and left a
space. The rest of the phrase has been added by another scribe (Schuller and Stegemann, *1QHodayotᵃ* [DJD XL], 139).

50. סבבום (line 27 of the manuscript). According to Schuller, the original text
must have been סבבוני, "they have surrounded me." Some text editions, including
DSSSE, read the participle סבבים.

51. כאש (line 28 of the manuscript). Some text editions have באש, "with fire." It
appears that the one version results from a scribal correction of the other (Schuller
and Stegemann, *1QHodayotᵃ* [DJD XL], 139).

(14i) ואני במוס לבי כמים ותחזק נפשי בבריתך

(15i) והם רשת פרשו לי

(16i) תלכוד רגלם

(17i) ופחים טמנו לנפשי

(18i) נפלו בם

(19i) ורגלי עמדה במישור

(20i) מקהלם אברכה שמכה

Translation of 1QH^a X 22–33

(1i)   I thank you, Lord

(1ii)   because you have placed my soul in the bundle of the living

(2i)   (And) you protect me from the snares of the pit

(2ii)   because vicious men sought my soul when I relied on your covenant

(3i)   But they are a council of futility, the congregation of Belial

(4i)   They did not know

(4ii)   that from you comes my steadfastness

(5i)   And in your kindness you save my soul

(5ii)   because from you are my steps,

(5iii) they are from you

(6i)   (They)[52] have attacked my soul for the sake of your Glory in the judgment of the wicked

(7i)   But you have shown your strength through me in the sight of men

(7ii)   because my standing is due to your kindness

(8i)   But I said:

(9i)   Heroes have besieged (me),

(10i) they have surrounded me with all kinds of weapons:

(11i) Arrows[53] destroy with no healing, and a flaming spearhead like fire consuming trees

(12i) Like masses of water is the noise of their voice; an inundation of rain (in order) to destroy many

(13i) To the stars[54] do wickedness[55] and deceit burst forth in the self-exaltation of their waves

---

52. The subject of this clause must be the vicious men mentioned in clause (2ii) and referred to again in (3i) and (4i).

53. I follow Schuller and Stegemann, *1QHodayot^a* (DJD XL), and others having "arrows" as the subject here, whereas "the heroes" is the subject in *DSSSE*.

54. למזורות: I translate this phrase "to the stars" in accordance with Schuller and Stegemann, *1QHodayot^a* (DJD XL). The text seems to rely on Job 38:32 and its con-

(14i) As for me—when my heart melts like water, then you strengthen
       my soul with your covenant
(15i) As for them—a net they spread for me
(16i) but it entangled their own feet
(17i) and traps they hid for my soul
(18i) —they fell into them
(19i) but my foot stood firmly[56]
(20i) From their assembly I bless your name

I shall give a brief account of the genre and register of the text and
analyze it for transitivity on the clause level. A clause may be verbal or
nominal. It may be related to other clauses hypotactically or paratactically,
and it may be connected to the main clause asyndetically or synthetically.
The range of possible functions for a specific hypotactic clause within its
sentence is determined by its first conjunction. As far as we are aware of
the semantic meaning of the various conjunctions in the Dead Sea Scrolls,
there are limited options. The grammatical function of paratactic clauses
in the sentence may be somewhat more difficult to define; it may even be
difficult to decide whether it should be regarded as a main clause or as a
subordinate clause. In the following paragraphs, I am going to investigate
the roles of the participants in the hymn through transitivity analysis.

---

text. See also Mansoor, *The Thanksgiving Hymns*, 109 n. 7. This translation allows for
a grammatical parallelism with the following clause. See Berlin, *Dynamics of Biblical
Parallelism*, 21–22; Niccacci, "Analysing Biblical Hebrew Poetry," 81. Conceptually, the
interpretation borders on the Self-Glorification Hymn (1QH[a] XXVI and parallels).
See chapter 6. Bonnie Kittel, on the other hand, translates "wickedness" because this
would better mirror the meaning of Isa 59:5, in which the whole phrase למזורות יבקעו
אפעה is probably rooted (*The Hymns of Qumran*, 42–43). This solution is lexicograph-
ically dubious because a masculine form would be expected.

55. אפעה: In biblical Hebrew this word has the meaning of "viper," apparent in
the phrase למזורות יבקעו אפעה of Isa 59:5 (והזורה תבקע אפעה, which shares some
homographic elements with our text even where the meaning is different). See the preceding note. However, it is often translated "wickedness" or the like, probably because
it forms a hendiadys with the following ושוא. See Kittel, *The Hymns of Qumran*, 43;
Holm-Nielsen, *Hodayot*, 44.

56. The words עמדה במישור have been added in the margin by another scribe,
but are probably part of the original text; the first scribe had left an open space after
ורגלי, and thus the text did not make sense. The extant text also adds up to a nearly
complete reuse of Ps 26:12. See Schuller and Stegemann, *1QHodayot*[a] (DJD XL), 139;
Holm-Nielsen, *Hodayot*, 44.

2.5.1. The Genre and Register of the Hodayah

The text of 1QH[a] X 22–32 is a prayer. This is signaled by the tenor of the text, *a human addressing God.* It can be classified more narrowly as a thanksgiving hymn according to its similarities with a subclass from the book of Psalms. However, as the transitivity analysis will demonstrate, some of the central elements found in the biblical psalms of thanksgiving may not function in the same way in the hodayah. In both cases, however, the field can be described as *motivated thanksgiving.*

This text, like the Hodayot in general, has the characteristics of a written text: it does not consist of words scribbled randomly, but seems to be well-planned, reflected, and polished. Its mode, then, is *written to be read.* Can the mode be defined more precisely? The thanksgiving formula at the very beginning, "I thank you, Lord," could signal that an offering is being made here. The same goes for the very last clause, "I bless you." These two formulas signal that the commodity of this text is in the form of *goods and services* (as opposed to information). Possibly, the words were meant to accompany an act of offering. However, it should be mentioned that the thanksgiving formula of the Hodayot, אודכה אדוני, distinguishes itself from biblical thanksgiving formulas because it is in the indicative or cohortative mood.[57] Constructions equivalent to אודכה אדוני are rare in the biblical psalms, where thanksgiving formulas usually have the form of jussives or imperatives directed to fellow worshipers.[58] In contrast, the construction so typical in the Hodayot has the effect of focusing on the relationship between hymnist and God, with little or no attention paid to fellow worshipers who might be present during singing or recitation—if

---

57. The verbal form does not distinguish between the modal and indicative functions. "Strictly speaking, a distinction must be made between the (syntactical) *cohortative mood* and the *cohortative form*. Sometimes, indeed, the syntax clearly indicates the cohortative mood even though the form is not cohortative" (Joüon and Muraoka, *A Grammar of Biblical Hebrew*, 2:374).

58. In this respect, Pss 9:2 (אודה יהוה), 108:4 (אודך), and 138:1 (אודך) are parallel to the Hodayot in using the formula אודכה אדוני which implies an "I" offering thanks directly to God. At the beginning of Ps 75, a plural subject, "we," offers thanks in the same manner, but later in the psalm this "we" becomes a praising "I." In other psalms, thanksgiving is ordered or exhorted through the use of imperatives (i.e., Pss 105; 107; 118; 136). It is also possible just to state the appropriateness of thanksgiving, as in Ps 92. Praise is not offered "just like that"; most often it is expressed as an imperative or jussive (Pss 47; 66; 106; 111–113; 117; 135; 146–150).

the compositions were at all meant for that kind of use.[59] So, seen as a tendency in the Hodayot, the consistent choice of this particular thanksgiving formula *may* point to a setting that is not liturgical in the sense of involving a big audience, singing, or recitation.

A final remark relating to the tenor of the text: All the clauses between the opening and ending formulas are declaratives, and there are no insertions of volitionals or exclamations of joy or grievance, often found in biblical hymns and prayers. I do not want to make too much of this in the interpretation of this particular text, but this is an aspect of the tenor that might reflect a less immediate relationship between the thanksgiving and the personal experiences of the speaker than what one finds in several biblical thanksgiving psalms. Could this "lack" of affective elements be an expression of a situation in which theoretical reflection (a situation of study and learning) takes priority over experience and reaction (a liturgical situation)?

2.5.2. Analysis of Transitivity

The Speaker

Three times the speaker of this text is the subject of a verbal process. In his very first and last words—"I thank you, Lord" (1i) and "from their assembly I bless you" (20i)—the speaker enacts material processes.[60] First and last, he takes on the role of an Actor. God, as an additional participant, is the Goal of these processes. In the middle of the text (8i), the speaker takes on the role of a Sayer in a verbal process: "But I said...." There is no other participant in this clause. Maybe the process also can be perceived as a mental process. In that case the following line expresses the thoughts of the psalmist. It seems at least to introduce an "introverted" part of the hymn.[61]

---

59. In Ps 108:3, a psalmist says, "I (will) thank you, Lord, amongst the people," thus signalling the witnessing function of thanksgiving and pointing to a social context for the thanksgiving. A similar picture emerges from Ps 9, and possibly also from Ps 138.

60. "I thank you" and "I bless you" are accented verbal processes, which are very close to material processes. See Halliday, *An Introduction to Functional Grammar*, 254. Cf. "I give you thanks," in which "thanks" is in fact *goods* handed over to a recipient.

61. This understanding of the verbal process is reflected in *DSSSE*, "I thought,"

In five other instances, however, the hymnist conducts himself as
an obligatory participant in other types of processes through the use of
a stand-in, be it his heart, his foot, his steps, or his steadfastness. I shall
deal with the four of them together because, in spite of (as well as because
of) differences between them, they are closely knitted together. In section
2.3.1 we found that there is a lexical string of standing/walking; the clauses
now to be analyzed for transitivity are all connected through this lexical
string as beads on a string. Three of them are nominal clauses located in
the first part of the text:

(4i) They did not know (4ii) that *from you comes my steadfastness.*
(5i) And in your kindness you save my soul, (5ii) because *from you are
my steps.*
(7i) But you have shown your strength through me in the sight of man,
(7ii) because *my standing is due to your kindness.*

As the SFL theory describes texts in English, the occurrence of a finite verb
is needed if we want to carry out a transitivity analysis. However, Hebrew
nominal clauses of the kind met in these three instances (pronominal
phrase + nominal phrase) actually realize relational processes (existential
processes can likewise be realized in nominal clauses in Hebrew). As participants in these processes, the subjects ("my steadfastness," "my steps,"
and "my standing") are Carriers of the attributes expressed by the prepositional clauses. In effect, it is the speaker that is being characterized in this
way as the Carrier. By way of lexical elements referring to body parts or
their functions (standing, steps), the use of stand-ins supports the picture
of him as a rather passive participant.

Each of these parallel clauses is part of a sentence that relates to the
reality of the speaker and provides additional knowledge and meaning:
1) The steadfastness of the speaker is something that "they did not know."
"They" refers to the "vicious men" mentioned earlier (2ii). The steadfastness of the speaker being something they did not know is, as far as they
are concerned, a *secret* quality. 2) The steps of the speaker, his walking,

---

but most translators choose the neutral, "I said." Michael Douglas ("Power and Praise,"
119) translates, "I, I declared," thus reflecting a different idea altogether. He suggests
that the text describes certain events evolving because of a conflict between the
Teacher of Righteousness and his opponents. See also Douglas, "The Teacher Hymn
Hypothesis Revisited," 264–65.

are seen as related to God, his mercy and act of saving. According to my translation above, the fact that the speaker's steps are from God has actually caused God's act of salvation.[62] They have a redeeming quality. In any case, in this setting the theme of standing/walking concerns the mutual relationship between the speaker and God. 3) Lastly, the theme of standing/walking is put into a much wider perspective as it is concerned with how God acts toward humanity; he does this *through the speaker*. To summarize the contexts of these three clauses, they embed the walking/standing of the speaker in three different situations: from that of isolated secrecy through that of God's salvation of the speaker to that of God's salvation of men through the speaker. The walking/standing of the speaker is a *quality* that he shows in all three phases on the initiative of God.

The fourth clause is a verbal clause also expressing a relational process in which the speaker, represented by his foot, is the Carrier of an Attribute.

(19i) *But my foot stood firmly.*

This utterance serves to conclude the theme of the speaker's walking/standing, and there is a different feeling to it that is an effect of linguistic variation. Unlike the former clauses, this one is independent. Also, where the former clauses focus on the circumstances of the standing/walking,[63] this clause leaves out circumstances and focuses instead on the quality of the Carrier itself.[64] It sums up the effect of God's influence upon the speaker.

To sum up the results of the transitivity analysis carried out so far: In the opening and concluding words of this hymn, where the speaker gives thanks and blesses God, he is the one who brings action into the world (he is performing speech acts). But throughout the composition he speaks—indirectly—of himself in the third person and as someone who does not act but is gifted with some qualities. He is seen in three different settings, none of which can be seen as the prioritized one. In this way, the walking/standing theme very much defines his relationship with God as one of

---

62. It could also be the other way around: If we take the כי to be an adverbial conjunction, the nominal clause could express a consequence of God's saving act. However, syntactically the option chosen here is the more likely.

63. They are a subcategory of relational processes, in SFL terminology called *circumstantial* attributive processes. See Eggins, *Introduction*, 245–47.

64. Ibid., 239–40. This subcategory is called *intensive* attributive processes.

steadfastness and security, whatever phase he is going through. He seems to see himself as a worshiping object, rather than as an acting subject.

God

On the other hand, God enacts material processes upon the hymnist four times: He has *put* the hymnist "in the bundle of the living (1ii); he *protects* (2i), *saves* (5i), and *strengthens* (14i) him. The speaker's act of thanksgiving and blessing thus takes place on the basis of God's actions toward him. We have seen that God stages the text as an Actor, or rather as an Agent, in one additional clause, in the process of *showing his strength* (7i).[65] In this clause, the speaker is still explicitly involved, but in a different role—reduced to a circumstantial element—since God is said to have shown his strength *through* him. But how does this fifth clause, in which God puts action into the world, relate to the others? Like clause (1ii), it has the verb in the perfect, whereas the other clauses have the verb in the imperfect. Clause (1ii) informs the audience of the reason for the thanksgiving, and the use of the perfect in this instance reflects the all-embracing meaning of this clause. The process of placing the speaker "in the bundle of the living" sums up and includes a number of processes that have taken place, such as the protection of the speaker "from the snares of the pit" (2i), the saving of his soul (5i), and the strengthening of it with the covenant (14i), all in the imperfect. The description of how God has shown his strength through the speaker parallels clause (1ii) in its use of the perfect. That, too, is a perfect, all-embracing description of how God puts action into the world according to this prayer.

The Opponents

Now for the vicious men who carry out a series of material processes, all directed at the hymnist: At first sight all these material actions on their part produce an impression of a very potent and powerful group of people. However, if we look at the context of these processes, we may have our doubts about this picture. The first clause, "vicious men sought my soul"

---

65. The causative, *hiphil* verb makes God an Agent who shows his strength through the hymnist. A rather more literal translation of the clause would reveal this: "You will make yourself great through me." God, who in this translation appears to be Goal as well as Agent, remains the one who causes action in the world.

(2ii), is followed by a relational process in which the vicious men are described as "a council of futility, the congregation of Belial" (3i). In itself, this characterization may simply mean that they are essentially evil, but there is more to it. The mental process following it, "*They did not know that from you comes my steadfastness*" (4i + 4ii), is not just an arbitrary additional piece of information; it has the function of giving a wider perspective on the vicious men and their actions. What they did not know was the fact that "from you comes my steadfastness," and I shall argue that this means they did not realize what kind of powers they were challenging, and that they in fact did not realize what they were doing.

The context of their second material process, "They have attacked my soul" (6i), points in the same direction. The adjunct phrase, "for the sake of your Glory in the judgment of the wicked," points to the termination, the final result of this action. The glory of God is hardly what the attackers intended to achieve,[66] and therefore the adjunct phrase serves to expose the futility of their deeds.

Then comes the clause, "Heroes have besieged me" (9i), having again the vicious men as Actors in a material process. What is important to note in this case is the preceding clause, "But I said" (8i), in which the speaker refers to himself as the participant Sayer in a verbal process. What does it mean that the speaker reintroduces himself in this manner, referring to another (earlier) instance of his speaking? He makes room for a different perspective, a perspective that he himself once had, but which is not necessarily the perspective he holds as he utters the prayer. Besides the idea that the vicious men had besieged him, what comes next in the text is a dreadful scenario expressed through apocalyptic images of war and chaos (9i–13i). It is possible to see this whole scenario the way most scholars do, as a description of terrible events that had happened to the speaker in the past and from which he had been eventually saved with the help of God. I am going to discuss the justification for this option in the next paragraph. For now, I want to underscore the point that by the choice of a verbal process displaying the speaker retrospectively as a Sayer, the author of this prayer has taken the liberty to deviate from the real-time perspective of the speaker. The implications of this will also be discussed in the next paragraph.

---

66. This is a variant of the rhetorical technique of using transformation as a means to point out the essential value of someone of something, as described by Burke, *A Rhetoric of Motives*, 10–20.

The last two material processes effectuated by the vicious men with the speaker as a goal are "the net they spread for me" (15i) and "traps they hid from my soul" (17i). But as the context shows, these actions are in vain because eventually the vicious men are the ones that are hit. The entangling of "their own feet" (16i) and their falling into their traps (18i) serve to contrast the vicious men with the speaker; through the theme of walking/standing he has been pictured as safe and belonging to "the bundle of the living" through the various phases of the text.

The overall picture given in the transitivity analysis is that of a worshiper offering thanks to God, not so much because he has been saved from disturbances caused by his earthly enemies, but to celebrate his situation; namely, that he has once and for all been put into the "bundle of the living" by God. This interpretation does not deviate from the theological ideas held by the Dead Sea community, but it does deviate from interpretations carried out by other Dead Sea Scrolls scholars, as will be seen in the last paragraph.

2.5.3 Discussion of 1QH[a] X 22–32

There is no consensus as to whether this composition, placed at the beginning of the block of so-called Leader Hymns, is a leader hymn or a community hymn.[67] Regarding the structure of the composition, the independent personal pronouns found in initial position in clauses (3i), (8i), (14i), and (15i) are usually perceived to mark the beginnings of new sections. Bonnie Kittel in particular stresses the structural and thematic significance of these pronouns, calling them the "chief thematic device of the poem." She describes how the repeated "I" and "they" create a polarity of

---

67. Jeremias (*Der Lehrer*, 171) did not include 1QH[a] X 22–32 within his group of eight so-called Teacher Hymns; Kuhn (*Enderwartung*, 24) also doubted that it belonged there; Newsom (*Self as Symbolic Space*, 232–40) treats it as a hymn of the community. Others again argue that it is a so-called teacher or leader hymn. Tanzer ("The Sages at Qumran," 61) argues this on the basis of "thanksgiving offered to God for deliverance from enemies, the description of persecution, and the personal context of the first person pronoun 'I,' set in opposition to 'they' (והמה)." Likewise Douglas ("Power and Praise," 119–22; 319–50), who focuses on the phrase והגבירכה בי and other elements that this hymn shares with compositions usually interpreted as teacher hymns.

"war between the wicked and the righteous and the corresponding battle between life and death."[68]

In 1960, Svend Holm-Nielsen described the genre of this composition as a mixture of biblical psalms of thanksgiving, complaint, and trust, primarily because the narrative motive, which is a typical trait in biblical thanksgiving psalms, "does not seem to relate safely ended past events," but rather deals with events that "are past, but whose consequences still exist in the present."[69] This difference in the narrative element in comparison to the biblical thanksgiving psalms could have been expected to provoke questions about difference in function, but this has generally not been a significant issue. Unlike Holm-Nielsen, Bonnie Kittel stresses the great resemblance between the apocalyptic imagery, which is a substantial part of this narrative section of the hymn, and biblical psalms such as Pss 29, 69, 93, and 107.[70] Newsom, more in line with Holm-Nielsen, does note the difference and describes it as follows:

> As in the thanksgiving psalms, the events narrated belong to the realm of symbolic expression and are not literal descriptions. In contrast to the thanksgiving psalms, however, the narrative is not a symbolic representation of a genuinely recollected anomic experience (illness, conflict, bad fortune) but a representation of the speaker's situation within a quasi-mythic account of the world. The function of the description in the hodayah is normative. Situating the speaker within the account of contending forces, the hodayah gives him a subject position within this symbolic order. The threat and deliverance is not a moment of the past but an integral part of the speaker's fundamental condition, one that the hodayah enables to be experienced over and over again.[71]

Newsom goes on to point out the opposition made by using the independent personal pronouns, but then claims that the fundamental opposition is not between speaker and enemies, but between enemies and God, on whose "account" the enemies have been acting badly. Newsom contrasts this with the biblical psalms, in which "the opposition between the psalmist and his enemies … remains fundamentally a human conflict, in relation to which the psalmist actively seeks divine aid, giving as his reason

---

68. Kittel, *The Hymns of Qumran*, 37.
69. Holm-Nielsen, *Hodayot*, 46.
70. Kittel, *The Hymns of Qumran*, 41.
71. Newsom, *Self as Symbolic Space*, 235.

the fact that he is on God's side and his enemies are not."[72] The speaker of the hodayah, in Newsom's view, is but a battlefield for God's fight against impious people.

This passive role of the speaker is partly in line with what I have found by way of transitivity analysis. However, I find it difficult to agree that the speaker is the battlefield, because apparently there is no proper battle at all. Contrary to what Newsom has to say about the vicious men, they do not make much of an opponent for God in the analysis undertaken here, but are pictured as rather impotent.

The author's use of a mental process in clause (4i) and a verbal process in clause (8i) serves to distinguish this composition from the genre of thanksgiving psalms by which it is so inspired. It is striking that whereas the independent personal pronouns are generally seen as significant to the sectioning and meaning of this composition, not much attention has been paid to how the apocalyptic scenario in clauses (9i)–(13i) is related to the independent pronoun marking the whole section.[73] In SFL terminology, that whole scenario is projected as the Verbiage of the verbal process, of which the independent personal pronoun is the participant Sayer. It represents a perspective that the speaker once held, but which is not in line with the perspective he now holds; namely, the overall perspective of the composition.

The result of the SFL analysis undertaken here differs quite substantially from other interpretations of 1QH[a] X 22–32. Its affinities with the well-established category of Psalms of Thanksgiving have been highlighted by several scholars. However, there is a tendency to ignore the differences or make very little of them. As a consequence, we may miss important points about the ideas as well as the functions of the composition. I suggest that analyses of the kind undertaken here make a good starting point for investigating the Hodayot from the perspective of genre: What can the particular form of the genre found in these particular compositions tell us about the ideas, the function, and the settings of the Hodayot?

---

72. Ibid., 236.

73. ואני אמרתי is usually translated neutrally; e.g., "And I said." Michael Douglas, who does not discuss this phrase in particular, is to my knowledge the only one to make something of it. He translates the clause, "I, I declared," thus picturing the hymnist's act of uttering something as a part of the narrative sequence of events itself ("Power and Praise," 119).

3
Leadership and Credibility: 1QH^a VI 19–33

1QH^a VI 19–33 is generally considered a community hymn because of the formal feature of the reconstructed introductory (or resuming) formula, the formal structure, and some less formal criteria. Due to the exceptional similarity between this text and certain parts of 1QS, many see the initiation ceremony described in 1QS V as its *Sitz im Leben*. This social setting also serves as an argument for interpreting it as a hymn of the community.[1] Others, however, disagree with this prevailing assessment. In her 2004 monograph, Carol Newsom, who does not ascribe the so-called Leader Hymns to any specific leader but rather to institutional leadership, holds the text to be such a leadership hymn.[2] Interestingly, her argument also rests on similarities to the language in 1QS, namely, the descriptions of the *maśkîl* (1QS IX 14–16) and the *pāqîd* (1QS VI 14).

Newsom's analysis makes a good starting point for the interpretation of the hymn. In Newsom's view, two particular features are of special

---

1. According to Svend Holm-Nielsen (*Hodayot*, 224), the lack of references to biblical psalms shows that this is a hymn of the community, and this impression is strengthened by line 17, which he sees as a reference to the cultic setting of the initiation ceremony described in 1QS. The general viewpoint is repeated by others: Kittel, *Hymns of Qumran*, 152–53; Tanzer, "The Sages at Qumran," 93, 96. Also seeing the composition as a hymn of the community (*Bekenntnislieder*) and belonging in a liturgical situation, Kuhn believed the covenant renewal was the original *Sitz im Leben* (*Enderwartung*, 29–33).

2. Newsom, *Self as Symbolic Space*, 282–83. Newsom does not include lines 12–18 in this composition. The view that the hymnist portrays a leader rather than an ordinary worshiper is not unprecedented. Menahem Mansoor, who in his time did not distinguish between the so-called Leader Hymns and the so-called Hymns of the Community, gave lines 17–19 as an example of an utterance that would serve to identify the author with the Teacher of Righteousness, the way he is presented in 1QpHab and CD (*The Thanksgiving Hymns*, 48).

interest. First, she sees in the hymn an attempt to "connect the rhetoric of
the formation of the self as it is developed in the Hodayot with the rhetoric of community formation as it occurs in the Serek ha-Yahad."[3] Secondly, she points out that although the hymn is formally directed to God,
it implicitly addresses the community members. This prompts a question
about the rhetorical situation of the text. Newsom refers to a situation
in which the very real, however informal, addressee is the community
member: The speaker, being a leader in a community setting, reveals
himself in such a way that everything he stands for seems to be derived
from God. This way he can implicitly urge his audience into compliance
without actually presenting a decision or decree to be obeyed. As will be
seen, transitivity analysis will confirm Newsom's point about the deriva-
tion of divine support for the speaker, but will not necessarily support her
conclusion that in this hymn a leader is addressing his flock. Is it possible
that this is simply an edificatory hymn by and for the whole or part of the
leadership of the Dead Sea community?[4] According to most translations
of this composition, including the one by Carol Newsom in the recent
DJD edition by Schuller and Stegemann, the indicative is the prevailing
mood in this text (as in other hodayot). Translators perceive the speaker
as someone who puts forward plain statements about God and whoever
appears in the hymn, including himself. What the hymnist engages in
throughout the hymn is making claims about the world and its values.
This seems somewhat peculiar given the poetic form of the text and the
communicative situation it portrays: a human address to God. Would it
not be natural for a praying person to display some degree of hesitation,
doubt, hope, or insecurity? The answer to this question depends of course
on the analyst's attitude toward the text. Does she see it as a text of worship or as a theological or rhetorical statement?

---

3. Newsom, *Self as Symbolic Space*, 278.

4. In order to address this question adequately, we shall have to consider more
closely the question of experiential distance, or put in other words, how the hymnic
text is related to a social situation. This question is not identical but related to the quest
for a *Sitz im Leben*. We can address it linguistically in terms of how social reality is
embedded in the text and can be analyzed in its different linguistic layers. However, we
can also turn to theories about ritual and performance in the search for a reasonable
understanding of the relationship between the hymnic text and a situation in which
hymns might be expected to have been used. Eventually, we shall do both.

In the following I shall address the question of what is actually going on in the text. Instead of searching for answers in its similarities to the 1QS material, I am going to concentrate my attention on the text itself. The processes performed and their participants will be analyzed for transitivity. Because there is disagreement on the role and function of the speaker, his attitude will be approached through modal analysis. It has been stressed by Ken Penner, whose analytical categories are employed in the present treatment of modality, that to some degree, modality must be inferred from context and knowledge about the world.[5] This is what I shall attempt to do regarding 1QH[a] VI 19–33. It may be an advantage to readers of the following analysis to have acquainted themselves with the excursus on modality in Hebrew at the end of this chapter (sections 3.4–3.4.3). Before I proceed with the analysis, I shall make a few comments on the extent of the composition.

3.1. EXTENT AND DELIMITATION

Until recently, 1QH[a] VI 19–33 (VI 8–22/*XIV 8–22*) has generally been considered a separate hymn. In 2003 Hartmut Stegemann argued that lines 12–18 belong to the same hymn, and this is confirmed in the recent DJD edition by Schuller and Stegemann.[6] Their argument rests on the occurrence in line 20 of the demonstrative pronoun אלה, which, wherever it occurs in the Hodayot, refers to preceding textual elements.[7] Since no such elements are found between the blessing formula and the demonstrative pronoun, it must point to the text before the blessing formula. If their division of the text is accepted (including the extant lines 12–18 of col. VI, which may even be a continuation of the hymn starting as early as 1QH[a] V 12), we have in line 19 not an incipit but a resumption of an earlier incipit used to introduce a subsection of the hymn. Schuller and Stegemann's preference for reconstructing the phrase ברוך] אתה אדוני in line 19 is connected with this argument because the alternative, אודכה

5. Penner, "Verb Form Semantics," 112–14.

6. Schuller and Stegemann, *1QHodayot[a]* (DJD XL).

7. Stegemann, "The Number of Psalms," 214; Schuller and Stegemann, *1QHodayot[a]* (DJD XL), 89–90. In 1QH[a] XIX 35–36 the almost identical expression, "Blessed are yo[u], O Lord, for you have done these things," likewise introduces a subsection.

אדוני, is nowhere used to introduce only a subsection,[8] whereas ברוך אתה
אדוני sometimes is.[9]

The argument is in itself reasonable, and lexically there is a high degree
of cohesiveness in the text even with the suggested addition. Still, there are
problems with this interpretation. If one follows Stegemann's use of *vacats*
as a criterion for divisions between hymns, the fact that line 18 doubtlessly
ends with a *vacat* and line 19 begins with one indicates the incipit of a new
hymn in line 19.[10] Stegemann notes that the use of *vacats* in lines 18 and 19
taken together is exceptional within a composition, and he speculates that
something in the *Vorlage* of scribe A must have caused this. A similar case
is found in connection with the formula in 1QH^a XVIII 16, "Blessed are
you, O Lord (ברוך אתה אדוני), God of compassion and [abundant] kindness, for you have made known to me these things (אלה)."[11] Here, the fact
that the whole of line 15 is left blank would also indicate the beginning of a
new composition in line 16. The demonstrative pronoun אלה, popping up
just after the formula, highlights the principal resemblance between this
place and 1QH^a VI 19. That, too, refers to elements occurring before the
formula and before the long *vacat* that would appear to signal the break
between two compositions. Here Stegemann finds support for his assessment of the divisions of col. VI. I doubt, however, that 1QH^a VI 19 and
XVIII 16 introduce subsections of the same caliber as those very small
subsections beginning in XIX 30, 32, and 35. In accordance with what is
signalled[12] by the use of *vacats*, I would like to suggest that a new hymn is

---

8. In favor of the reconstruction of Schuller and Stegemann is the fact that אודכה
אדוני ("I thank you, Lord") is invariably followed by the particle *kî* rather than by a
participle. See Holm-Nielsen, *Hodayot*, 220 n. 1.

9. ברוך אתה is doubtlessly used to introduce a subsection in 1QH^a XIX 30, 32,
35 (XIX 27, 29, 32). The discussion of these three instances is summarized in Schuller
and Stegemann, *1QHodayot^a* (DJD XL), 242–44. It is questionable, however, whether
Stegemann is correct to include the instance found in 1QH^a XVIII 16 (XVIII 14).

10. According to Stegemann, scribe A (cols. I 1 to XIX 25) lets the introductory
formula of a new hymn be preceded by a *vacat* in the same line whenever half or more
of the line above is filled up with text. If less than half of the line ending a hymn is
filled with text, the new hymn starts at the very beginning of the following line ("The
Number of Psalms," 209–10). Examples regarding ברוך אתה אדוני are found in 1QH^a
VII 21 and VIII 26, and ones regarding אודכה אדוני in X 22, 33; XI 20, 38; XIII 7, 22;
XV 9.

11. Translation by Newsom (Schuller and Stegemann, *1QHodayot^a* [DJD XL]).

12. See Gérard Genette, *Paratexts*, esp. 312–16 on various functions of intertitles.

indeed introduced in VI 19, however, a hymn that *evolves from* the preceding hymn. Perhaps "independent subsection" is a more appropriate label, if a label is needed. In other words, I endorse the view that the text of 1QH^a VI 19–33 in its present form did not constitute a unity that was completely independent of the text preceding it in 1QHodayot^a. When discussing divisions between compositions, we tend to perceive them as independent texts that someone has placed in a particular succession at a particular point in time.[13] We should not disregard the possibility, however, that compilers or redactors not only juxtaposed previously independent compositions but simultaneously composed additional material in order to make the collection an apt expression with a view to particular rhetorical, didactic, or liturgical needs. The text of 1QH^a VI 19–33 could be one such later addition to a composition starting either in the lost lines 1–11 of col. VI or as early as in V 12. There is no decisive proof to confirm this proposal. Nevertheless, it is plausible due to the fact that it offers an explanation of both the meaning of אלה and the meaning of the *vacats* in lines 18 and 19.[14] More importantly, however, these arguments are in favor of seeing 1QH^a VI 19–33 as a unit that is self-contained, at least to some degree, and that can be analyzed as such in a meaningful way. This is how it will be treated below.

3.2. Text, Transitivity, and Modality

Translation of 1QH^a VI 19–33

19   [ ] *vacat* [Blessed are you,] Lord, who gives insight to the heart of [your] servant

20   so that he may understand all these things and per[ceive] and may restrain himself from deeds of unrighteousness and may bless

21   [in] justice those who prefer your will, [to choose all th]at you love[15] and abhor all that

---

13. A typical example of this is found in Angela Y. Kim's treatment of 1QH^a XVIII 16–XIX 5 when she considers the full *vacat* of line 15 as a distinction between the so-called Teacher Hymns preceding it and the Hymns of the Community following it ("Signs of Editorial Shaping," 142).

14. And, similarly, if we make the same suggestion for 1QH^a XVIII 16, it can explain the total absence of writing in line 15.

15. This is an instance of the gnomic perfect.

22   [you hate]. And may you teach your servant [*b*… lo]ts of humanity.
      Because according to the spirits you cast (the lot) for them between
23   good and wicked; [and may you ap]point [ ] *tm* their actions. As
      for me, I know by your understanding
24   that according to your delight in m[a]n you incr[ease his allot-
      ment] in the spirit of your holiness, and (that) therefore you bring
      me[16] to your insight. But in accordance
25   with my closeness I have become angry[17] with all the evildoers
      and the men of fraud. For no one close to you would alter your
      commandment
26   and no one among those who know you would change your words.
      Because you are righteous, and true are all of your chosen ones.
      And every wickedness
27   [and gu]ilty person you will destroy forever, and your righteous-
      ness will be revealed to the eyes of all your creatures. *vacat*
28   As for me, I have knowledge thanks to your plentiful goodness.
      And by an oath I have enjoined my soul from sinning against you
29   and from doing anything that, in your eyes, is evil. Therefore, I
      have been brought near to the community of all the men of my
      counsel. According to
30   someone's[18] [un]derstanding, let me draw him near, and according
      to the amount of his inheritance, let me love him. Let me not turn
      my face to the evil and not acknowledge an unrighteous, corrupt-
      ible person.
31   Let me not exchange your truth for riches or any of your judg-
      ments for a bribe. For according as [a ma]n

---

16. I read תגישני with Sukenik and others. Schuller and Stegemann read תגישנו,
arguing that the suffix must point back to איש. However, this solution forces them to
read ולפי קורבו קנאתו ("but in accordance with his closeness") in the following text,
despite the fact that according to them the Hebrew text is in fact ולפי קורבי קנאתי
(*1QHodayot*[a] [DJD XL]). The phrase, "as for me, I know by your understanding,"
introduces the sentence, and this makes the speaker the natural referent. Finally, the
occurrence of הוגשתי in line 29 strengthens this interpretation, according to which
the speaker is ingeniously identified as someone in whom God delights.

17. Schuller and Stegemann argue that one should continue to read a third-person suffix, קורבו קנאתו, as a natural way to continue from תגישנו in the preceding line
(*1QHodayot*[a] [DJD XL]).

18. לפי שכלו: The third-person masculine singular suffix seems to refer to an
unspecified member of the community, mentioned in line 29.

32   [let me lo]ve him, and according as you keep him at a distance, let
      me abhor him.
33   And let me not bring into the council of [your tru]th [anyone] who
      has not taken account [of] your [c]ovenant.

The Structure of 1QH^a VI 19–33

> VI 19–22: *Praise*, including blessing formula and characterization
> of God as giver of knowledge.
> VI 22–23: *Plea* for God to give understanding.[19]
> VI 23–27: *Cognitive section*, containing
> — the speaker's realization of general conditions and the
>   consequence on his part (23–24)
> — the speaker's realization of (cognitive) disharmony (24–
>   26)[20]
> — resolution of disharmony, including the speaker's foresee-
>   ing the final resolution in the form of judgment and uni-
>   versal acknowledgement (26–27).
> VI 28–33: *Commitment*
> — resumption of cognitive section, including the speaker's
>   assertion of his obligation toward God (28–29)
> — the speaker's wish to fulfill the ensuing obligation toward
>   men of the council of God (29–33).

Various pragmatic criteria lie behind the division and labeling of the structural units: formulaic expressions; *vacats*; comparative, classical (form-
critical) categories; changes of perspective (namely, alternation between
first- and second-person discourse); ensuing of new processes and process types. The structural outline is based on the different *processes* that
take place in the text rather than, for instance, conventional patterns and
forms in prayers of the period. The purpose of this approach is, first, to get
closer to an understanding of whom the text is about and, second, to find
out whom the text addresses. In addition to the choice of process types,
modality has an important role to play as it allows the language user to
"intrude on her message, expressing attitudes and judgments of various

---

19. The verbs involved are ותשכל and תכן[ו], *jussive* forms.
20. Including amplification of general condition (25–26).

kinds."[21] Is it possible, by analysis of modality, to reveal something about *attitude* in the hymns? Because the indicative and modal forms are in most cases morphologically indistinguishable, it can be quite difficult to analyze modality in Hebrew, particularly in an unvocalized text. It is necessary to add syntactical criteria to the morphological ones, as suggested by by Niccacci and by Talstra and Bosma.[22]

VI 19–22: Praise

In the words following the reconstructed blessing formula, God is characterized as the giver of knowledge through the use of a participle. He is the one who gives knowledge to "the heart of [your] servant," the servant of God. The subsequent chain of infinitives outlines the intended course of action on the part of the servant.

Since the infinitives in lines 20–22 actually determine for what purpose God gives knowledge—and thus what is subsequently expected from his receiving servant—we must analyze the content and scope of these infinitives. This will be done by means of the transitivity analysis introduced in chapter 2.[23] The first infinitive, "that he may understand," pictures a *mental process* in the servant—a direct effect on him of God's blessed agency. Secondly, the servant is expected to "restrain himself." This is a *behavioral process* also involving only the servant. However, by his virtue as a "behaver," it is not only his state of mind, his internal situation that is pictured, but also his external appearance—his (potentially) observable behavior. Finally, the servant is supposed to bless the ones chosen by God and, apparently, to choose what God loves and abhor what he hates. On the surface, these are mostly mental processes, taking place in the speaker's mind.[24] However,

---

21. Eggins, *Introduction*, 172.

22. Alviero Niccacci, "A Neglected Point of Hebrew Syntax," 7–19; Eep Talstra and Carl J. Bosma, "Psalm 67: Blessing, Harvest and History; A Proposal for Exegetical Methodology," 290–313.

23. See Eggins, *Introduction*, 206–53. In some cases, it is reasonable to analyze infinitives for transitivity. Here, we have instances of infinitive phrases functioning as subordinate clauses expressing purpose. They are called infinitivals and have no temporal features. The subject, however, can be inferred from the context. See Hatav, *The Semantics of Aspect and Modality*, 200. In Hebrew, the infinitive construct may function as a verb when a subject is implied by the context (Waltke and O'Connor, *Biblical Hebrew Syntax*, 598–612, esp. 609). See also my discussion in section 4.2.3.

24. See Eggins, *Introduction*, 225–33.

the blessing is a material process because in the Hebrew Bible blessing ultimately comes from God and is the cause of "concrete, tangible actions" that change reality.[25] The infinitive "to abhor" may also be interpreted as a material process because idiomatic usage of this verb and its synonyms in the Hebrew Bible implies not only sentiments but also actions.[26] Thus, God's giving of knowledge potentially has a spectrum of effects ranging from change of thought and attitude to concrete and measurable actions.

We must keep in mind that this string of infinitives pictures not a real situation but *a potential outcome of God's* giving of knowledge. It is due to his giving of knowledge that God is praised by the speaker. The use of the participial phrase, "who gives insight" (line 19), to characterize God gives the impression that the giving of knowledge—the raison d'être of the blessing—is a generic condition rather than a historical event. Knowledge is as fundamental to the unfolding of the life of those receiving it as it is to the unfolding of the thanksgiving text. Thus, when the subsequent infinitives express the *opted for* outcome of God's giving of knowledge, we must ponder whether in the remaining text expression is given to a fulfilling of all this potentiality.[27] For now it suffices to note that God's giving of knowledge is meant to affect the mentality of its receiver, as well as his behavior and its effects on his surroundings. The cognitive section and the section following it actualize and concretize the processes referred to here.

VI 22–23: Plea[28]

The following verbs, having God as their logical subject, are in the jussive. The hymnist is requesting that God will teach and give understanding to

---

25. Ibid., 215. The fatherly blessing of Jacob and Esau in Gen 27 illustrates this perfectly, as in effect it transfers Esau's birthright to his younger brother, Jacob. When God blesses the patriarchs, this means that their descendants may multiply and live in the promised land (Gen 12:1–3; 26:2–5; 28:13–15).

26. Thus, to *love*, which is the opposite of hating and abhorring (Ps 119:163), is juxtaposed to keeping the commandments (Deut 10:12–13; 11:1). Amos foretells unbearable consequences for those who hate justice, and only on those who "hate evil and love good" does he envision the possibility that God will have mercy (Amos 5:10, 14–15).

27. In accordance with Newsom's interpretation of this text as a leader hymn, the latter three infinitives (including the reconstructed one) may be perceived as desired sentiments of *leadership*, but it is not necessarily so. I shall deal with this question later.

28. The verbs involved are the short, jussive forms תשכל and [ו]תכן.

him. In spite of the damaged character of this brief section, the purpose of asking for knowledge seems to be his concern for a whole group of people.

VI 23–27: Cognitive Section

I have termed this section *cognitive* because it begins and ends with the words "I know."[29] In terms of SFL transitivity analysis, this makes the speaker the *Senser* in a mental process.[30] Just like verbal processes, mental processes make room for subjective evaluation: it is "the speaker's processes of consciousness" that are reflected in a mental process.[31] Therefore, we consider the contents of the speaker's knowledge as recounted in lines 24–27 as a source of his self-perception and awareness rather than as his ideological belief.[32] The speaker in the cognitive section confesses[33] his special bond with God and also acknowledges the attitudes and the conduct it entails. Thus, his sentiments regarding ensuing events and other people in real life are defined, and his commitments are made, on this basis. Accordingly, we must understand the descriptions of the speaker's actions in the following section (*commitment*) in the light of the confessional contents of the cognitive section.

The cognitive section presents a mixture of fundamental and experienced knowledge, which explains the speaker's stance toward his social environment. First, there is a swift move from the principal statement in line 24 about men in whom God delights to the speaker's personal experience of belonging among this kind of men. The text does not make a big point of the speaker's status at this point. Rather, this information is offered in an almost imperceptible way by simple means. Instead of a repeated use of the third-person pronominal suffix, which in the first clause, "You increase his allotment" (הרב[ב]יתה נחלתו), refers to a man in

---

29. The speaker's concluding statement about having knowledge is located at the very beginning of the ensuing section; it functions as a resumption and a transition.

30. More specifically, this verb belongs to the class of cognition. Verbs expressing mental processes can be divided into three classes: verbs of cognition, affection, or perception. See Eggins, *Introduction*, 225.

31. Halliday, *An Introduction to Functional Grammar*, 198.

32. In terms of action, the section can also be referred to as a creedal statement because the speaker in it confesses his bond with the deity. See section 3.4.3 Criteria for Defining Chains of Propositions.

33. This expression should not be confused with the form-critical category of confession. I use the term to designate a mode of cognition.

whom God delights, the second clause, "therefore you bring me to your insight" (וכן תגישני לבינתך), has the first-person pronominal suffix, thus including the speaker.[34] The logic is that the nearness of the speaker to God, briefly mentioned in a prepositional phrase (ולפי קורבי) in the following line, is a consequence of how God deals with men of his delight and is also a prerequisite for the following scenario.

Only now, in his prudently established capacity of being near to God, does the speaker refer to himself as an acting subject. He recalls that he has become angry at "deeds of unrighteousness" and "men of fraud." Thus, to use SFL terminology, he depicts himself as a Behaver in the behavioral process of being angry, and this is the first appreciable outcome of his confession of bonding with God. A tight, causative connection has been made in the text: "But in accordance with my closeness I have become angry."

The speaker identifies "the men of fraud"—again subtly—as something that he himself is not. This interpretation rests on my reading of the clauses כי כול קרוביך לא ימרו פיך וכול יודעיך לא ישנו דבריך (lines 25–26) and differs from most translators' interpretation of them. Usually, and probably because of the repeated use of קרוב as an adjectival characterization of the subject (namely, the angry subject of the preceding clause), these clauses are understood as declaratives about those who, like the speaker, are close to God and know him. The negated *yiqtōls* ימרו and ישנו are seen as indicative forms, for example, in Holm-Nielsen's translation: "[F]or all who are near Thee are not obstinate against Thy commandment, and all who know Thee do not pervert Thy word."[35] According to Holm-Nielsen's translation, an apparently undisputed, positive judgment on the speaker and his kind is offered here. This rendition of the text, however, creates a static expression of something that was originally dynamic, and does not really move the text onward the way it should. Interestingly, Penner ascribes modal value to the verbs, but only the weaker kind (habitual). Thus he confirms the idea that ימרו and ישנו express the usual situation among righteous people.[36] What is actually going on, however, is that the clauses under discussion disclose the paradoxical situation that people who *seemingly* are close to God and know him act in a way that is incompatible with such people. This is a chal-

34. See note 185.
35. Holm-Nielsen, *Hodayot*, 219.
36. Penner, "Verb Form Semantics," 270.

lenging situation. Seen as a continuation of the preceding clause about the speaker's anger, what we have here is the outline and negation of the hypothetical situation that people close to God and genuinely familiar with him could ever think of altering or changing his words. The statement is a condensed expression of something which could have been put in a more elaborate conditional clause, like this: "If they were close to you and knew you, they would not alter your commandment or change your words." The subsequent nominal clauses, "because you are righteous" and "true are all of your chosen ones," constitute the axiomatic basis and support of this opinion.

To round off this paragraph on the cognitive section, I wish to stress its character as a creedal statement, in which the speaker confesses his nearness to God and consequently refutes his allegiance to men who, in his opinion, change the words and commandments of God. Doing this, I also relate the cognitive section to other prayer literature, since confession is a natural part of hymns and prayers. Praise of God is confessional in character as are petitions for help and confessions of guilt.

In the first section, we saw that one of the purposes of God's giving of knowledge was that his servant would abhor what God hates and choose what God loves. The speaker's anger in the cognitive section is a concrete fulfillment of the first purpose. The next section conceptualizes the fulfillment of the second purpose; namely, to love what God loves, and so on.

VI 28–32: Commitment

The opening phrase, "as for me, I have knowledge thanks to your plentiful goodness," functions as a closure to the preceding section and as a transition. Immediately following it, the hymnist declares to have taken an oath and to have been brought near to the community. The oath involves an obligation on the part of the speaker. His claim to possess knowledge is expressed in the exact same Hebrew words in line 23 (ואני ידעתי)—and yet there is a difference in meaning. The verb ידעתי of line 23 governs two object clauses in line 24, and thereby the contents of his knowledge are elaborated. In line 28, on the other hand, ידעתי is not followed by any such information; the speaker simply states that he has knowledge. Furthermore, the speaker's reference to his oath-taking provides a different context for the expression, "I know," a context in which the oath of the speaker appears to be a consequence of his knowledge.

The remainder of the text consists of a chain of utterances in which the speaker commits himself to fulfilling his obligations.[37] The first-person singular verbs of this section are in the *yiqṭōl*, and their clauses are usually translated as declaratives in the present tense or as future statements. It appears from the translations that the verbs are thought to be declarative rather than modal.[38] As long as translators do not make it clear that the verbs have a modal nuance, it must be presumed that knowingly or unknowingly, they perceive the statements as declaratives. In some translators' comments on the composition, this situation is obvious. Holm-Nielsen, for instance, characterizes the bulk of this text as "a sort of *declaration of righteousness* [my italics], which one could compare to the '*Fürstenspiegel*' in the Psalms, e.g. in Ps. 101."[39] The purpose of this declaration would be to evaluate "one's own righteousness ... on the basis of certain definite circumstances, since the underlying motif of the psalm is the matter of acceptance into the community and of the relationship of the righteous to those within and outside the community."[40] Thus, according to Holm-Nielsen, the text displays the relationship of the righteous person to his surroundings and presents this relationship as an *argument* for his acceptance into the community of fellow righteous people. In their capacity as a rhetorical argument to this end, the utterances in lines 28–31 about "the relationship of the righteous to those within ... the righteousness of God" are statements about the speaker's member status.

Agreeing with Holm-Nielsen on the issue of *Sitz im Leben*, Kittel describes these lines and their context in terms of "declaration" and "statement."[41] On the basis of similarities to a particular section in 1QS V, she proposes that "these lines are creedal statements, or are drawn from vows taken by the community."[42] Like Holm-Nielsen, Kittel presents these lines as arguments with a purpose; she links them to the yearly covenant

---

37. Most translators render this series of *yiqṭōl* verbs as indicatives. Would it be reasonable to see them rather as "non-perfectives" in a modal function? See Waltke and O'Connor, *Biblical Hebrew Syntax*, 506–9, esp. 509.

38. Most translations are into English. See Mansoor, *The Thanksgiving Hymns* (generally the present tense); Holm-Nielsen, *Hodayot* (the future tense); Kittel, *The Hymns of Qumran* (the future tense).

39. Holm-Nielsen, *Hodayot*, 224.

40. Ibid., 224.

41. Kittel, *The Hymns of Qumran*, 152–53.

42. Ibid., 153. Kuhn (*Enderwartung*, 131) also ascribes this section to the speaker's entrance into the community at some time in the past. Does this, then, imply that the verbs under discussion are part of strong assertions?

renewal, which she describes as the occasion on which community members were examined and then ranked according to their insight.[43]

According to the clause הוגשתי ביחד in line 29, the speaker has already entered into the community. What I would like to suggest is that the ensuing verbs under discussion are modal in the sense that they express his willingness or commitment, rather than a declaration. Regarding the following discussion, I refer the readers to the excursus on modality in Hebrew at the end of this chapter. Within the confines of the applied theory of modality, it is unproblematic to suggest that these verbal forms are modal in the sense of *habitual*. Penner suggests this, too.[44] My suggestion, however, goes further because it resorts to a stronger (that is, nonepistemic) form of modality found in Palmer's category *dynamic modality* and expresses willingness and ability. I suppose it resembles the deontic modality of *obligation* in strength;[45] perhaps the most significant difference is that modality of obligation is used in second- and third-person discourse, whereas modality of commitment works in first-person discourse. In the words of Palmer, deontic modality is concerned with "language as action," and with "the expression by the speaker of his attitude towards possible actions by himself and others."[46] I suggest that this is also what we get in 1QH^a VI 30–32. My proposition, which is based on the argument that the preceding sections of the text have presented God's purpose and the speaker's acknowledgement of it, is that now the speaker has the fulfillment of this purpose in his heart. Therefore, his response to God's acknowledged purpose is not a declaration of what he is going to do, but an attitude of willingness and commitment. This interpretation is in accord with my understanding of the immediately preceding reference to an oath (שבועה) taken by the speaker in line 29, which I shall explain in the next paragraph. The oath is referred to, not as something fulfilled here and now in the moment of speech, but as the basis of what the speaker intends to do in the future.

---

43. There is a difference in nuance between, on the one hand, simply stating, perhaps in response to a request, what one expects will take place at some point in the future, and, on the other, expressing an assertion in connection with a vow. Palmer, however, treats these nuances as *different functions of the declaratives*; namely, assertion and strong assertion (*Mood and Modality* [2001], 68–69).

44. Penner, "Verb Form Semantics," 270.

45. *Obligation* is a stronger type of modality than the *habitual*. See ibid., 123–24.

46. Palmer, *Mood and Modality* (1998), 121.

As regards the logic of the text, however, even direct expressions of hopes and desires to fulfill the acknowledged purposes would actually be viable here, since they would also fit into a situation characterized by the acknowledgement of purposefulness, but not yet of fulfillment. *Wish* is not part of the modal categories outlined by Penner at all. The nearest extant category is the cohortative, which is also deontic and a very strong type of modality. Even if an ungrammaticalized modality of this caliber were included in the employed linguistic model for modality, it could be difficult to argue on the grammatical level that this is what we have in the text, in part because the verbs under consideration are not clause-initial,[47] and in part because the negation לא is generally used with the indicative.[48] However, there are examples from the Dead Sea Scrolls in support of a modal understanding. In 1QSb III 22–25 a series of blessings is introduced. The blessings proceeding from line 25 and well into the next column all have the asyndetic *yiqṭōl*, sometimes clause-initial, sometimes not. It is of course possible to argue that the latter cases are merely the result of stylistic inversion so typical of parallelism, especially since the very first blessing is verb-initial. On the other hand, the distribution of clause types is uneven, and the parallelistic pattern does not appear to be very strict. Therefore, I do not find this objection entirely convincing. In 1QS II 2–17, there are a series of blessings and curses, introduced with clause-initial *yiqṭōl*s. Whenever the proposition is negated, the negation is לא. In this context, ending with "Amen Amen," there can be no question about the modal value of the propositions and thus about the use of לא in modal propositions.[49]

---

47. Thus, they are less likely to express a wish or desire, unless the word order is purely poetic and conditioned by parallelism, which is hardly the case here. See Niccacci, "A Neglected Point of Hebrew Syntax," 7–9.

48.Purely grammatical analyses will tend to insist on the indicative (or prohibitive) meaning of לא + *yiqṭōl*, and the slender evidence against this is atypical and confirms the rule. In one of the two instances of this construction in the hortatory parts of the *War Scroll* (1QM XI 10), Søren Holst, on grammatical grounds, sees a volitive verbal form (jussive) rather than an indicative (*Verbs and War Scroll*, 111). A similar usage is found in Ben Sira (Sir 42:10), where לא seems to be used in an "expression of fear that something will *not* take place" (Peursen, "Negation in the Hebrew of Ben Sira," 239). In the Dead Sea Scrolls, אל is the negation normally used to express negative wishes, for instance in apotropaic prayers (11QPsᵇ frg. 4–5 14–15; 11QPsᵃ XXIV 12–13).

49. "Amen" functions as an additional factor (adverbial adjunct) for determining

3.2.1. Agency

Whichever kind of modality, exactly, is expressed, the speaker clearly refers to his own agency for the fulfillment of God's purpose. Instead of the broader range of processes opted for on the part of the "servant" and the "chosen" in lines 19–22, the speaker now refers to material processes that he is willing and ready to undertake now or in the future. These material processes are distinguished by having human targets (Goals in SFL terminology), people other than the speaker that are or may become affected by the actions that he undertakes on behalf of God; as God has drawn the speaker near, it falls upon the speaker to draw others near. An *agency hierarchy* is outlined in which God is the initiating agent behind the acting speaker, whose actions affect other people in various ways.

This structure, with God as the initiator, in fact pervades the prayer. Except for the words of blessing in the very first and last lines, which establish a ritual frame for this literary structure, the entire text unfolds as a "special agency" scenario, to use the terminology of McCauley and Lawson.[50] This concept means that divine agency is pictured, in this case as it unfolds through a human mediator, as an *instrument*. The concept of agency entails that what unfolds in the text is not only a series of events, but rather a complex of *intended* actions: "While all actions are represented as events, not all events are represented as actions. Human beings have the capacity to distinguish between those types of (intentional) activities which involve agents and those which do not."[51] McCauley and Lawson base their concepts of agency on cognitive psychology and on the assertion that from their early childhood human beings read agency into events; analyzing events for agency involves identifying *agents* (human or divine),[52] *acts*, *instruments*, and *patients* (that is, goals, targets).[53] The rec-

---

the modal value of verbs. Gesenius's lexicon (s.v.) expresses its meaning like this: "Its proper place is where one person confirms the words of another, and expresses a wish for the issue of his vows or predictions."

50. Lawson, "Cognition"; McCauley and Lawson, *Bringing Ritual to Mind*, 8–37.

51. Lawson, "Cognition," 310.

52. As far as nonhuman agents are concerned, McCauley and Lawson name them CPS-agents; that is, "culturally postulated superhuman agents" (*Bringing Ritual to Mind*, 8).

53. When we speak of *agents* and *patients* in relation to this theory, these concepts should not be confused with the grammar-related concepts of Agent and Goal (with capital letters) from SFL terminology, used in transitivity analyses of verbal processes

ognition of agencies is therefore a fundamental function of human beings' perception and ordering of the world.[54] Accordingly, the function of the speaking "I" as both Goal and Actor in the divine agency must affect the self-perception of anyone who utters the words, as he must think they are in fact representing himself in some way. The text of 1QHᵃ VI 19–33 is about the divine agency and the speaker's place within it. Embedded in the framework of a blessing, this divine agency is acknowledged and sanctioned by the speaker. Schuller has described how *acknowledgement* is a general function of the thanksgivings and blessings in the Hodayot:

> These psalms are full of repeated expressions of gratitude for what God has done, wonder at being chosen, and acknowledgement of divine graciousness and righteousness. Even in those passages where the psalmist graphically describes the weak and sinful condition of all humankind, including himself, this too is an acknowledgement of what God has determined; it is God who created the psalmist as "a shape of clay, kneaded with water, a ground of shame, and a source of pollution, a melting-pot of wickedness and an edifice of sin." (1QHᵃ 9:23–24 [1:21–22].[55]

In the context of 1QHᵃ VI 19–33, the divine agency and the speaker's place(s) in it are acknowledged in the blessing. This means that the speaker also acknowledges God's purposes for him.[56] Within the outlined agency

---

in clauses. Nevertheless, transitivity analyses can contribute to the identification of the kind of agency structures discussed in this paragraph.

54. In fact, it is seen as a kind of knowledge that exceeds what can be taught culturally. See Lawson, "Cognition," 317.

55. Schuller, "Petitionary Prayer," 38.

56. According to the theory, special agent rituals (God = agent) are irreversible and unrepeatable (for example, funerals and circumcisions). Special patient rituals (God = patient), on the other hand, are not (for example, blessings and sacrifices). See Lawson, "Cognition," 314. How does this correspond with the identification of a special agency scenario in this hodayah? Potentially the prayer was repeatedly used by the same persons and did not have the quality of a once-in-a-lifetime ritual. The human blessing of (or thanksgiving to) God is a special patient ritual in itself. As such it can be used repeatedly in a meaningful way. The special agency scenario is *embedded in* this ritual, but is not in itself a ritual. It expresses a permanent condition, rooted in the dualistic and deterministic character of the world as it is established by God *once and for all* from the beginning (1QS III 17–21; IV 25–26; 1QHᵃ VI 27–33; IV 29; IX 10–13). This condition, the validity of which remains intact, is captured in the Hodayot. With recourse to his knowledge, the speaker sees his experiences from the perspective of the general, durable condition; for example, in the cognitive section

structure, embedded in the blessing, there is plenty of room for the speaker's sense of obligation and willingness to fulfill God's purposes. But there is less room for a rhetorically motivated pledge uttered by the prospective member in the hope of acceptance into the community, or for an assertion by the leader hoping for the loyalty of ordinary members. Regardless of the fact that the hodayah has many affinities with 1QS V, which is generally assumed to have been used at the initiation ceremony, it may have had a completely different *Sitz im Leben*. The Hodayot genre contemplates a broad field of issues, such as the nature of humanity, righteousness, knowledge and access to God, and may *generally* have been used in other situations in the life of the community. It is quite possible that the text of 1QH^a VI 19–33 *reflects* on events that took place in the initiation ceremonies, but its *function* may have been completely different from that of a pledge or an oath uttered on that specific occasion. Perhaps its function was rather edification and contemplation of what it meant to belong in the community.

Before concluding the analysis of 1QH^a VI 19–33 with a summarizing outline of the argumentation of the text, I wish to broaden the perspective and look at it in the light of cognate literature. This will be done first with a view to biblical psalms in which agency hierarchies like the one found in 1QH^a VI 19–33 are revealed only by glimpses, and secondly in intercessory prayers and related literature distinguished by similar agency hierarchies. The purpose of this is to provide a literary basis and scale for a typological definition of the Hodayot and to show what support there is for the modal analysis undertaken.

3.2.2. In the Light of Biblical Psalms

The relationship of the Hodayot to the biblical Psalms is significant with regard both to similarities and differences.[57] Two particular elements in

in 1QH^a VI 23–27. See particularly lines 23–24, where the speaker clearly interprets his experience of being brought near to the insight of God from the perspective of his dualistic worldview.

57. With respect to concrete references, Holm-Nielsen mentions a few possible links to various texts, such as Ps 73:3 regarding the speaker's anger in line 25 (*XIV 14*) and Isa 56:1 regarding the righteousness of God in line 27 (*XIV 16*). See Holm-Nielsen, *Hodayot*, 223. If there is a link to Ps 73, it is not a very strong one. The perspective held throughout the psalm is indeed different from the perspective held in 1QH^a VI 19–33. In the former text, the anger is retrospectively regarded as the result of the speaker's misapprehension (cf. vv. 2 and 21–22).

the text of 1QHᵃ VI 19–33, נגש and שבועה, will have our attention here because of how they accentuate typical biblical situations and yet display deviation from the Bible through their use of these elements. Because of this situation they are eligible for an analysis of the situational context and mode of the prayer. On the surface, the references to an oath (שבועה in VI 28) and to "drawing near" (נגש in VI 24, 30) may echo or bring to mind a cultic setting. I argue, however, that the use of נגש and שבועה points to a situational context where cult is not the issue, but where agency or leadership on behalf of God is.

The verb נגש (hiphil, "to draw near") is connected with the priestly status as well as the role of a mediator on behalf of God both in the Bible and in other Dead Sea Scrolls. The importance of this concept in the Hodayot text should be seen in the light of the fact that not even once is it found in the biblical Psalms, which prefer the root קרב to describe the nearness of God to those loyal to him, often with no explicit indication of who takes the initiative to create nearness.[58]

Elsewhere in the Bible נגש is mostly used of people's *approaching* superiors and, in many cases, whatever they might bring with them; for example, food, taxes, and sometimes even people.[59] Frequently, the superior of the transaction is God, and the fact that references are made to food offerings being *brought* to him points to a cultic setting.[60] In the cases that refer to cultic offerings, נגש is in the *hiphil*, and the actors are typically priests performing their cultic duties.[61] There is ample biblical evidence of the priests as grammatical subjects of the verb נגש, and the audience of the Hodayot might very well have these connotations in mind. The use of נגש elsewhere in the Dead Sea Scrolls, however, bears witness to a changed perspective on the priestly identity.

CD III 21–IV 4 cites and interprets the text of Ezek 44:15, which says that in spite of Israel's going astray, the priests, the Levites, and the sons of Zadok had maintained the temple service and would continue to do so in the future. The interpretation claims that this is about the Dead Sea com-

---

58. Pss 34:19; 65:5; 69:19; 73:28; 75:1; 119:151; 145:18.

59. Gen 27:25; 48:10; 1 Kgs 5:1; Exod 21:6. Most instances are in the *qal*, but the *hiphil* is used as well.

60. 2 Sam 13:11 and 1 Kgs 5:1 exemplify approaches to a human superior. Several instances talking about approaching God are found in the prophetic works—Isa 29:13; 41:1, 21, 22; 45:20, 21; 49:20; 65:5; Jer 30:21; 42:1; 46:3; Ezek 44:13.

61. Exod 32:6; Lev 2:8, 14; Mal 1:7, 8, 11; 2:12; 3:3.

munity itself (in one form or another), its history, and its eschatological future: "The priests are the converts of Israel who left the land of Judah; and <the Levites are> those who joined them; *Blank* and the sons of Zadok are the chosen of Israel, the men of renown, who stand (to serve) at the end of days."[62] In the quotation, CD has replaced להקריב in Ezek 44:15 for יגישו, showing that this term was indeed perceived in the Dead Sea community as valid in relation both to the priestly temple service and to the priestly legacy and function of the community itself.[63] The implication is that in CD the priestly identity was transformed and transferred to the community's life away from Jerusalem.[64] According to Maxine Grossman, the priesthood in this and other passages in the CD sometimes served as a metaphor for the members of the covenant.[65] This point is relevant regarding the relationship of 1QH[a] VI 19–33 to the biblical Psalms because it suggests an ideational framework for the reuse of the Psalms genre that left little room for traditional (cultic) interpretations of the Psalms, even when the terminology used mirrored an originally cultic context. Choosing to use the term נגש alongside קרב, which was also used in the biblical Psalms, the author accentuated aspects of nearness that were absent or weak in the biblical Psalms, but suitable and meaningful in the different situational context of CD and other Dead Sea texts.

It is not the cultic aspects of the "drawing near" in order to bring offerings that are prominent in 1QH[a] VI or elsewhere in the Dead Sea Scrolls.[66] In the text of 1QH[a] VI 19–33, the hymnist is drawn near to the community by God, and he draws others near according to their understanding. In line 24, it is God who "draws near," as in the other occurrences of נגש in

---

62. CD IV 2–4.

63. נגש is used in Ezek 44:13 in relation to priests who had not lived up to their obligations and who were not to approach God again.

64. This is not to say that the community members or some of them were originally temple priests, but that is a possibility.

65. For this particular passage, Grossman claims that its concern "is not for a hereditary or ritual priesthood but rather for the members of the community who have taken on a metaphorical priestly identity" ("Priesthood as Authority," 127).

66. Thus, Hopkins, supported by Lange, is only partially correct when she assumes that references to thanksgiving in the Hodayot, where a "sacrifice of thanksgiving" would have been mentioned in the book of Psalms (for example, Ps 116:12–19), bear witness to the preservation of "sacrificial rules … for a future time" in the community that had abandoned the sacrificial cult in Jerusalem ("The Qumran Community and 1QHodayot," 326). See also Lange, *Weisheit und Prädestination*, 202–3.

1QHᵃ VIII 24 (VIII 21) and XX 26 (X 23).[67] In line 29 the speaker is the subject of הוגשתי and therefore the *Goal* of the process, to speak in terms of SFL transitivity analysis. It is not apparent who the Actor is, but the context suggests it is God. In line 30, on the other hand, the speaker is the subject and Actor in the process. This usage of נגש is closely paralleled in the thematically and linguistically related text of 1QS IX–XI.[68] In 1QS IX 16 it is the *maśkîl* (in the third person) who will draw someone near "according to his insight," while in 1QS XI 13 God will draw him, the *maśkîl*, near. The juxtaposition of these two variants in the text of 1QHᵃ VI hints at their subtle semantic relatedness. As God draws the speaker near, the speaker will draw other people near (according to their insight). The common denominator of the two variants is the act of leadership in the sense that the speaker duplicates the role of God vis-à-vis other people when he draws them near, or that he acts as the substitute for God. This leadership aspect is more easily grasped in the reading of 1QS because there it is the explicit duty of the *maśkîl* to draw God's chosen ones near.[69] This meaning of נגש is far from prominent in the Bible, but there are a couple of analogous instances. In Gen 48:10 Joseph brings his sons to Jacob in order to have them blessed by him. In the legal context of Exod 21:6 it is made clear that a Hebrew slave, who after seven years in slavery declares he does not wish to be set free, must be brought before God and then be appointed a slave for the rest of his lifetime. In both cases, then, someone brings someone else to a superior (human or divine) in order that a particular lasting condition may be established for him. This aspect should be kept in mind, insofar as both 1QHᵃ VI 19–33 and the related 1QS text are often situated by scholars in the social context of covenant renewal.[70]

To sum up, the use of the term נגש in 1QHᵃ VI 19–33 creates a difference from the concept of nearness between God and psalmist as it appears in the Psalms. It calls to mind the community's appropriation of the priestly identity and accentuates the importance of mediation or leadership, which

---

67. In the first case the hymnist himself is the object, in the second a plural entity, "they." See also 1QS XI 13.

68. On the relatedness, see Newsom, *Self as Symbolic Space*, 278 n. 117.

69. The larger context of 1QS IX 16 is ambiguous as to the identity of the people whom the speaker should draw near. See section 4.3.1.

70. See Arnold, *The Social Role of Liturgy*, 188–90; Delcor, *Les Hymnes*, 267; Kuhn, *Enderwartung*, 131–32.

is present in the usage of נגש in other scriptural texts, but absent in the talk of nearness between psalmist and God in the biblical psalms.

The occurrence of a reference to an oath (שבועה) in 1QH[a] VI 28 points in the same direction. The term שבועה is used only this once in the Hodayot, and it occurs only once in the Psalms, where it refers to a promise made to Isaac by God.[71] In the hodayah, the speaker refers to an oath that he has taken not to sin. As he recalls his own promise in the face of God, a situation is created that resembles the one met in several psalms; there the psalmist refers to another kind of promise, a vow (נדר), that he has taken and will fulfil. There is a semantic difference between the two concepts of vow and oath.[72] The vow is an individual person's conditioned promise to God, made in a time of distress. The fulfilling of it takes place in response to God's saving action. The psalms imply a cultic setting involving offerings or thanksgivings as part of the fulfillment.[73] The oath, on the other hand, is unconditional and can be made by God as well as men. The meaning of שבועה is multifaceted and has a broad range of usages, often with juridical significance.[74] This is the case also in the Dead Sea Scrolls, where in 1QS V 8 and CD XV 5–10 שבועה is the oath to return to the law of Moses, which should be taken by all upon their entering into the community and the covenant.[75] Because of its general similarities to these texts, it is reasonable to infer that the hodayah also refers to the situation of entering the covenant and the community (but this in itself is not to say that the composition was used liturgically at initiation ceremonies).

Nevertheless, because of the Hodayot's dependence on the genre of psalms, the speaker's reference to his own promise in this prayer evokes

---

71. Ps 105:9. The oath made by God to Isaac is juxtaposed to the covenant made with Abraham through parallelism.

72. See Cartledge, *Vows in the Hebrew Bible and the Ancient Near East*, 14–18. For a discussion of vows in the biblical psalms, see ibid., 150–60, esp. 154.

73. For example, by way of explicit mentioning of the temple or the city of Jerusalem. See Pss 22:26; 50:14; 56:13; 61:6; 65:2; 66:13; 116:14, 18.

74. It can refer to oaths taken by humans vis-à-vis God (Num 30:3, 11, 14), sometimes in a distinctly cultic context (Jer 11:15); to juridical or other agreements between humans (Exod 22:10; Gen 24:8; Josh 2:17, 20); to curses (Judg 21:5); to the covenant God made with Abraham (Gen 26:3) and the covenant of Moses. As Holm-Nielsen has pointed out, it is likely that Num 30:3 is referred to here (*Hodayot*, 221 n. 19).

75. In other places the juridical aspects of oath-taking dominate—for example, CD IX 8–12; XVI 7–12; 11Q19 LIII 13–16; LIV 2, all of which build on Num 30:7–9. Vows also appear in these contexts as part of juridical deliberations.

the vows of the psalms and creates a difference: To some degree he conforms to the fulfilling of a radically different promise *as if* he was fulfilling
a vow, thus potentially bringing to mind the concept of vow-taking and the
events and ideas revolving around it. The promise he refers to, however, is
the unconditional abiding by the law, which is intrinsically connected with
his community membership. The point is that the reference to oath-taking
by means of the noun שבועה in fact produces a distance from the cultic
universe met in the relevant biblical psalms. It creates a contrast between
the psalms and the Hodayot, and it emphasizes the radically *different* character of the situation of the Hodayot.

The two details discussed in this paragraph reveal an interesting playing with the genre of psalms. The choice of the terms נגש and שבועה in
the place of typical psalms vocabulary accentuates issues not present in the
book of Psalms: agency or leadership on behalf of God, on the one hand,
and the community's exclusive promise to return to the law of Moses, on
the other. This creation of difference is an important feature and an indication that the Hodayot were bound to meet the requirements of a different social situation than those of the classical psalms. The accentuation of
human agency on behalf of God will be pursued in the following section,
which looks at how this feature has found its way into other post-scriptural prayer texts in Jewish antiquity.

3.2.3. In the Light of Prayers of the Time

There is ample material in later hymns and prayers outside the Dead Sea
Scrolls and in the New Testament showing that the speaker of intercessory prayer expresses his hopes and desires in modal propositions. Quite
a few instances of this occur in hymns acknowledged to be ideologically
and linguistically rather close to the Hodayot,[76] and it is possible that
the Hodayot manifest a general tendency in intercessory prayers of the
period. Thus, for instance, the speaker in the Psalms of Solomon uses the

---

76. The Psalms of Solomon were related to Qumran and Essenism in Eissfeldt,
Einleitung, 827–28 n. 2; Dupont-Sommer, *Écrits Esséniens*, 347, 359; J. H. Charlesworth has pointed out some major points of contact between the Odes of Solomon
and the Dead Sea Scrolls, the Hodayot in particular. He suggests that the similarities
may have come about not only because the texts were composed in similar Jewish
milieus, but also because the author might have been personally acquainted with the
Dead Sea society ("Odes of Solomon," 728).

optative to express wishes on behalf of "the devout" and their intimida-
tors, respectively:

> May God remove the lips of criminals in confusion far from the inno-
> cent, and (may) the bones of the slanderers be scattered far from those
> who fear the Lord. May he destroy the slanderous tongue in flaming fire
> far from the devout. May the Lord protect the quiet person who hates
> injustice: may the Lord guide the person who lives peacefully at home.
> May the salvation of the Lord be upon Israel his servant forever; may the
> wicked perish once and for all from before the Lord. And may the Lord's
> devout inherit the Lord's promises.[77]

The Lord may also be addressed directly: "Lord, let your mercy be upon all
those who love you" (Pss. Sol. 4:25).[78] Even if the second or third person
is used throughout the pseudepigraphic material, and not the first person
as in 1QH^a VI 28–32, there is good reason to perceive them as parallel
phenomena as regards their modal value. There is a particularly illumi-
nating passage in one of the Odes of Solomon (Odes Sol. 14:5) where, in a
modal proposition, the speaker begs that he himself may "be pleasing" to
God. It appears from the context that the aim of this and similar requests
is that the speaker "may produce fruits" in the Lord. There is no visible
sign of people who would benefit from the intercession, but clearly some
sort of outcome is expected or hoped for, other than the well-being of the
speaker himself.

The texts mentioned here are in agreement with each other in that
they focus not on the situation of the speaker per se, but on the situation of
followers or fellow worshipers. This pattern is seen also in the New Testament in reports of prayer activity, wishes made for human addressees in
the epistolary literature, and in prayer texts having the verbal actions in
the subjunctive or the optative.

---

77. Pss. Sol. 12:4–6, in the translation of Charlesworth, *The Old Testament Pseudepigrapha*.

78. Further examples can be seen in Hellenistic Synagogal Prayers (Hel. Syn. Pr.) 8.6.5–8 (Funk, *Didascalia et Constitutiones*); Pss. Sol. 4:6, 14, 24; 11:9; 17:45–46 (Wright, *The Psalms of Solomon*); Odes Sol. 5:4–7; 14:5–8 (Charlesworth, *The Odes of Solomon*). For comments on the modal translation of 5:4–7, see Majella Franzmann, *The Odes of Solomon*, 34 and 113–14. A similar variant is found in a Hellenistic funeral prayer, where the speaker expresses wishes on behalf of the dead (Hel. Syn. Pr. 8.41.2–5).

Matthew Gordley has surveyed Jewish hymns and prayers of the Second Temple period in order to contextualize the Colossian hymn (Col 1:15–20). He finds similarities throughout the material and concludes about the Dead Sea Scrolls material and the Hodayot that they continue the biblical psalms tradition and at the same time serve the doctrinal and didactic purposes of articulating the new theological developments of the community.[79] The doctrinal and didactic developments mentioned by Gordley are not the only ones. As in the intercessory prayers mentioned above, there is clearly a concern in the Hodayot for the followers of the speaker or his fellow worshipers. He sees himself as responsible with regard to them, both in in the text under discussion and in some of the so-called Leader Hymns. New social situations and different social structures must have created a need for other perlocutionary effects of the praying activity. This, too, must have prompted the creative development of existing patterns (*Gattungen*) of hymns and prayers. If, like Gordley, we look for parallels between the Hodayot and the New Testament, we find comments in the New Testament on the meaning and purpose of prayer that are pertinent to how we read the Hodayot. Thus, in the Letter to the Ephesians, we find Paul's appeal to them to pray for him in order that he may get knowledge of and also "make known with boldness" the mystery of the gospel; in other words, that he may fulfill his function in the Christian community:

> Pray also for me, so that when I speak, *a message may be given to me* to make known with boldness the mystery of the gospel, for which I am an ambassador in chains. Pray that *I may declare it boldly*, as I must speak.[80]

Likewise, Paul claims that he and Timothy pray on behalf of the Colossians:

> We have not ceased praying for you and asking that you may be filled with the knowledge of God's will in all spiritual wisdom and understanding, so that you *may lead* lives worthy of the Lord, fully pleasing to him, as you bear fruit in every good work and as you grow in the knowledge of God. *May you be made strong* with all the strength that comes from his glorious power, and *may you be prepared* to endure everything with

---

79. Gordley, *The Colossian Hymn in Context*, 100.
80. Eph 6:19–20 (my italics).

patience, while joyfully giving thanks to the Father, who has enabled you
to share in the inheritance of the saints in the light.[81]

Clearly, there is a close connection in these examples between having
knowledge and leading a life that brings about related and optimal effects.
It also seems clear that the one situation does not automatically lead to
the other. Insecurity about one's own or fellow worshipers' ability to fulfill
duties within the religious community prompts prayer, and is expressed by
using modal verbal forms, which are clearly recognized in the Greek text
(and put in italics in the examples just quoted).

Even the very dense language of the Lord's Prayer produces a subtle
expression of this tendency to connect supplication with yet unfulfilled
duties of the praying person. But there is a certain insecurity on the part
of the speaker inherent in the expression of Matt 6:10 (but missing in the
version of Luke), "your will be done, on earth as it is in heaven." The seri-
ous-minded and attentive person uttering these words must acknowledge
his own responsibility for their fulfillment, but also his limited capacity.[82]
Patrick Miller describes how the first three petitions of the prayer, "hal-
lowed be your name; your kingdom come; your will be done, on earth as
in heaven," control the meaning of the subsequent ones:

> The intent and effect of these petitions are to subordinate all prayer to the
> will and purpose of God. The starting point of the Christian prayer on
> this model is the prayer for the effecting of God's purpose, not the prayer
> for our needs. The order is important in that the petitions for ourselves
> come only after and under the petitions for God to do and be what God
> will do and be and for God to accomplish through human and divine
> action the will and purpose that God seeks. We do not begin, according
> to this model, with the prayer for ourselves, but we place our words to
> God in the service of the work and purpose of God.[83]

Similarly, the speaker of the hodayah places his words "in the service of
the work and purpose of God." God's purpose is expressed already in the
continuation of the introductory blessing, where it is made clear that God
gave his servant insight in order that he should love what God loves and

---

81. Col 1:9–12 (my italics).
82. See Nissen, "Fadervor—håbet og bønnen om en ny verden," 79–93.
83. Miller, *They Cried to the Lord*, 331.

hate what God hates—actions that are included in the speaker's list of actions that he claims or wishes to undertake in the commitment section.[84]

In conclusion, there is ample evidence of intercessory prayers revolving around the optimization of God's agency through human beings in other post-scriptural texts. Even if petitions with the verb in the first person are unusual, this evidence is in support of the proposed reading of verbal forms in 1QH^a VI 28–32.

We have seen examples of nonbiblical intercessory prayers in Jewish literature outside of the Dead Sea Scrolls. A few examples can be found also in the book of Psalms.[85] However, it is generally difficult to decide whether the psalmist is included in or distinct from the people he is concerned about, and only by glimpses do the Psalms reveal that he may have some sort of mediating or leading role vis-à-vis them.[86] This suggests that intercession occurred in the biblical psalms in undeveloped form but evolved into a central function of hymns and prayers in the Dead Sea Scrolls and in other (New Testament and—anachronistically labeled—extrabiblical) literature.

3.2.4. The Argumentation of the Text

When praising God and uttering the blessing formula, the speaker endorses God's giving of knowledge and its general purpose. The characterization of God found within the praise fulfils an important function in the text: It epitomizes the main theme of the hymn, the giving of knowledge and the outcome opted for—to affect the receiver's sentiments, behavior, and readiness to act in the world. The string of infinitives expresses purposes, not fulfillment, and bears witness to an open-ended situation where God's purpose may be achieved or may fail. The infinitive forms thus add to the dynamics of the text.

The speaker's plea in the following section confirms this and anticipates the cognitive section in which the speaker acknowledges that he

---

84. God's purpose is similarly made clear through a number of infinitives in the thematically and linguistically related instruction to the *maśkil* in 1QS IX.

85. Pss 53:7; 69:7; 122:6; 125:4; 128:5–6.

86. In Ps 69:7, it turns out that the hymnist worries that false allegations raised against him will also dishonor those "who hope in" and "seek" God. In Ps 119:79, the rare situation occurs that the speaker discloses himself as someone with a mediating role vis-à-vis other people: "Let those who fear you turn to me, so that they may know your decrees."

is one of those people whom God has endowed with knowledge and, by implication, God's purpose with him. Again, the cognitive section is confessional in the sense that the speaker in it embraces his situation of being close to God. In order to understand the place of the cognitive section in the logic of the composition, it is important to keep in mind that it is an expression of the speaker's *awareness* rather than a statement of the facts. The speaker's awareness of closeness is at the same time an awareness of God's purpose with him. There is also open-endedness connected with this awareness because it does not, by itself at least, fulfill the purpose outlined in the previous section.

With reference to theories on modality in Hebrew and to comparable prayer texts only a little later than the Dead Sea Scrolls, I have argued that in the last section of 1QH[a] VI 19–33, the speaker expresses his acknowledged obligation or wish to fulfill the purpose of God's giving of knowledge. I do not deny the possibility that the speaker could be instead *pledging* to fulfill the purpose. In that case he would be seeking the *closure* of the open-ended situation outlined from the beginning, *anticipating* the positive outcome of God's giving of knowledge, and the concluding structural unit would represent some kind of resolution (that is, the pledge would signal that God's purpose was now, indeed, being fulfilled). I rather wish to suggest, however, that the open-endedness is kept intact throughout the text. I see the whole composition as a *momentum* of acknowledged obligation and wish to fulfill God's purpose, rather than the unfolding of a psychological development or a rhetorical argument concluded by a neat resolution. The confessional statements of praise and cognition emerge from this momentum, as does the will of the speaker, or his stance toward his situation. It is a situation in which the speaker realizes God's purpose with him, and as he acknowledges God's purpose it is something that he wishes to fulfil. His hope—and prayer—are that he is capable of doing so.[87]

---

87. At two points in the text the speaker looks back on completed actions or situations. In line 25 he mentions his anger, "[I]n accordance with my closeness I have become angry with all the deeds of unrighteousness and the men of fraud," and in line 28 he refers to a pledge already taken, "[A]nd by an oath I have enjoined my soul not to sin against you." The anger and the pledge are provisional closings of the text as they materialize the incipient fulfillment of God's purposes. A pledge does not imply fulfillment. On the contrary, the risk of treachery is inherent in the pledge. The hope and prayer to be able to fulfill God's purpose thus follow quite naturally.

The interpretation I have just offered differs from the ones mentioned earlier in this chapter because it downplays the significance of rhetorical argument directed to an ideal audience (for example, God, the congregation, community members) for some implicit purpose (for example, acceptance into the community or establishment of leadership authority). Duh Instead, my starting point is prayer as an act of communication with God. Read this way, the text of 1QHᵃ VI 19–33 reveals itself as the prayer of someone acknowledging his God-given leadership duties toward his community and facing the challenges with hopes and perhaps fears. Accordingly, I suggest that this composition is the prayer of a religious elite, directed not to subordinate community members, but to fellow, elite worshipers facing the same challenges of fulfilling God's purpose. But I thought it wasn't rhetorical

The purpose of introducing comparative material is not to establish only directed to God a historical and genealogical development of the genre of intercessory prayer, starting with the Hodayot. The prayers discussed here are most relevant in spite of their different languages and later time of composition and use simply because they, by speaking with the voice of an intercessor, are paralleling the tendency discerned in 1QHᵃ VI 19–33 and other Hodayot compositions to include more participants and to place the speaker in a mediating function. This development represents a pronounced change of attitude in comparison with the biblical psalms, and ultimately betrays an evolving, new outlook different from the biblical one.

Sociologically, the distribution of this feature in and outside the Dead Sea documents suggests that the Dead Sea community was shaped by sociohistorical conditions that were formative also for other communities; for example, Christian groups that developed a little later. Guy Stroumsa, who describes the development of religions in Hellenistic-Roman antiquity as a process of individualization and internalization due to the end of official, sacrificial state cults, sees this development as a process anticipated in Diaspora Judaism by Jews who had been debarred from participation in the sacrificial cult. This was a development of communitarian fellowships with new roles for participants, as well as for their leaders, who were not to act as priests. According to Stroumsa a "new model of religion" developed:

> In the new model, subjective forms of religion such as faith or piety are dominant, and they model the objective forms that it might take. If religion remained, as formerly, a social (that is to say, collective) fact, in the new circumstances the community was (in principle) chosen by the individual; belonging to the group was based on the conversion of the

individual person, or his repenting. And finally, the reading of Scripture had become a personal duty. All this means that the principle of authority rested largely on the individual.[88]

There is reason to believe that Diaspora forms of religious organizations and practices had repercussions on Palestinian Judaism.[89] Synagogues seem to have been in use for assembly and Torah studies in Palestine in the Second Temple period, although they did not function to substitute for temple worship as did the Diaspora synagogues.[90] According to some, their architectural design suggests they did not develop *sui generis* but were examples of a wider, social phenomenon in the Hellenistic world, the *collegia* or voluntary assemblies.[91] The implication of all this is that along with its hostile break from the temple authorities and its distinct beliefs, the Dead Sea community was not unaffected by general tendencies in the Hellenistic world but, as one might expect, would resemble both contemporary and later groups in their development of new strategies for worship and community life. Therefore, we should not be surprised to learn that member and leadership roles changed and were realized in literature and ritual performance in analogy with manners we recognize in later Jewish and Christian literature.

3.3. The Prayer Seen in a Performance Perspective

The ideal audience's general knowledge of the use of hymns and prayers will have rendered some interpretations more appropriate to the partici-

---

88. Stroumsa, *End of Sacrifice*, 92.

89. Stroumsa does not preclude the possibility that Palestinian Judaism developed in a similar way. Remains of synagogues in Palestine point to the existence of communitarian life there also (ibid., 87–88).

90. See Inger Nielsen, "Synagogue (synagogé) and Prayerhouse (proseuché)," 69–81, for a presentation of archaeological findings, architectural analysis, and written sources. Seven buildings from before the destruction of the temple in 70 CE are generally discussed as possible synagogues, one of which dates from the Hasmonean era (Jericho) and one shortly after (Gamla). Others have been more reluctant to accept the existence of synagogues in Palestine before the very late, post-Maccabean Second Temple period. See Grabbe, "Synagogues in Pre-70 Palestine: A Re-assessment," 17–26; Flesher, "Palestinian Synagogues before 70 C.E.: A Review of the Evidence," 27–39.

91. Richardson, "Early Synagogues as *Collegia* in the Diaspora and Palestine," 90–109; Nielsen, "Synagogue (synagogé) and Prayerhouse (proseuché)," 91–94.

pants than others. Likewise, *our* knowledge of the genre in general and in Jewish circles in the Second Temple period in particular, allows us to render some historical and sociological interpretations more likely than others. Given that the genre of the Hodayot is hymn or prayer, the question is which social and rhetorical situations may possibly be addressed in them? In the light of the preceding analysis, I shall approach this issue by analyzing 1QH^a VI 19–33 from a performance theoretical perspective. I have suggested that the composition of 1QH^a VI 19–33 is an edificatory prayer spoken by and directed to people who saw themselves as a religious elite dealing with issues of leadership and responsibility. This means that I reject the prevailing view of the text as a community hymn giving voice to a collective of "rank and file" worshipers. I also reject the idea that the leadership of the Dead Sea Scrolls addresses such ordinary members through the composition, as suggested by Newsom. However, I find Newsom's rhetorical analysis of this and other Hodayot texts refreshing and methodologically helpful. Unlike earlier approaches to the Hodayot, it seriously considers the rhetorical potential and advantages of the genre.[92] For this reason, I shall wrestle with it a little more.

After a brief consideration of the genre of the Hodayot in a ritual theoretical framework, I will sketch out Jeffrey Alexander's theory of cultural pragmatics, in which he provides adequate tools for discussing the relation of a text, or *script*, to its social context within the confines of *authentic performance*. Finally, I am going to take up Carol Newsom's interpretation with reference to Alexander's theory.

3.3.1. Hodayot and Ritual Theory

When it comes to defining the ritual genre of the Hodayot, the texts could belong in a rite of exchange or communion, as described by Catherine Bell, because thanksgiving is a central and formative element. Two distinct aspects are handled in such rites: the human-divine relationship and the organization and well-being of the community itself. "Ritual acts of offering, exchange and communion appear to invoke very complex relations of mutual interdependence between the human and the divine. In addition, these activities are likely to be important not simply to human-divine rela-

---

92. Because of this, Newsom's article, "Kenneth Burke Meets the Teacher of Righteousness," seriously prompted my interest in the Hodayot several years ago.

tions, but also to a number of social and cultural processes through which the community organizes and understands itself."[93]

As we shall see, Carol Newsom attaches a great deal of weight to the latter aspect (namely, the community organization) because she treats the so-called "Leader Hymns" as hymns composed and performed by the leadership with the purpose of maintaining the loyalty of the community members. She treats the hymns as pieces of rhetoric in which the speaking hymnist performs an act of leadership for an (ideal) audience consisting of ordinary members. She hardly makes an effort to scrutinize the meaning of the formal address to God, which permeates the Hodayot. The basic meaning of thanksgiving to the deity—the way this sort of transaction between humans and God affects the speaker and his audience—is not explained. In her treatment, then, Newsom lets the organization of the community overshadow the human-divine relation as she prioritizes the texts and their rhetorical situation over any ritual meaning that might be expressed simultaneously on occasions of reading or performing the texts. Admittedly, we only have the texts; we do not have the community. On the other hand, it is reasonable to assume they belonged in some sort of ritual setting in which exchange or communion between humans and the deity took place.

If we are aware of these (not further defined) ritual settings, we may get some valuable guidance for assessing the rhetorical potential of the texts. The so-called Leader Hymns may also originate in political rituals in which certain power relations were promoted, as suggested by Newsom, and this option should not be excluded in advance. However, the question is whether such interpretations are compatible with an understanding of the compositions as thanksgiving prayers, and whether they are sustained by close linguistic readings accounting for formal traits, like the thanksgiving formulas, as well as subtle and minor details. This is a question of the credibility needed for rhetoric to work.

Within ritual theory, performance theorists are often preoccupied with political aspects of ritual.[94] James Fernández even describes ritual performance as a further development of rhetorical persuasion.[95] Jeffrey Alexander has developed a theory on the authenticity of performance and ritual, which can be of help in a discussion of Hodayot texts and their aptness to express hegemonic agendas; that is, their political capacity and

---

93. Bell, *Ritual*, 109.
94. Ibid., 128–30.
95. Fernández, "Persuasions and Performances," 39–60.

rhetorical potential. Below, I shall give a brief introduction to Alexander's theory, which will eventually be applied to the discussion of 1QH^a VI 19–33 in the effort to determine the communicative patterns of the text.

3.3.2. Theoretical Framework of Social Performance

Saying that the Hodayot Leader Hymns are rhetorical actions of leadership, Newsom in effect treats them as textual remains of performances. It is a basic notion in Alexander's theory of cultural pragmatics that, in complex societies, the cultural function of symbolic action is sustained through performance, whereas in smaller, less complex societies it is sustained by ritual. Whereas ritual communicates the "shared understanding of intention and content"[96] between participants and audience and revitalizes their natural sense of relatedness and identification, a performance reproduces the authenticity of the ritual with the purpose of creating a similar effect on audiences in a less homogeneous and simple society. Alexander does not see ritual and performance as opposite poles. Performativity is at the core of every ritual, but increases with the degree of complexity of a society. Thus, performativity prevails in modern society but is highly present also in, for example, the Dead Sea community, which can be described as a complex, premodern society. Performance *seems* ritualistic,[97] and its success is contingent on its ability to re-create ritual-like conditions. To be more precise, it must *re-fuse* the following elements, which are naturally and "seamlessly" present in the rituals of less complex societies, but have become de-fused in larger, segregated communities:[98]

— *Actors*, performers who display social meaning and do so skilfully and convincingly.
— *Audiences*, who may also be "participants observing themselves and their fellow performers."[99] In successful perfor-

---

96. Alexander, "Cultural Pragmatics," 29.

97. Alexander proposes that this is because rituals in earlier societies "were not so much practices as performances," and that "all ritual has at its core a performative act" ("Cultural Pragmatics," 38). This is a reversal of R. Schechner's proposition that "all performance has at its core a ritual action" (Introduction to *The Anthropology of Performance* by Victor Turner, 7–20).

98. Alexander, "Cultural Pragmatics," 32.

99. Ibid., 35.

mance, the members of the audience identify psychologically with the performers, and cultural extension takes place in the sense that emotions and textual patterns are projected onto the audience "as moral evaluations."

— *Collective representations* of the world, including both deep background representations (i.e., myths, oral traditions) and scripts designed more specifically for the performance (i.e., liturgy, speech, play). These must be *enacted* and many rhetorical devices are employed.

— *Means of symbolic production* in the form of clothing and other material equipment.

— *Social power*; that is, possessors of political and economic power and status determining who may act out or attend a performance, the means of symbolic production allowed, the cultural text to be promoted, and so on.

— *Mise-en-scène*,[100] meaning that the performance must *take place*, or be staged—and unfold in temporal sequence and with spatial choreography.

These elements were naturally fused in rituals performed by simple communities with a limited group of members. Their rituals were closely connected with the mundane activities and the organization of the community, which had only a few social roles; they rested mostly on background representations like myths and religious beliefs. In such communities, the performing actors "have little self-consciousness about themselves as actors," and a ritual is not perceived as a performance but rather as "a natural and necessary dimension of ongoing social life."[101]

This is different in complex societies with a high degree of segregation, an increasing number of social roles (including more "specialists"), and hierarchical power structures. In such societies elements of performance are *de-fused*, while ideology and rationalization become means in the efforts to gain from technological developments.[102] The innovation of written text is one of the most important social innovations causing this kind of cultural change, because it makes the decontexualization of collective representations possible. In Jack Goody's words, it allows written abstrac-

---

100. Ibid., 40.
101. Ibid., 39.
102. Ibid., 42–45.

tions of laws and rules "to be abstracted from particular situations in order to be addressed to a universal audience out there, rather than delivered face-to-face to a specific group of people at a particular time and place."[103] Thus, according to Alexander, the innovation of written texts allows for the considered and planned production of cultural scripts and produces performative actions that are "more achieved and less automatic."[104]

In addition to this separation of written, cultural scripts from the background collective representations, de-fusing is found in the separation of performing elites from the mass audiences as well as in the fact that social powers, rather than the performing actors, control the means of symbolic production. In actual fact, performances in complex societies are politicized expressions of hegemonic agendas, often averse to other people, agendas, and perspectives.

As mentioned, the success of social performance depends on a high degree of re-fusion of the de-fused elements, a seamlessness that invests the performance with authenticity. Rather than rehearsing all the details of re-fusing performative elements here, I shall now turn to the necessary presentation of 1QH^a VI 19–33 in order to undertake eventually a discussion of it as a performative text. Along the way, I shall touch upon two criteria given by Alexander of a successful re-fusing that I find particularly relevant to the understanding of this text and its social situation: the *frequency* of its performance and the fact that it must be *mis en scène*.

3.3.3. Is 1QH^a VI 19–33 a Credible Leader Hymn?

Newsom's interpretation, when expressed according to Alexander's performance-theoretical terminology, makes up the following scenery: ordinary community members constitute the *audience* (are they participants or observers?) that the speaking *actor* addresses in order to secure their continued support for his and his colleagues' community leadership. The text of 1QH^a VI 19–33 and perhaps additional texts constitute the cultural *script* of the performance, allowing the speaker to *act* the role of someone who is in perfect relationship to God and therefore has special commissions and duties towards the member group, and also to dissidents, whom

---

103. Goody, *The Logic of Writing and the Organization of Society*, 13, quoted by Alexander, "Cultural Pragmatics," 43.

104. Alexander, "Cultural Pragmatics," 45.

he denounces.[105] We do not know the means of symbolic production since none are mentioned. Neither do we know how the performance was *mis-en-scène*, when and in which location it took place. What we do know, however, is that its authenticity or credibility depended also on how it was *mis-en-scène*. Newsom suggests the Hodayot may have been performed at banquets similar to the kind used by the Therapeutae, where the head of the community would rise and sing to God.[106]

Would such a performance convince those who participated in it of what was hoped for by the social powers behind it? Would it re-fuse all the elements constituting the performance so that it could pursue its rhetorical goal successfully? Did it feel authentic? Since we were not there, we are unable to give definite answers to these questions. By looking more closely at some of the criteria for a successful performance, however, it should at least be possible to explore the probability of its success.

First, we must consider how the performance could be *mis-en-scène*. Being a prayer, the text is a script for religious activity belonging in a religious rather than a secular setting. As we saw, the text signals that it belongs in (or perhaps imitates?) a rite of exchange and communion. Therefore, it must have been *mis-en-scène* in a similar way to rites of exchange and communion proper in the cultural milieu. Whatever the location was, it must have constituted an appropriate *scène* for religious rituals of exchange and communion, and participants must have gathered there at specific times expecting to be part of religious activity—in a meeting between the heavenly and the mundane. Members of the audience must have seen themselves as participants in a rite of communion or exchange. It is not difficult to imagine this audience consisting of ordinary community members, being subject to social control by their leaders to some degree. Carol Newsom has forcefully demonstrated this in terms of rhetoric, making use in particular of Kenneth Burke's thoughts on rhetoric in poetry, but I shall not rehearse the arguments here.[107]

One obstacle or restrictive feature of performance may be pointed out, though. Repetition must have weakened the forcefulness of the symbolic re-fusion. Since the prayer was written—that is, planned and placed in a

105. Newsom, *Self as Symbolic Space*, 277–86.
106. Ibid., 202–3. Reike ("Remarques sur l'histoire de la forme [Formgeschichte] des textes de Qumran") first proposed that the Hodayot might have been used in connection with similar communal meals in the Dead Sea community.
107. Newsom, "Kenneth Burke Meets the Teacher of Righteousness."

collection of similar texts—one does not get the impression that it grew out of spontaneous creativity on one occasion, not to be performed ever again. The fact that it has been carefully kept in the library, rather, witnesses to the community's fondness for and repeated use of it. If it was actually the case that the speaker, through a series of declarative propositions in the last lines of the text, told his audience of community members that he was acting out his God-given duties toward them in order that they should stay loyal to his (and his colleagues') leadership, this in itself would be a token of a complex social situation. Accordingly, the text must be seen as scripting a performance in which the seamlessness of performative elements, inherent in the genuine rituals of simple communities, could only be achieved with difficulty. If re-fusing had been successful at some point, a successful repetition would be even harder to achieve:

> We are aware that very central processes in complex societies are symbolic, and that sometimes they are also integrative, at the group, inter-group, and even societal level. But we also clearly sense that these processes are not rituals in the traditional sense. Even when they affirm validity and authenticity and produce integration, their effervescence is short-lived. If they have achieved simplicity, it is unlikely they will be repeated. If they are repeated, it is unlikely that the symbolic communication can ever be so simplified in the same way again.[108]

In the fused, integrated ritual of an early society, leadership would be naturally felt and hardly an issue. By repeated staging of the leadership's legitimacy, there was a risk of creating a crack between leadership and audience; the elements of performance would be insufficiently re-fused and their persuasive effort would be weakened.

However, the greatest difficulty with the scenario of Newsom's theory does not relate to its perception of the audience, but to the performing actor and his attitude to the performance. As he belonged in a genuinely religious community whose worship was an indispensable activity, he would hardly be capable of detaching himself repeatedly and systematically from the religious meaning of his acting—an act of transcendent communion and of thanksgiving to God—in a performative effort to affect the organization of the community. Therefore, given that the text of 1QH^a VI 19–33 permits *both* translations promoting the speaker as part of a legitimate

---

108. Alexander, "Cultural Pragmatics," 31.

leadership *and* translations focusing on the communication between the
speaker and God, the latter is preferable because such a script would better
contribute to an efficient re-fusing of the elements of performance.

It is my suggestion, then, that 1QH[a] VI 19–33 as a prayer or hymn of
thanksgiving was used repeatedly as an edificatory mantra dealing with
the *ongoing* challenge of a religious group defining itself as elite. The audience was not found among ordinary community members, but in community leadership itself, or, rather, in a community whose members generally held special responsibilities. In this scenario, there is no conflict
between the explicit act of prayer and the implicit, community-regulating
function. In his act of prayer the speaker acknowledges his God-given
responsibility and simultaneously expresses his desire to live up to it. In
the same way, his fellow participants also oblige themselves to God and
the community. This scenario seems to provide a re-fused, thus credible,
performance, and in this way the performance-theoretical approach provides external support for the linguistic arguments about modality presented above in this chapter.

3.4. Excursus: Modality in Hebrew

From a general linguistic perspective, the speaker's attitude toward what
he is saying is indispensable to the understanding of a text. In SFL terminology, modality in this sense is one of the major factors of a text's capabil-
ity of producing meaning.[109] However, the SFL method of analyzing mood
and modality has been developed for modern English and is inapplicable
with a view to immediate use on the Hebrew language. Therefore, a theoretical and practical framework for modal analysis in Hebrew will be outlined on the following pages.

Apart from the jussive and cohortative moods, which can be expressed
morphologically and syntactically, modality is not necessarily grammaticalized in Hebrew. It is complicated even to describe modality and categorize it since only the jussive and the cohortative forms are grammaticalized.

In the Hodayot, grammatically distinctive jussive and cohortative
forms are few. The *yiqṭōls* of the thanksgiving formulas אודך / אודכה
found in the Hodayot[110] may be perceived as cohortatives that are not

---

109. Eggins, *Introduction*, 174. Palmer describes modality concordantly, saying it
reveals the speaker's *attitude* to an event (*Mood and Modality* [1998], 15–17).

110. 1QH[a] VI 34 (VI 23); X 22 (X 20), 33 (32); XI 20 (XI 19), 38 (37); XII 6 (XII

morphologically distinct. Alviero Niccacci argues that *yiqṭōl* forms in biblical Hebrew discursive texts always have a jussive function (that is, not indicative) when placed at the beginning of a sentence. They may in fact begin a sentence even in cases where they *seem* to be in a second position.[111] The only clause-initial asyndetic *yiqṭōls* extant in 1QHᵃ are the אודכה / אודך of the introductory formulas.[112] There are clause-initial *wāw-(X)-yiqṭōl* forms, but according to Niccacci, for these to have a jussive value, they must follow a jussive *yiqṭōl* in a series of two or more jussives. If this applies also to Qumran Hebrew discourse, does this imply that, apart from the possible cohortatives of the introductory formulas, modal forms are not employed in the whole document of 1QHᵃ? This is hardly the case, and we must surmise that criteria other than morphology and syntax may apply to the jussive and the cohortative.

Apart from the distinct jussive and cohortative forms, modality and volition can be expressed through finite verbal forms formally indistinguishable from the indicative, particularly the *yiqṭōl*. These occurrences must be inferred from "other indications in the context,"[113] such as adverbial modifiers and syntax. For modern interpreters of texts written in ancient Hebrew, both recognizing a volitive form and grasping its semantic meaning may be difficult tasks. Like the jussives and the cohortatives, the modal value of these volitives is often described in terminology stemming from non-Semitic languages (for example, subjunctive, optative, *irrealis*). This may not be a huge problem regarding the grammatically distinguishable jussives and cohortatives, but when it comes to the modal and volitive verbal use, such confusion of language systems, with their different semantics, may utterly blur our understanding.[114]

volitive

---

5); XIII 7 (XIII 5); XV 9 (XV 6), 29 (26); XVI 5 (XVI 4); XIX 6 (XIX 3), 18 (15) (in this last case possibly a *wāw-X-yiqṭōl*, and not the usual asyndetic clause-initial *yiqṭōl*).

111. According to Niccacci, the *wāw-(X)-yiqṭōl* form has a jussive function when preceded by an asyndetic *yiqṭōl* ("direct volitive form") or followed by a syndetic *wǝyiqṭōl* ("indirect volitive form") ("A Neglected Point of Hebrew Syntax: Yiqtol and Position in the Sentence," 7–19).

112. A single exception is found in 1QHᵃ XIX 18 (XIX 15/ XI 15), in a verbal phrase parallel to that of the preceding introductory formula. See Vegas Montaner, "Some Features of the Hebrew Verbal Syntax in the Qumran Hodayot," 277.

113. Waltke and O'Connor, *Biblical Hebrew Syntax*, 507. Their viewpoint is largely a repetition of the one found in Driver, *A Treatise on the Use of the Tenses*, 48, 58–62.

114. Merwe stresses the need for revisions of linguistic categories in the wake of

For the purpose of understanding modality in the Hodayot, I take my starting point in Ken Penner's recent dissertation on verb form semantics in the Dead Sea Scrolls.[115] Penner takes a text-linguistic approach to modality and other issues of verbal use, which works well with the systemic-functional-linguistic methods that I use.[116] He also uses a theory of verb semantics developed by Galia Hatav for both English and biblical Hebrew, which is a good reason for employing the theory that she developed.[117] However, in due time we shall see that the modal values Penner ascribes to verbs in Hodayot contexts are in several instances disputable and may be biased by customary expectations of the texts.

3.4.1. Modality in Relation to the Event Model

According to Penner, not aspect but time-reference is the prevalent value of the verbal forms. Saying this, however, he does not refer to tense solely in an absolute sense; that is, the occurrence of a happening before (the past), simultaneously with (the present), or after (the future) the moment of speech. Rather, the temporal categories (past, present, future) are relative also to a reference time, which may exist simultaneously with the act of speaking but may also be projected into the future of the speaker or recalled by her as past. There is a speech time (S), an event time (E), and a reference time (R) relative to which the event takes place. This depiction of tense, called the Event Model, was first put forward by the philosopher Hans Reichenbach.[118] Building on the Event Model, Penner describes modality in terms of "a constantly branching time line."[119] According to

---

computerized, linguistic description, which may require subtler distinctions between categories ("Some Recent Trends in Biblical Hebrew Linguistics," 9).

115. Ken Penner, "Verb Form Semantics in Qumran Hebrew Texts: Tense, Aspect, and Modality between the Bible and the Mishnah".

116. He thus emphasizes that context rather than the verb form itself should be used for determining the semantic meaning of a verb (ibid., 79).

117. Galia Hatav, *The Semantics of Aspect and Modality*.

118. See Hans Reichenbach, *Elements of Symbolic Logic*.

119. Penner, "Verb Form Semantics," 97. According to Hatav (*The Semantics of Aspect and Modality*, 118–19), this concept has been invented by Saul Kripke and subsequently developed by tense logicians such as Richmond H. Thomason, "Indeterminist Time and Truth-Value Gaps"; David Dowty, *Word Meaning and Montague Grammar*; James McCawley, *Everything that Linguists Have Always Wanted to Know about Logic but Were Ashamed to Ask.*

this version of the Event Model, modality is about the way in which clauses express uncertainty about the reality of an event. Penner gives the following examples in order to illustrate this:

> The statement "John *must* go to the beach" is true if and only if in *every* branching option subsequent to the Speech Time John goes to the beach. "John *may* go to the beach" is true if *in at least* one branching option John goes to the beach. "John *will* go to the beach" is true if in every branching option that turns out to be the *actual option*, John goes to the beach. In this way, future statements may also be considered modal.[120]

If a verbal action is projected into the future, it is not (yet) real, and there is uncertainty about its realization. In the words of Galia Hatav, whose work on modality in Hebrew Penner relies heavily on, "time is considered as non-linear, branching towards the future, where the different branches are thought of as alternative futures."[121] This does not mean that the future tense is a precondition of modality. Rather, it is the relationship of the reference time to the speech time that conditions the modal verb use.[122] However, even verbs expressing absolute future events (the future tense) are modal according to this model. Uncertainty about the actual realization of an event rules out the possibility of indicative statements about the future, even if the clause looks and feels like a declarative ("I will do it tomorrow"). According to Hatav, all *yiqṭōl* and *wəqāṭal* forms "exhibit modality of some kind,"[123] including when they are employed in conditionals or generic statements and even in expressions of past habituality.

---

120. Penner, "Verb Form Semantics," 97.

121. Hatav, *The Semantics of Aspect and Modality*, 119.

122. Note that Hatav has developed her conception of modality based on biblical Hebrew, saying that tense is not particularly relevant to the semantics of biblical Hebrew verbs (thus the title of her book, *The Semantics of Aspect and Modality*). In spite of his conception of Qumran Hebrew as tense-prominent rather than mode- or aspect-prominent, Penner is able to use the same analytical model because, like Hatav, he refers to time in terms of sequentiality and relative tense rather than in terms of absolute tense.

123. Hatav, *The Semantics of Aspect and Modality*, 198. In taking this position, Hatav differs from classical grammars where the indicative function of the *yiqṭōl* forms predominates over the modal functions. See, for instance, Joüon and Muraoka, *A Grammar of Biblical Hebrew*, 2:366–73.

This is because all the differing usages of *yiqṭōl* and *wəqāṭal* are semantically related—in short—through "the notions of necessity and possibility."[124]

The concept of modality outlined above and applied by Penner in his analysis of verb semantics in Qumran Hebrew is a broad one. It acknowledges modality in verbal forms that do not grammaticalize modality morphologically (like the jussive, the cohortative, and the imperative), and it involves contextual factors such as genre, syntax, and the use of adverbial modifiers in the assessment of each verb. Even so, Penner's conception of modality may not be sufficiently diversified. By making tense logic a criterion of modal verbal use in the Dead Sea Scrolls, Penner is perhaps unwittingly too concerned with the meaning of *possible worlds* for the understanding of the verbs in their contexts—because there is very little room for discussions about the speaker's will within Penner's theoretical framework.

3.4.2. The Relevance of Wishes and Hopes

According to both Hatav and Penner, modality in Hebrew may be deontic or epistemic. These two categories belong in cross-linguistic modal systems as described by F. R. Palmer in *Mood and Modality*.[125] Deontic modality implies that something *ought to happen* and thus expresses something about the speaker's will. It belongs to the category of Event modality, which refers to "events that are not actualized, events that have not taken place but are merely potential."[126] Epistemic modality, on the other hand, belongs to the category of Propositional modality, which may be described as modality "concerned with the speaker's attitude to the truth-value or factual status of the proposition."[127] Through expressions of epistemic modality, the speaker makes speculations, deductions, or assumptions about the truth of a proposition.

Penner arranges Hatav's list of modality types according to their degree of modality, starting with highly modal deontic categories. He characterizes epistemic modality as weaker than deontic modality.[128]

---

124. Hatav, *The Semantics of Aspect and Modality*, 117.
125. Palmer, *Mood and Modality* (1998), 51–125.
126. Palmer, *Mood and Modality* (2001), 8.
127. Ibid.
128. The model is reproduced on the basis of Penner, "Verb Form Semantics," 123–24.

The modality expressed by the imperative, the jussive, and the cohortative moods is included in the deontic group. The ungrammaticalized types
of modality in this group are restricted to expressions of *obligation* and
permission similar in meaning to the imperative and the jussive, respectively, because they express the will of someone external to the (grammatical) subject/Agent. If I understand Penner's categories correctly, these
forms of modality, even if deontic, express the speaker's attitude in terms
of his *evaluation* of a situation (its branching opportunities) rather than in
terms of what he hopes for. This understanding is even truer for the group
of epistemic types of modality. I argue, however, that modal values similar
in meaning to the cohortative forms may also be found in the *yiqṭōl* forms
of the Hodayot.

Dividing the nonindicative functions of the finite verb[129] into the
modal and the volitive uses, Waltke and O'Connor make more room for
the speaker's subjective will than does Penner. According to them the
speaker's will is involved in both the modals and the volitionals.[130] However, whereas "the judgment about the factuality of a situation" is prominent with the modals,[131] the speaker's imposition of "an obligation on the
subject addressed" is prominent with the volitionals.[132] The speaker's will
is thus brought more explicitly to the fore in the latter situation. Within
these confines, Waltke and O'Connor operate with a modal category called
"non-perfective of desire," in which room is made for the speaker's wishes

---

129. In their treatment, only the *yiqṭōl*, in their terminology the "non-perfective,"
is considered.

130. Both categories are ungrammaticalized; that is, outside the *volitional class* of
the jussive, the imperative, and the cohortative.

131. "Whereas tense (Latin *tempus*) refers to the absolute temporal relationship of
the situation to the speaker, mood refers to *a subjective judgment about the factuality of
the situation* [my italics]. It may be regarded as real (i.e., indicative in the classical languages) or other than real (irreal or unreal mood, i.e., subjunctive and optative in the
classical languages). A situation may be regarded as irreal for one of two reasons: (1)
because the speaker is uncertain about the reality of the situation itself, or (2) because
the speaker is uncertain about the reality existing between the subject and its predicate
in the situation" (Waltke and O'Connor, *Biblical Hebrew Syntax*, 506–7).

132. "Closely related to the modal nuances of the non-perfective, which express a
situation wherein the action of the subject is contingent on the will of the speaker, is its
use in situations wherein the speaker imposes an obligation on the subject addressed.
In this use it approximates the imperative mood and is, in fact, frequently found in
conjunction with an imperative form" (ibid., 509).

	Type of Modality	Hebrew Example	English Translation	Source
Deontic	Imperative/Directive	ועתה שמעו	"And now, listen!"	CD I 1
	Cohortative	ונעבדה אלוהים אחרים	"let us serve other gods"	11QT LIV 10
	Jussive	יברככה בכל טוב וישמרכה מכל רע	"may he bless you with all good and guard you from all evil"	1QS II 2–3
	Obligation	הוא אם עבר יעשה אשמה והתודה	"if he transgresses, he will be guilty and must confess"	CD XV 4
Epistemic	Permission	יקדם או יאחר	"he may advance or retreat"	CD XI 23
	Possibility	להלכה יחד לא יוכל	"they cannot walk together"	1QS IV 18
	Rhetorical Questions	מי יוכל	"Who is able to…?"	1QS XI 20
	Protasis of Conditionals	ואם במחנות ישבו	"if they live in camps"	CD VII 6
	Relative Future	עד לא ימלאו ימיהם	"before they would complete their days"	CD X 10
	Absolute Future	המשפט בעשה	"he is going to pass judgment"	CD I 2
	Present or Past Habitual	ואת אשר שנא התעה	"those that he hates, he causes to stray"	CD II 13
	Present Generic/Gnomic	אל אהב דעת	"God loves knowledge"	CD II 3
Nonmodal	Declarative (indicative)	ויתנם לחרב	"he gave them up to the sword"	CD I 4

ought to happen

attitude toward truth

and hopes.[133] Furthermore, in addition to the forms of *instruction* and *pro-hibition*, the volitional verbal use includes forms of *injunction*, expressing "the speaker's will in a positive request or demand."[134]

Waltke and O'Connor's references to other-than-indicative functions of *yiqṭōl* forms reflect their awareness of aspects of the perlocutionary force of modal (nonindicative) use, which is not discernible in Penner and Hatav's Event Model outside the grammaticalized modal forms. Due to its strong focus on the degree of factuality in verbs, it neither distinguishes the speaker's will as an essential factor in modal verbal use, nor analyzes the vast variety of modal expressions of volition. Apart from the grammatical moods, the speaker's will is only discernible in the modal types of obligation and permission, their meaning being related to the moods of imperative and jussive. On the other hand, it seems that the meaning of the cohortative can only be expressed through the grammaticalized cohortative mood.

Hatav's model, used by Penner, does not discuss the possibility of an ungrammaticalized modal verbal expression of the speaker's will or desire, even if this is a *cross-linguistic* possibility. Palmer observes that besides the deontic modality there are non-epistemic variants of modality implying "varying degrees of involvement of the speaker"; namely, subjectivity. He suggests supplementing the categories of deontic and epistemic modality by the category of *dynamic modality*, which involves "notions of willingness and ability," adding that "WILL still retains its earlier meaning of wishing."[135] Referring to Palmer on other matters, Hatav and Penner both disregard this contemporary conception of the speaker's will apart from the otherwise grammaticalized categories. I suggest supplementing the Event Model by a dynamic category of willingness and ability. Such a category is relevant to biblical Hebrew, and I believe modal analyses of the Hodayot will prove it applicable to Qumran Hebrew as well. As

---

133. Their example involves only second- and third-person discourse.

134. Waltke and O'Connor, *Biblical Hebrew Syntax*, 509. Similarly, Christo van der Merwe, Jackie Naudé and Jan Kroeze name one modal function of the *yiqṭōl*, "the (un)desirability of events" (*A Biblical Hebrew Reference Grammar*, 149).

135. Palmer, *Mood and Modality* (1998), 102–3. Palmer also mentions "commissives" and "volitives" as types of modality that are neither strictly deontic nor epistemic. They are expressions of commitment and wishful feelings and attitudes, respectively (ibid., 115–16). As these forms of modality are apparently more specific and typically formally expressed modality types, the broader category of dynamic modality seems more relevant here.

will be seen later, a dynamic category of willingness will not be in conflict with the basic principles of the Event Model. Penner sees tense as the prominent aspect expressed in verbal forms of Qumran Hebrew, and in his opinion the modal nuances are embedded in the future-oriented branching possibilities.[136]

The modal expression of willingness and ability may be intended in several translations of wāw-(X)- yiqṭōl forms of the type "and (X) will." Contrary to earlier English usage, the verb "will" is used with indicative meaning (like, formerly, "shall" in British English) just as much as in modalized utterances. However, in many translations of the Hodayot, the reader must infer the meaning of the verb from information outside the translation, because it is simply not clear how one is supposed to understand the various verbal clauses. There seems to be a general preference among translators and interpreters of the Hodayot for indicative translations of yiqṭōl forms. The question is whether or not this preference is justified. It could be biased by anterior expectations on the part of the interpreters.[137]

3.4.3. Criteria for Defining Chains of Propositions

The approach of this study to modality goes hand in hand with Penner's work when it comes to defining the criteria of modality analysis. We need to look beyond grammar and involve both the relation between sequences of text and our general "knowledge about the world," including our knowledge of the genre of prayer of the time. In addition, some fixed criteria are needed for this work. First, we need to define chains of propositions that correlate with the structural logic of such chains as they are generally found within the genre of prayer. Each proposition must perform a feasible function within its structural unit, as must each structural unit within

---

136. This does not mean that the verbal system of the Dead Sea Scrolls has yet become tense-prominent the way Mishnaic Hebrew has, according to general convention. In any case, even the tense-prominence of Mishnaic Hebrew does not exclude modal nuances in verbal usage according to several studies. See A. Bendavid, *Leshon miqra ulshon hakhamim*, 535–36; Kutscher, *A History of the Hebrew Language*, 131; Penner, "Verb Form Semantics," 4 n. 16.

137. This is a general problem pertaining also to the interpretation of poetic compositions in the Bible, according to Eep Talstra and Carl J. Bosma, "Psalm 67: Blessing, Harvest and History: A Proposal for Exegetical Methodology," 290–313.

the overall structure of the composition. Second, since the Hodayot are prayers—that is, ritual acts of communication with God—their logic and argumentation must be seen as unfolding *between the speaker and God.* I am going to clarify this point only after I have defined the meaning of the first criterion.

As for the first criterion, the various (modal) propositions must be explicable on the basis of *similar logical structures* found in other psalms and prayers. Poetic literature in the Hebrew Bible will serve as the starting point of a comparison because the Hodayot, when assessed from a form-critical perspective, share some of the basic elements found in the categories (*Gattungen*) of biblical psalms. Thus, two of the central elements of biblical thanksgivings are typically present: the *thanksgiving (offertory) formula* and the *praise*. Other unit types typically found in biblical thanksgivings, on the other hand, are practically nonexistent in the Hodayot (invitations to give thanks, exhortations). Some elements from psalms categories other than thanksgivings are used as well. Finally, some structural units cannot be defined according to biblical categories but seem to be molded upon biblical unit types and transformed into something new. For instance, the speaker may recall a promise that he has made (1QH^a VI 28) without actually making a promise in the course of the prayer. Thus, there is no vow formula of the kind occurring in biblical psalms of complaint and thanksgiving, but a reminder that a promise had been made. By looking at the context of vows and oaths in the Hodayot and in the biblical Psalms, we may determine whether they function in a similar way.[138] The sections of 1QH^a VI 19–33 that I have termed "cognitive" are found in several of the 1QHodayot^a texts and also exemplify a transformation because they seem to fill the function of typical form categories in the book of Psalms; namely, "accounts of trouble and salvation" in biblical thanksgiving psalms or "affirmation of confidence" in complaint psalms. In their respective form categories, these unit types are creedal statements in the sense that they confess an existential binding to the divine authority,[139] and this is also the basic meaning of the cognitive sections in the Hodayot. To

---

138. Vow formulas in biblical psalms tend to portray cultic life because they hold out prospects of thanksgiving to God (Pss 22:26 [NRSV 25]; 56:13 [12]; 61:6, 9 [5, 8]; 116:14, 18). We have seen that traces of oath-taking in the Hodayot do not contain promises of cultic action but rather point to ethical obligations. See section 3.2.2.

139. This formulation of the meaning of creedal statements is a rough translation of Aage Pilgaard's words on confessions ('*bekendelser*') in *Gads Bibel Leksikon*:

recapitulate, the structures and their units in the Hodayot do not simply copy biblical structures and their units, but we must strive to make use of similarities and take account of deviations. This work involves comparisons with prayer texts from outside the Hebrew Bible; namely, literature not necessarily written in Hebrew. Some Hodayot structural units have more in common with units found, for example, in pseudepigraphic or New Testament hymns and prayers, the overall structures of which are in some instances more enlightening for our appreciation of what is going on in the Hodayot.

The second criterion is the need to see the Hodayot primarily as communication between a speaker and God. It is related to the first criterion, because the second criterion also is rooted in the need for a valid interpretation. I insist on detaching my interpretation from the rhetorical situation of the text, of which we know very little. What we are looking for is a *typical situation*, in the sense that the choice of genre mirrors not primarily ad hoc realities but some sort of typical practice. This does not rule out the possibility that at the same time, through their sequences of propositions, the texts unfold arguments or structures meant to persuade also the ideal human audience. However, such arguments must not come into conflict with the basic, genre-controlled superstructure and its object.[140] In an article on rhetoric in biblical lamentations, Dale Patrick and Kenneth Diable point to the relation between the Psalter's addresses to God and its truth-seeking, *non-manipulative* character.

> In principle, prayer should be the purest form of persuasive speech. The supplicant seeks to persuade God to intervene on his behalf, and since the auditor knows all the relevant facts and possesses unsurpassable wisdom, the speaker cannot win by manipulation.
>
> One of the functions of the Psalter is to provide prayers which speak honestly and forthrightly about the supplicant's condition and mood within the bounds of propriety and the community's implicit theology. In other words, the Psalms provide the supplicant with truthful words to speak with God.[141]

"I religiøs sprogbrug er b. som handling en offentlig kundgørelse af et eksistentielt forpligtende forhold til en guddommelig instans" (Hallbäck, *Gads Bibel Leksikon*, 76).

140. See the genre definitions presented in section 1.3.

141. Patrick and Diable, "Persuading the One and Only God to Intervene," 31.

Here Patrick and Diable touch upon an aspect of prayer that is immensely important if one wishes to avoid biased rhetorical interpretations. If it is to have any sort of persuasive or edifying effect upon a human audience, a prayer must be perceived as authentic and undivided in its address to God. Better This, too, must be taken into account in an analysis of modality in propositions. In the context of 1QHodayotᵃ, as I read it, this means that the speaker, insofar as he perceives himself as belonging in a religious leadership, must be attentive to God's will, which he is both dependent upon and supposed to help fulfill.

To recall and sum up, the investigation of modal propositions in the Hodayot must be based not only on grammar, but also on syntactical features in the texts and general knowledge of their situational and literary contexts. Propositions and structural units must be seen as elements in an argumentation directed to God and be selected on the basis of similar and comparable arguments in related biblical and extrabiblical literature.

4

TWO COMPOSITIONS SPOKEN BY A *MAŚKÎL*: 1QHª XX 7–XXII 39 AND 1QS IX 12–XI 22

It is commonplace to point to the similarity of 1QHª XX 7–XXII 39 to the last three columns of 1QS (IX 12–XI 22), but the similarities are rarely used to throw light on 1QHª XX 7–XXII 39 and the group of so-called Community Hymns in general. The similarities between the two hymnic compositions under consideration are considerable with respect to both form and content. Most of the hymn in 1QS speaks of God in the third person, but in XI 15 there is a change: "Blessed be you, my God, who opens the heart of your servant to knowledge." The remainder of the hymn follows particularly closely the pattern of those Hodayot that according to Sarah Tanzer contain many wisdom elements and are generally placed in the group of so-called Community Hymns.[1] Among the most significant similarities identified by Tanzer are the *blessing* of God in 1QS XI 15 in his role as *giver of knowledge;*[2] *the rhetorical questions* displaying mankind's inability to have understanding;[3] the *Niedrigkeitsdoxologie* picturing mankind's lowliness in terms of dust, ashes, and so forth, and contrasting it with the righteousness of God.[4] The concluding hymn of 1QS also shares some rare expressions exclusively with the Hodayot.[5] With regard to the

---

1. Tanzer, "The Sages at Qumran," 163–65.
2. This trait is an integral part of the Hodayot, where it can be formulated either as a blessing or thanksgiving.
3. Such rhetorical questions, found in the conclusion of 1QS (XI 20–22) are typical for the so-called Hodayot of the Community and dominate large parts of the hodayah to be discussed (more precisely, the large section XX 30–XXII 34).
4. Found twice in the 1QS text (1QS XI 9–11 and again in XI 15–22), which addresses God in the second person. This is a typical (and exclusive) trait in the so-called Hodayot of the Community, which is found also in 1QHª XX 27–30.
5. For instance, the verb שׁעׁן with a noun designating one of God's properties,

1QS hymn and the hodayah under consideration in this chapter, they are both spoken by a *maśkîl* and share the *combination of prayer and calendrical material*. A closer analysis of the texts and their rather complex agency structures will confirm the fundamental affinity between the compositions but also reveal some significant differences. Elements from SFL, primarily transitivity analysis but also lexical strings, will be employed in order to describe and compare the ideational contents of the two documents.

Another common feature, which will get attention in the latter part of the chapter, is the references to the *maśkîl* in both compositions. Like a handful of the so-called Community Hymns, the hodayah in question is introduced by the superscription למשכיל, and at one point the speaker also refers to himself as a *maśkîl*. In 1QS IX the instruction to the *maśkîl* is also introduced by the superscription למשכיל. The speaker of the subsequent hymn does not refer to himself as such; yet, it is common to assume that the *maśkîl* of the instruction *is* the implicit speaker of this hymn. I shall turn to my reasons for endorsing this point of view in section 4.2.2.

At this point, I would like to draw attention to the paradoxical situation that, according to scholarly interpretations, the identity of the *maśkîl* is radically different in the two documents. In spite of the strong affinities between the texts, the *maśkîl* of 1QH[a] XX 7–XXII 39 is generally seen as a representative of the ordinary community member, whereas the speaker of the hymnic 1QS composition, running from 1QS X 6 to XI 22, is seen as an institutional leader with special assignments in the community. I will give a survey of *maśkîl* references in the Dead Sea Scrolls in order to reconsider the common perceptions of the *maśkîl* in the two documents. Even if in some Dead Sea texts the *maśkîl* seems to refer to a specific, institutional office, more often he appears to be simply a wise and learned person. In some cases, he is expected to instruct others, like the *maśkîlîm* of Dan 11:33 and 12:3; possibly 1QH[a] XX 7–XXII 39 operates with a similar concept of the *maśkîl*.

---

such as "goodness," "truth," "mercy," or "love," is seen only in 1QS X 16 (and in the parallel text of 1QS[d]), in 1QS IV 4, and in the Hodayot (XII 37; XIV 28; XI 21; XVIII 19; XIX 35; XXII 12, 32). In 1QS X 16 and the Hodayot examples, the expression is used by the speaker in the first person. The closest, but not identical, use of שען is found in two hymnic/prayer documents: 4Q379 18 3 (4QApocryphon of Joshua) and 11Q11 II 8 (11QApocryphal Psalms). But there the terminology is different; it is God himself ("you") and his name that are the objects of reliance.

In the following paragraphs, I am going to analyze 1QH^a XX 7–XXII 39 and 1QS IX 12–XI, respectively, in order to further highlight the coherence between the texts and consider its implications for their contextualization. I shall proceed to survey various understandings of the *maśkîl* in the Dead Sea Scrolls and consider the meaning of this concept in the analyzed texts.

4.1 INTRODUCTION TO 1QH^a XX 7–XXII 39

Even if למשכיל הודות ותפלה ("For the *maśkîl*. Thanksgivings and prayer"), which has been reconstructed at the beginning of 1QH^a XX 7 on the basis of two parallel texts from Cave 4,[6] is an unusual introductory formula in the Hodayot, it is probably correct to see it as the beginning of a new composition. The parallel Cave 4 texts both "establish that there is a point of transition from one composition to another one after line 6 in 1QH^a col. XX."[7] The text probably runs all the way to the ending of col. XXII. Some scholars have suggested that the composition ends earlier—namely, in the damaged beginning of XXII 34—because there is a blessing formula (ברוך אתה אל הדעות אשר החינות[ה]) in the latter part of the line, which could introduce a new section.[8] Schuller and Stegemann argue for two reasons that the composition continues into the missing lines at the bottom (XXII 40–42). First, scribe C, who is responsible for all material from 1QH^a XIX 29 onwards, starts other compositions at the very beginning of a line. Second, there is a demonstrative pronoun in line 35, which could only

---

6. 4Q427 8 ii 10 and 4Q428 12 ii 3 both have למשכיל in the corresponding position. In addition, fragment 54, which in 1988 Puech had placed at the upper right part of the column just above line 7, has remains of the upper part of the *lamed*. Therefore Puech reconstructed the text as [למשכי]ל ("Quelques aspects," 50). Several scholars earlier suggested that the text of column XX started somewhere in the missing lines at the top of the column or with one of the several blessing formulas in column XIX, but their suggestions were put forward before the placement of fragment 54, which, according to Schuller, renders their various nonformulaic reconstructions of XX 7 far less probable.

7. Schuller and Stegemann, *1QHodayot^a* (DJD XL), 252. 4Q427 has another composition preceding the introductory formula parallel to 1QH^a XX 7, whereas 4Q428 has the very same order of compositions as 1QHodayot^a.

8. See Carmignac, *Les textes de Qumrân*, 280; Puech, "Quelques aspects," 53.

refer to the lines preceding the formula.[9] Schuller and Stegemann's arguments are hardly decisive, but taken together they are quite convincing.[10]

Translation of 1QH[a] XX 7–39

7.   [For the *maśk*]*îl*.[11] [Th]anksgivings and prayer, for prostration and entreaty continually, from one appointed time to another:[12] with the coming of light

8.   until its dominion in the courses of day, according to its plan (and) according to the laws of the big light, at the turn of the evening and the going forth of

9.   light[13] at the beginning of the dominion of darkness, until the nighttime,[14] at its courses to turn into morning and at the end of

---

9. Schuller and Stegemann, *1QHodayot[a]* (DJD XL), 271. See also Holm-Nielsen, *Hodayot*, 265 n. 13. Schuller and Stegemann compare this way of resuming the preceding text in a subsection to the use of the demonstrative pronoun אלה or זאת/זות elsewhere in the Hodayot. For a discussion and references to other occurrences in the Hodayot, see *1QHodayot[a]* (DJD XL), 89–90.

10. First, there are only two other introductory formulas by scribe C—namely, XX 7 and XXV 34—and therefore there is not enough material to see a habit in it. Second, it is conceivable that a pronominal reference to the preceding text in a written collection of prayers results from a deliberate redactional attempt to link originally independent compositions. See my suggestion in section 3.1 regarding the beginning of 1QH[a] VI 19–33.

11. The reconstruction is supported by the parallel text in 4Q427 8 ii 10 and probably also 4Q428 12 ii 3. See Schuller and Stegemann, *1QHodayot[a]* (DJD XL), 255.

12. The term קץ, which is repeatedly used in this composition, is translated "time" in accordance with general usage in the Dead Sea Scrolls and Late Biblical Hebrew, and not "end" as in most biblical instances. See Qimron, *Grammar*, 296. The phrase מקץ לקץ (lit., "from one appointed time to the other") may refer to the fact that "everything in the world—from the past to the present, and into the distant future—is fixed and classified according to their times" (Brin, *The Concept of Time*, 275). In a context like this, where the phrase is followed by details of the parts of the days and the years, I agree with Brin that it also refers to the fact that prayers take place at set, or appointed, times (ibid.).

13. The Hebrew phrase translated, "and the going forth of light," is ומוצא אור. Even though מוצא is typically used of the sunrise (and of the morning), the text presumably speaks of the lights, the moon, and the stars. Cf. Ps 65:9, which uses מוצא as a designation of both morning and evening.

14. למועד לילה: When used in relation to the times of the days and years, מועד tends to refer to holy time, such as religious festivals. According to Gershon Brin, the meaning of the word in this instance is time in general because it "is not used on the

10. its gathering into its refuge before lightening by the end of night and coming of day, continually, with all

11. the births of time, the foundations of the seasons, and the course of the festivals[15] after their plan according to their signs, for all

12. their dominion according to a plan, steadfast from the mouth of God, and a witness to that which exists; this is what shall be,

13. and there is no end (to it). Besides it there is nothing, and nothing else shall be; for the God of knowledge

14. has established it and nobody is with him. But I, a *maśkil*, know you my God, because of the spirit

15. that you have given me, and faithfully I have listened to your wondrous counsel. In your holy spirit

16. you have opened up within me knowledge concerning the secret of your understanding[16] and (likewise) a source of your streng[th   ] h in the midst of

17. [those who fear y]ou, for an abundance of compassion but also zeal for destruction, and you have made an end[...

18. [   ] *l* [ ] in the splendor of your glory for an eternal lig[ht...

19. [from] fear of wickedness, and there is no deception and[*wl*

20. [   ] times appointed for desolation, for there is no m[ore...

21. [and] there is no more oppression, for before your ang[er...

22. [   ] (they) flee, and there is no one righteous with you[   ]*kh*

---

level of the day"; i.e., time regulated according to a festival calendar (*The Concept of Time*, 257).

15. ותקופת מועדים: In this context מועד designates holy time, i.e., a time appointed for festivals. See the preceding note and Brin, *The Concept of Time*, 256–57.

16. פתחתה לתוכי דעת ברז שכלכה: I take "the secret of your understanding" to be part of the first object, which is knowledge (as to the interpretation of *bet*, see Clines, *Dictionary of Classical Hebrew*, 2:85, section 12 on this preposition). This suggests that the speaker claims to have been given a share in the secret of God's understanding. Newsom's translation in DJD XL, on the other hand, interprets this phrase, and thus the secret, as the instrument through which God opens up the knowledge. It is not clear from her translation what status the following phrase about the source of God's strength should have. I see the "source" (מקור) as an object parallel to "knowledge," not least because מקור is commonly seen as the object of פתח, whereas דעת as the object of פתח looks a little peculiar (semantically, the closest parallel is found in 1QS XI 15, where a prepositional phrase is used).

23.   and [to] have insight in all your secrets and to provide an answer [to your judgments...

24.   by your rebuke, [17]and they will look out for your goodness. For in [your] compassion [al]l

25.   who know you. And in the time set for your glory they will rejoice, and according to [fo]r according to their insight

26.   you have drawn them near, and according to their dominion they will serve you in [their] classe[s not to] turn from you

27.   or transgress your word. As for me, from dust [you] took [me and from clay I was ta[ken

28.   as a source of filth and shame, a heap of dust, kneaded [with water, a council of magg]ots and a dwelling of

29.   darkness. And the return of dust to a creature of clay in the time of [your] wrath wi]ll dust return

30.   to where it was taken from. But what dust and ashes reply [to your judgment, and how can (it) understand

31.   [its a]ctions. How can (it) stand before the one who reproves it and [ ]holiness

32.   [ ] eternal and a pond of glory and a source of knowledge and the [wonder]ful strength. But [they] are not

33.   [ab]le to recount all your glory and to stand up before your anger, and there is no one who can reply

34.   to your rebuke, for you are righteous, and nobody is comparable to you—what, then, is he who returns to his dust?

35.   As for me, I am mute. How can I speak about this? According to my knowledge I have spoken, as someone stirred,[18] a creature of clay. But how

---

17. בתוכחתכה: Following Sukenik, commentators generally substitute *tav* for *bet*, seeing it as a scribal error. See Schuller and Stegemann, *1QHodayot[a]* (DJD XL).

18. מצורוק: The appearance and meaning of the word are debated. It is found also in 1QH[a] XXIII 28, 36; 1QS XI 21//4Q264 1 9; 4Q511 28–29 3. Sukenik and others read צדק. See Holm-Nielsen, *Hodayot*, 207 n. 71, who accordingly translates: "I speak with the right that that hath which is made of clay." Carmignac suggested it is a foreign loanword but did not offer a concrete suggestion ("Compléments," 555). According to Schuller and Stegemann (*1QHodayot[a]* [DJD XL], 258–59), it is almost certainly to be read מצורוק, as if from the nonexistent Hebrew root צרק. Their solution—to take it as a Hebrew variant of the Aramaic root טרק ("to mix" or "stir up")—seems reasonable because this makes it a parallel concept to מגבל found elsewhere in the Hodayot. In fact, the two words occur together in 4Q511 28–29 3–4 and 1QS XI 21. It is difficult

36. can I speak unless you open my mouth? How can I understand unless you give me wisdom? And how can I sp[eak]

37. if you do not uncover my heart? How can I keep the way straight, if you do not establi[sh my]ste[p? And how]

38. can [my] step stand firm [if there is no stre]ngthening empowerment? And how can I rise up[unless

39. and all [   ]my step unl[ess

40. *t*

41. *k*

42. *w*

Translation of 1QHᵃ XXI 1–38

1. [...

2. [s]in, someone born of a w[oman

3. [   ]your [ ] your justice

4. [h[o]w can I disce[rn] if I have n[ot] seen this

5. [ho]w[19] can I behold if you have not opened my eyes and hear[20]

6. [ʕ   ]   the name [by] myself, for to an uncircumcised ear a word has been opened, and the heart...

7. [w]onders, and I know that for your sake you have done these things to me. And what is flesh

8. [   ] to make wonders and in your thought to confirm and appoint everything for your glory.

9. [   ] an army of knowledge to recount to flesh mighty deeds and foundational laws to someone born

10. [by a woman   ] you brought into the covenant with you, and you uncovered a heart of dust in order (for him) to take heed

11. [   ] from the snares of judgment ... your compassion. As for me, I am a creature

---

to distinguish beyond doubt between *yod* and *wāw*, and thus מצירוק, "spat saliva," is another possibility. See *DSSSE*, 1:192.

19. Based on a comparison of the text with 1QHᵃ XVIII 19, Schuller and Stegemann (*1QHodayot* [DJD XL], 263–64) suggest the schematic restoration ואבין באלה] בלוא השכלתני ואיכ[ה.

20. The translation rests on the assumption that the interrogative in front of the preceding verb is implicitly still in force.

12.   [of clay   d]ust[21] and the heart of stone. With
      whom shall I be reckoned until this? For
13.   [you] have given to an ear of dust, and that
      which will be forever you have engraved into the heart
14.   [of stone   ] you have removed in order to
      bring (it) into the covenant with you[22] and that (it) may stand[23]
15.   [in the judgment of witnesses[24]] in the eternal dwelling of the
      light of dawn[25] for eternity. And the darkness will flee
16.   [*wt*°°*l*   witho]ut[26] end and peaceful times
      without se[arching[27]...

---

21. Based on a comparison of the text with 1QH[a] V 32, Schuller and Stegemann
suggest the schematic restoration ‎[חמר ומגבל מים מבנה ע]פר (*1QHodayot[a]* [DJD
XL], 264).

22. ‎השבתה: This verb is probably a *hiphil* of ‎שבת, and not ‎שוב or ‎ישׁ, as suggested by some. See Schuller and Stegemann, *1QHodayot[a]* (DJD XL), 265; Holm-
Nielsen, *Hodayot*. These are in disagreement with Licht, *The Thanksgiving Scroll*, 218;
Mansoor, *The Thanksgiving Hymns*, 193 n. 6. Against Newsom's translation (*1QHo-
dayot[a]* [DJD XL], 268), "you have refrained from bringing into covenant with you,"
I am in favor of Holm-Nielsen's suggestion that the object of "restrained" (‎השבתה)
was a negative word like "ungodliness" or the like, placed in front of the verb—i.e., in
the lacuna (*Hodayot*, 257 n. 46). It is unusual to have the *hiphil* of ‎שבת governing an
infinitive; typically the preposition ‎מן or ‎לבלתי would be expected. Rather, the infinitive expresses the *purpose* of the restraining; cf. ‎תגלה לב עפר להשמר (line 10). Furthermore, the fate of the speaker and his peers is in focus throughout the composition.
Antagonists are mentioned only a couple of times, and then their threatening acts, not
their own fate, appear to be the issue. See 1QH[a] XXI 28; XXII 27.

23. ‎להביא בברית עמצה ולעמוד: An implicit "it" (or "him"), having the same referent as "an ear of dust" and "the heart of stone" (lines 13–14), is the object of ‎להביא
and the subject of ‎ולעמוד. Cf. 1QH[a] XX 30–31, where "dust and ashes" is the subject
of all the verbs.

24. The text has been reconstructed on the basis of the overlapping text in 4Q427
10 4.

25. I accept Schuller's reading (‎אור אורתים), which is supported by the paleographical analysis of Malachi Martin, against other proposals. See Martin, *Scribal
Character*, 489. Regarding the translation, Schuller and Stegemann's argument that
‎אורתים is a (pseudo-)dual of ‎אורה and is a phenomenon parallel to ‎צהרים ("early
light"/"dawn") and ‎ערבים ("dusk"), seems the most plausible. For a full discussion
with references, consult Schuller and Stegemann, *1QHodayot[a]* (DJD XL), 160–61.

26. The reconstructed elements are based on 4Q427 10 5 and are followed by
most scholars. Cf. Schuller and Stegemann, *1QHodayot[a]* (DJD XL), 265.

27. ‎לאין ח]קר: The occurrence of this phrase elsewhere (e.g., 1QH[a] XI 21; XIV 6;
XVI 18) substantiates the reconstruction.

17. [   ]As for me, I am a creature of the
    dust...

18. [to ble]ss[28] your name. I will open [my]
    mouth[...   ']

19. [   ]creature[29][
    d'l]

20. [dust *tḥh nh*   a hidden trap...

21. [*h*] the net of [a pit spr]ead out [and on its ways the snare of an
    abyss...

22. °°[ ]°°*h w'* [ ]°°*h* opened a way *l*° [*ym* to walk[30]...

23. on paths of peace and to make wonders with flesh [like these ones,
    for   lest][31]

24. my steps trudge on the hiding places[32] of its snares, the outspread
    n[et and the heap of   How][33]

25. can I, a creature of clay, be guarded from[34] dispersing and dissolv-
    ing[35] (like) wax when it me[lts before the fire...

---

28. ולברכ]ד שמכה: The occurrence of this phrase elsewhere (e.g., 1QH[a] X 32; XIX
9; XXII 36) substantiates the reconstruction.

29. "Creature" or "inclination." The *yod* and in particular the *resh* of יצר are
uncertain, but this reading is preferable based on the parallel text of 4Q428 13 1–2.
Reconstructions in lines 19–24 (as well as the *aleph* at the end of line 18) are also based
mostly on 4Q428 13 1–2.

30. See the note on line 19 regarding the basis of the reconstruction.

31. See the note on line 19 regarding the basis of the reconstruction.

32. מטוני is probably a scribal error for מטמוני (cf. line 28).

33. ר]שת וערמת: The reconstruction is based on the parallel text of 4Q427 11 2.

34. איכה אשמר ביצר עפר מהתפרד: I follow the majority, who perceive the verb
as a *niphal* and ביצר עפר as a characterization of the implicit subject, "I." The meaning of the clause is then in agreement with the larger context. See Schuller and Stegemann, *1QHodayot[a]* (DJD XL), 268; Dupont-Sommer, *Le livre des hymnes*, 106; Martin,
Scribal Character, 255 n. 15. There are some grammatical obscurities in connection
with this reading: Treating ביצר עפר as a phrase in apposition to the speaking subject
is a little odd, since there is no explicit subject. Usually in the Hodayot this kind of
phrase, including "creature" (יצר), is the predicate of nominal sentences having "I" as
the subject ("As for me, I am a creature of..."). See 1QH[a] XI 24; XXI 11, 31; XXII 19.
יצר עפר and similar phrases can be used like this also in a verbal clause (1QH[a] XXII
12) or in a rhetorical question (1QH[a] XII 30). Furthermore, the preposition ב is a little
difficult to explain away. By itself, the construct noun יצר followed by a noun (e.g., עפר
or חמר) can be used in order to characterize human beings by what they consist of; if
this had been the purpose of the phrase ביצר עפר, the preposition would have been
superfluous. The parallel text of 4Q428 13 8 is identical and therefore of little help.

26.   and a heap of ashes. How can I stand up against the stor[my] wind?[36]
        [But as for me, he establishes me[37] in…

27.   And he preserves him[38] for the secrets of his delight, for he knows[39]
        lm… [*l*…

28.   [ ]*r* destruction and snare upon snare. They bury traps of wicked-
        ness …[…

29.   [ ] *w* with iniquity they accomplish every fraudulent desire, because
        to the anger […

30.   [ ]*l*[40] vanity and nothingness, wicked desire and fraudulent actions
        […

Holm-Nielsen translates the sentence in the active, making יצר עפר the object
(thus the Goal of the process, if the clause is analyzed for transitivity) and distinguishing it thoroughly from the speaking subject (*Hodayot*, 262). This reading seems
to contradict the general impression that the speaker focuses on his human nature
rather than seeing himself as someone who acts, with other human beings as objects.
Alternatively, one could see the prepositional phrase ביצר עפר as controlled by the
verb and translate: "How can I pay heed to a creature of dust, (so) that it does not
disperse…." Compare the use of שמר in the *niphal* in 2 Sam 20:10. Theoretically, the
speaker could include himself in the category "creature of dust," and therefore this
solution may be more in tune with the context.

    35. It makes best sense to take this as a defectively written nominal form of נתך.
See Schuller and Stegemann, *1QHodayot[a]* (DJD XL), 266.

    36. The expression "stormy wind" is seen also in Pss 107:25; 148:8; Ezek 1:4; 13:11
and in 4Q381 46 6.

    37. יכיני: If the reconstruction, which is based on overlapping material in 4Q427
11 1–5, is correct, it means that either God is suddenly spoken of in the third person
here and in the following lines, or someone else whose identity is lost in lacunae. It is
difficult to distinguish between *yod*s and *waw*s, and יכננו, "he establishes him," is also
theoretically possible. See Schuller, "Hodayot" (DJD XXIX), 266.

    38. וישמורהו: The identities of both the subject and the suffixed object are uncer-
tain, but presumably the subject of this verb and the following one is identical to the
subject of the reconstructed יכיני in the preceding line. God is the subject of an overwhelming majority of active forms of כון in the Hodayot, including this composition,
so in all likelihood God is the implicit subject here. In that case, the second-person
address to God is broken in lines 26–27. Possibly, these (and the surrounding lines
with no extant address to God) were not originally part of the composition.

    39. Concerning the identity of the subject of this verb, see the preceding note.

    40. Schuller and Stegemann (*1QHodayot[a]* [DJD XL], 267) reconstruct מגב]ל,
"kneaded," but without giving a reason. Since the word און occurs only here, they are
probably correct that this line is based on Isa 41:29, which contains this word in a similar lexical environment. In light of this, כ]ל may be a more plausible reconstruction.

31.   [   ] °ᶜ   *vacat*   But I, a creature of *h*°[…
32.   [   ]how can[41] he be established for you? You are the God of knowl-
       edge. Al[l …
33.   [   ] You have done to them, and except for you no *p*°°°° […
34.   [And I, a cr][42]eature of dust, know because of the spirit that you
       have given to me that[…
35.   [   ] ° *mh* ev[er]y wickedness and deception attack together in
       pride[…
36.   [all a]cts of impurity to sickness and judgments of calamity and
       [eternal] destruction […
37.   ] °°*ḥ*°°°°° *ś*°°°° to you anger and reve[nging] ardor…
38.   [   ]the creature of clay ° […

Translation of 1QHᵃ XXII 5–39

1.   …
2.   …
3.   …
4.   …
5.   [h]oly as in heaven
6.   [   ] great, and this is the miracle; and they cannot
7.   un[derstand these things or tell of [your] won[ders]. And they are
      unable to know of all
8.   [tu]rn to dust. As for me, I am
      a man of sin and enrolled
9.   [   ]the guilt of wickedness. As
      for me, in the times of wrath
10.   [r]ise up before calamity and
      guard myself
11.   from[you t]each me, my God, for
      there is hope for a man
12.   [   ]*m'l* As for me, a creature
      of clay, I lean
13.   on your strong a[rm and   ]my foot. And I
      know that the truth of

---

    41. In agreement with Schuller and Stegemann (ibid., 268), I interpret the letters
following the lacuna as an interrogative.
    42. This reconstruction is likely because of similar occurrences; e.g., 1QHᵃ IX 23;
XXI 11, 17, 31.

14.   your mouth [and your word will not turn] back.[43] As for me, in my
      life span I will adhere

15.   to [your] covenant   ] *mh*   in the position you
      have made me stand, because

16.   [   ] a man, and you will make him
      turn, and by what *yt* [...

17.   [   ]*hš°°°th*   you are powerful °°*p*°

18.   [   ]°*b yš*° without ho[pe

19.   [   ]And I am a creature[...

20.   [   ]you have divi[ded...

21.   [   ]' who °[...

22.   [ev]ening and morning with
      the co[ming...

23.   [pa]in of a man and from
      the sorr[ow of a human]

24.   [you br]ing to joy, [because] they look out [for forgive]ness, and on
      their guard they [stand firm].

25.   And the willing do not f[ail   ]for you rebuke every destructive
      adversary and *mrṣ* [...

26.   for me ever since I was established at *l*°[   ]°*bh* As for you, you have
      opened my ear *k*°[...

27.   he will not come because °[   ]°°*w* And the men of the covenant
      have let themselves be persuaded by them, and will come[44][...

28.   into my body[45] and bowels[46] [in rep]roof before you. As for me, I
      have feared your judgment...

29.   [bef]ore you. Who can become pure in your
      judgment? And what, then, is h[e]

30.   [   ]°'*nw* in judgment and return to his dust.
      What can he underst[and]?

43. The reconstruction is based on 1QH^a V 35 and 36, because this is the only
other place in the Hodayot where אחור occurs.

44. It is not possible to decide whether the verb is plural or singular and thus
whether it has the "men of the covenant" as its subject.

45. The noun מבנית has the basic meaning of "building" or "structure," but it can
be used to depict the human body. See Licht, *Thanksgiving Scroll*, 249.

46. The word תכמים seems to be a Dead Sea Scrolls invention. See Qimron,
Grammar, 302.

31. [for you,] my Go[d] have opened my heart to your understanding, and you uncover [my e]ar
32. [   ] to have confidence in your goodness. But my
heart grumbles *k*°°°...
33. [   ]° my heart is like melting wax because of transgression and sin
34. [unto] its end. Blessed be you, God of knowledge, who
have established [it]
35. [   ] And this happens to your servant because of you.
For I know
36. [   ] your [kindness][47] I will await my whole life, and your name
I will bless continually.
37. [   ]hope for your servant. But do not leave
him in the time of
38. [   ]*h* and your glory
and goodness.
39. [   ] concerning *b*[...

The Structure of 1QH[a] XX 7–XXII 39

XX 7–14:   Introduction with calendrical information
XX 14–26: Cognitive confession of the *maśkîl*: In this section,
   God is addressed by the *maśkîl* in acknowledgement of God's
   actions toward himself and all others who "know" God.
XX 27–30: The speaker's acknowledgement of his lowly status.
XX 30–XXII 34: Rhetorical questions and statements about the
   speaker and those of a lowly status and lacking ability.[48]
XXII 34–39: Blessing and entreaty

It is difficult to outline the structure of the prayer in its entirety because
lengthy passages are missing. The effort made here is therefore tentative,
particularly regarding the latter part of the text.

---

47. The reconstruction, based on the common combination of the verb יחל with
חסד, is widely accepted.
48. This lengthy section could probably be divided into smaller units, but due
to the poor condition of the text this cannot be done in a meaningful way. However,
the focus seems to be alternately on people of a lowly status in general, the speaker,
and humankind.

The relatively well-preserved beginning of the text contains plenty of information for a comparison with 1QS IX 12–XI. The integration of calendrical material in a prayer text is one significant characteristic that the two texts have in common. In the analysis of 1QHᵃ XX 7–XXII 39, therefore, I am going to attend to the calendrical introduction. I would like to pay attention to the fact that there are no parallel witnesses indicating that the calendrical material should have been inserted into an already existing prayer. On the contrary, 4QHᵃ 8 ii 10–21 confirms its place within the composition.

From 1QHᵃ XX 27 onward, the prayer is very much concerned with the anthropological issue of mankind's inability to obtain true wisdom, and it is saturated with typical wisdom elements and the rhetorical questions so characteristic of many of the so-called Community Hymns.[49] As we shall see in a later paragraph, it definitely makes good sense to parallel the general anthropological outlook expressed here with the one expressed in 1QS IX 12–XI 22. In both texts the speaker's figure is influenced by this general outlook, and we shall see that to some degree the speakers resemble each other because of this. There are, however, some aspects of the speaker in 1QS IX 12–XI that are not visible in the speaker of 1QHᵃ XX 7–XXII 39. This will be demonstrated along the way and discussed toward the end of the chapter. In the discussion of 1QHᵃ XX 7–XXII 39, I shall take my starting point at the beginning of the text by looking at the introductory section and its function in the prayer, and will let the analysis unfold from there.

4.1.1 Textual Cohesion and Agency Hierarchies

I would like to approach the linkage between the introductory section and what follows by focusing on textual cohesion with the help of lexical strings. The purpose of this is in part to show cohesion in spite of the manuscript's poor condition, and in part to establish that the calendrical information given in the introductory section is a meaning-making, integral part of the composition, not simply a dispensable list of times for praise. I find two lengthy lexical strings running from the very beginning

---

49. See Tanzer, "The Sages at Qumran," 23–56.

of the text—I call them *time* and *giving*[50]—both very dense in the first two sections and weaker in the latter sections:

Time: XX 7) continually – time – *c* coming of light – 8) dominion – *c* courses of day – plan – *c* turn of the evening – 9) *c* beginning – *c* dominion of darkness – *c* nighttime – courses – *x* turn into morning – *c* end – 10) – *c* lightening – *c* end of night – *c* coming of day – continually – 11) *c* births of time – *c* seasons – course of the festivals – plan – 12) dominion – plan – steadfast – 13) *c* end – 18) eternal – 20) *c* times appointed for desolation – 25) *c* the time set for your glory – 26) dominion – 29) *c* return of dust – *c* the time of your wrath – *x* return – 32) eternal 34) – *x* returns – XXI 13) forever – 15) eternal dwelling – *c* dawn – eternity – 16) *c* end – *c* peaceful times – 27) *x* preserves – 36) *c* eternal destruction (and so forth)

Giving: XX 7) thanksgiving – prayer – prostration – entreat – 10) – gathering – 11) *x* births – festivals – *x* signs – 12) *x* witness 14) established – *x* spirit – 15) – given – faithfully – listened – *x* counsel – *x* spirit 16) opened – *x* knowledge – *x* source – 17) *x* abundance of compassion – 23) *x* insight – provide *x* an answer 24) rebuke – goodness – compassion – 25) *x* glory – rejoice – *x* insight 26) – serve – 27) took – was taken – 28) *x* source of filth and shame – 29) return of dust – *x* creature of clay – return – 30) taken – reply – 31) reproves – 32) *x* pond of glory – *x* source of knowledge – 33) recount – reply 34) rebuke – 35) say – spoken – *x* creature of clay – 36) say – open – give – say 37) uncover – establish *x* my step – 38) *x* strengthening empowerment – XXI 5) opened 6) *x* name – word *x* has been opened – 8) make wonders – confirm – appoint – 9) *x* knowledge – recount – *x* foundational laws – born – 10) brought – *x* covenant – uncovered *x* a heart of dust – 11) compassion – *x* creature – 13) have given – engraved – 14) removed – to bring – *x* covenant – 17) *x* creature of dust – 18)

---

50. Regarding the lexical strings, readers are reminded that relationships of classification (co-hyponomy/class-subclass/contrast/similarity) are not marked, relationships of composition (meronomy and co-meronomy) are marked with *c*, and relationships of expectancy are marked with *x*. The numbers do not refer to a division of the text into clauses, as they usually do in SFL representations of lexical strings, but to the lines of text in the manuscript in order not to spoil the readers' orientation in the text.

bless – open – 19) *x* creature – 22) opened *x* a way – 23) make
wonders – 25) *x* creature of dust – 26) establishes – 27) preserves
– 29) desire 30) desire – 31) *x* creature – 32) – be established – *x*
knowledge – 34) *x* creature of dust – spirit *x* have given – 38) *x*
creature of clay (and so forth)

The introductory section (XX 7–14) is replete with references to the cultic
divisions of time. As it runs through the section, the lexical string thema-
tizing *giving* is tantamount to *offering* because, within this part of the text,
practically all items of the string share that semantic field. The references
have to do with cultic giving from humans to God, whereas in the following section there is never such a narrow, unambiguous field covering all or
most items of the string.

In the remainder of the text, the giving continues to take place verti-
cally across the boundary between the divine and the human spheres, but
now in the opposite direction. God is the participant Actor or Agent of all
material processes taking place, most of which are about *giving*, whereas
the speaker is the participant Goal. This experience is communicated by
the processes that materialize throughout the text: God is someone who
gives to the speaker;[51] he *has established* his plan;[52] he *has opened* or *uncovered* the speaker's heart, ear, and eyes so that he can receive, and his mouth
so that he can speak.[53] In addition to the recurring verbs just mentioned,
several others are used occasionally and likewise render God as the giver
in the relationship.[54] In addition to what can be extracted from transitivity
analysis, the knowledge spoken of is clearly from God,[55] just as creation
(that is, life)[56] and judgment[57] are obviously God-given things.[58]

---

51. 1QH[a] XX 15, 36; XXI 13, 34.

52. 1QH[a] XX 14; XXII 34.

53. 1QH[a] XX 16, 36, 37; XXI 5; XXII 26, 31.

54. God has also recompensed, drawn near, showed something, engraved something, restored, preserved, acquainted, and rebuked.

55. 1QH[a] XX 15–16, 32, 36; XXI 32, 34.

56. 1QH[a] XX 27, 29, 30; XXI 11–12.

57. 1QH[a] XXII 28.

58. The endless references to humankind as a creation of dust and clay in the
Hodayot are often, and correctly so, interpreted as expressions of a *Niedrigkeitsdoxologie*. Nevertheless, the semantic range of a word like "creation" is much broader, and
other aspects of the word will always be in play and add meaning to the text. To place
the word in a network of items in one or several lexical strings is to take notice of and

The speaker is correspondingly rendered as a confident and await-ing receiver,[59] but most of all as someone who, as a human being created from clay, is incapable of doing anything at all. The speaker of the hodayah appears to be rather passive: he is the Senser of several mental processes, most of which express that he *knows* something;[60] he is the Behaver of behavioral processes (*listening, beholding*);[61] and he is the Existent of a number of relational processes, characterizing him as "a creature of clay," as "mute," and so forth.[62] None of these processes express concrete, tangible action; they reveal aspects of the speaker's self-understanding and of his state of being, rather than of his doing. There are also a number of mate-rial processes depicting the speaker as speaking,[63] keeping his way straight,

---

pay attention to one or more of those additional meanings in the light of contextual information. This is how "creation" and "creature of dust" also witness to the role of God as giver in this text.

59. 1QH[a] XXII 12, 36.

60. 1QH[a] XX 14, 36; XXI 4, 7, 34; XXII 13, 28, 35.

61. 1QH[a] XX 15; XXI 5.

62. 1QH[a] XX 35; XXI 11–12, 17; XXII 8, 12, 19.

63. דבר: e.g., 1QH[a] XX 35–36. The definition of these processes may be ambigu-ous: דבר can be translated "speak" or "talk." When describing the process of speak-ing as *material*, I interpret the verb as referring to the concrete, tangible action of uttering something; I accentuate its (potentially) manifest character. Theoretically, one could instead focus on the physiological aspects of speaking or talking and categorize clauses with דבר as behavioral processes. According to Eggins, the behavioral pro-cesses are processes of *physiological* or *psychological* behavior, which is experienced by a conscious being (*Introduction*, 233). Silviu Tatu's definition of behavioral processes is broader than that of Eggins, and it includes talking as an example of a *social* behavioral process (*Verbal Sequence*, 122). His rather inclusive definition of behavioral processes makes it possible to distinguish between meanings that are semantically related, but not identical; e.g., to see speaking as a material process and talking as a behavioral process. However, in order not to end up arguing about the meaning of the various verbs in each of their different contexts (e.g., walking, waiting, and grumbling in the text under discussion), I prefer to keep the behavioral category narrow and the mate-rial category broad. With regard to this discussion, it is essential to keep in mind that the behavioral aspects of a process do not preclude the possibility that the process has material or mental qualities: The behavioral processes reveal meanings that are "mid-way between materials on the one hand and mentals on the other" (Eggins, *Introduc-tion*, 233). In Tatu's words, they "blend the material and mental into a continuum" (*Verbal Sequence*, 122).

Eggins categorizes talking as a verbal process, and in Tatu's work speaking and talking are also defined as verbal (i.e., not only behavioral). This is problematic

rising up, opening his mouth (that is, speaking), standing up, adhering to the covenant, and waiting.[64] Two observations about these material processes are relevant to the impression of the speaker. First, most of them do not have a Goal; the processes are *intransitive*, and this means that the material processes do not express actions affecting objects other than the speaker himself.[65] Secondly, some of the processes occur in the lengthy section of rhetorical questions, such as: "How can I keep my way straight?" (XX 37); "And how can I rise up?" (XX 37); "How can I stand up?" (XXI 26). Thus, there is some uncertainty about the factuality of the speaker's ability to walk, stand, speak, and so forth. Taken together, these observations lead to the impression that the doings of the speaker concern his own being, his (in)ability to move or to speak—and not external action. The impression remains that God, the one who gives, is the only one to initiate action.

The lexical string of *time* is one that pictures both continuance and division—the continuing division of time according to the God-given schedule. Particularly in the first section, these two aspects of time concur; the days and seasons are divided by the cultic act of prayer in a rhythm that goes on "continually" (XX 7, 10), with "no end" (XX 13), and is "established" by God (XX 14). The string of time changes after that. Unlike the unchanging cyclic time outlined at the beginning, time is now stretched out by means of references to beginning ("creation") and ending ("judgment," "destruction," and "salvation"). Between these two extremes, there are references to "real time," particularly in the rhetorical questions and the speaker's statements about his own condition and about God.[66] This temporal template has much in common with the idea of רז נהיה as used in 4QInstruction. It is an elusive concept, difficult to firmly define, proba-

---

because processes of speaking and talking do not project clauses. With very few exceptions, the verb דבר is absolute in the sense that it does not project a representation of what someone talks *about* or speaks *of*. (See, however, Exod 32:7; Dan 2:4. In these and similar cases, one should probably reckon with an implicit ויאמר / לאמר introducing the speech.) See Eggins, *Introduction*, 235–36; Tatu, *Verbal Sequence*, 122–23.

64. 1QH[a] XX 35, 37, 38; XXI 18, 26; XXII 14, 36.

65. Strictly speaking, the clause "I will open my mouth" is a transitive process. In its figurative sense of speaking, however, it is intransitive: "I will speak."

66. E.g., "As for me, I am mute. What can I say about this?" (XX 35); "and I know…" (XXI 7); "I am a creature of clay" (XXI 11); "I am a man of sin" (XXII 8); "I am confident" (XXII 12); "But my heart grumbles" (XXII 32); "for you are righteous, and nobody is comparable to you (XX 34); "You are the God of knowledge" (XXI 32); "And now you have opened my ear" (XXII 26).

bly because it is a "comprehensive word," as Elgvin has put it. In his under-standing, the expression comprehends "God's mysterious plan for creation and history, his plan for man and for redemption of the elect."[67] From its use in its various contexts within 4QInstruction, Daniel Harrington has deduced that it "clearly concerns creation, behaviour in the present, and the coming of judgement," or, put in other words, "cosmological, ethical, and eschatological aspects."[68]

Toward the end of the calendrical outline, it becomes clear that its division of time is in accordance with a plan (תכון) ordered by God (1QH[a] XX 12). Following this, "a witness to that which exists" (תעודת הווה) is mentioned. This witness is also referred to as that which "shall be" (namely, is to last eternally), and as something established by "the God of knowledge."[69] It seems to be identical either with God's plan or with the temporal (calendrical) unfolding of the plan.[70] The plan is comparable to the esoteric concept of רז נהיה in 4QInstruction[71] and to

---

67. Elgvin, "The Mystery to Come," 135. Elgvin believes some of this compre-hensiveness is encapsulated in the word נהיה itself, as this form may be either a *niphal* perfect (*nihyâ*) or a participle (*nihyeh*) (ibid., 133).

68. Harrington, "Two Early Approaches to Wisdom," 35.

69. Another possibility is that the pronoun refers not to one specific noun, but includes "the whole order of the world as portrayed in the previous lines" (Holm-Nielsen, *Hodayot*, 204 n. 33).

70. According to Holm-Nielsen, the witness is "of this world, created and orga-nized by God, the witness of its existence being the actual expression, while God's word is the theoretical expression, of the regular changing of the times" (ibid.).

71. The immediate context of the expression could give a clue as to the correctness of this assumption. Elgvin has pointed out some typical features of the environment of רז נהיה in 4QInstruction: In seven instances one is admonished to meditate on / search for / gaze on רז נהיה with use of the verbs לקח, נבט, דרש, הגה. The meditation is to take place continually, "day and night." The purpose or consequence of this activ-ity is that the meditating person would receive knowledge; this is seen from the recur-ring apodosis of the type ואז תבין, ואז תדע ודע. Finally, as many as eight times it is said that God will "open the ear" (גלה אוזן) of the understanding one to רז נהיה ("The Mystery to Come," 133). The *immediate* context of והיאה תהיה in 1QH[a] XX 12 does not contain any of these features. However, the wider context has several references to how God will "open the ear" of the speaker, a phrase that Armin Lange (*Weisheit und Prädestination*, 222) interprets as "eine teilweise Offenbarung der in diesem Text mit רז נהיה bezeichneten präexistenten Ordnung des Seins." Collins (*The Apocalyptic Imagination*, 151) also makes this connection. The introductory section with all its calendrical directions parallels, in extended form, the admonitions in 4QInstruction to *meditate day and night*. In fact, the difference in genre accounts for the differing

the idea expressed in 1QS III 15 that "all that is and all that shall be" is that which God has designed and established from the very beginning.[72] The lasting plan contains all that is and all that shall be, and this means creation, judgment, and all ethical life unfolding between them, very

much like רז נהיה in 4QInstruction. This "lasting plan" is universal and, regardless of its occurrence at the end of the list of seasons and prayers, it entails much more than the establishment of liturgical order. It signals that liturgical order, *too*, is part of God's plan.

By implication, praise and prayer—undertaken according to the divinely planned seasonal order outlined with all its transitions—are then "a witness to that which exists" and at the same time a realization of aspects of God's plan. This applies also to the prayer of the *maśkîl* unfolding immediately after the conclusion of the introductory section (1QH[a] XX 14). It is a witness to and a meditation on God's plan in all of its above-mentioned aspects: beginning, end, and whatever comes in between. Much attention is paid to the latter throughout the prayer—the human condition and humankind's fundamental lack of ability to meet the requirements on the one hand, and God's grace and giving of understanding to human beings on the other.

A passage in 4QInstruction describes reiterated meditation as a means to obtain knowledge of God's secret. Earlier studies have shown that 4QInstruction and the Hodayot share a large stock of concepts and vocabulary.[73] It is therefore conceivable that a similar understanding to the one expressed in this example also lies behind our text:

---

representations in the two texts of the network of ideas belonging with the concept of רז נהיה and, in the case of 1QH[a] XX 12, the clause היאה תהיה.

72. Holm-Nielsen connects והיאה תהיה with 1QS III 15 (מאל הדעות כול הויה ונהייה ולפני היותם הכין כול מחשבתם) and 1QM XVII 5 (*Hodayot*, 204 n. 33). The affinity between 1QH[a] XX 7–XXII 39, 1QS III–IV, and 4QInstruction is also implied in Armin Lange's interpretation of מחשבה in these texts. The concept, as met in 1QH[a] XXI 8 and 1QS III 15, designates the preexistent plan for the world and everything that exists in it (in some Hodayot compositions it denotes human plans and devices). See Lange, *Weisheit und Prädestination*, 219.

73. Matthew Goff has made a comprehensive study of literary and linguistic features shared by the two corpora in "Reading Wisdom at Qumran." See further comments on Goff in section 4.3.3. Tigchelaar discusses a number of parallels between 1QH[a] V and 4Q417 and considers the correspondences that exist between these two texts and a part of the Tractate on the Two Spirits (1QS III 13–18; IV 14–26). He suggests that the 4QInstruction text and the closely related Two Spirits text belonged in

... day and] night meditate on the mystery of existence, [and seek continuously. And then you will know truth and injustice, wisdom ... understand the work of ... in al]l their paths together with [their] visitations for all eternal periods, and eternal visitation. And then you will know (the difference) between good and evil in their works, for] the God of knowledge is the foundation of truth, [and through the mystery of existence, he expounded its basis ...] (4Q418 frgs. 43+44+45 i 4–6)[74]

Again, God is the only Agent in 1QH^a XX 7–XXII 39. This is a major point that has materialized through transitivity analysis and awareness of the patterns of *time* and *giving*. Another major point is that the introductory section, with all its details on calendrical timing, invites reflection on the act of praying. The calendrical material is much more than a simple guide to correct prayer times.[75] As it projects reiterated prayer as part of God's plan, it encloses it, so to speak, in his all-encompassing agency. Potentially, this could in turn endow the praying person with a strengthened sense of confidence and understanding and make the language about such matters come alive. In other words, the introductory section with its calendrical material could trigger the meditative quality of a prayer session.

Since the text displays God as the Actor opposite a receiving *maśkîl*, the role of the praying *maśkîl* must be rather passive, and indeed it is. In the following section we shall meet another praying *maśkîl*, but in this case we can more easily connect him with the idea of the *maśkîl* as a leader. The question is whether, in principle, there is any difference between the *maśkîlim* of the two texts.

---

the same milieu, and that "1QH^a V–VI was influenced by both *Instruction* and *Two Spirits*" (*To Increase Learning for the Understanding Ones*, 207).

74. Translation of *DSSSE*, 2:869. The reconstructions are based on the parallel text of 4Q417 2 i 6–9 and 4Q418a 11.

75. This is how the calendrical section has often been regarded. Based on this text as well as 1QS X and 1QM XIV, Weise (*Kultzeiten und kultischer Bundesschluss*, 24) actually finds that "[u]nsere Gruppe ist aufs höchste interessiert an der Exaktheit der zeitlichen Fixierung der täglichen Gebetszeiten." Both in this section and the very similar section at the beginning of 1QS X, Leaney (*The Rule of Qumran*, 239) finds an injunction "probably founded upon the twice-daily offering of a lamb in the Temple (Ex 29:38–42)."

4.2. 1QS IX 12–XI 22 for Comparison

The text of 1QS IX 12–XI contains instructions *for* a *maśkîl* and a hymn or speech explicitly spoken *by* a *maśkîl*. Not only does it share a considerable amount of lexical items with 1QH[a] XX 7–XXII 39, but also the merging of hymnic and calendrical material (1QS X–XI) is a special feature that the two texts have in common.

There are many translations of this text, but in order to support the close analyses provided here, I have produced my own translation, which I believe is fairly consistent with my translations of Hodayot texts. At the same time, it is much indebted to the one by Qimron and Charlesworth.[76]

Translation of 1QS IX 12–26

12. These are the rules for the *maśkîl*; that he should walk together with every living being according to the order of each period and the weight of each man;

13. he should do the will of God in all that has been revealed for each period and learn all the wisdom found through the periods, and the

14. rule of the (current) period; he should distinguish and weigh out the sons of Zadok *vacat* according to their spirit and strengthen the chosen of the period according to his

15. will, such as he has commanded; and he should judge each man[77] according to his spirit; receive each man according to the purity of his hand, and depending on his insight

---

76. Qimron and Charlesworth, "Rule of the Community," 1–51. Other translations and comments consulted are Vermes, *The Dead Sea Scrolls in English*, 82–89; Wernberg-Møller, *The Manual of Discipline*, 35–39, 135–56; DSSSE, 1:92–99; DSSR, 1:34–43.

77. ואיש כרוחו כן לעשות משפטו ואיש כבור כפיו לקרבו: Even though Qimron and Charlesworth clearly perceive the *maśkîl* as the subject of the infinitives in lines 12–14, they translate this passage differently: "And according to a man's spirit (is) justice to be done to him, and according to the cleanness of a man's hands he may approach." "Each man" is made into an object for the latter of these infinitives, and of the following infinitive, להגישו, in line 16 ("Rule of the Community," 41). But there is really no indication that such a shift takes place. Rather, the row of infinitives all function as modal verbs expressing obligations on the part of the *maśkîl*. This is in accordance with Knibb, *The Qumran Community*, 146; Newsom, *Self as Symbolic Space*, 283; DSSSE, 1:93.

16. draw him near. Thus should his love be, and his hate.[78] *vacat* But he must not rebuke or argue with the men of the pit[79]

17. but hide the counsel of the Torah among the men of unrighteousness and rebuke (with) true knowledge and just judgment the chosen ones of the way;

18. Each man he should lead into knowledge in accordance with his spirit and the plan for the period, and teach wonderful and truthful secrets among

19. the men of the *yaḥad*, so that each man can walk perfectly with his neighbor in all that has been revealed to them. This will be the time of preparing the way

20. in the desert. He should teach them all there is to be performed in this time and separate himself from anyone who has not departed

21. from all evil. *vacat* These are the norms of the way for the *maśkîl* in these periods regarding his love and his hatred: eternal hatred

22. against the men of the pit in the spirit of concealment. He should leave riches and the labor of the hand to him, as does a servant (to) his ruler and an afflicted one before

23. his oppressor, and become a man jealous for the law and prepared for the day of revenge. He should do the will (of God) in every business[80]

24. and in all his dominion, as he has commanded it; and he should delight willingly in all that is done and desire only the will of God.

25. And in all the words of his mouth he should delight, and not wish for anything that God has not commanded; he must watch out for the judgment of God perpetually

---

78. In the translation of Qimron and Charlesworth, the love and hate spoken of are clearly of the men drawn near by the *maśkîl*. The reference to love and hate serves to summarize and characterize the actions prescribed for the *maśkîl* himself through the infinitives spread throughout lines 12–16 (see the preceding note). This whole section, which is logically rounded off by a *vacat*, clearly deals with the duties of the *maśkîl* vis-à-vis potential and de facto insiders of his community.

79. אנשי השחת, "the men of the pit," could possibly be a contrast to בני השחר, "the sons of the dawn," occurring in 4Q298 in connection with משכיל. Hempel, who made this suggestion, believes that those concepts may be part of a *maśkîl* tradition that has also influenced the core of rules about the *məbaqqēr* in CD XIII 7b–XIV 2. The phrases would then have been a means to distinguish between outsiders and insiders by way of "changing one crucial letter" within this tradition (*The Laws of the Damascus Document*, 125).

80. בכול משלח כפים: lit., "in every sending of the hands."

26.   [And in afflict]ion he should praise his Creator, and in everything
         he should rec[ount   ] his lips. He should praise him[81]

Translation of 1QS X 1–26

1.   in accordance with the times that he has decreed; at the beginning
         of the dominion of light according to its circuit; at its withdrawal to
         its ordained dwelling at the beginning of the

2.   watches of darkness—for he opens its[82] treasure and spreads it upon
         (earth) *vacat*[83] —and at its circuit, at its withdrawal before light, at
         the radiation of

3.   the luminaries from the residence of holiness, at their withdrawal to
         the dwelling of glory; at the coming of set times for the days of the
         month together with their circuit

4.   and the transmission from one to the other at their renewal. (Every
         time it is) a great day for the holiest of holy and a sign of the release[84]
         of his everlasting merciful deeds at the heads of

5.   appointed times in every time to come *vacat* At the beginning of
         the months at their set times, and on the holy days after their plan
         as a memorial of their set times.

6.   (With) offering of the lips I will bless him in accordance with the
         rule forever; at the heads of the years and in their fixed circuits; at
         the fulfilment of their regular

7.   plan—each day having its ordinance, one after another—from har-
         vest season to summer, from seedtime to first sprouts, and from the
         seasons of the years to the weeks of years,

8.   at the head of their weeks of years until the jubilee. In all my life a
         law will be inscribed on my tongue, as a fruit of praise and a portion
         of my lips.

9.   Let me sing with knowledge,[85] and all my singing will be to the
         glory of God; my string instrument will be in accordance with the

---

81. This reading is generally agreed upon. The context renders Wacholder's translation, "He will bless us," unlikely (*The New Damascus Document*, 129).

82. The suffix probably refers to darkness, not God (mentioned in IX 26 as "Creator"). See Wernberg-Møller, *The Manual of Discipline*, 140.

83. This *vacat* is unusually small and not recognized by all.

84. Lit., "opens."

85. דעת: I refrain from the justified translation "skill" used by others in order to
emphasize the technical aspect of musical performance. See Qimron and Charles-

plan of his holiness; and the flute of my lips I will lift in tune of[86] his judgment.

10.   At the coming of day and night, let me enter the covenant of God. And with the end of evening and morning, I will recite his laws. Where they are, I will set

11.   my boundary—there is no turning back. (By) his judgment I am rebuked according to perversities, and my sins appear before my eyes like an engraved rule. Then I say to God: "My righteousness!"

12.   and to the Most High: "Founder of my goodness, source of knowledge, and spring of holiness! Pinnacle of glory and strength of all in eternal splendor!" I will choose

13.   what he teaches me and be delighted when he judges me. From the moment I stretch out my hand and foot I will praise his name; from the moment I leave or enter,

14.   sit or stand, and when I lay on my bed I will rejoice. I will bless him with an offering issuing from my lips, in the row of men.

15.   And before I lift my hand in order to enjoy[87] the delightful fruit of the earth, in the beginning of fright and terror, and in the foundation of distress and nothingness

16.   I will bless him for the wonder (with) thankfulness.[88] On his strength I will meditate and upon his compassion I will lean all day—and I will know that in his hand lies the judgment of

---

worth, "Rule of the Community," 45; Wernberg-Møller, *The Manual of Discipline*, 37. Instead, I accentuate knowledge as an element adding cohesion to the text with reference to the occurrences of דעת in 1QS X 12, 24, 25, as well as adding textual coherence with the Hodayot. See also translations in Vermes, *The Dead Sea Scrolls in English*, 84; DSSR, 1:39; DSSSE, 1:95.

86. בקו: The expression indicates musicality, "in tune," as well as morality, "lawfully."

87. להדשן: The form is a *hithpael* with assimilated *tav*. See Qimron, *The Hebrew of the Dead Sea Scrolls*, 55.

88. אברכנו בהפלא מודה: The phrase is difficult. For a summary of suggestions, see Wernberg-Møller, *The Manual of Discipline*, 146. I follow Wernberg-Møller in his opinion regarding מודה, but do not entirely adopt his solution, "I will bless him by giving thanks distinctly." I find his reading of בהפלא problematic because it represents a usage of the root (verbal as well as nominal) that is anomalous in the larger context, where it characterizes God and his actions (cf. 1QS IX 18; XI 3, 5, 19, 20). Therefore it is not the speaker's act that is characterized. The definite article not being assimilated into the enclitic preposition is probably a more acceptable irregularity, as it occurs elsewhere in Qumran Hebrew. See Muraoka, "Morphosyntax and Syntax of Qumran Hebrew," 202.

17.   every living being and that all his doings are true. At the commence-
       ment of distress I will praise him, and at his salvation I will rejoice.
       I will not repay anyone for

18.   a wicked action; with good I will pursue a man. For with God
       belongs the judgment of every living being, and he will pay man his
       reward. I will not be jealous in a spirit of

19.   wickedness, and my soul will not wish for riches of violence. And
       in a quarrel with a man of the pit I will not engage until the day of
       vengeance. But my anger I will not

20.   hold back from men of deceit, and I will not delight until he has
       established judgment. I will not keep (my) anger toward those who
       turn from sin and not have affection

21.   for those who defy the way. I will not grieve over the smitten[89] until
       the perfection of their way, and Belial I will not preserve in my
       heart. Neither will foolish things or depraved falsehood

22.   be heard from my mouth, nor fraud or lies be found on my lips. But
       the fruit of holiness will be on my tongue, whereas abominations

23.   will not be found on it. With thanksgivings I will open my mouth;
       continually my tongue will tell of God's righteous actions and the
       treachery of men—up to the completion of

24.   their sinfulness. Vanities I will remove from my lips, filthiness and
       perversities from the thought of my heart. In the counsel of wisdom
       I will hide[90] knowledge,

25.   and with prudent knowledge I will fence it in with a firm border
       in order to safeguard faithfulness and a strong judgment of God's
       righteousness. And I will measure out

26.   a rule by the guiding line of times ... righteousness, love, and com-
       passion for the submissive ones and to strengthen the timid ...[91]

---

89. I translate like Vermes, *The Dead Sea Scrolls in English*, and *DSSR*, seeing
נכאים as a passive participle of נכה. Others prefer "obstinate." See Wernberg-Møller,
The Manual of Discipline, 38; Qimron and Charlesworth, "Rule of the Community,"
47. For a brief summary of different options, see Wernberg-Møller, *The Manual of
Discipline*, 148.

90. אסתר: The text has been altered, possibly by a later scribe. By placing a dot
under the *tav* and adding a supralinear *pe*, he has altered the text into אספר, "I will
recount."

91. It is common to presuppose a word denoting teaching; e.g., להודיע.

Translation of 1QS XI 1–22

1. insight to those erring in spirit; to teach those who grumble[92] with knowledge, and to respond gently to the haughty of spirit, and with a broken spirit to the men of

2. oppression[93] who stretch the finger, speak evil, *vacat* and acquire riches. As for me, with God belongs my judgment, and in his hand is the perfection of my ways, as well as the uprightness of my heart.

3. And in his righteousness he forgives[94] my sin. For from the source of his knowledge he has let out[95] his light.[96] Then my eyes looked at his wonders, and the light of my heart at the mystery

4. of what will become and exist forever. Support is to my right; on solid rock is the way of my footstep. Not by anything will it be shaken,[97] for the truth of God, it is

5. the rock of my footstep, and his strength is the staff (in) my right hand. From the source of his righteousness (comes) my judgment, a light into my heart from his wonderful mysteries. At that which exists forever

6. my eyes have looked: salvation which is hidden from man; cunning knowledge and counsel (hidden) from the sons of Adam; a source of righteousness, a well of

---

92. Several translators follow H. L. Ginsberg's proposal and read רוגנים instead of רוכנים. E.g., Qimron and Charlesworth, "Rule of the Community," 47; Brownlee, *The Dead Sea Manual of Discipline*, 43 n. 1; Wernberg-Møller, *The Manual of Discipline*, 150 n.1. The first part of the line seems to be inspired by Isa 29:24, using רוגנים. The substitution of *kap* for *gimel* follows a pattern known from Samaritan and other sources. See Qimron, *The Hebrew of the Dead Sea Scrolls*, 27.

93. On the basis of the clear allusion to Isa 58:9 ("If you remove the yoke from among you, the pointing of the finger, the speaking of evil"), Wernberg-Møller (*The Manual of Discipline*, 38) and others rightly translate "oppression" as a figurative rendering of מטה (lit., "yoke").

94. Lit., "wipes off."

95. Lit., "has opened."

96. It is difficult to decide on the basis of paleography whether the text is אורי, "my light," or אורו, "his light," and there is no consensus on the matter. Qimron and Charlesworth read אורי but translate "his light," making no further comment ("Rule of the Community," 47). The reading אורו has been chosen here because this fits with the context in the sense that God is presented as a provider in this clause and the preceding clauses.

97. יזד עזר: a damaged *hithpalpel*, יזדעזע, of the root זוע. See Wernberg-Møller, *The Manual of Discipline*, 151, for a brief discussion.

7.   strength, and a fountain of glory (hidden) from the assembly of flesh. To the one that God has chosen he has given an eternal possession, and he has made them inherit the lot of

8.   the holy ones. Together with the sons of heaven he has gathered their assembly into a council of the community. And the assembly is a sanctuary for the eternal planting during every

9.   time to come. But I (belong) with the wickedness of Adam and with the assembly of evil flesh. My depravities, my sin, my transgression, as well as the perversities of my heart

10.   (belong) in the assembly of worms and those who walk in darkness. For to Adam belongs my[98] way, and a man cannot establish his own footstep. For to God belongs judgment; from his hand

11.   (comes) the perfection of the way; in his knowledge is that which will be; everything that exists he establishes by his plan, and without him nothing can be done. *vacat* As for me, when

12.   I totter, the compassion of God is my salvation forever; when I stumble in the depravity of my flesh, my judgment (lies) in the righteousness of God—it endures forever.

13.   When my affliction starts,[99] he delivers my soul from the pit; he establishes my footsteps for the way. In his compassion he draws me near and in his mercy he brings

14.   my judgment. In the righteousness of his truth, he judges me. In his great goodness he atones for all my depravities and in his righteousness he cleanses me of the impurity of

15.   man and the iniquities of the sons of Adam—in order (for me) to give thanks to God for his righteousness, and to the Most High for his splendor. Blessed be you, my God, who opens the heart of your servant to knowledge.

16.   Establish, in your righteousness, all his doings; erect the son of your handmaid, like you wanted (it to happen) to the chosen ones of Adam in order that they could stand up

17.   before you forever. For without you there is no perfection of the way; without your will nothing can be done. You have taught

---

98. I read דרכי with Qimron and Charlesworth, whose text edition actually has דרכו ("Rule of the Community," 48–49). Most reading difficulties in 1QS pertain to the fact that *wāw* and *yod* are generally indistinguishable in the document. See Metso, *Textual Development*, 16.

99. Lit., "opens."

18.   all knowledge, and everything that shall be is according to your will. And there is no one except you to respond to your counsel, or to give insight

19.   into all of your holy plan, to look into the depth of your mysteries, or to perceive any of the wonders (performed) with the power

20.   of your strength. Who can comprehend your glory? And what is, really, the son of Adam among your wondrous works?

21.   Born of a woman—how can he dwell[100] before you—he whose kneading is from dust, and whose body[101] is nutrition for worms? He is squeezed moisture,[102]

22.   nipped-off clay, the longing of whom is dust. How can clay and handicraft respond? How can (it) understand the counsel? *vacat*

The Structure of 1QS IX 12–XI 22

IX 12–X 5: Instruction for the *maśkîl*
X 6–XI 22: Hymnic speech of the *maśkîl*
    X 6–XI 15a: speaks of God in the third person
    XI 15b–22: addresses God directly with a blessing

This rough division of the text is based on contents and formal criteria: The first main part is an instruction regulating the conduct of a *maśkîl*,

---

100. There are different opinions about the reading. Vermes (*The Dead Sea Scrolls in English*, 88), Wernberg-Møller (*The Manual of Discipline*, 39), DSSSE (1:98), and DSSR (1:43) read an emended מה יחשב instead of מה ישב. The reading of Qimron and Charlesworth ("Rule of the Community," 50–51) followed here leaves the text intact and pictures a scenario not unlike the one found in the preceding text in the expression להתיצב לפניכה (lines 16–17).

101. Lit., "habitation" or "dwelling place."

102. מצירוק: This word or phrase is difficult to analyze. Qimron and Charlesworth ("Rule of the Community," 51 n. 304) as well as Wernberg-Møller (*The Manual of Discipline*, 39) argue along somewhat different tracks that semen is actually what is meant here. Their opinions are supported by later, rabbinic material, particularly ʾAbot 3:1, which is early, possibly pre-70 CE. The word could be a contraction of two roots, רוק ("spit," "saliva") and a form of מצה (to "press" or "squeeze" moist liquid or moisture), possibly a passive participle. Even if the construction obtained by combining two roots may be correct, this sort of interpretation seems a bit forced; my translation allows for a less specific understanding, which in turn sticks with the imagery of clay in someone's creating hands found in places like Gen 2:5–7; Job 4:19; 10:9–10.

who is spoken of in the third person. The speaker of this instruction is impersonal. The second main part consists of a hymnic speech, in which a personal "I" at first speaks of God in the third person. Then there is a change, and the text becomes a prayer addressing God directly.

The structure outlined here does not quite correspond to the divisions usually made on the basis of a comparison of the different S recensions found in 1QS IX 12–XI and the parallel texts in 4QS[b] (4Q256); 4QS[d] (4Q258); 4QS[e] (4Q259); 4QS[f] (4Q260); 4QS[j] (4Q264). On redaction-critical grounds, most commentaries prefer to divide the text into two main parts consisting of IX 12–26a and IX 26b–XI 22.[103] The main reason for this is that manuscript 4QS[e], which is regarded as older than 1QS, had a different text, the calendrical 4QOtot (4Q319),[104] following the text equivalent to 1QS IX 26a. As to the connection between the instruction in col. IX and the speech in the latter part of col. X, some scholars believe they originally belonged together[105] whereas others do not.[106] According to some, the calendrical material of 1QS X 1–8 "sticks out" from both the preceding and the following text. It is regarded by many as originally separate material.[107] However, it is not the redaction-critical background of the text that is of interest here. Rather, it is the coherence and meaning of the extant text, the recension of 1QS. Due to the change in perspective appearing in the middle of the calendrical passage (X 6), I prefer to divide it here.[108] The first part, 1QS X 1–5, is distinct and could be an originally independent unit. As it is placed in 1QS, however, it is a logical continuation of the immediately preceding instruction to "watch out for the judgment of God perpetually" and "praise" the Creator (IX 25–26). Seen in the light of this instruction, the calendrical section, with all its references to proper times for prayer, reminds one of the passage quoted above from 4QInstruction, where regular prayer is taken as a means to obtain knowl-

---

103. For details and references, see Metso, *Textual Development*, 108 n. 2.

104. This conclusion is made on grounds of the same, distinctive handwriting and physical features like form and damage patterns. See Alexander and Vermes, *Serekh ha-Yahad* (DJD XXVI), 150.

105. See Weise, *Kultzeiten und kultischer Bundesschluss*, 5–7; Murphy-O'Connor, "La genèse littéraire," 529–30.

106. See Leaney, *The Rule of Qumran*, 115–16.

107. See Falk, "Qumran Prayer Texts and the Temple," 115; Falk, *Daily, Sabbath, and Festival Prayers*, 104; Murphy-O'Connor, "La genèse littéraire," 529–32, 544–46.

108. See the argumentation below.

edge.[109] This focus is expressed further down in the speech: "For from the source of his knowledge he has let out his light. Then my eyes looked at his wonders, and the light of my heart at the mystery of what will become and exist forever" (1QS XI 3–4).[110] In any case, the people responsible for the recension of 1QS found in the calendrical material an appropriate response to the instruction and a suitable expansion of the duties outlined there. The latter part of the calendrical passage, X 6–8, is spoken in the first person and belongs with the ensuing hymnic speech. That, too, may have existed independently, but like the calendrical material of 1QHᵃ XX 7–XXII 39, it fits into the hymnic discourse.

Formal Structure	Location of Calendrical Material	
Instruction (impersonal) 1QS IX 12–X 5		
	X 1–5	*Calendrical Outline*
Hymnic Speech (First-person discourse) 1QS X 6–XI 22	X 6–8	

4.2.1. Order and Coherence

Of particular interest concerning the coherence between the main sections is the theme of *order* occurring in the many circumstantial elements throughout the text. Most of these references allude to God's orderly plan, discussed in connection with 1QHᵃ XX 7–XXII 39. The *maśkil* is instructed to act on "all that has been revealed for each period" and to undertake his duties in accordance with "all the wisdom found through the periods, and the rule of the (current) period," and so forth.[111] These phrases are echoed in the *maśkil*'s speech when he says that "everything that exists he [God] establishes by his plan, and without him nothing can be done" or "everything that shall be is according to your will."[112] The speaker's eyes will look at "the mystery of what will become (רז נהיה) and exist forever"

---

109. 4Q418 frgs. 43+44+45 i 4–6, cited in section 4.1.1.
110. See also 1QS XI 5–6, 15.
111. 1QS IX 12–14, 18.
112. 1QS XI 11, 17.

and at that which is hidden from mankind.[113] All of these circumstantial elements, both in the instruction and the speech, reflect the concept of רז נהיה, or God's lasting plan discussed in connection with 1QH[a] XX 7–XXII 39.[114] Prayer according to calendrical order is also part of this plan. As mentioned, it was seen as a source of divine knowledge in 4QInstruction, and this is probably also the case here. In sum, the text of 1QS IX 12–XI 22 is coherent regardless of its composite nature and redactional history, and in the following analysis I take this as the starting point.

At this point, a brief comment on the meaning of the calendrical material is appropriate. It is commonplace to see the calendrical section as one of the clearest expressions of the obligation to perform prayer at fixed times in the community.[115] The calendrical section can even be seen as an extension of the regulation in 1QS IX 3–6 to perform prayer at ordained times for the sake of atonement,[116] but I am not convinced that the function of the calendrical section in this literary context was primarily prescriptive. Any text outlining a time frame for prayer activity must be looked at with regard to its function in its literary context before it is taken as proof that the practice it outlines was "obligatory" in a particular community at a particular time.[117] We have to ask if it is prescriptive, descriptive of an existing practice, meditating upon the meaning of reiterated prayer, or something else. I am inclined to prioritize the meditative quality that the calendrical section may have added to both the instruction and the speech.

---

113. 1QS XI 3–4, 6.

114. This applies also to instructions to the effect that the *maśkil* will deal with men "according to their spirit" (1QS IX 14, 15, 18).

115. See Leaney, *The Rule of Qumran*, 239; Knibb, *The Qumran Community*, 144. The case is thoroughly argued by Nitzan, "The Idea of Holiness."

116. According to Nitzan, 1QS IX 3–6 is a regulation containing two revolutionary ideas: 1) that atonement for sin could take place without sacrifice and outside the temple, and 2) that prayer could have the same atoning function as sacrifice ("The Idea of Holiness," 131).

117. According to Falk, even the following section of X 9–14 is calendrical in its contents. The language employed is different but outlines four types of prayer praxis that are all extant in the textual material found at Qumran: recital of the Shema and Decalogue, blessings added to the Shema, confession of sin, and songs of praise (*Daily, Sabbath, and Festival Prayers*, 112–23). If he is correct that such concrete occasions for prayer are also mirrored here, this encourages the viewpoint that the calendrical sections under discussion functioned to improve the meditative quality of the text.

Although I acknowledge the text divisions based on duplicates in parallel manuscripts, I hold to the division outlined above. It is actually because of its apparently consciously composite nature that 1QS IX 12–XI makes such an interesting parallel to 1QHª XX 7–XXII 39.

4.2.2. The Identity of the Speaker

With a view to the comparison with the speaker of the Hodayot text, I am interested in the role of the *maśkîl*. The instruction presents the ideal role of a *maśkîl*. This is made clear in the heading, "These are the rules for the *maśkîl*." The speaker of the second main section subsequently personifies such a *maśkîl*. As mentioned in the introduction to this chapter, he does not refer to himself as a *maśkîl*. Yet, based on the coherence of the text, this is what he appears to be. Some central elements of the instruction to the *maśkîl* are picked up in each of the following sections regardless of their differing provenances.

Immediately before the beginning of the calendrical section, the instruction says that the *maśkîl* should "not wish for anything that God has not commanded"; he must "watch out for the judgment of God perpetually" and "praise his Creator," presumably undertaking such activities "with his lips" (IX 25–26). Thus, the instruction makes it clear that *worship should be undertaken always because of God's will*. The first part of the calendrical section concretizes the implication of this instruction by adding a number of adverbial elements mentioning the times for praise: morning and evening, at the beginning of new months, on holy days, and so forth. The second part of the calendrical section is spoken in the first person by a speaker who blesses God "with the offering of the lips … in accordance with the rule forever"—namely, "at the head of the years and in their fixed circuits," "at the fulfilment of their regular plan," and "from the seasons of the years to the weeks of years" (X 6–8). In effect, the personal speaker of the calendrical section claims to be fulfilling the instruction outlined above. The calendrical section then concludes like this: "In all my life a law will be inscribed on my tongue, as a fruit of praise and a portion of my lips" (X 8). This formulation quite clearly makes one recall the words of the instruction. In other words, the speaker seems to take it upon himself to fulfil the final instruction to the *maśkîl*. He takes it upon himself to *be a maśkîl*. The first-person discourse then continues into the hymn where the speaker claims that his singing (and his reciting of the law) will be "in accordance with the plan of [God's] holiness," "at the coming of day and night" and "with the end of evening and morning" (X 9–10). And again, further on in the text, the speaker claims that he will praise God when he leaves or enters, sits or stands, and when he lies on his bed (X 13–14). In sum, the concluding instruction to the *maśkîl* in 1QS IX 25–26, to *worship* God *always* according to *the will of God*, is elaborated both in the calendrical section and in the ensuing hymn:

Instruction 1QS IX 12–X 5		Hymnic speech 1QS X 6–XI 22
1QS IX 12–26b	**1QS X 1–8** *Calendrical section*	1QS X 9–XI 22
Impersonal	Contains a change to first-person discourse	First-person discourse
• praise (worship) • command (God's will) • perpetually (always)	• blessing (worship) • rule (God's will) • forever/all my life (always)	• singing (worship) • plan (God's will) • coming of day and night (always)

The structure of the extant text, with its formal transitions and retrieving of earlier themes, suggests that the speaker of the hymn is ideally the *maśkîl* spoken of in the instruction. In the following, I shall assume this is the case. We shall see, however, that the appearance of the speaking *maśkîl* is slightly different from the ideal *maśkîl* outlined in the instruction. At the same time, he has affinities with the speaker of 1QH[a] XX 7–XXII 39.

4.2.3. 1QS IX 12–X 5a: Instruction

The bulk of the infinitives outlining the ideal conduct of the *maśkîl* envisage his responsibilities for other human beings. Expressed according to the *transitivity* terminology of Systemic Functional Linguistics (SFL), he is ideally the Actor in a row of *material processes* with concrete, often personal, Goals. For instance, he is supposed to "distinguish" and "weigh out" the sons of Zadok, to "strengthen" the chosen ones, to "receive" and "draw near" each man according to "the purity of his hand" and his "insight," whereas "the chosen ones of the way" he is to "rebuke" (IX 14–17). These are all transitive, material processes, involving human Goals. Basically, it is against the SFL rules to analyze nonfinite verbal forms for transitivity because, in principle, infinitives express only an action or a condition; they do not express a temporal aspect and they do not give any information about the subject, which would constitute an obligatory participant in the transitivity analysis. When this information is provided by the context, however, the Hebrew infinitive construct may in fact function as a verb in various syntactical environments.[118] The infinitives to be discussed here function as modal verbs expressing obligation.[119] Therefore, to analyze them for transitivity is a necessary adaption of SFL to the Hebrew language.

In addition to the concrete tasks of the *maśkîl*, the instruction provides information about the social context in which he is to be working. The instruction is very much a window to the ideal interaction between a *maśkîl* and the different people belonging in the social context spoken of: "every living being," "the sons of Zadok," "the men of the pit," "the men of unrighteousness," "the men of the *yaḥad*."

The three infinitives at the very beginning of the instructions (IX 12–13) relate to the relationship between the *maśkîl* and God. The *maśkîl* is to "*walk* ... according to the order of each period," "*do* the will of God," and "*learn* wisdom" (from God). The "will of God" and "wisdom" are impersonal objects that seem to be strived for in general. Walking and doing are concrete, tangible actions, which we recall are a part of the definition of material processes. However, they have not yet been specified in terms of concrete actions taken vis-à-vis concrete, tangible persons.[120]

---

118. See the discussion in section 3.2 (n. 23) and section 4.2.3.

119. See Waltke and O'Connor, *Biblical Hebrew Syntax*, 598–612, esp. 609. See also the translations of Qimron, *The Hebrew of the Dead Sea Scrolls*, 41; DSSSE, 1:93.

120. In English, the verb *walk* behaves grammatically like both material and behavioral processes. The unmarked present tense is the present continuous. Behaviorals are "in part about action, but it is action that has to be experienced by a conscious being. Behaviourals are typically processes of physiological and psychological behaviour" (Eggins, *Introduction*, 233). With this as background, it may be argued that walking occurs in behavioral processes; it illustrates that there is no hard and fast boundary between these process types. According to Eggins's example (216), "So you walk round weak-kneed for three days," walking is a *material* process, but one that is then *intransitive*.

The third process mentioned here, למוד את כול השכל, is a mental process. Both the Hebrew verb למד and the English "learn" act as mental processes; that is, they

Instead, they serve as a sort of heading defining the meaning of all the material processes listed subsequently in the text, actions to be undertaken in the social world surrounding the *maśkîl*.

Following the rows of infinitives, there is finally a series of finite verbs: the *maśkîl* should "desire," "delight," and "wish" in a particular way (IX 25–26). These processes are mental and relate to the ideal ethos of the *maśkîl*, his attitude and (by implication) conduct. They become concretized in the verbal processes of IX 26, obligating the *maśkîl* to praise God.

Up to this point, we have seen a multifaceted set of virtues that are expected from the *maśkîl*. To be a *maśkîl* is in theory a question of: 1) generally living according to the rules of God, 2) performing specific tasks vis-à-vis specific segments of people, 3) having particular attitudes, and 4) praising God. The virtues expected from the *maśkîl* are thus multifarious and include aspects of personal attitude and conduct on the one hand, and leadership responsibilities vis-à-vis other people on the other.

4.2.4. Transition: The Calendrical Outlines of 1QS IX 26b–X 8

The remainder of the instruction (IX 26b–X 5, according to my division) is somewhat different in character. It includes most of the calendrical section (IX 26b–X 8), which several commentators judge to be formerly independent material. It unfurls the temporal circumstances under which the praise of God is to take place. The passage is calendrical, but not in the meticulous and monotonous way of the above-mentioned 4QOtot.

Based on the overwhelming amount of overlapping vocabulary, 1QS IX 26b–X 5 may be compared to 1QH[a] XX 7–14, in which the performance of blessings had been "established" by God and was expected to take place "continually" and with "no end" to it.

---

behave in some of the same ways as verbs of mental processes. For instance, they project clauses. Regarding this and other criteria, see Halliday, *An Introduction to Functional Grammar*, 197–206. It seems to me, however, that in some instances English "learning" represents material processes because of the use of the continuous or progressive present ("It is difficult, but *I am learning*"), and this may complicate our perception of the Hebrew expression.

Shared Vocabulary	1QHᵃ XX 7–XXII 39	1QS IX 12–XI
קץ	1QHᵃ XX 7, 9, 11, 25, 29; XXI 16; XXII 9, 14, 37	1QS X 1, 5, 9
אור	1QHᵃ XX 7, 9, 10, 18; XXI 15	1QS X 1, 2; XI 3, 5
ממשלה	1QHᵃ XX 8, 9, 12, 26	1QS X 1
מועד	1QHᵃ XX 9, 11, 20	1QS X 3, 5, 6, 7, 8
לילה	1QHᵃ XX 9, 10	1QS X 10
בקר/בוקר	1QHᵃ XX 9; XXII 22	1QS X 10
מעון	1QHᵃ XX 5 (4QHᵃ 3 2; 4QHᵇ 12 ii 1)	1QS X 1, 3, 12
מוצא	1QHᵃ XX 8, 10 (4QHᵃ 8 ii 13)	1QS X 10, 14
יום	1QHᵃ XX 8	1QS IX 23; X 3, 4, 5, 7, 10, 16, 19
תקופה	1QHᵃ XX 8, 9, 11 (4QHᵃ 8 ii 14)	1QS X 1, 2, 3, 6
תכון	1QHᵃ XX 8, 11, 12	1QS IX 12, 18, 21; X 5, 7, 9
אות	1QHᵃ XX 11	1QS X 4

The rate of common words, particularly with 1QHᵃ XX 7–14, is very high. Time is important in both texts, but the quality of ceaselessness and continuity of blessings is expressed in different words in this text. According to the objective perspective expressed in 1QS X 1, the blessing should take place "in accordance with the times that he (God) has decreed." On the other hand, the words used by the speaking *maśkîl* in 1QS X 8, "in all my life," express his subjective perspective on how and when blessings were to be spoken. The foci of both the Hodayot and the Serekh text seem to be something other than the mere listing of the exact times for blessings.[121] A concern for the perpetuity of the blessings, both on the universal and the personal level, is brought forward.

---

121. Falk (*Daily, Sabbath, and Festival Prayers*, 191) sees no hint of the contents of the prayer in the calendrical material of 1QS IX 26–X 8a, but sees the material as

The structure of the text underscores this. As mentioned, the calendrical material runs from IX 26b through X 8, but both the communicative situation and the perspective of the text change along the way. In X 6, if not before, there is a switch from impersonal to first-person discourse. It is possible that even line 5b, which is disconnected from the preceding text by a *vacat*, should also be reckoned to this first-person discourse.[122] The calendrical vocabulary also actually changes at this point. The calendrical designations preceding the *vacat* are made with reference to the movements of celestial bodies. After the *vacat*, the intervals for blessings are spoken of in terms of changing seasons as they may be observed, for example, in rural life and agriculture.

It is also worth considering that the string of references to celestial bodies ends with a concluding remark in 1QS X 4 about the meaning of the blessings: "(Every time it is) a great day for the holiest of holy and *a sign of the release of his everlasting merciful deeds* at the heads of appointed times in every time to come." This remark is placed midway into the calendrical section, which it divides into 1) the preceding, impersonal section focusing on celestial or cosmic movements, and 2) the subsequent, first-person discourse focusing on calendrical and seasonal changes as they are perceived on earth. One could say that the calendrical section overlaps both the first main section with its impersonal instruction for the *maśkîl* (IX 12–X 5) and the second main section, the personal speech of the *maśkîl* (X 6–XI 22). In this way, the calendrical section holds the two main sections together.

4.2.5. 1QS X 5b–XI 14: The Speech of the *Maśkîl*

Since the first and second main sections of 1QS IX 12–XI are merged in this recension, I find that the ways in which the *maśkîl* has been depicted by the two sections must have been perceived as mutually compatible by those responsible for knitting them together. When analyzed for transitivity, this section can tell us something about how the authors perceived the

---

a statement about the duty to perform prayer at set times. He relates the elements of calendrical information from X 9 onward to various liturgical texts in the Dead Sea Scrolls and argues that it gives a broad reflection of the varied prayer practices found at Qumran, which were probably based on temple practice (ibid., 103–7).

122. This part of the text is verbless, and theoretically it could belong with the following text.

concept of the *maśkîl* (analysis is generally restricted to verbal processes in which the *maśkîl*/"I" is a participant or part of the circumstantial information). If we start by taking a look at the material processes having God as the Actor and the speaker as a Goal, we may get a somewhat confusing picture of the *maśkîl*: God "delivers" his soul, "establishes" his footstep, "draws [him] near" (XI 13), "judges" him, and "atones" for him (XI 14). Furthermore, he "opens the heart of" his servant (XI 15), is to "establish" his work and "erect the son of [his] handmaid" (XI 16). In some of the propositions, the speaker is not represented by a pronoun ("him" or "me"), but by the phrases "my soul," "my footstep," "the heart of your servant," and "the son of your handmaid." In those propositions, the speaker is also the implicit Goal of the outlined processes.

The potential source of confusion lies in the fact that these exact processes are common in literature generally believed to address the relationship between God and ordinary community members. The speaker of 1QH^a XX, who designates himself as a *maśkîl* yet pictures himself as any human being made from dust and clay, is the Goal of exactly identical processes. Likewise, the speaker of 1QH^a VIII, of whom nothing extraordinary can be said, pictures God as drawing him near,[123] cleansing him,[124] and establishing him;[125] he also reels off other, similar processes with himself as the Goal and God as Actor. In summary, a particular experience—that of being the subject of God's mercy and his atoning, judging, and redeeming actions—is unfolded in very similar language in the genre of prayer in two otherwise rather diverse text traditions, those of the Serekh Hayaḥad (S) and the Hodayot (H). The speaker refers to himself as a *maśkîl* in both traditions. In H, scholars usually regard him as an ordinary community member. In S they interpret him—with some reservation—as a community leader in office.[126] The reservation is that the

---

123. נגש: 1QH^a VIII 30.

124. טהר: 1QH^a VIII 30. See also XIX 13, 33.

125. עמד: 1QH^a VIII 31 ("causing [my feet] to sta[nd...]").

126. Thus Knibb, *The Qumran Community*, 96, 118; Newsom, "The Sage in the Literature of Qumran," 374–75. This position can be argued from several angles. On the formal level, the occurrences of phrases very similar in wording to material in the Damascus Document on the *maśkîl* or *məbaqqēr* (מבקר), which in that material is apparently the designation for an official community leader, have promoted the idea that משכיל is generally to be understood this way, as also in S. For instance, almost exactly the same wording as 1QS IX 12, אלה החוקים למשכיל להתהלך בם עם כל חי לתכון עת ועת, is found in CD XII 20–22 within a passage on the *məbaqqēr*: ואלה

speaker also embodies the ideal conduct of ordinary members. According to this logic, the *maśkîl* presents himself in a language cognate with that of any son of light or ordinary community member for rhetorical reasons. The use of "ordinary" prayer language has the didactic purpose of offering the ordinary members the opportunity to identify with the *maśkîl* and adopt his exemplary attitude and conduct. This explanation is viable in the light of a theory defining *maśkîl* in 1QS and other texts as something other than an ordinary member, that is, as a unique figure with particular communal functions, someone different from those who would normally read, recite, sing, or meditate upon the texts in question. I am not convinced, however, that this theory and its rhetorical model can explain everything there is to explain. We need to reconsider the situation of the concluding hymn of 1QS in the light of 1QH[a] and other similar, so-called community hymns, and we must reconsider those Hodayot in the light of 1QS as well. I shall turn to this discussion after a brief look at verbal processes starring the speaker as the participant Actor.

The bulk of verbs having the speaker as grammatical subject represent mental and verbal processes. In 1QS X 6–17 as many as fourteen verbs display such processes in the speaker's expression of how he will bless God, delight in him, rejoice, and so forth. Not only are these perfectly concordant with both the concluding instructions in col. IX and the calendrical section, but they represent the fulfilment of what is outlined

---

החקים למשכיל להתהלך בם עם כל חי למשפט עת ועת. Kosmala ("Maśkîl," 154), by way of comparing the concept of משכיל in the Dead Sea Scrolls with occurrences of it in the Bible, holds that it is the Danielic idea of a *maśkîl* as teacher or instructor that is prevalent in the Dead Sea Scrolls: "[I]t is in this sense that the word maśkîl became a technical term in the scriptures of Qumran, singling out the teacher who not only instructs the members and the novices of the sect in the knowledge of God and His ways with man, but also teaches them the way of life which God wants them to pursue so that they may escape the oncoming judgement." Kosmala does not say explicitly that there could only be one *maśkîl* at a time, but he makes clear that for anyone to qualify as a *maśkîl*, he must not only have the "necessary mental and spiritual qualifications" but he also must have "distinguished himself by a perfect way of life." He also contrasts the concept in the Dead Sea Scrolls with the collective understanding of the concept held by the later Karaites (ibid., 154–55). With reference to the obvious similarity between the final hymn of 1QS and the Hodayot, particularly with regard to the "utterances of deep personal devotion with creedal assertions of warm conviction," Leaney suggests that the Teacher of Righteousness, who according to him could very well be the author of those texts, was also the author of this final prayer or hymn (*The Rule of Qumran*, 115–16).

in those earlier parts and add much to the inner coherence of the text. It is logical to see the instructed *maśkîl* as the speaking voice here. At the same time, however, all of these verbs represent processes in which any ordinary member would be an appropriate Actor. Seen in isolation from its redactional milieu in 1QS, the propositions referred to here could have been spoken by anyone in the community.

Other verbs and processes in the text are also ambiguous, and in the remainder of cols. X and XI an uneven picture of the speaker appears. On the one hand, he describes himself as a lowly man belonging "with the wickedness of Adam" (1QS XI 9). On the other hand, he says he will take it upon himself to "*teach* those who grumble with knowledge" (1QS XI 1) and thus to perform a clear task of leadership. It is not perfectly clear whether the same can be said of his *hiding* and *fencing in* of knowledge, or of his *pursuing* a man with what is good, but it is quite likely (1QS X 18, 24–25).[127] In any case, these are all material, transitive processes making the *maśkîl* a doer of tangible actions. The propositions made in this part of the text generally concern the speaker in his social world. For instance, he will not "wish for riches" or "engage in a quarrel with a man of the pit,"[128] nor will he hold back his anger from men of deceit or grieve over the smitten until the perfection of their way (1QS X 19–21). In line with this, the following propositions about how the speaker will give thanks and tell others of God's righteousness are contrasted with lowly affairs, such as speaking foolishly, in which he will not engage. It is not very clear from the outset if these propositions would be typical from a leader or rather from an ordinary member, as the language is not distinctly idiomatic.[129] To sum up, the speech of the *maśkîl* is permeated with neither leadership language nor "corporate" language. It has some conventional

---

127. In the Dead Sea Scrolls, it is normally God who "fences in" someone or something for protection (e.g., 1QHᵃ X 23; XVI 12).

128. אנש שחת: Apart from this place and the parallel passage in 4Q260 (4QSᶠ) IV 8, this phrase, or rather its equivalent אנשי שחת, occurs twice in col. IX and in its parallel passages in other S documents (1QS IX 16, 22; 4Q258 [4QSᵈ] VIII 1, 6; 4Q259 [4QSᵉ] III 14). As there are no other extant occurrences, and as we know that this part of 1QS had been merged with S at some point, it could very well have been added to the text as a means to create cohesiveness.

129. For instance, the expression "to bear resentment" (נטר אף/נטר) is used of the *məbaqqēr* in CD XIII 18 in the rather large context that also refers to the *maśkîl*. However, it is not in any way typical in the depiction of leadership. In most other instances, particularly in the Damascus Document, bearing resentment is depicted as corporate

wisdom language and concludes with a *Niedrigkeitsdoxologie*, typical of
the so-called Community Hymns of the Hodayot. Nonetheless, it also
refers to some actions normally belonging in the realm of leadership,
especially ולהשכיל (1QS XI 1).

In sum, the text of 1QS IX 12–XI 22 can be divided into two main
parts, an instruction to the *maśkîl* and a speech by the *maśkîl* (including a blessing). The calendrical section overlaps both. It provides a thematically meaningful extension of the instruction and runs well into the
speech. It smooths over the undeniably composite character of the text
by picking up the themes of time and order in the first section and by
providing a frame for the blessings promised and performed in the subsequent text: prayer at preordained times as a means to obtain divine,
mysterious knowledge. Thematically, it adds to the inner coherence of
the text. The ideal *maśkîl* sketched in the introduction has various duties,
among others to deal with men in various social contexts. The *maśkîl*
speaking in the latter part of the text also refers to such duties, but most
of the time he appears to have the same place in the agency hierarchy
as any speaker of the so-called Community Hymns of the Hodayot. The
people behind the redaction of 1QS seem to have been at ease with a concept of the *maśkîl* as someone who is at times the Goal of God's agency, at
times an Actor on behalf of God. He can be found at the bottom of God's
agency hierarchy, but he also can be positioned higher up in it. In other
words, the author of 1QS tolerates the *maśkîl* having several, seemingly
simultaneous roles.

4.3 1QH[a] XX 7–XXII 39 IN THE LIGHT OF 1QS IX 12–XI 22

Before proceeding to conclusions about how our understanding of 1QH[a]
XX 7–XXII 39 could be affected by the comparison with 1QS IX 12 –XI
22, I want to outline the main results of the transitivity analysis of the two
texts. In both texts, God is the initiator of action; he is the Actor or Agent,
as exemplified below (the relevant clauses are in italics):

God in 1QH[a]
  You *have opened up* within me *knowledge*. (XX 16)

---

behavior (CD VII 2; VIII 5; XIX 18)—perhaps even a corporate behavior that ought
not to take place, as it is appropriate only for God (CD IX 2, 4, 5).

Fo]r according to their insight *you have drawn them near.* (XX 25–26)

And I know that for your sake *you have done these things* to me. (XXI 7)

You brought into the covenant with you, and *you uncovered the heart of dust.* (XXI 10)

For you,] my Go[d] *have opened my heart* to your understanding, and *you uncover [my] ea[r].* (XXII 31)

God in 1QS

When my affliction starts, *he delivers my soul* from the pit; *he establishes my footsteps* for the way. In his compassion *he draws me near,* and in his mercy *he brings my judgment.* In the righteousness of his truth *he judges me.* In his great goodness *he atones for all my depravities* and in his righteousness *he cleanses me* of the impurity of man and the iniquities of the sons of Adam—in order (for me) to give thanks to God for his righteousness, and to the Most High for his splendor. Blessed be you, my God, *who opens the heart of your servant* to knowledge. *Establish,* in your righteousness, *all his doings; erect the son of your handmaid,* like you wanted (it to happen) to the chosen ones of Adam in order that they could stand up before you forever. (XI 13–17)

It also appears from the examples that the speakers (the *maśkîl*) of *both* texts are the Goal of God's material actions. However, when participating as the doers of processes, they are not quite as similar.

In the 1QH^a text, the speaker is mostly an Actor of intransitive material processes, a Senser, or a Behaver. Therefore, with a few exceptions of minor importance,[130] the processes of the *maśkîl* do not generally affect objects other than himself (see the figure below).

According to the instruction of 1QS, the *maśkîl* should accomplish transitive material processes. We have seen that the speaker of the hymnic

---

130. In the literal meaning of דרך אישר, "how can I keep the way straight," (1QH^a XX 37), the way is the Goal in a transitive material process. By using this expression instead of (for example) "walk straight," which is the figurative meaning of the expression, the author accentuates the proactive aspect of the action.

The process of blessing God (XXII 36) has God as Goal; it concerns the prayer situation itself, and not actions directed at Goals in the speaker's social world.

speech also pledges to do such things. Thus, contrary to 1QHᵃ XX 7–XXII 39, this text envisages the *maśkîl* as someone whose actions may have Goals in, and effects on, the social world.

The Speaker of 1QHᵃ

As for me, *I am mute. How can I speak* about this? According to my knowledge *I have spoken*, as someone stirred, a creature of clay. But *how can I speak* unless you open my mouth? How *can I understand* unless you give me wisdom? *How can I sp[eak]* if you do not uncover my heart? How *can I keep the way straight* if you do not establi[sh my] ste[p? (XX 35–37)

How] *can I, a creature of dust, be guarded* from dispersing and dissolving (like) wax when it me[lts before the fire] ... How *can I stand up* against the stormy wind? (XXI 24–26)

As for me, a creature of clay, *I lean on*[131] [your strong] a[rm. (XXII 12–13)

I will await my whole life, and your name I will bless continually. (XXII 36)

The Speaker of 1QS Hymnic Speech

I will not repay anyone for a wicked action; with good *I will pursue a man.* (X 17–18)

I will not hold anger toward those who turn away from transgression; but *I will not have compassion* for all those who deviate from the way. *I will not console* those who are being obstinate until their way is perfect. (X 20–21)

In the counsel of wisdom *I will hide knowledge*, and with prudent knowledge *I will fence it in* with a firm border in order to safeguard faithfulness and a strong judgment of God's righteousness. And *I will measure out a rule* by the guiding lines of time ... righteousness, love, and compassion for the submissive ones and to strengthen the timid ..." (X 24–26)

The Hodayot hymns of the *maśkîl* are reckoned among the so-called Hymns of the Community by general consent, regardless of the fact that one of them is explicitly spoken by a *maśkîl* who, when met in other

---

131. *נשענתי: fig., "I repose confidence (in)."

Dead Sea Scrolls, is mostly interpreted as part of the community leadership—a functionary.

This peculiar situation reaches almost paradoxical dimensions if we take into consideration the considerable accordance between these Hodayot texts and passages in the Community Rule that explicitly deal with the *maśkil*. Although the coherence of the texts is generally agreed upon, this has not led to a renewed discussion of whom the speaker in those Hodayot texts may represent. Perhaps the problem lies in the apparent contradiction between the general scholarly perception of the concept and the meaning of *maśkil* in the Damascus Document (CD), S, and 1QS[b] on the one hand, and H, on the other. Scholars often work with questions pertaining to one or few of these traditions, and cannot manage to analyze the usage of a concept in every tradition. In the following sections, we shall look at various concepts of the *maśkil*—with particular reference to the highly relevant S tradition—in order to reassess the meaning of that word in the context of the Hodayot.

4.3.1 A Survey of *Maśkil* References in the Dead Sea Scrolls

The understanding that in the S tradition the term *maśkil* designates an institutional leader bears much on some of the CD material. It is common among scholars to see the *maśkil* as identified with the *məbaqqēr* in CD and 1QS. This position is based on redactional analyses showing that smaller, independent units concerning the *maśkil* have been incorporated into these large corpora.[132] The *maśkil*, of whom relatively little is said in those formerly independent units, is perceived (among scholars at least) as the holder of an institutional office in the thoroughly organized community. Hempel argues that material on the *maśkil* (represented in CD XII 20b–21a; XIII 7c–8; XIII 22) had circulated independently and was fused into the rules for the "overseer" or *məbaqqēr* (מבקר) in CD XIII 7b.12–13 and 15b–16a.[133] So, according to Hempel, both CD XII 20b–21a, which mentions the *maśkil*, and both XIII 7c–8 and XIII 22, which do not, are

---

132. Hempel, *The Laws of the Damascus Document*, 114–30. See also Wacholder, *The New Damascus Document*, 263. On the basis of the overlapping text of 4Q259 III 6–7, Metso (*Textual Development*, 49, 67) similarly concludes that the *maśkil* material in 1QS IX 26b–XI 22 has at some point been incorporated into the S tradition.

133. Hempel, *The Laws of the Damascus Document*, 105–6, 114–30.

remains of a tradition on the *maśkîl* later worked into a text talking about
the *mᵊbaqqēr*. The text of CD XII 20b–21a explicitly refers to a *maśkîl*:

CD XII 20b–21a[134]

ו﬩ﻻ החקים למשכיל להתהלך בם עם כל חי למשפט עת ועת
וכמשפט הזה יתהלכו זרע ישראל ולא יוארו

And these are the rules for the *maśkîl*, (he is) to walk by them with every
living being, according to the judgment for every time. And in accordance with this judgment the seed of Israel shall walk and (it will) not
be cursed.

It is remarkable that the context in which the activities of the *maśkîl* are to
take place is the broad context of "all the living" and the relatively broad
context of "the seed of Israel." As Charlotte Hempel has pointed out, this
could indicate that the original setting of this passage was presectarian.[135]
The superscription is identical to the superscription of 1QS IX 12, and the
passages are similar in form and content:

1QS IX 12

אלה החוקים למשכיל להתהלכ בם עם כל חי לתכון עת ועת למשקל
איש ואיש

These are the rules for the *maśkîl*, (he is) to walk by them together with
every living being according to the order of each period and the weight
of each man.

As for the passage in CD XIII 7b–8, quoted below, it is part of a section on
the *mᵊbaqqēr*, running from XIII 7b–XIV 2.

CD XIII 7b–8

וזה סרך המבקר למחנה ישכיל את הרבים במעשי אל ויבינם בגבורות
פלאו ויספר לפניהם נהיות עולם בפתריהם

---

134. See also the parallel text in 4Q266 9 ii 7–8.
135. See the summary of her argument below.

And this is the rule for the *məbaqqēr* over the camp, (he is) to instruct the many in the works of God and give them insight into his wonderful mighty deeds and recount before them those things that will be forever with their interpretations.

The latter passage does not seem to fit very well into its immediate literary context. Hempel has given the following reasons. First, it is theological in its orientation, whereas the remainder of the text is pragmatic in its regulations.[136] Furthermore, the superscription, וזה סרך המבקר למחנה ("And this is the rule for the *məbaqqēr* over the camp"), introduces the *məbaqqēr* and the camps as main subjects of the whole section, but these are only met again much later in lines 13 and 16. Meanwhile, the passage under consideration has introduced tasks of the *məbaqqēr*, which in 1QS IX 12–26 are assigned to the *maśkil*. Finally, yet importantly, this passage admonishes the *məbaqqēr* to instruct "the many" (רבים), a surprising term in a text dealing with the *məbaqqēr's* assignments vis-à-vis the camps.[137] There is a discrepancy, then, between the orientation of the *məbaqqēr* material compared with that of the inserted *maśkil* material, and the two traditions seem to speak of differing social entities—the narrowly defined "camps" on the one hand, and the broader "every living being," "the many," and "Israel" on the other.[138]

With respect to the provenance of the *maśkil* material in CD and S, Hempel suggests that "both documents independently drew upon pre-Qumranic material." She continues: "In the case of the Laws of the Damascus Document parts of this material were merged with the material on the overseer and parts may have been lost."[139] Hempel's argumentation is persuasive, and one should take care not to transfer automatically the interpretation seen in CD—that the *maśkil* is an official equivalent to the

---

136. See also the occurrence of משכיל in two different settings within the context of 4Q266. The words of 4Q266 5 i 17, "these are the rules for the *maśkil*," known also from 1QS IX 12, occur in a setting where the overriding theme is the inclusion of members in accordance with their spiritual lot. In 4Q266 9 iii 15, however, *maśkil* is used in a context rehearsing regulations pertaining to lowly matters, such as divorce (in a society including women).

137. See Hempel, *The Laws of the Damascus Document*, 116–18.

138. See also CD XIII 22, another *maśkil* phrase that has been worked into this material on the *məbaqqēr*: "These are the regulations for the instructor, [to walk in them]...."

139. *The Laws of the Damascus Document*, 106.

məbaqqēr—to other Dead Sea Scrolls such as the Serekh texts. In particular, caution must be exercised when dealing with the concept of *maśkîl* in any passage of uncertain origin that has been (or may have been) worked into an overall sectarian composition.

Other nonsectarian literature also refers to the *maśkîl* in a nontechnical sense. 4Q418 (4QInstruction[d]) 81 + 81a 17, a text that has affinities with 1QS XI 3 and several of the Hodayot,[140] refers to *maśkîl* in the plural: ומיד כול משכילכה הוסף לקח, "And from all your teachers get more understanding." In 4QInstruction, which is an extensive sapiential work found in at least six copies, someone is instructing "an understanding person" (מבין) in matters pertaining to daily life in a community consisting of both men and women, and it apparently is *not* a sectarian text.[141]

> Depending on how one views the history of the Qumran community, one can regard 4QInstruction as a book that influenced the language and theology of the Qumran group from the outside, as a witness to a broader Jewish movement that has come to light through the Qumran discoveries, or as evidence for the beliefs and practices of group- or sect-members (Essenes?) living in situations other than the isolated settlement by the Dead Sea.[142]

In light of the affinities of this text with S and H, the reference to several *maśkîlîm* or "instructors" is interesting, not least because the affinities are found in the parts of the traditions that are under discussion in this chapter. It suggests a situation where these sections have been highly influenced by early, nonsectarian traditions treating *maśkîlîm* as a group; and perhaps these parts of S and H have even been created within the very same, nonsectarian milieu. It is not possible to say what, exactly, was the function of those *maśkîlîm*: Were they "wise men" acting inde-

---

140. Goff ("Reading Wisdom at Qumran," 264–88) discusses a number of terminological and theological overlaps and other similarities—as well as differences—between 4QInstruction and the Hodayot, and also draws some lines to 1QS.

141. The composition can be dated as early as 160–130 BCE. See Elgvin, "The Mystery to Come," 116–17. Harrington ("Two Early Jewish Approaches to Wisdom," 25) suggests that an even earlier date may be possible. Joshua E. Burns ("Practical Wisdom in 4QInstruction," 12–42, esp. 15, 19) argues that some aspects of the practical wisdom teachings in 4QInstruction, especially about economic matters, are uncharacteristic of the Dead Sea community and suggestive of its origin elsewhere.

142. Harrington, "4QInstruction and 4 Ezra," 344.

pendently, assigned officials, or something else? In any event, there has
indeed been some sort of group identification. Because of the suffixed possessive pronoun ("your"), the meaning of *maśkîl* in ומיד כול משכילכה הוסף
לקח is clearly transitive. However, Strugnell and Harrington remark that
4QInstruction knows משכיל in "both the senses of 'acting intelligently' …
and of 'making someone intelligent.'"[143] Furthermore, Harrington softens
the distinction between the instructing *maśkîl* and the instructed *mēbîn*
by suggesting that the latter was "groomed to exercise leadership" and
that 4QInstruction might have been "intended as a handbook for train-
ing leaders within a Jewish movement."[144] The question is if this *mēbîn*
was trained to undertake *institutional* leadership or rather assignments of
leadership placed in the community of wise people as a whole. Tigchelaar
hints at the latter possibility, saying that 4QInstruction "apparently intends
to admonish people from all layers of society to behave according to their
God-given ordained position."[145] Nevertheless, there are indications of a
rather broad *maśkîl* concept in 4QInstruction, not too distanced from the
multifaceted representations of a *maśkîl* found in S and H.

Finally, I would like to mention the use of למשכיל in 4Q433a 2 2,
which has been designated a "pseudo-Hodayot" and "Hodayot-like."
Schuller compares its usage of למשכיל to that of 1QH[a] XX 7 (// 4QH[a] 8 ii
10 // 4QH[b] 12 ii 3) because in none of them is God addressed directly, but
is spoken of in the third person.[146] She makes the following remark, apparently presupposing that the text must be sectarian: "Apart from the designation למשכיל there is little that is specifically sectarian in the vocabulary
or content, though terms such as בליעל and the expectation of the eschatological fire of destruction can readily fit into a sectarian composition."[147]
This suggests that the text may well be nonsectarian, in the sense that it
need not be written by a member of the Dead Sea community. Perhaps it
was one of the texts of unknown origin that became sectarian, so to speak,
because of the way it was read and used by community members. On a
hypothetical level, this could explain similarities between this text and the
Hodayot. Apart from the comparable usage of the superscription למשכיל,

---

143. Strugnell and Harrington, "4QInstruction[d]" (DJD XXXIV), 310. See 4Q418
21 2 and 4Q418 80 + 81 17, respectively.

144. Harrington, "Two Early Jewish Approaches to Wisdom," 36–37.

145. Tigchelaar, "The Addressees of 4QInstruction," 75.

146. See also 1QH[a] XXV 34.

147. Schuller, "Hodayot" (DJD XXIX), 239.

Schuller also singles out the image of a planting, which recalls substantial passages from 1QH^a XIV and XVI.[148]

In conclusion, we have evidence of literature that refers to the concept of *maśkîl* both in passages of presectarian provenance merged into sectarian material, and in independent, presectarian works. In this material the term *maśkîl* does not seem to be the technical designation of an institutional office, and even if the authors of CD happened to interpret it as such, it is questionable whether this understanding characterizes the sectarian texts in general. However, it is a widely-held opinion that it does. In the following section, we shall consider the possibility that the *maśkîl* material in the Hodayot has also been brought in from broader, nonsectarian strands of literature.

4.3.2. The Identity of a *Maśkîl*

Henry Morisada Rietz has argued that the Songs of the Sabbath Sacrifice were composed by members of the Dead Sea community and, based on the superscriptions to the *maśkîl*, that "the Sabbath Songs were used in the community, *apparently by important functionaries* [italics mine]."[149] Not only is the use of the superscription למשכיל taken as evidence of sectarian origin and usage, but it also instantly leads to the assumption that it was used by prominent, institutional leaders. By implication, the למשכיל superscriptions in the so-called Community Hymns of the Hodayot should lead one to the conclusion that they were also used by "important functionaries," but this is rarely the case.[150] Russell Arnold is among the few exceptions when he advocates the view that the term *maśkîl* consistently designates the office of the person whose duty it was to rank the members of the community according to God's will.[151] In Arnold's opinion, 1QH^a

---

148. Ibid.

149. Rietz, "Identifying Compositions and Traditions," 51.

150. Rietz suggests that this may be the case in 1QH^a XX 14 (XX 11/*XII 11*), as well as in CD XII 21 (ibid., 46). Based on numerous similarities of 1QH^a VI 19–33 with 1QS, Newsom (*Self as Symbolic Space*, 277–78 and n. 117) suggests that a community leader must be the speaker of the former text, even if it does not have a למשכיל superscription. She does not go into a discussion of the meaning of the למשכיל superscriptions occurring elsewhere in the Hodayot in this context, but see pp. 287–300.

151. Arnold, *The Social Role of Liturgy*, 189–90.

VI 19–33 and XX 7–XXII 39 both reflect how the *maśkil* was to undertake this task at the yearly ceremonies meant to initiate new members and renew the covenant. They express the ideological basis of his office in the following way:

> The speaker is not an agent, acting according to God's will, but is, instead, the site of divine activity. The speaker is nothing more than an opportunity for God to be glorified and to show strength through the speaker. God acts not for the speaker but through him. Based on this ideology about the function of the *Maskil*, the membership has no means of disputing the decisions made by him. The *Maskil*'s leadership and authority on questions of rank is absolute, because he actually has nothing to do with it. At the same time, the *Maskil* is represented as the ideal member, a model for all members to emulate.[152]

In his interpretation of these prayers, Arnold portrays the *maśkil* also as an institutional leader and sees his "ordinary" characteristics as a function of his serving as a model for ordinary community members. He treats the duties of the *maśkil* in connection with "political rites" and apparently sees the community members as the ideal audience and the spectators of his performance. As will be recalled from my previous discussion of 1QH[a] VI 19–33, I find the orientation of such interpretations to be overly political and rhetorical because they fail to account for the communicative patterns of the genre of prayer.

The prevailing view, however, is that these hymns represented ordinary community members, and in most interpretations no institutional leader is in sight. For example, Newsom remarks about the so-called Hymns of the Community, including those that contain an introductory dedication to the *maśkil*, that "they seem quite different in tone and self-representation from the psalms of the persecuted leader," and for this reason she is reluctant to "merge" the two categories of hymns; that is, to see leadership hymns in both groups.[153] This opinion is based on a more nuanced view of the concept of the *maśkil* in the Dead Sea Scrolls; namely, that most, but not all, instances of the word *maśkil* reflect the institutionalized leadership role.[154] Generally, the superscriptions in the Hodayot seem to be regarded

---

152. Ibid., 190.

153. Newsom, *Self as Symbolic Space*, 198.

154. Newsom (*Songs of the Sabbath Sacrifice*, 3) holds that משכיל is for the most part used to "designate a particular office or functionary in the Qumran Community."

as some sort of technical designation either to indicate that the hymns were technically authored by a *maśkîl*, or to give them the uniform appearance suitable for items belonging to the same collection of hymns.[155] Thus, the term *maśkîl* in the Hodayot is not seen as a designation of the speaker as such, or of the ideal audience of Dead Sea community members that would identify with this speaker.

In 1QS the noun *maśkîl* is often translated *either* into "wise man" (or a cognate term indicating outstanding intellectual skills), *or* into "instructor" (or the like) to indicate not only cleverness but also *function*. In the instruction (1QS IX 12–26a) we saw that the *maśkîl* is apparently expected to fulfil the role of instructing other people—this is the goal of instruction. In Naftali Wieder's understanding, this meaning of the word is "transitive" since it indicates the occurrence of verbal action with an object.[156]

In the following I wish to focus on what scholars read into the word in its transitive meaning. Usually this is not merely about the function of instructing someone, but rather the institutionalized task of instruction—in the role of a functionary.[157] As we saw in the preceding section, however, it is not evident from the S text we have analyzed here that the *maśkîl* is such a functionary. It is possible to argue on the basis of other parts of 1QS that he is, and CD has some passages that understand *maśkîl* in this way.

In this major group she includes 1QS III 13; 1QSb I 1; III 2; V 20; 4Q511 2 i 1; 8 4, as well as the instances found in the Songs: 4Q400 3 ii; 5 8; 4Q401 1–2 1; 4Q403 1 i 30; 1 ii 18; 4Q405 20 ii 6; 4Q406 1 4. On the other hand, in 1QHᵃ XX 14 (XX 11/*XII 11*) and CD A XII 20–21, the term is considered to have a nontechnical meaning. Rietz ("Identifying Compositions and Traditions," 46 n. 83) questions this interpretation of the latter examples.

155. Puech (*Les données qumraniennes*, 337 n. 11) suggests that the (presumably five) dedications to the *maśkîl* functioned to divide 1QHodayotᵃ into sections, so as to mirror the division of the book of Psalms into five parts.

156. Wieder, *The Judaean Scrolls and Karaism*, 104–6.

157. Because of the heading in IX 12, "shall walk with every living being according to the rule appropriate to each time," Knibb associates the *maśkîl* with the *overseer* (מבקר) of CD XII 20b–21. He translates *maśkîl* as "the wise leader," and describes his role as follows: "the exercise of pastoral oversight, the selection and admission of new members, and the avoidance of contact with outsiders" (*The Qumran Community*, 142). See also Newsom, *Self as Symbolic Space*, 171; Tukasi, *Determinism and Petitionary Prayer*, 74–77; Arnold, *The Social Role of Liturgy*, 188–90.

Long ago Wieder advanced propositions that point to other, less institutional aspects of the *maśkîl*. In spite of certain reservations that we may have about his approach, some of his observations are worth reconsidering here. He suggests that in the Dead Sea Scrolls the term *maśkîl* draws on the concept of *maśkîlîm* in the book of Daniel. Wieder demonstrated that, much later, the Karaites merged corporate interpretations of the Suffering Servant of Isaiah and the *maśkîlîm* of Daniel, seeing their own spiritual leaders as simultaneously fulfilling both roles as atoners for Israel.[158] Based on substantial analogies between Karaite documents and the Dead Sea Scrolls, as well as indications of allusions to Daniel in the latter, Wieder felt that a similar interpretive approach might be found there as well, but this was not yet "sufficiently substantiated."[159] His suggestion involves identifying a collective of community members with the *maśkîl* or, as in the book of Daniel, several *maśkîlîm*. This collective, then, perceived itself as atoners for Israel having "certain soteriological functions." To my knowledge, Wieder's suggestion has not yet been substantiated by way of a detailed analysis of allusions to Daniel in texts employing the concept of the *maśkîl*, and the scheme may be too simplistic.

However, Hempel has systematically compared the concepts of *maśkîlîm* and *rābbîm* in the book of Daniel and in 1QS. She warns against seeing the book of Daniel as the source of any of the Dead Sea Scrolls, but suggests that there is "a strong case for a common milieu behind both groups of texts."[160] Interestingly, she finds that the most relevant text in this respect is the instruction in 1QS IX 12–25.[161] Based on the parallel material, she concludes that this is probably early material tradition-historically, with some of it, however, earlier than other parts. Instead of references to *the many*, as in the book of Daniel, groups called by other names are affected by the activities of the *maśkîl*. The variegated labelling of these people is used by Hempel to divide up the instruction and to suggest a redactional layering of it. The introduction to the instruction, 1QS

---

158. Wieder, *The Judaean Scrolls and Karaism*, 113–14.

159. Ibid.

160. Hempel, "Maskil(im) and Rabbim," 139.

161. Ibid., 137–38. Due to the special connection between the concepts of *maśkîlîm* and *rābbîm* in Dan 11, the parts of S containing references to both concepts are usually regarded as more relevant. Hempel, however, finds that none of the numerous references in S to the *rābbîm* is related closely enough to the *maśkîl* to be of significance (ibid., 143).

IX 12–14a, directs the *maśkîl* to deal with every living being and according to the weight of each man. Here the designations signal a universalistic perspective, which in part is also found in the Treatise on the Two Spirits (1QS III 13–IV). Such a universalistic perspective is absent in the book of Daniel with its distinctly nationalistic perspective and its talk about "the people" (עם). The following section, 1QS IX 14b–18a, resembles the book of Daniel on this point by using designations that signal the election of a delimited community ("chosen ones" vis-à-vis "men of the pit"). This is the section typologically closest to Dan 11–12. Finally, even exclusiveness is suggested in 1QS IX 18b–21a ("the men of the *yaḥad*"), but this is a sectarian twist not known in the book of Daniel.[162]

Hempel's conclusion that the Dead Sea community *shared* the language of Daniel, in the sense that both authorial milieus drew on common sources, is significant. It implies that from the beginning the *maśkîl* in 1QS IX was construed with the help of language and ideas shared by the Dead Sea community and broader Jewish circles. Wernberg-Møller also remarks that the use of the term *maśkîl* in 1QS IX 12–21 corresponds to its use in Daniel and pseudepigraphic literature and naturally applies to "the community as a whole."[163] Another feature shared by the book of Daniel and 1QS IX 12–XI is their reinterpretations of the Lord's Servant in Isaiah. William Brownlee demonstrated that Dan 11–12 is a corporate interpretation of the Lord's Servant in Isaiah.[164] There is ample evidence of the

---

162. Ibid., 152–55.

163. Wernberg-Møller, *Manual of Discipline*, 66 n. 39. Armin Lange rejects this position because in his opinion the duties of the *maśkîl* in 1QS are far more multifaceted than those of the concept of a *maśkîl* in precommunity literature. In addition to the catechetical and liturgical functions known beforehand, the Dead Sea community ascribed halakhic and magic-mantic functions to their *maśkîl* (*Weisheit und Prädestination*, 146–48). However, Lange's insistence on the *maśkîl* as an officeholder complicates the matter because it leads to the assumption that 1QS IX is an all-embracing official document and therefore incompatible with similar yet deviating documents.

164. Brownlee, "The Servant of the Lord in the Qumran Scrolls I," 12–15. According to him, the term *maśkîlim* in Daniel is in itself an allusion to הנה ישכיל עבדי in Isa 52:13, and this should be apparent from Dan 12:3 ("Those who are wise [המשכלים] shall shine like the brightness of the sky, and those who lead many to righteousness [ומצדיקי הרבים], like the stars forever and ever"), itself an allusion to Isa 53:11b ("The righteous one, my servant, shall make many righteous" [יצדיק צדיק עבדי לרבים]). However, *the many* are in Daniel interpreted "not merely as the recipients of the Servant's instruction, but as themselves suffering as God's servants. They too must be

reinterpretation of the Servant also in the Dead Sea Scrolls, including both Serekh literature[165] and the Hodayot.[166]

In sum, the Dead Sea community, including the authors and the redactors of 1QS, has drawn on sources that it shared with the book of Daniel. This background material apparently included a corporate concept of the *maśkîl*. In the preceding section, we concluded that the term *maśkîl* is generally *not* used to designate a functionary with authority to maintain ritual purity and keep unwanted persons outside of the community. Even if in some instances *maśkîl was* used in this way in CD and S, there is reason to believe that the term had other connotations, inherited from the broader cultural milieu—also in these large, sectarian documents.

The implication of this is that the difference between the concept of the *maśkîl* in 1QHodayot[a] and in 1QS may not be as huge as often assumed. In both of the texts analyzed, the *maśkîl* is the Goal of God's agency. How-

---

'refined' by suffering, and they too are 'wise' (Dan 12:10). Thus, the corporate interpretation of the Servant of the Lord in Daniel embraces all the hasidim" (ibid., 13).

165. See the discussions of the influence of Isaiah and the Servant on 1QS in Brownlee, "The Servant of the Lord in the Qumran Scrolls II," 33–38.

166. Dupont-Sommer (*Le Livre des Hymnes*, 13–19) connects several passages of the Hodayot, especially from col. XVI, to passages in Isaiah on the Suffering Servant of God; e.g., 1QH[a] XII 9, 24 (XII 8, 23/ *IV 8, 23*) and XVI 27–28 (XVI 26–27/*VIII 26–27*) to Isa 53:3–4; 1QH[a] XIV 13–16 (XIV 10–13/ *VI 10–13*) to Isa 49:6–8 and 42:6. Julie Hughes finds that the composition of 1QH[a] XVI 5–XVII 36 (XVI 4–XVII 36/*VIII 4–IX 36*) was influenced by the whole section of Isa 44–66, and that the "suffering and vindication of a righteous person" in the former text was in part built on Isa 50:4–6 and 52:13–53:12 (*Scriptural Allusions*, 181). Holm-Nielsen, who also remarks that the book of Isaiah, particularly Isa 40–55, must be a favorite in the community, warns against overstating its significance: "The time of coming of glory after the degradation of the exile, as prophesied in Deutero-Isaiah, has obviously not been difficult for the community to apply to itself. But this is not to say that the concept of the Servant of the Lord from these chapters has played any particular part in the community, as many would reckon, either by considering the community to be the incarnation of this concept, or by realising it in a definite figure, the 'Teacher of Righteousness,' to such an extent that he has even had at times Messianic rights conferred upon him" (*Hodayot*, 310). Chamberlain ("Toward a Qumran Soteriology," 309) takes a less reserved position when he asserts that the council of the community, as described in 1QS VIII 5–10, was seen as the corporate agent of God with an atoning function vis-à-vis the rest of the Dead Sea community. Delcor (*Les Hymnes*, 69–70) maintains that references in the Hodayot to the Suffering Servant pertain to one person, the Teacher of Righteousness, although he acknowledges that corporate interpretations of the concept exist in other Dead Sea documents.

ever, the hymnic speech concluding 1QS creates a rather more multifaceted concept of the *maśkîl* than does 1QH[a] XX 7–XXII 39. He participates in material, transitive processes as well as in the process types dominating 1QH[a] XX 7–XXII 39. Thus, he is rendered not only as the Goal of God's agency, but also as someone playing an active part in it. At the same time, the author of the hymnic speech is clearly familiar with the ideas, the language, and the literary norms of the Hodayot. He can manage more than one concept of the *maśkîl*, but he focuses upon the *maśkîl* in his capacity to act (on behalf of God) with other people as Goal.

Similarly, even if the author or redactor of 1QH[a] XX 7–XXII 39 and other of the so-called Community Hymns did not present the *maśkîl* in this way, it is likely that they, too, share the broad *maśkîl* concept of 1QS. In the last section of this chapter, I shall look at some indications that the Hodayot—or some of them—are also rooted in or inspired by presectarian thinking: perhaps the ideas and thoughts inherited from the past—including the concept of a *maśkîl*—continued to put their imprint on the literary works of the community, and perhaps they had a larger impact than we usually think.

4.3.3. The Hodayot and Their Past

As mentioned in the survey of references to the *maśkîl*, there are numerous overlaps and similarities between the Hodayot and 4QInstruction. Concerning our interest in the speaker of 1QHodayot[a] as cast in the role of a *maśkîl*, some of the most interesting observations by Goff concern the numerous similarities between the speaker in the Hodayot and the *mēbîn* in 4QInstruction, as well as the differences between them. For instance, both corpora liken human beings to angels, but not quite in the same way. The *mēbîn* in the wisdom instruction belongs in the lot of angels, in the sense of being elect, and accordingly is to *behave like* an angel, whereas the speaker of the Hodayot actually claims to *join* the angels in liturgical prayer (4Q427 7 i 17).[167]

This picture applies to both groups of Hodayot, but Goff seems to discern the largest "twist" away from 4QInstruction in the so-called Leader Hymns. With regard to the so-called Community Hymns and their affinities with wider wisdom circles, his observations about the occurrence of

---

167. Goff, "Reading Wisdom at Qumran," 283–85.

the phrase "spirit of flesh" (רוח בשר) in connection with being elect is interesting, particularly since it is found only in these textual corpora. Spirit of flesh cannot obtain knowledge of the mysteries of God. The *mēbîn*, as someone who has understanding, is distanced from this concept, whereas the elect one in the Hodayot continues to be burdened by its effects and continues to refer to himself as "dust" and "a creature of clay." In this light, Goff suggests that texts like 1QH^a V and 1QS XI are "product[s] of further reflection"; in other words, they represent a later stage of development than the one reached by 4QInstruction.[168]

Angela Harkins also considers the origins of the Hodayot, thinking we should consider the possibility that community hymns were brought in from a noncommunity context. She pays attention to the uneven distribution of terms that have a distinct sectarian usage[169] and to their absence only in community hymns that are not physically close to the collection of "Teacher Hymns."[170] The predominance of generic language may also be suggestive of a noncommunity origin, but neither this nor sectarian terminology provides conclusive evidence. In Harkins's view, the use of generic language, which can easily be adopted in new settings, may reflect the need to invest innovative literature with credibility and authority. The same argument applies to the use of scriptural language.[171] The occurrence of expressions that are not generic but rather in conflict with strictly sectarian ideas and language, however, is a convincing argument for the incorporation of material originating in a "parent group." Harkins suggests two compositions in 1QH^a IV as candidates for such noncommunity material, based on their nonsectarian character and the occurrence of some remarkably nonsectarian elements in them. The expression "human/ Adamic covenant" (ברית אדם) in 1QH^a IV 39 clashes with the normal usage of ברית in the Hodayot. It is an expression not seen in the Bible or

---

168. Ibid., 282–83.

169. Harkins, "The Community Hymns Classification," 141–50. The terms she discusses are "community" (יחד), "many" (הרבים), and "Belial" (בליעל). These terms are found within the so-called Leader Hymns and mainly there. However, ביחד is found in some parts of the Community Hymns, and is found once in col. VII.

170. The general picture that emerges, according to Harkins, is that "[t]he sections of the Community Hymns that show the strongest alignment with the terminology known from the sectarian text 1QS are the second *LeMaskil* grouping (5:12–7:20) and the third *LeMaskil* grouping (7:21–20:6, the Teacher Hymns material is embedded in this grouping)" (ibid., 145).

171. Ibid., 149.

elsewhere in the Dead Sea Scrolls.[172] "Glory of Adam" (כבוד אדם) in 1QH[a]
IV 27 is another expression otherwise unseen in the Hodayot, but found
in 1QS IV 34—a part of S that is often regarded as originally presectarian.[173]

Harkins is probably correct to see these phenomena as indications
of presectarian material. Rhetorically, it is difficult to explain such odd
expressions as resulting from a process of authorization. Even if we cannot
derive similar conclusions about other so-called community hymns on the
basis of the findings in col. 4, it is important to note the likelihood that
some of the material was not only inspired by literature stemming from
wider circles in Jewish society, but also originated there.[174]

This possibility—that the so-called Community Hymns, or a considerable part of them, were not produced by the Dead Sea community but
were taken over by it and embedded in a new social and literary setting—
also provides new questions and considerations. Why would the community adopt these compositions and juxtapose them with writings of their
own? What was the connecting factor in the composers' opinion? Whom
were the incorporated texts understood to represent, ideally? Did redactors and, subsequently, community members and leaders adopt them on a
par with more "sectually" flavored literature?

These are difficult questions that can only be answered tentatively.
Some of them coincide with the major questions of this book, namely, the
basically rhetorical question of *how* some compositions in 1QHodayot[a]
were made to function in a rhetorical situation different from the one in
which they originated. This question does not presuppose the idea that
the *maśkîl* hymns (or other "community hymns") originated outside the
Dead Sea community, but that idea may be part of the answer. The crucial
point of this question and Harkins's suggestion is that 1QHodayot[a] is a collection of variegated texts, which at one point and for some reason were

---

172. Ibid., 147–48.

173. Ibid., 146.

174. In the period when huge amounts of Cave 4 material, including wisdom literature, came to the knowledge of the public, Dimant expressed her expectation that
these findings would "modify our understanding of the community in significant
respects" ("The Qumran Manuscripts," 33). Harkins's suggestions about the origins
of the *maśkîl* hymns represent such a significant modification; they provoke critical reflection on the traditional Hodayot categories and the sociohistorical reality
behind them.

merged into one, heterogeneous collection by people to whom this made sense in some way or another.

In the following chapter I shall attempt to explore the meaning of merging wisdom material stemming from wider circles in Jewish society with distinctly sectarian material. I am going to do that by analyzing one text that was defined by Sarah Tanzer as a hybrid.

5

MERGING OF TRADITIONS IN A CLASSICAL HYBRID: 1QHᵃ XII 6–XIII 6

As long as teacher or leader hymns have been recognized among the Hodayot, there has been no doubt about the place of 1QHᵃ XII 6–XIII 6 within the category. The composition has phrasings close to some of the passages on the Teacher of Righteousness in the Habakkuk commentary, so it could easily be imagined that the speaker of this composition was the Teacher himself. Nonetheless, it cannot be denied that the composition is a composite. Tanzer has suggested that "the material adapted from the Hymns of the Community … extends from 4:29 [XII 30] to the end of the composition."[1] Similarly, Douglas argues at length that this part of the text is a secondary addition.[2] Their points of view will be confirmed by my reading. Of the compositions analyzed in this book, 1QHᵃ XII 6– XIII 6 is the only one defined as a hybrid by Tanzer's criteria. She calls it a "hymn of the Teacher" in which there is a limited presence of wisdom elements. The wisdom elements, both formal and thematic ones, are located in the latter part of the text, which in Douglas's view is secondary (XII 30–XIII 6).[3]

In the preceding chapter I concluded that the difference between the *maśkîl* concepts in 1QS IX 12–XII 22 and 1QHᵃ XX 7–XXII 39 may not be as huge as often assumed, and I suggested that both 1QS and 1QHodayotᵃ consist in part of Jewish wisdom traditions in which the *maśkîl*'s identity is

---

1. Tanzer, "The Sages at Qumran," 111.
2. Douglas, "Power and Praise," 106–12.
3. On the formal level, this part of the composition is characterized by rhetorical questions and on the thematic level by "terminology and themes from the biblical and postbiblical wisdom corpus" (Tanzer, "The Sages at Qumran," 114). According to Tanzer (ibid.), the wisdom elements are concentrated in 1QHᵃ XII 30–34.

corporate and involves active participation in God's agency. Even if 1QH[a] XII 6–XIII 6 is a so-called leader hymn with a limited presence of wisdom elements, we shall see that this one too is influenced by a Danielic *maśkîl* concept. In fact, this applies even to the part of the hymn that is characteristic of the so-called Leader Hymns.

In this study of hybrid compositions, 1QH[a] XII 6–XIII 6 is the only one by consensus regarded as a so-called leader-hymn.[4] It is also the only composition classified as a "classical" hybrid as defined by Tanzer. Like this, it exemplifies on a microlevel the composite nature of the collection as a whole. Here lies the special relevance of this text with a view to understand the redaction of 1QHodayot[a]. The analysis of the hybrid characteristics within this clearly delimited composition will strengthen the hypothesis that the heterogeneity of 1QHodayot[a] is the result of a conscious, interpretive endeavor. Having acknowledged the composite and hybrid character of the composition, I want to stress that it is the extant text, and not its redaction history, that is the object of this study.

The text of 1QH[a] XII 6–XIII 6 is firmly delimited by an introductory formula in XII 6 and again in XIII 7. It can be divided into three sections on the basis of formal distinctions. It is because of the first main section that the composition is by consensus counted among the so-called Leader Hymns—or Teacher Hymns as they have often been named. In the following first part of the chapter, I shall investigate the hybrid character of the text rather closely. After going over the sections one by one and, as in previous analyses, focusing on the character of the speaker, I am going to attempt an all-encompassing reading of the text and consider whether there is a rhetorical meaning inherent in its composite character.

As it happens, there are some structural affinities with material on the *maśkîlîm* in the book of Daniel in the first main section. This is interesting, particularly in light of the findings of the preceding chapters on *maśkîl*-related material in some of the Community Hymns. In the second part of the chapter, I shall therefore consider the possibility that the concept of the *maśkîl*, in one of its forms outlined above, has had a role to play in the identity formation of the people behind this compound composition and in the redactional logic behind 1QHodayot[a] in its entirety.

---

4. This category covers all texts traditionally labelled "hymns of the teacher," "hymns of the leader," or equivalent titles. They are located within cols. X–XVII.

Structure of 1QHᵃ XII 6–XIII 6 (XII 5–XIII 4/IV 5–V 4)

XII 6–7 Introduction
XII 7–30 Retold drama
XII 30–34 Anthropological section
XII 34–XIII 6 Contemplation of God's salvation

Translation of 1QHᵃ XII 6–7: Introduction
6.   I thank you, Lord, for you have enlightened my face by your cov-
       enant, and […]
7.   […] I seek you.[5] And like a perfect sunrise with its refulgence you
       have shone for me.

Translation of 1QHᵃ XII 7–30: Retold Drama
7.   And they, your people […]
8.   …[…] have flattered them. And those who interpret deceitfully
       [have led] them astray, so that they perish unknowingly.
9.   For in folly they have [carried out] their deeds, because I was rejected[6]
       by them, and they do not appreciate me when you show your strength
       through me,[7] for they have expelled me from my country,
10.   like a bird from its nest. And all of my friends and acquaintances
       have been driven away from me and now they appreciate me like a
       breaking vessel. But they are deceitful

---

5. Holm-Nielsen (*Hodayot*, 80 n. 4) suggests that אדורשכה is either a faulty reading or an otherwise unknown *poel* of דרש with an intensive meaning, but a *qal* is
probably what we have here. Qumran Hebrew has a pattern for the imperfect that
admits both יקטול- and יקוטל- in forms with pronominal suffixes. See Qimron, *The
Hebrew of the Dead Sea Scrolls*, 51–53.

6. נמאסי: Most commentators see this as a scribal error for נמאסתי and do not
follow Sukenik's reading (*The Dead Sea Scrolls of the Hebrew University* [1955], 40),
נמאסו.

7. The translation, "when you show your strength through me," is a rather neutral
rendering of בהגבירכה בי. The phrase articulates how something is at stake when God
acts through the speaker. It marks the culmination of the big drama that is unfolding.
Therefore, one could justify the translation, "when you conquer/prevail through me."
This understanding of the phrase is supported by its occurrence in the militaristic context of 1QHᵃ XIII 17. There are variants of the phrase in the hymn: XII 24 עד הגבירכה
בי; XII 28 ותגבר עד לאין מספר; 29 הגברתה עמדי. Due to the rather diverse contexts
it is difficult to achieve consistency in the translations.

11.   intermediaries and fraudulent seers. They have made malicious
       plans against me in order to change your law, which you have
       engraved into my heart,[8] for flattery

12.   for your people. And they prevent the thirsty ones from drinking
       knowledge, and for their thirst they give them vinegar, in order to
       watch

13.   their mistake: acting foolishly at their festivals and getting caught in
       their nets. But[9] you, God, reject all of Belial's

14.   schemes. Because your council shall last and the plan of your heart
       shall be maintained forever. But they, hypocrites, have the malice of
       Belial

15.   on their minds. With a double heart they seek you and they are not
       steadfast[10] in your truth. There is a rod in their plans, which brings
       forth poison and wormwood.

16.   And with their stubborn hearts they scrutinize. They seek you
       among idols and have placed the stumbling block of their injustice
       before themselves. They go

17.   to seek you from the mouth of false prophets, seduced by delusion.
       And [with] a st[ammering] language and an alien tongue they speak
       to your people

18.   in order to belie all their deeds by way of fraud. For they did not
       choose the way of your [hea]rt[11] and did not listen to your words,
       for they said about

19.   the disclosure of truth, "It is not reliable," and about the way of
       your heart, "It is not like this." But you, God, will answer them,
       judging them

---

8. The Shema is alluded to here, as the phrase שננתה בלבבי combines elements
from Deut 6:6–7.

9. Because in this case כי has an adversative sense, the previous description of the
opponents and their doings appears even more negative.

10. The verb is a *niphal* of כון. This is the case also for "shall be maintained" in the
previous line. Holm-Nielsen (*Hodayot*, 82–83 n. 31) has also rendered the two verbs
in different ways. This is in agreement with his view on the use of כון in the Hodayot;
it is only the thoughts of God that can genuinely be established. Human beings can be
established provided that God accomplishes this. The use of כון in both lines 14 and 15
intensifies the contrast between God and the hypocrites.

11. The reconstruction has turned out to be the only viable one after the placement of fragment 43. The expression בדרך לבכה also occurs in XII 19, 22, 25; XIV
10, 24.

20. in [yo]ur power [a]ccording to their idols and the abundance of their sin, in order that they who have deviated from your covenant may be caught by their own plans.

21. And in judgment you will destroy all men of fraud, and there will be no erring seers anymore. For there is no folly in any of your actions,

22. and there is no fraud [in] the will of your heart. Those who are in accordance with you will stand before you perpetually. And those who follow the way of your heart

23. will stand firm forever. [An]d I, as I hold on to you, I get up and rise[12] above those who mock[13] me, and my hand is against all those who scorn me. For

24. they do not appreciate me, even [though] you show your strength through me. But you reveal yourself to me in your strength as perfect light and do not hide in shame the face

25. of all who are soug[h]t by me, those who come together in accordance with your covenant and listen to me, those who walk on the way of your heart and muster before you

26. in the assembly of holy ones. For you make their judgment a triumph,[14] and truth into justice for them. You will not let them err by the hand of scoundrels,

27. like someone who plots against them. But you will infuse your people with fear of them, and see to the scattering of all the people of the countries in order to destroy in judgment all those

---

12. אתעודדה ואקומה are likely to have the force of the indicative because the cohortative forms (נקטלה/אקטלה) in the Dead Sea Scrolls often denote the indicative. (In fact, in the nonbiblical texts the cohortative form is used almost exclusively in first-person imperfects with consecutive or conjunctive *waw*.) See Qimron, *The Hebrew of the Dead Sea Scrolls*, 44.

13. For this translation of מנאצי, see Jer 23:17 and Pss 10:3, 13; 74:10.

14. ותוצא לנצח משפטם: This expression and the immediate context are probably based on Isa 42:3. The translation given here is not consistent with the translation of לנצח in XII 14 ("forever"), nor with the meaning of לנצח in combination with the verb יצא in 1QS IV 19, which also seems to build on Isa 42:3. Yet, I have chosen this inconsistent reading in agreement with Holm-Nielsen's argument that one should maintain the sense of parallelism with the following "and truth into justice" (*Hodayot*, 84 n. 58). *DSSSE*, 169, and Newsom (in Schuller and Stegemann, *1QHodayot*[a] [DJD XL], 166) follow the same logic in their translations. However, I am inclined to believe that the author was aware of an ambiguity in this expression. See the usages in Prov 16:3; 19:21; 20:18; Isa 46:10.

28.   who violate words of your mouth. Through me you have enlightened the face of the many and you have increased (them) without
number.[15] For you have let me know your wonderful

29.   secrets and in your wonderful council you have shown strength in
me;[16] and the wonder (takes place)[17] in the presence of the many for
the sake of your glory and to make known

30.   your mighty deeds to all the living.

5.1. 1QH[a] XII 7–30: RETOLD DRAMA

The content of this comprehensive opening section has persuaded scholars that the Teacher of Righteousness must be the author of the hymn.
The speaker, repeatedly referring to circumstances and experiences in his
life, seems to be a distinct individual. The text outlines a drama involving four different parties. In addition to the speaker and God, who is the
formal addressee, there is a group that adheres to the speaker and a group
of antagonists. It appears from XII 24c–26a that judgment will be good for
those adhering to the speaker: "(You) do not hide in shame the face of all
those soug[h]t by me, those who come together in accordance with your
covenant." Indirectly, the speaker insists that he acts for the benefit of this

---

15. ותגבר: I follow the translation by Newsom in Schuller and Stegemann (*1QHo-dayot*[a] [DJD XL], 166). Because there is no object of the verb, it is also possible to translate "and you have shown endless strength." See, e.g., Vermes, *The Dead Sea Scrolls in English*, 202; Holm-Nielsen, *Hodayot*, 78. This would be in line with the use of the verb elsewhere in the text; e.g., the following line. See 187 n. 7. Either way, the sentence can function as a kind of heading to the final text of this section. The first part focuses on the speaker: "For you have let me know (הודעתני) your wonderful secrets (ברזי פלאכה) and in your wonderful council (ובסוד פלאכה) you have shown strength (הגברתה) in me." The second part widens the perspective: "and the wonder (הפלא) (takes place) in the presence of the many for the sake of your glory and to make known (ולהודיע) your mighty deeds (גבורותיכה) to all the living." The repeated use of פלא, גבר, and הודיע underscores the twofold movement and the widening perspective; the fundamental act of showing strength involves the strengthening and increasing of the many.

16. הגברתה עמדי: The translation in *DSSSE* (1:169), "you have strengthened my position," obviously takes the verb as a transitive, but this is unusual in the Hodayot.

17. הפלא: Several interpreters have analyzed this word as an infinitive or a finite verb. I take it as a definite noun in a verbless clause functioning to give additional information about the action introduced by the verb ותגבר in line 29 and unfolding through the remainder of the section. See the previous note.

group of people. Subsequently (XII 28), the speaker describes himself as the mediator through whom God communicates: "Through me you have enlightened the face of the many and you have increased them without number." In several of the Leader Hymns, the speaker depicts himself as someone who (ideally) acts for the benefit of others different from himself:

> You have maintained my steps in the land of wickedness. And so I became a snare to transgressors but healing to all who repent of transgression, prudence for the simple, and a resolute purpose for the eager. You made me an object of reproach and a derision to the treacherous, (but) a foundation of truth and understanding to those whose way is upright. (1QHᵃ X 10–12)[18]

> And you have made me a father to the children of kindness and like a foster-father to the people of good omen. (1QHᵃ XV 23–24)[19]

> Though you made the tongue strong in my mouth, unrestrained, it is not possible to lift up (my) voice to make (my) disciples hear, in order to revive the spirit of those who stumble and to support the weary with a word. (1QHᵃ XVI 36–37)[20]

This trait clearly distinguishes the so-called Leader Hymns of the Hodayot from hymns in the Hebrew Bible, but we have seen it appear also in one so-called hymn of the community, 1QHᵃ VI 19–33, where the speaker is supposed to "draw near" the chosen ones.

In this first section of the text much attention is paid to the antagonists of the speaker. They have expelled the speaker from his country "like a bird from its nest" (XII 9–10), and they mock him (XII 22). It comes as no surprise that they are a menace not only to the speaker but also to his followers, whom they purpose to harm and misguide (XII 8, 12–13). In fact, the speaker expresses quite clearly how his antagonists plot against him to get at the people of God: "They have made malicious plans against me in order to change your law, which you have engraved into my heart, for flattery to your people" (XII 11–12). Not only is the speaker a medium for the communication of God with his chosen ones, but is also potentially a

---

18. Translation by Newsom in Schuller and Stegemann, *1QHodayotᵃ* (DJD XL), 142.

19. Ibid., 214.

20. Ibid., 224–25.

tool in the hands of the antagonists. The ending of the drama points to the eschatological future when God will pass sentence on the antagonists of the speaker (XII 19–21) and bring salvation to his followers (XII 26–28).

This outline is in accordance with the pattern of the social world *and* the communication of the text as seen by Newsom in her 2004 monograph, *The Self as Symbolic Space*.[21] In its simplest form, her graphic display of the structure can be reproduced as in the figure below:

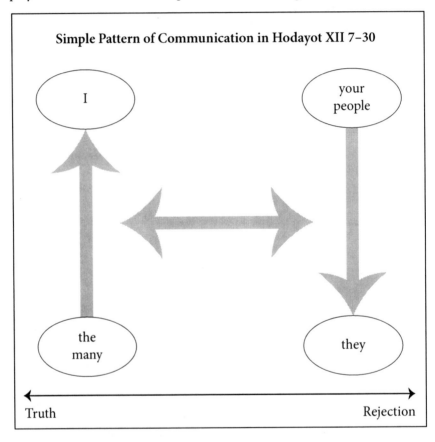

Simple Pattern of Communication in Hodayot XII 7–30

I

your people

the many

they

Truth   Rejection

Two of the four groups represented in the text mediate their values to the two other groups. Insofar as the metaphors of *light* and *enlightening* (XII 6–7, 24 and 28) denote giving of knowledge, it is correct to say that the speaker ("I") teaches knowledge to his followers ("the many"). Truth,

---

21. Newsom, *The Self as Symbolic Space*, 320–22.

according to Newsom, is what is being conveyed in this relationship. The antagonists ("they"), on the other hand, teach false teachings to the people of God ("your people").[22] They are rejecters of truth who keep the truth of the speaker from the people of God. These two "channels" of communication are in conflict with each other and represent opposite ideologies.

If we disregard the social world contained in this drama and analyze the agency hierarchy of the text, we must include God in our considerations. God and the antagonists are clearly the proactive participants acting out a series of material processes. The material processes having God as Actor (or Agent) have a wide range of Goals (the strength of God, the speaker, the traitors, the people of God, and so forth), whereas the antagonists always target the speaker or the people of God.

The role of the speaker is not overly outgoing, and this may be a bit surprising as one quickly senses the animosity between the speaker and his opponents. He is the grammatical subject of no more than two verbs, in both cases intransitive material processes. In addition, his hands are the grammatical subject of a relational process functioning to attribute the quality of cogency to the speaker himself.[23] All these processes are found in XII 23: "[An]d I, as I hold on[24] to you, I *get up* and *rise* above those who mock me, and my hand *is against* all those who scorn me." Seemingly, these processes are contingent on the speaker's holding on to

---

22. According to Puech (*Les données qumraniennes*, 417), the intended audience of the Hodayot generally does not identify itself as the "people of God," but rather as "the rest" (or as here, "the many").

23. וידי על (lit., "my hand is against"): This verbless clause may have the positive meaning of *helping* or *facilitating*, but here it must have the meaning of *turning* or *striking against* someone. God is usually the subject. For transitivity structure, see Tatu, *Verbal Sequence*, 212.

24. The prepositional phrase with a participle and suffix is a *circumstantial of manner* or *contingency*. See Tatu, *Verbal Sequence*, 224–27. This description of the phrase applies also to its English translation which, having a finite verb, will be subject to analysis of the clause complex, rather than to transitivity analysis. See Eggins (*Introduction*, 283–84) for examples. Tatu (*Verbal Sequence*, 229) offers Exod 25:40 as another illustrative example where, with the use of a participle, even the circumstantial element of the *Hebrew* text resembles a finite clause. To relegate the phrase, "[An]d as I hold on to you," to the status of a circumstantial is not to say that it does not convey any experiential meaning. However, "a circumstantial element in a clause contains only a minor process, not a major one; so unlike a clause it cannot construe a figure, it cannot enact a proposition/proposal and it cannot present a message" (Halliday, *An Introduction to Functional Grammar*, 368).

God. Interestingly, the phrase "my hand is against" also suggests a process dependent on God; in the Hebrew Bible when, not the hand of God, but someone else's hand is referred to by this expression, it is often in connection with an action initiated by and thus undertaken on behalf of God.[25]

One should think that the receivers of truth and untruth, "the many" and "the people of God" respectively, would be the least active parties, and this is in part true. The one thing said about the people of God in this respect is that they "will perish." Of the adherents ("the many"), however, it is said that they will both "stand before" God perpetually (line 21) and "stand firm" forever (line 22), and they "listen to" the speaker and "muster before" God (line 24). They are the Actors in *intransitive* material processes ("stand," "muster") and the Behavers in behavioral processes ("listen to"); in this case, it means that their *attitude* is in focus and that their conduct does not affect any other participant.[26]

The most important thing to observe in this brief analysis of transitivity is that God initiates a large share of the processes, and in many cases he works through the speaker. This is seen most clearly toward the end of the section (XII 28–29). The declaration that God has "enlightened the face of the many" through the speaker is qualified by the following series of reasons: 1) "For you have let me know your wonderful secrets"; 2) "you have heightened my position"; and 3) "you have worked wonders in the presence of many." These utterances display several aspects of God's working through the speaker. A more indirect, but nonetheless clear example is found in XII 24–25: "But you reveal yourself to me in your strength as perfect light and do not hide in shame the face of all who are soug[h]t by me, those who come together in accordance with your covenant and listen to me, those who walk on the way of your heart and direct themselves toward you in the assembly of holy ones." The people affected by God's revelation to the speaker are those who connect with the speaker in a specific way ("are soug[h]t by me" and "listen to me") and *simultaneously* connect with God through adherence to his covenant and his will. Furthermore, circumstantial information (XII 9, 24) depicts God as someone who shows his strength through the speaker.[27]

---

25. The hand of Moses is referred to in the numerous instances where God bids Moses to cast plagues over the Egyptians. See, e.g., Exod 9:22; 10:12, 21–22; 14:16, 27.

26. See Eggins, *Introduction*, 233.

27. ‎עד הגבירכה בי and ‎בהגבירכה בי.

Since the agency of God takes place through the speaker, the speaker's mediation to "the many" becomes a "communication of truth," whereas the mediation of the antagonists is a rejection of truth. It is not difficult to discern this pattern within the text. In Newsom's interpretation, the very same pattern appears to apply to the text itself as an act of communication within its social situation. The communication of truth unfolding in the text between the speaker and "the many" implicitly becomes the same communication of truth that unfolds between the speaker and the real, extratextual audience. This transmission of the literary pattern into the communicative situation in which it is being used lies implicitly in Newsom's interpretation when she concludes that the text "not only defines leadership within the community but serves as an act of leadership."[28] I am not quite convinced by this transmission of a textual pattern into the communicative situation of the text, and we shall consider it more closely after a look at the second and third sections of the text.

5.2. 1QHª XII 30–34: Anthropological Section

Translation of 1QHª XII 30–34
30. What is flesh compared to this? What creature of clay can work great wonders? For it is in iniquity
31. from the maternal womb and until grey hair (old age) in faithless guilt. But I know that justice does not belong to man and a way of perfection not to a human being.[29]
32. With El Elyon are all deeds of justice and the way of man is not established, except for the spirit God has created for him
33. in order to make a perfect way for the human beings so that they will know all the deeds of his mighty strength and all his mercy on the children of
34. his will.

In the dramatic first section, the speaker repeatedly declared that through him God had shown his strength, and this theme was rounded off by a reference to God's "mighty deeds" (XII 30). The ending of the section thus emphasized God's power and served to contrast with the opening of the following anthropological section: "What is flesh compared to this? What

---

28. Newsom, *Self as Symbolic Space*, 325.
29. בן אדם: lit., "son of man."

creature of clay can make great wonders?" These rhetorical questions draw attention to a general human condition. From the very moment of birth, members of the human race are morally impotent and unable to live their lives in justice. This is seen from the following words about the so-called "creature of clay": "For it is in iniquity from the maternal womb and until grey hair (old age) in faithless guilt" (XII 30–31). We have met these sorts of expressions already, particularly in 1QH^a XX 7–XXII 39, and also in the concluding hymn of 1QS. It is a significant expression of the *Niedrigkeits-doxologie* so prominent in the wisdom material.

This anthropological section differs from the preceding one, not only by virtue of its broader perspective, but also because of formal criteria. The speaker does not address God directly but speaks of him in the third person. The section also appears more impersonal even though the speaker refers to himself with the words "but I know" (XII 31), thus recalling in passing how he possesses knowledge about God and human beings. Other than this the speaker is silent about himself.

At the very end of the section, the concept of mercy is introduced. God has created a spirit "in order to make a perfect way for the human beings so that they will know all the deeds of his mighty strength and all his mercy on the children of his will" (XII 33–34). The introduction of mercy narrows the perspective. God's mercy is not for the whole of humankind but is reserved for those who are "children of his will." This wisdom language, with its introduction of mercy, prepares his audience for the third section of the hymn. The third section leaves the anthropological perspective and picks up a personal perspective, probably that of a child "of his will."

5.3. 1QH^a XII 34–XIII 6: Contemplation of God's Salvation

Translation of 1QH^a XII 34–41

34. But I, trembling and terror have gripped me and all my bones break in pieces. My heart melts like wax before the fire and my knees give way like water

35. running down a slope because I came to remember all of my iniquities and the faithlessness of my fathers when scoundrels rose against your covenant

36. and wretched ones against your word. And I said: "Because of my sin I have been abandoned from your covenant." But when I remembered the strength of your hand together with

37.   your plentiful mercy I stood up and remained standing, and my spirit stood fast against ... since I reposed trust

38.   in your compassion and in your plentiful mercy, because you forgive iniquity, and it belongs to your righteousness to purify man from his guilt.

39.   It is not for man to [...]... you have made, for you have created righteous as well as vicious [...]

40.   [...] I will hold on to your covenant until [...]

41.   your [...] because you are truth and just are all [your deeds...]

Translation of 1QHª XIII 3–6:

3.   Until the day with [...]

4.   your forgiveness and [your] great [compassion]

5.   And when I realized these things [I] was comforted[...] ... [...]

6.   In accordance with your will and in your hand is the judgment of them all [...]

In the third and concluding part the speaker once again addresses God in a direct and personal manner. The text displays two levels of consciousness in the speaker, both with the help of bodily metaphors. First, his sense of dissolving and his awareness of being abandoned due to his sin have been temporally delimited to a previous time by the verbal process, "and I said"[30] (XII 34–36). Then a change occurs in XII 36–38, beginning with the circumstantial information, "but *when I remembered* the strength of your hand together with your plentiful mercy." The speaker's remembrance marks a turning point, and from now on he adopts a completely new attitude, which is signalled by a series of material processes: he "stood up," "remained standing," and "rested" in the mercy of God.

These two levels of consciousness refer to general levels of truths presented in the anthropological section. First, the nothingness of humankind (XII 30–31) justifies the speaker's awareness of his sin and his feeling of being abandoned. Second, the justice of God, his mercy, and creation of a spirit in man for the sake of his perfection (XII 32–34) justify the change of attitude in the speaker. Structurally, thematically, and theologically, then, the latter two sections, dealing with a general, anthropological level and a personal level respectively, fit together very well. Both of these

---

30. The context allows for the more freely translated "I thought," and it is perhaps more correct to see this process as *mental*; it refers to an inner discourse in the speaker.

sections have the wisdom language and other features that are so characteristic of the so-called Community Hymns according to Tanzer's definition, and Tanzer is convinced that they have been "adapted from material
belonging to the Hymns of the Community."[31] The coherence between
the two suggests that they may have belonged together before they were
incorporated into the composition we now have in front of us.[32] We need
to consider how these latter two sections relate to the first section and the
social drama unfolding there.

5.4. The Speaker as a Unifying Factor

Of particular interest with regard to the unity of the composition is the
relationship between the speaker recounting the drama of the first section
and the speaker contemplating his salvation in the concluding section. In
both sections, the speaker displays his experience in a subjective manner,
but in different ways. The speaker of the first section has the role of a mediator on behalf of God. He fulfils a function among those who adhere to
the covenant and are in accordance with the will of God (XII 24); he is not
identified completely with this group but stands out from it. In the concluding section, however, the details of the social situation are out of sight.
Instead, the inner feelings of the speaker, his guilt, and his confidence that
God is a merciful savior are in focus. He does not stand out as before, but
is included in the group that in the middle section was referred to as "the
children of his will." At this point, then, the speaker seems to be expressing
himself in a similar manner as any worshiper in the group would express
himself, and not in the capacity of mediator. Thus, one may get the impression that the speaker of the last section represents someone entirely different from the speaker of the first section—even if there are terminological
parallels that connect them. I suggest that, rhetorically, the speakers are to
be seen as one, even if they do not constitute a perfect literary unity.

Technically, it is because of the composite (redacted) nature of the
text that the speaker, too, appears to be a composite person. In connection with compositions previously analyzed, I have already acknowledged
that the so-called Community Hymns had been inspired by nonsectarian

31. Tanzer, "The Sages at Qumran," 114.
32. Both sections are intensively preoccupied with creation, spirit, and mercy.
The *Niedrigkeitsdoxologie* of the anthropological section is echoed in the disheartened
awareness of sin and perdition in XII 36.

or noncommunity circles and may have originated outside the Dead Sea community. Obviously, this aspect must be part of any explanation of the relationship between this sort of wisdom-related material and distinctly leader material found in the first section of the hymn under discussion—and also of the identity of the speaker. For the sake of that discussion, however, it may be wise first to attend to the inner coherence of the text.

There are connecting factors irrespective of changes of form, perspective, contents, and style. Douglas, who basically argues for the composite nature of the text, still recognizes some lexical connections suggesting the opposite.[33] Tanzer remarks that there are several references to knowledge within the otherwise "non-wisdom" material of XII 7–30.[34] I am going to take a closer look at the role of knowledge throughout the composition because, thematically, it is what holds the composition together.

5.5. KNOWLEDGE AS A UNIFYING FACTOR

Knowledge is a recurring element in the hymn. In the introduction, we are told that the thanksgiving is due to the *knowledge* that the speaker has received from God. This hymn and the Hodayot in general differ from the many scriptural hymns that have the speaker express gratitude for deliverance from all sorts of hardship. In the Hodayot, the perception of divine knowledge has replaced experience of deliverance. Knowledge is part of, or even identical with, salvation.

Knowledge is introduced from the very beginning of the composition, because it is for God's giving of knowledge that the speaker wishes to express his thankfulness: "I thank you Lord, for *you have enlightened my face* to your covenant, and [...] I seek you. And *like a perfect sunrise* with its lightening you have shone for me" (XII 6–7). The sunrise and the lightening of the speaker's face are metaphorical expressions of how God has given knowledge to the speaker. This metaphor of light is resumed toward the ending of the first section (XII 24, 28) and frames the whole drama unfolding there. The drama itself expands the theme of

---

33. The covenant, בריתך/בריתכה, occurs three times within XII 7–30 and three times within XII 30–XIII 6. The word חלכאים, "scoundrels," which is rare in the Hodayot, occurs both in XII 26 and 36 (for reasons of translation and syntax it is placed in line 35 in the translation above). The phrase אתעודדה ואקומה (XII 23) is echoed in התעודדתי ואקומה (XII 37). See Douglas, "Power and Praise," 107–8.

34. Tanzer, "The Sages at Qumran," 115.

knowledge, focusing primarily on its negative aspects. The text mentions deceitful interpreting and leading astray (XII 8), "deceitful intermediaries" and "fraudulent seers" (XII 10–11), and the prevention of drinking of knowledge (XII 12).

The theme of knowledge recurs in the second section in the swift reminder that it is the speaker's knowledge that is being presented, "As for me, I know..." (XII 31); and again in the third section where it is hard to decide on the connection due to the damaged and fragmentary text: "And when I realized these things (ובדעתי אלה) [I] was comforted..." (XIII 5). But besides this direct reference, knowledge is also made the topic in an indirect way in the third section through references to—and dissociation from—a scriptural idea of sin.

Immediately before the speaker expresses his confidence in God (XII 36–38), he recalls his sin and the sin of his ancestors. He also illustrates the impact of this recollection, describing how parts of his body *tremble, break in pieces, melt,* and *give way* (XII 34–35). Here the author combines scriptural language from poetic texts like Mic 1:4, Ezek 7:17, and Ps 22.[35] Psalm 22:15 forms part of a passage in which the speaker complains, "I am poured out like water, and all my bones are out of joint; my heart is like wax; it is melted within my breast." The use of language from Micah and Ezekiel functions to recall the idea that sin in the form of violations causes human suffering. In these texts there is specific reference to the idolatry of Israel. Therefore the reference to these texts serves to contrast with the conception of degradation held in the Hodayot; namely, that human beings are in a state of imperfection from the moment of birth. Psalm 22, on the other hand, is interesting for another reason; namely, that it does not ascribe the speaker's suffering to his trespasses, as happens in other scriptural lamentations.[36] On the contrary, the speaker gives the impression that he does *not* assume the responsibility, and so does the speaker of our hodayah. In both texts the speakers express their confidence in the mercy of God.

We have seen in 1QH^a XII 36–37 how the speaker moves from the feeling of guilt and agony to calm assuredness at the very moment he *remembered*. At no point is there a reference to God's rescue of the speaker; he is

---

35. In Mic 1:4 it is mountains, valleys, and waterfalls that are "melting," rather than parts of the body.

36. See Ps 32:5, where the connection between suffering and previous trespasses is particularly clear.

not saved from his agony like the speaker in Ps 22, but he rises through his own effort by virtue of his knowledge of God's power and mercy.

Even though the author borrows expressions from a scriptural lamentation here, lamenting is not a motif. The speaker does not seem to go through the common process of trespassing–suffering–confession–supplication–salvation. Rather, he has left his state of agony and now contemplates his troubles retrospectively *from his position as possessor of knowledge.*[37] As to the use of Micah, Ezekiel, and Ps 22, those texts refer to a view that is prominent in the scriptural universe, but one that is not held by the author of this hymn. It serves to contrast with and throw into relief the view held by the author, that man is in sin from his birth.

In sum, the theme of knowledge pervades the text and is built into it in various ways. Epistemologically, knowledge works differently in the first section than in the latter two because it is revealed to and through the speaker.[38] In the remainder of the composition, knowledge is *wisdom,* apparently obtainable without revelation. The circumstantial information contained in the phrase, "but when I *remembered,*" is an indicator of this. Wisdom themes, such as references to the compassion of God,[39] his righteousness and truth, also point in this direction. The different epistemologies spring to a large degree from differences in origin and need not be contradictory when juxtaposed within this composition. On the contrary, it may explain in part why these pieces of text were joined together. Each section contains a duality or dualism, and we can assert that there is a correspondence between them:

---

37. For the same reason he does not beseech God or present him with promises of praise to make him intervene, as is often the case in the biblical lamentations. This is in harmony with a general tendency in the Hodayot. These hymns contain thanksgivings and praises but no preceding plea for deliverance.

38. See Jeremias, *Der Lehrer,* 211.

39. Jeremias lists רחמים among the words that occur primarily outside the so-called Leader Hymns. Out of twenty-eight occurrences, he finds that only four are found in a leader hymn. The fact that רחמים occurs four times in the latter two sections of 1QHᵃ XII 6–XIII 6 suggests, then, that this word genuinely belongs in compositions influenced by wisdom ideas and language (ibid., 172).

1QH[a] XII 7–30: Drama	Nontruth	Truth
1QH[a] XII 30–34: Anthropological section	Nothingness	Mercy, spirit, and knowledge from God
1QH[a] XII 34–XIII 6: Contemplation of God's salvation	A person's potential belonging in this realm	A person's belonging in this realm

There is nothing significant about this duality in itself—dualism and duality are part of both the apocalyptic perspective behind the first section and the wisdom perspective behind the latter two. The importance of it here is its relationship with the theme of knowledge. It is, in fact, the object of knowledge. We have seen that knowledge in cognate wisdom literature pertains to God's plan in all of its duality. According to the sapiential perspective held in the latter two sections (1QH[a] XII 30–XIII 6), at least in their original milieu, this sort of knowledge was commonplace and part of ordinary wisdom teaching. This does not mean that it was meant for everyone, but it was part of the curriculum taught within wisdom circles.

What happened to the text when this knowledge and wisdom ethos was juxtaposed with the apocalyptically flavored first section, pointing to revelation as a condition for this sort of knowledge? The juxtaposition served to fence in that kind of wisdom knowledge, secure it for a narrowly defined group of people and assert that it was unavailable to others.[40] I suggest that such an epistemological change served to give a twist to the culturally inherited wisdom worldview and *maśkîl* identity held by a particular community (the Dead Sea community) and infuse it with new ideas. This point, pertaining to the rhetorical aspect of the particular redaction of this text, will be concretized in the following section.

5.6. Who is Persuading Whom?

The recognition of so-called leader or teacher hymns in the Hodayot has put its mark on the interpretations of 1QH[a] XII 6–XIII 6 since long ago.

---

40. For this function of apocalyptic, see Nickelsburg, "The Nature and Function of Revelation," 116–17.

As regards Jeremias, this composition was the principal reason for beginning to think that the Teacher of Righteousness had authored some of the Hodayot prayers,[41] and scholars who do not agree with his opinion of the authorship do still recognize the leadership perspective in this text.[42] As regards setting and communicative pattern, therefore, it is often seen as a leader's admonition to his followers.

Tanzer gives this text and 1QH^a X 5–21 *(II 3–19)* and XIII 22–XV 8 *(V 20–VII 5)* the heading "admonition not to be seduced away from the psalmist," and proposes their *Sitz im Leben* to be the speaker's "battling against a splinter group within the community."[43] According to her, the function of the wisdom elements is to support the attempt to warn followers not to turn from the right way represented by the leader. However, she does not explain in any detail how this was expected to work in the social context. A more serious objection to her theory is that none of the compositions placed in the group actually admonishes anyone; they are all directed to God. It is of course possible that the text was implicitly addressed to an ideal audience consisting of the speaker's followers, but this is not something that we know. Newsom argues at length along the same lines as Tanzer, proposing that the composition is the institutional leadership's appeal to community members for loyalty.[44] In the following, I shall approach these readings critically through a discussion with Newsom.

Rhetorically speaking, a text is someone's effort to persuade a target group into acting in a specific way or into adopting a certain attitude. All the components of the text—words, ideas, composition, and genre—can be explained as part of the rhetorical project and inner logic of the text. This understanding of text lies behind Newsom's work on the Hodayot. She operates with the concept of *suture*, an important mechanism that must take place if the text is to successfully achieve its rhetorical goal.[45]

---

41. Jeremias, *Der Lehrer*, 211.

42. See Licht, *The Thanksgiving Scroll*, 24; Nitzan, *Qumran Prayer*, 326 n. 19.

43. Tanzer, "The Sages at Qumran," 109.

44. Newsom, *Self as Symbolic Space*, 294–98, 325–28.

45. Ibid., 198–201. Suture takes place in the consciousness of the reader or listener when he or she connects textual elements with persons and things in the real world. The function of the text is to symbolize and order reality with all its actors and components. The concept of suture applied by Newsom is developed by literary and film critic Kaja Silverman on the basis of linguist Émile Benveniste's categories of "speaking subject" (the person producing the speech) and "subject of speech" (the "I" as signifier and representation of the speaker), which Silverman supplements with

Suture works roughly as follows. In the consciousness of the reader, textual elements seem to apply to things, persons, or groups of people in the real world as he or she experiences it. The function of the text is to symbolize and order reality for the audience. Suture occurs in the process of reading or listening, the very moment the reader or listener agrees that a particular element in the text—a pronoun, a name, a noun, a concept—is a representation of himself or herself.

Prayer texts naturally invite the implied audience, who in a liturgical setting would be the actual worshipers, to identify with the speaking voice.[46] In the dramatic first section of 1QH[a] XII 6–XIII 6, as well as in other so-called leader hymns, the speaker may appear as an individual who distinguishes himself from a group of followers. According to Newsom, this group of followers is the textual element offered to the ideal audience as an object of identification. Newsom's view on the Leader Hymns as a whole is actually that they are the general, institutional leadership's effort to persuade the Dead Sea community into staying loyal. The ideal audience thus will see its community leaders as represented by the self-sacrificing hymnist, and it will see itself as the followers for whose sake the sacrifice takes place. In the schematic structure outlined above, this is the group referred to as "the many." When and if suture worked like this, the hymn might become a successful *appeal* from community leadership for the loyalty of the ordinary members.

The problem with this interpretation is that it puts too much weight on the drama and does not take enough interest in the latter parts of the hymn, the unfolding description of the general human condition and the condition of belonging to "the children of his will." In those sections there is no reference to the leading function of the speaker. On the contrary, he

the category of "spoken subject" (the subject that is constituted in someone who—by way of suture—identifies himself or herself with the subject of speech). See Émile Benveniste, *Problems in General Linguistics*, 217–30; Kaja Silverman, *The Subject of Semiotics*, 43–53, 194–201.

46. The speaker may represent any member of a worshiping collective in one of two ways: 1) The worshiper may identify *as* the speaking "I," making the speech of the "I" totally his own. 2) The worshiper may identify *with* the speaking "I," seeing it as belonging to someone who is perhaps slightly above himself, an ideal worshiper, whose pious attitude the worshiper tries to adopt. This ideal figure may be someone who is reciting on location, or it may be an *ideal* speaker, in the mind of the worshiper. Recitations of collective compositions and individual compositions are likely to fit into these two patterns respectively.

is hardly distinguishable from the speaker met in the compositions generally recognized as the Community Hymns proper. Is it still the community leadership that is raising its voice here, or may some less prominent community member have taken over? We can only speculate about the realization of suture in connection with the use of the text, and I believe that is exactly what we need to do.

A few years ago, I argued that two distinct voices are raised in the text of 1QH^a XII 6–XIII 6.[47] I followed Newsom's outline of the structural pattern of the composition, which is in fact based on the drama of the first main section. However, I insisted on the significance of the different second and third sections and suggested that the speaker of the latter two represented the group of people that the speaker of the first section had referred to as attentive to his words and loyal to God's covenant (XII 25). I argued, in other words, that the composition speaks on behalf of both a leading or mediating figure and a group of people for which this first speaker had expressed his concern. That solution is not very satisfactory, especially since there are no indicators in the text of a liturgical situation with participation of successive participants or the like. Suture, while a part of my solution, is also part of the problem. I presupposed that ordinary community members would have identified first with the followers addressed by the speaking voice of the first section, and, secondly, with the speaker of the third section.[48] However, another realization of suture is both possible and far simpler. Perhaps the situational context of the text allowed a member of the ideal audience to identify with the speaker all the way through. In that case, he would perceive himself simultaneously as someone mediating on behalf of God and as someone included in God's mercy.

We have previously seen that the *maśkîl* concept, as traced in 1QH^a VI 19–33 and XX 7–XXII 39, encompasses two roles or functions in the agency hierarchy of God. The *maśkîl* may be an active participator in God's agency, and he may be the goal of it. Both functions need not be present simultaneously. In 1QH^a VI 19–33 they are, but in 1QH^a XX 7–XXII

---

47. Hasselbalch, "En retorisk analyse," 253–54.

48. This solution is in accord with how one pictures the performing of psalms in a liturgical setting. The psalm may either be representative of a leader (e.g., a king David) or of the collective of worshipers attending the ritual performance. The members of this collective may then identify either *with* the leader, seeing him as the ideal worshiper, or *as* the speaking "I," feeling it speaks on their behalf.

38 the active or mediating function is not visible—it is uninscribed background knowledge. I suggest that the latter two sections of the composition under discussion, which in all likelihood stem from the same wisdom circles, also represent such a *maśkîl* ethos. No agency on behalf of God is visible, but it is implied in the general knowledge of the owners of this literature, who shared a complex idea of a *maśkîl* ethos and defined themselves by it. On this background, another piece of text, different in character and origin, has been added to the two wisdom sections. The drama has now been placed at the beginning of the composition. In its own way and with recourse to apocalyptic epistemology, it picks up and accentuates the agency theme that lies implicit in the wisdom sections; namely, the mediating function included in the *maśkîl* ethos. In the latter part of this chapter, I am going to analyze more closely the meaning of merging the apocalyptically flavored drama with wisdom literature. For now, I have made these points because they affect my understanding of the communicative situation of this composition and the way that suture may have worked with its ideal audience.

The suggestions made here have a bearing on how suture might have worked, not only in connection with this particular composition but also in the use of the so-called Leader Hymns in general. Instead of being the leadership's admonition to ordinary, lower-ranking members about their obligation to stay loyal, the composition could very well have been the meditative or edificatory prayer of a group defining itself within the boundaries of a *maśkîl* ethos. As far as *suture* is concerned, it is not crucial to know whether the usage was liturgical or rather didactic. What matters is that the setting allowed for an edificatory experience. The members of the group understood themselves as elite and took it upon themselves to play an active part in the preservation of the covenant people. Suture could have worked like this: The implied audience, members of a religious elite group, would see themselves as represented by the speaker in the text. In that case, the prayer was spoken, not by a leader to the lower-ranking members, but by community members sharing a collective leadership responsibility. While general aspects of the *maśkîl* ethos were inherited and lay implicit in the wisdom parts of the composition, the leadership or mediator function was underscored by their juxtaposition with the dramatic first section. Just as the drama itself pictures a stressful situation, perhaps one of societal breach, the merging of texts may have been motivated by just such a rhetorical situation and the need for a sharpening of the community's profile.

This reading has two advantages over the readings by Tanzer and Newsom. First, the traditional categories "leader hymns" and "community hymns" are not of much help when one wants to explain the hybrid nature of this text. By detecting in the one category an accentuation of aspects held in the other, we have come into a position where we can suggest rhetorical motives behind the merging of features from each category. Secondly, this reading is far less instrumental in its rhetorical understanding. Instead of seeing the composition as primarily a subtle rhetorical device to maintain loyalty to the community leadership, it accounts for the fundamental meaning of the genre of prayer and the fact that the speaker directs his words to God. It renders the text meaningful as a hymn or prayer directed to God, but does not deny its rhetorical advantages. The edificatory and rhetorical functions of the text are two sides of the same coin: to legitimize this particular community as inheritor and keeper of the covenant. George Brooke makes a similar point in relation to the significance of scriptural allusions in the Hodayot. As far as he is concerned, the Hodayot's allusive character is similar in function to that of the parabiblical texts—which he prefers to call *hypertexts*—on "Mosaic discourse" in the Pentateuch (the *hypotexts*). The hypertexts keep the Mosaic discourse alive and authentic in ever new social settings.[49] Likewise, he suggests that the Hodayot might be "as poetically inspired and as revelatory as anything in Mosaic discourse."[50] Brooke clearly contrasts his point of view with Newsom's analysis of 1QH[a] XII 6–XIII 6, of which he remarks that it secularizes the composition and avoids speaking of its

---

49. Brooke (*Reading the Dead Sea Scrolls*, 73–76) outlines the function of these hypertexts in terms of authority (the hypertexts receive authority from the hypotexts [underlying biblical texts] and give them authority by using them), authenticity (the hypertexts renew the authenticity or integrity of hypotexts in new generations), immediacy (hypertexts make the events that took place in the hypotext contemporaneous with and relevant to new generations), and continuity (the hypertext represents itself as being continuous with the pentateuchal hypotext—sometimes even prior to it).

50. Brooke, *Reading the Dead Sea Scrolls*, 82 n. 48. Elsewhere Brooke connects the "scripturalization of prayers" in poetic anthologies of scriptural allusions with the development of prayer as a means to express personal devotion, and he indicates that the participants in prayer would be prepared to grant authority to the recited scriptures: "Even in synagogues today it is the ritual reading from the Torah scroll with its acclamatory blessings that most clearly indicates the authority of the text for the member of the community" ("Aspects of the Theological Significance of Prayer and Worship in the Qumran Scrolls," 46).

theological aspects.[51] As it seems, not only the genre of prayer but also the extensive use of scriptural allusions indicate that 1QH[a] XII 6–XIII 6 and other of the so-called Leadership Hymns had edificatory purposes beyond the leadership's need to perform social control. The leadership-membership dichotomy stands in the way of a fuller understanding of the Hodayot's edificatory function, and of how this function is reflected in 1QH[a] XII 6–XIII 6 and in 1QHodayot[a] in general.

So far my arguments largely rest on text-internal features and the assertion that the latter two parts of the composition should be seen as a continuation of the *maśkîl* ethos found in wisdom literature circulating within and around the Dead Sea community. In the remainder of the chapter, I shall substantiate my argument by involving some external evidence of the role of the *maśkîl* ethos in the merging of the sources.

5.7. MEDIATOR PERSPECTIVES IN 1QH[a] XII 6–XIII 6

Scholars generally perceive the speaker of the so-called Leader Hymns as someone who casts himself in the role of a leader. This impression stems to a large degree from apocalyptic epistemology that tends to materialize within those compositions. The speaker alleges to be the receiver of revelatory knowledge, and the secret and hidden character of this knowledge is expressed in language that brings to mind apocalyptic mediators such as Daniel and Enoch.[52]

> For you, my God, have concealed me (סתרתני) from the human beings, and your law you have hidden (חבתה) in [me] until the time when you reveal your salvation to me (עד קץ הגלות ישעכה). (1QH[a] XIII 13–14)

> As to the mystery that you hid in me (וברז חבתה בי), they go about as slanderers to the children of destruction. In order to show [your] strength in me, and for the sake of their guilt you have hidden the spring of understanding and the counsel of truth (סתרת מעין בינה וסוד אמת). (1QH[a] XIII 27–28)[53]

---

51. Brooke, *Reading the Dead Sea Scrolls*, 79.
52. The following textual examples are given in my own translation.
53. Other instances in which the hymnist expresses how God displays his power and strength to or through the hymnist are found in 1QH[a] IX 36; X 26; XII 9, 24, 28, 29; XIII 17, 27.

The relationship between the speaker, in his capacity as a locus for revelation, and the people is colored by the fact that ultimately he also *mediates* the secrets revealed to him. The mediation has purposes regarding the receivers of his revelatory messages and even eschatological consequences. Occasionally the contour of the final receiver of the revelation comes into sight:

> But you have set me as a banner for the chosen ones of your righteousness, and as a knowing mediator (מליץ דעת) of wonderful mysteries so as to test [the men] of truth and to try the lovers of instruction. (1QH^a X 15–16)

It is generally recognized that the speaker is also construed by way of allusions to biblical figures with prophetic qualities, particularly Moses. Douglas thinks that the drama, with its focus on true and false "mediums," is patterned on the promise of "a prophet like Moses" in Deut 18:9–22.[54] Hughes sees several allusions that point to Moses and the covenantal theme also in the prophetic books.[55] Allusions of this kind could both serve to underscore the revelatory character of the knowledge presented in the text, and to invest the speaker with the legitimacy of the renowned prophets in a new literary and social setting.[56]

---

54. Douglas, "Power and Praise," 293–95.

55. Hughes (*Scriptural Allusions*, 119–21) sees the phrase "You have enlightened my face (according) to your covenant" as an echo of Exod 34:29, where it is said of Moses on his return from Sinai that his face was shining because he had spoken to God. She also notices allusions to Deut 29:1–30:20, a text that foresees deviation from the covenant and restoration to it. Hughes finds that the majority of allusions in the composition "are drawn from prophetic books that stress the covenantal theme." For instance, she notes that the phrase also recalls the description of God's Servant in Isa 42:6, the only place in the Old Testament combining light and covenant. There is no verbatim quote, she says, but a "subtle typological allusion" (ibid., 105). Other examples discussed by her are Hos 4:1–6:3; Jer 23:9–40; Ezek 13:1–14:11 (ibid., 120–21).

56. As Douglas remarks, the allusions to a text like Deut 18 are paralleled in the literary construction of the Teacher of Righteousness in 1QpHab ("Power and Praise," 296). I have treated this issue in the article, "Skriftbrug i Habakkukkommentaren" (in Danish). One should be cautious not to take this as an expression of identity between the Teacher of Righteousness and the speaker of the Hodayot; rather, the texts share a typological pattern. George Brooke (*Reading the Dead Sea Scrolls*, 79) describes such use of scriptural allusions in the Hodayot in more general terms as "imitative pastiches of anthological allusion" that constitute "a move toward the widely used poetry of others for the construction of particular identities."

However, there is also a *structural* allusion to Dan 11:27–34, another text that revolves around loyalty and disloyalty to the covenant. The text is part of the last vision in Daniel (chapters 10–12) and deals mostly with the affairs of kings on the international scene of politics, diplomacy, and warfare. The perspective narrows as one of the kings involved rages and turns against the holy covenant because of his failing efforts in war. Suddenly, the international level is abandoned and the inner relations of the covenantal society come into focus. The textual unit is delimited by an *inclusio*, as parallel formulations in verses 27 and 35 relate the situation to the end of time. This text has an agency structure analogous to Newsom's structure of the drama of 1QH[a] XII 7–30 outlined above. It has four parties: 1) the king (who does not belong to the covenantal society); 2) those who had violated or forsaken the covenant; 3) the wise persons among the people; and 4) the many.

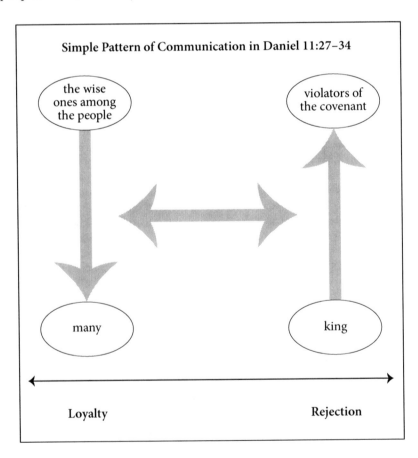

Simple Pattern of Communication in Daniel 11:27–34

the wise ones among the people

violators of the covenant

many

king

Loyalty   Rejection

The foreign king (Antiochus Epiphanes is probably the king to which the text alludes) turns against the holy covenant on his way home from unsuccessful negotiations. It is clear that he does so in part by flattering those within the covenantal society who have violated or forsaken the holy covenant. The king is then a *rejector* of the covenant, seducing those who have *abandoned* the covenant. These two parties are opposing the covenant. On the opposite side there are the "wise among the people" who *teach* "many." The latter two parties seen together mirror the king and the violators of the covenant, and they represent positive values, as did "truth" in Newsom's model of 1QH^a XII 6–XIII 6. Here, I find it correct to call that positive value "loyalty"; that is, loyalty to the covenant. I would like to recall that the covenantal theme is highly present also in 1QH^a XII 6–XIII 6, and Newsom's truth-and-rejection-of-truth scheme could easily be switched to a loyalty-and-disloyalty scheme.[57]

This superficial demonstration of a similar pattern in the two texts can be qualified by pointing out some significant lexicographical similarities. For the sake of clarity, I present them graphically and use identical headings to describe each typological group.

The model on page 212 and the next one on 213 display not only a common pattern but significant lexicographical equivalents between the text of Dan 11:27–34 and the retold drama in 1QH^a XII 7–30. The correspondences between the two models mainly speak for themselves. In both texts, the followers of the covenant are called the "many," and they are taught by the defender of the covenant. The opposer of the covenant flatters the abandoners of the covenant, and in both texts this "flattery" is rendered with the relatively rare word חלקות. In both cases that group's abandoning the covenant is explicit but expressed in different words.

A few comments and elaborations are required: Unlike the book of Daniel, the hodayah does not call the defender משכיל. Also, differing verbs are used to denote the defenders' teaching activity. Nevertheless, they function the same way in both texts; it is through the defender that God conveys understanding to the many, those who are loyal to his covenant:

Through me you have enlightened the face of the many and you have increased (them) without number. For you have let me know your won-

57. The introduction of the composition, "I thank you, Lord, for you have enlightened my face by your covenant," makes this clear, as does the speaker's nearly concluding statement in XII 40 that he will hold onto the covenant of God.

eaning and Context in 1QHodayot[a]

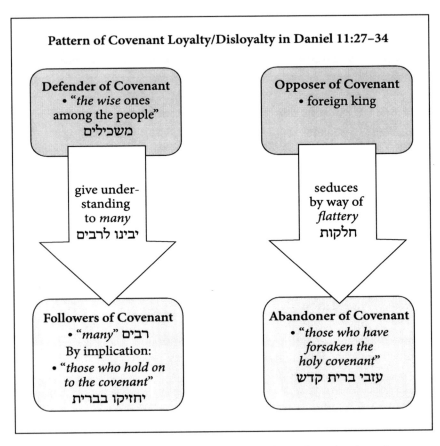

Pattern of Covenant Loyalty/Disloyalty in Daniel 11:27–34

Defender of Covenant
- *"the wise* ones among the people"
משכילים

Opposer of Covenant
- foreign king

give under-standing to *many*
יבינו לרבים

seduces by way of *flattery*
חלקות

Followers of Covenant
- *"many"* רבים
By implication:
- *"those who hold on to the covenant"*
יחזיקו בברית

Abandoner of Covenant
- *"those who have forsaken the holy covenant"*
עזבי ברית קדש

derful secrets and in your wonderful council you have heightened my position and you have worked wonders in the presence of the many for the sake of your glory and to make known your mighty deeds to all of the living. (1QH[a] XII 28–30)

Second, by implication both texts conceive of the group of followers of the covenant as "those who *hold on to* the covenant." Regarding the text of Daniel, my argument stems from the following formulation: Those who violate the covenant (ברית), he shall seduce with flatteries; but the people who are loyal to their covenant shall stand firm (יחזיקו) and take action. The verb יחזיקו in this syntactical environment does not have an object. It is plausible, however, that ברית in the preceding statement is actually the implicit object here; at least readers could easily have perceived it this way, knowing that החזיק, when transitive, has the meaning of holding on to

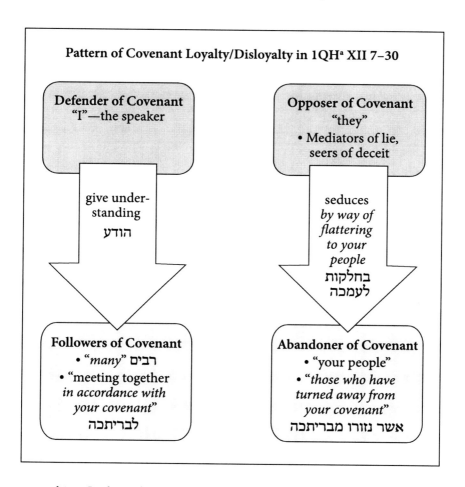

Pattern of Covenant Loyalty/Disloyalty in 1QH^a XII 7–30

Defender of Covenant
"I"—the speaker

Opposer of Covenant
"they"
• Mediators of lie,
seers of deceit

give under-
standing
הודע

seduces
by way of
flattering
to your
people
בחלקות
לעמכה

Followers of Covenant
• *"many"* רבים
• *"meeting together*
in accordance with
your covenant"
לבריתכה

Abandoner of Covenant
• *"your people"*
• *"those who have*
turned away from
your covenant"
אשר נזורו מבריתכה

something. In the Hebrew Bible, the concept of holding on to the covenant is rendered by other verbs in combination with ברית.

In the Hodayot text, the followers of the covenant are said to be meeting in accordance with the covenant of God, and another verb (נועד) is used in combination with ברית to express this idea. However, ברית and חזק are combined in 1QH^a XII 40, where the speaker says he will "hold onto the covenant" of God (אתחזקה בבריתכה), and in both 1QH^a X 30 and XXIII 10, likewise to express the idea of holding onto the covenant. Other sectarian texts clearly connect this behavior to the men of the community.[58]

---

58. See also 1QS V 3 and 1QSb I 2, where it is clearly the men of the community

5.8. MINGLED EPISTEMOLOGIES AND RHETORICAL MEANING

The common patterns and use of vocabulary in Dan 11:27–34 and 1QH^a XII 7–30 do not prove that one text was literarily dependent upon the other. What is obvious, however, is that they must at least have drawn on common literary sources. In the previous chapter we saw how some of the so-called Community Hymns have drawn on the same literary sources as Daniel and may even stem from the same social milieu. The finding of a similar situation in the so-called Leader Hymns is significant because we must assume the material was created in a sectarian setting, namely, in a milieu that, regardless of its possible affinities to wider Jewish wisdom circles, was different from it. Both this text and Dan 11 offer reinterpretations of a current, corporate *maśkîl* ethos, and they do it for similar reasons and in much the same ways. First, they display a situation of social crisis where the people of God do not cling wholeheartedly to the covenant because some of its members have abandoned it. I believe one is justified to see this literary outline as reflecting a social—and rhetorical—situation experienced by the authors as a situation of conflict and crisis.

Second, the texts place a *maśkîl* figure in this situation and make him the supporter of these people who are faithful to the covenant. In 1QH^a XII 7–30 this is done far less explicitly than in the book of Daniel, because not at any time does the speaker refer to himself as a *maśkîl*. As we have seen, the juxtaposition of the drama with the two wisdom sections is mainly what achieves this.

Thirdly, both texts resort to apocalyptic epistemology. At first sight, this may seem contradictory to the underlying wisdom ethos and epistemology, but in light of the particular rhetorical situation addressed in each text, I believe it is not. The apocalyptic epistemology serves to restrict the access to wisdom to those adhering to the covenant. It is an apt literary response to a stressful situation requiring rhetorical action. Rodney Werline's points regarding the dissonance between "apocalyptic determinism and conditional covenant theology" in Daniel also apply to 1QH^a XII 6–XIII 6 and provide an insightful perspective on the mingling of apocalyptic and sapiential epistemologies.

---

who are to hold onto the covenant. Other texts express the same idea by combining חזק with terms other than ברית. See 1QS V 1//4QS^d I 1; CD XIX 14; XX 27.

The *maskilim* have two traditions and social visions with which they must work: the apocalyptic and the covenantal. The apocalyptic tradition establishes the group's identity and distinguishes it from other groups. The covenantal traditions in the text—not just in the prayer but, as we have seen, elsewhere in Daniel 7–12—relate the group to a broader stream of Jewish tradition and temple practice, within which they also see themselves as standing. They need both—the apocalyptic traditions to be loyal to one another in the group and the covenantal traditions to be loyal to an older, broader tradition—and they must hold to and enact both. To lose the apocalyptic aspect of their faith would be a loss of identity; to lose the covenantal aspect of their faith would, for them, separate them from what they have received as part of the heart of the tradition.[59]

Seen this way, the epistemologies are part of rhetorical strategies employed in order both to anchor the owners of the texts in tradition and to make them, and not their religiopolitical rivals, true *maśkilim* and rightful heirs to the covenant. The retold drama of 1QH[a] XII 7–30, when merged with broadly grounded wisdom material, thus displays a subtle reinterpretation of the traditional *maśkil* ethos. Rhetorical need was probably the driving force behind this reinterpretation, and therefore we should be careful not to see sections or whole compositions displaying one or the other epistemological stance as static expressions of a particular set of ideas held by some social groups in isolation from others.[60]

Newsom also underscores the importance of reusing and interpreting discourses belonging in hegemonic circles for the formation of subjectivity. It enables text users to "create the sense that one is only now understanding the true meaning of words that had long been familiar and important. The subject who is called into being is also experienced as at once familiar and new, a self that is recognizable but truly known for the first time."[61] By implication, the reinterpretation of the *maśkil* ethos in 1QH[a] XII 6–XIII 6 has not only cast the speaker and those seeing themselves as represented

---

59. Werline, "Prayer, Politics, and Social Vision in Daniel 9," 31. Newsom also discusses the mingling of epistemologies in Daniel as an expression of discursive strategies (*Self as Symbolic Space*, 42–47).

60. Werline's warning to modern interpreters is pertinent in this respect: "Perhaps modern scholarship needs to reassess the notion that authors of ancient religious texts and ancient religious practitioners, and even religious technicians, first and foremost sought to present a coherent and systematic set of ideas" ("Prayer, Politics, and Social Vision in Daniel 9," 30–31).

61. Newsom, *Self as Symbolic Space*, 195.

by him in the role of a *maśkîl*, but has fused new meaning into the concept. The speaker of the drama personifies the *maśkîl* ethos in a conflict-ridden situation and accentuates aspects of the role that are less prominent, but not absent, in the so-called Community Hymns. Those aspects include his mediating function, which we have seen in 1QH^a VI 19–33 and 1QS IX 12–XI, and the task of distinguishing between righteous and unrighteous people within Israel.

Finally, I wish to suggest that the heterogeneous character of 1QHodayot^a also betrays such a rhetorically motivated interpretive endeavor. The group of so-called Leader Hymns has been embedded into a collection of hymns with a strong sapiential flavor and affinities with Jewish wisdom literature because the editors saw them as apt developments of this literature in light of the current social situation. In conclusion, then, I suggest that Werline's interpretation of the petitionary prayer spoken by Daniel in Dan 9 is suitable also for the prayers in 1QHodayot^a, because the speaker "[a]s one who possesses wisdom, knowledge, and understanding … functions in the text as a model of and for the *maskilim*."[62]

In the following chapter, the analysis of 4Q427 7 i 6–ii 23, with its parallel in the inferior text of 1QH^a XXVI 3–42, will show that the merging of differing texts and perspectives in the Hodayot also could take place in a much more explicit manner, through the reworking and reshaping of texts in new recensions.

---

62. Werline, "Prayer, Politics, and Social Vision in Daniel 9," 25.

6

Two Voices in Unison: The Self-Glorification Hymn and the Hymn of the Righteous

In this chapter I will discuss the so-called Self-Glorification Hymn and the Hymn of the Righteous. These two hymns appear together in 1QHo-dayot[a] and in other documents and therefore seem to have been treated as a unit. Accordingly, they will be treated here as one text. In quite its own way, this text invites a collective of worshipers to assume an elevated status, indeed to identify as someone with an active part to play in the agency of God.

The heterogeneous nature of 1QHodayot[a] is underscored by the presence of this text in the collection. Because of its exceptional character, John Collins and Devorah Dimant have questioned "the adequacy of the traditional division between Hymns of the Teacher and Hymns of the Community."[1] The speaker of the Self-Glorification Hymn boasts of himself in a way unseen in other Hodayot compositions: he calls himself a friend of the king and a companion of the angels and claims that nothing compares to his teachings. In the ensuing Hymn of the Righteous, the focus shifts as the speaker now addresses a collective of worshipers, encouraging them to participate in the praise of God. In this hymn, the speaker's ego slides into the background as he now highlights the magnificent acts of God. The presence of this text in 1QHodayot[a] underscores the heterogeneity of the collection, on account of both the text's composite character and its dissimilarity to other hodayot, especially in the case of the Self-Glorification Hymn.

The text is found in 1QHodayot[a] in the bottom part of col. XXV and in col. XXVI in a rather fragmentary form.[2] Remains of the beginning of the

---

1. Collins and Dimant, "A Thrice-Told Hymn," 155.
2. Based on the parallel texts of 4Q431/4Q271b and 4Q427, Schuller argues that

Self-Glorification Hymn are preserved in 1QH^a XXV 34–37 (frg. 7 i 6–9), and a few words from the ending of the hymn are visible at the beginning of lines 6–9 in col. XXVI (frg. 56 ii 1–9). The ensuing lines 10–17 have remains from the beginning of the Hymn of the Righteous (frg. 46 ii 1–5 and 55 ii 1–3), and some more substantial remains of the latter parts of the hymn are found in lines 26–38 (frg. 7 ii 1–13). Thus, even if the very first words of the Hymn of the Righteous are missing (it must have begun in the middle of line 11), it is clear that the Self-Glorification Hymn is immediately followed by the Hymn of the Righteous.[3] Of the sparse information given in the fragmentary beginning, it is worth mentioning that it begins with a dedication to a *maśkîl* (למשכיל) as in 1QH^a XX 7, instead of the characteristic formula of thanksgiving or blessing.

The Self-Glorification Hymn and the Hymn of the Righteous appear in other Hodayot texts. The best preserved manuscript of the hymns is 4Q427, consisting of a number of Hodayot compositions distributed on nine columns of text.[4] This document has other compositions from 1QHodayot^a, but in a different order, and the Self-Glorification Hymn and the Hymn of the Righteous are located as early as cols. III–IV. 4Q427 7 i–ii is going to be the basis for my analysis of the Self-Glorification Hymn and the Hymn of the Righteous. The extant text of the Self-Glorification Hymn is sparse, but much remains of the Hymn of the Righteous, and the transition between them is intact (4Q427 7 i 13).

A fragment from a third manuscript, 4Q431, contains a part of the Self-Glorification Hymn and the very first word of the Hymn of the Righteous: "Sing!" (זמרו). This fragment was initially treated as unidentified by John Strugnell and was published by Esther Eshel in DJD XXIX as 4Q471b. Eshel treated it as an independent document but nevertheless noticed that it might belong with 4Q431, a manuscript consisting of a fragment with text from the Hymn of the Righteous.[5] In the very same DJD

---

the composition probably continued into the third line of column XXVII, the beginning of which is missing. These parallel versions of the Hymn of the Righteous end with a triple doxology that, though not extant in 1QH^a XXVI, presumably rounded off the 1QH^a version. See Schuller and Stegemann, *1QHodayot^a* (DJD XL), 300.

3. The joining of frgs. 56 and 46 is justified because of a shared edge and the preservation in both of the right column margin. See Schuller and Stegemann, *1QHodayot^a* (DJD XL), 24, 292; Wise, "מי כמוני באלים," 205–6.

4. 4Q427 is edited by Eileen Schuller in *Qumran Cave 4 XX: Poetical and Liturgical Texts, Part 2* (DJD XXIX), 77–123.

5. *Qumran Cave 4 XX: Poetical and Liturgical Texts, Part 2* (DJD XXIX), 421–32.

volume, Schuller edited this fragment, 4Q471b, as belonging to 4Q431. In her reconstruction, it has become frg. 1 of that document, whereas the fragment containing remains of the Hymn of the Righteous has become frg. 2.[6] Apart from textual overlaps with 4Q427 7 ii and 1QHodayot[a], the very similar handwriting in the manuscripts is the basis for her assessment, which seems reasonable but not absolutely certain.[7] In any case, I follow the terminology of Schuller and refer to 4Q431 1 (identical to 4Q471b) and 4Q431 2, respectively. Important for the present study is that the texts of both fragments are very similar to the parallel texts in 4Q427 7 ii and 1QHodayot[a], and that 4Q431 1 witnesses the transition from the Self-Glorification Hymn to the Hymn of the Righteous. The transition is thus extant in three documents that can reasonably be designated Hodayot, or at least Hodayot-like.[8] The variants that appear between these manuscripts are minor.[9]

A different text of the Self-Glorification Hymn and the Hymn of the Righteous was published by Maurice Baillet in 1982, before any of the Hodayot manuscripts discussed up this point. Baillet designated this text, now labelled 4Q491c, as 4Q491 (4QM[a]) frg. 11–12 and treated it as War Scroll material.[10] On the basis of material, orthographic and paleographic evidence, Martin Abegg later divided the fragments of 4Q491 into three groups: the first contains a portion of 1QM; the second deals with eschatological warfare, but is not a copy of 1QM; and the third group, frg. 11–12 (4Q491c), he singled out from the second group and claimed on the basis

6. Ibid., 199–208.

7. I base this purely on the differences that Schuller herself mentions: appearance of the skin, letter size, and distance between the lines (ibid., 199).

8. Thanksgiving formulas and other terminology typical of Hodayot compositions are lacking in 4Q431 1 and 2.

9. See Schuller and Stegemann, 1QHodayot[a] (DJD XL), 301. With respect to the placement of the Self-Glorification Hymn and the Hymn of the Righteous, it differs from one document to another: in 1QHodayot[a] they are found toward the end of the manuscript, but in 4Q427 already in the third column. It is possible that the text of 4Q431 was at the very beginning of the scroll, and thus hypothetically at the beginning of a Hodayot collection. This is indicated by the right margin of frg. 1, which is wider than most margins between columns. See Schuller, "Hodayot" (DJD XXIX), 200.

10. Baillet, Qumrân grotte 4.III (DJD VII), 26–34. It was clear to Baillet, as well as to Hunzinger (who had previously published an article on a part of 4Q491), that this section of the document has no parallel material in 1QM. See also Hunzinger, "Fragmente einer älteren Fassung," 131–51.

of physical evidence that it belonged to an independent document.[11] On
literary grounds he decided that this portion of text could not be War Scroll
material and pointed instead to its affinities with the Hodayot.[12] Abegg's
division of the material has generally been approved by other scholars, but
Florentino García Martínez has disagreed with his decision that 4Q491c
is independent of the War Scroll context. Due to material, conceptual, and
linguistic similarities between 4Q491c and 4QM[a] (4Q491), he finds justification for the view that 4Q491c should be interpreted within the literary
context of War Scroll material, rather than with the Hodayot (with which
it is only generically related).[13]

4Q491c 1 contains a substantial part of the Self-Glorification Hymn,
whereas only four fragmentary lines remain of the Hymn of the Righteous—enough, however, to show the speaker exhort a group designated
"righteous" (צדיקים) to give praise to God.[14] The text of 4Q491c is briefer
than the text of the Hodayot manuscripts and is regarded as earlier.[15] The
Hodayot text is labelled recension A, and 4Q491c is called recension B.[16]

---

11. Abegg, "Who Ascends to Heaven?" esp. 61–73. Abegg's part III/4Q491c is the
same as 4Q491 frg. 11 i and 12. The physical grounds for singling out these two fragments were different line heights and paleographic observations.

12. Abegg even mentions the possibility that the text of 4Q491c originated within
a Hodayot context ("Who Ascends to Heaven?," 72).

13. García Martínez, "Old Texts and Modern Mirages," 327–29. García Martínez
has made his observations on the basis of all photographs now available: Emanuel Tov
et al., eds., *The Dead Sea Scrolls on Microfiche*; Timothy H. Lim and Philip S. Alexander, eds., *The Dead Sea Scrolls Electronic Reference Library*. In the photo of frg. 11 in
DJD VII (pl. VI), the two columns of frg. 11 seem to be physically joined, but Baillet
(*Qumrân grotte 4.III* [DJD VII], 27) notes that the joint is "seulement probable." Wise
directs attention to the fact that the photo has been masked and scholars have been
misled to see joints where there are none ("מי כמוני באלים," 179).

14. Wise ("מי כמוני באלים," 180–193) joins the seventeen fragments of 4Q491c
differently than Baillet. I do not want to enter into a discussion of the matter here,
but only remark that their reconstructions agree with respect to the beginning of the
Hymn of the Righteous (Baillet: lines 20–24; Wise: lines 13–17).

15. See Wise, "מי כמוני באלים," 214–16. He argues on the assumption that expansion is a common tendency in liturgical literature of the time, and also that recension A expands on themes and passages in 4Q491c. Eshel expresses the opposite view
but also mentions the possibility that both recensions draw on a common source ("A
Self-Glorification Hymn," 201). In her later DJD edition of 4Q471b ("4QSelf-Glori-
fication Hymn [= 4QH[c] frg. 1?]" [DJD XXIX], 420–32), Eshel does not discuss the
issue. Schuller, in her edition of 4Q427 ("Hodayot" [DJD XXIX], 101), also hesitates to
discuss the temporal aspects of the relationship between the two recensions.

The two recensions agree on two important points: the division of the text into two hymns and the impression that two different subjects speak them. This suggests not only that the two hymns were transmitted as a unit in the community, but also that the relationship between the two very dissimilar speakers was perceived as significant in some way. This duality, and its development in recension A, is intriguing as regards our concern for the hybrid character of 1QHodayotᵃ and its speaker(s): recension A takes the text of recension B in an interesting direction because it *makes more of* the relationship between the hymns and, accordingly, between their speakers.

6.1. The Identity of the Speaker

It was Baillet, in the first edition of 4Q491, who noticed that the material now labeled 4Q491c should be divided in two. The first part he called "cantique de Michel," the second "cantique des justes." According to him, these hymns belonged in the part of the War Scroll where the archangel Michael comes to the rescue of the righteous ones (1QM XVII 6–9). In this War Scroll context he interpreted the text as spoken by the archangel.[17] García Martínez has recently argued in favor of Baillet's position on the basis of a literary comparison with texts about eschatological war, but in general scholars have preferred to identify the speaker of 4Q491c as a human being.[18]

Morton Smith was the first to reject the possibility that 4Q491c could have been spoken by an angel. Because angels by nature belong in the heavenly realm, they would hardly find occasion to brag about their position or compare themselves to human nobilities. In his view, the Self-Glorification Hymn is proof that "fifty or sixty years before Jesus' crucifixion, men in Palestine were actually making claims of the sort that John was to attribute to Jesus."[19] Abegg's exclusion of 4Q491c from a War Scroll con-

---

16. See however García Martínez ("Old Texts and Modern Mirages," 330), who criticizes the use of the term "recension." In his view, the differences between 4Q491c and the Hodayot texts imply comprehensive reworking, not just revision.

17. Baillet, *Qumrân grotte 4.III* (DJD VII), 26–30. The text is edited as 4Q491 11 i. Baillet regards frg. 12 as belonging with the text of frg. 11.

18. García Martínez, "Old Texts and Modern Mirages," 336.

19. Smith, "Two Ascended to Heaven," 298. He also considers the possibility that the author of the Hodayot might be the speaker here. Because of its exceptional assertions about ascent to heaven, however, he prefers to see it as an extreme development of a tendency discernible also in the Hodayot; namely, to speculate about (and perhaps

text and the discovery of more complete Hodayot manuscripts in Cave 4 have pointed researchers in the same direction: most scholars see the speaker of the Self-Glorification Hymn and Hymn of the Righteous as an exalted human being. A very common position is that the speaker is a priestly figure. Esther Eshel argues on the basis of resemblances between the Self-Glorification Hymn and the Rule of Blessings (1QSb) that the speaker is the eschatological high priest.[20] Joseph Angel offers a number of observations to support this claim; for example, the speaker's repeated references to his "glory" (כבודי) and his emphasis on his own pedagogical proficiency, which is comparable to that of the eschatological high priest in other texts.[21] Some have argued that the speaker can be identified in a more specific way; for example, as Melchizedek.[22] Crispin Fletcher-Louis believes that the speaker was a contemporary priest who assumed angelic

---

experience) humans' "encounters with gods or angels" ("Ascent to the Heavens and Deification in 4QM[a]," 187–88). Abegg, in his remarks on 4Q471b (=4Q431), seems to believe the Self-Glorification Hymn originated in a Hodayot context as he asserts that the Teacher of Righteousness must be the speaker. See Michael Wise, Martin Abegg, and Edward Cook, *The Dead Sea Scrolls: A New Translation*, 404–5.

20. Eshel, "4QSelf-Glorification Hymn (= 4QH[e] frg. 1?)" (DJD XXIX), 422–27. See also Eshel, "The Identification of the 'Speaker,'" 630–34. It is particularly because of the following characteristics outlined in 1QSb IV 22–28 that Eshel identifies the speaker with the eschatological high priest: He is presented as a "*luminary* [...] for the world in knowledge" who is to "shine on the face of the Many" (1QSb IV 27); he shall be "*like an angel* of the face in the holy residence for the Glory of the God of the Hos[ts"; and he shall be "casting the lot *with the angels* of the face and the Council of the Community [...] *for eternal time* and *for all the perpetual periods*" (1QSb IV 24–26). Translations are taken from *DSSSE*, 1:107. Even if no references to the high priest are found in this part of the blessings, they are usually thought to apply to him and not to the sons of Zadok or any other group mentioned elsewhere in the text.

21. Cf. 1QSb IV; 4QShirShabb[a] 1 i; 4QInstruction[d] 81; 4Q541 9; Jubilees 31. See Angel, *Otherworldly and Eschatological Priesthood*, 137–41, esp. 139. See also Collins, *The Scepter and the Star*, 148.

22. See, e.g., J. C. O'Neill, "'Who is Comparable to Me in My Glory?,'" 24–28, 36. Like the eschatological high priest, Melchizedek is described in 11Q13 II 6–8 as having an elevated position and a role to play in the final redemption of the sons of light and the men of his lot. Thus, he resembles the high priest as described in, e.g., 1QSb. See Angel, *Otherworldly and Eschatological Priesthood*, 110–46. A similar pattern is seen in Heb 7:3, 15–17, where Melchizedek is made a model for the eschatological high priest and a symbol of Christ. Cf. Svendsen, *Allegory Transformed*, 140–51; Dalgaard, "A Priest for All Generations," 116–23.

status in a mystical experience during the liturgy.[23] With regard to recension A in particular, some consider the Teacher of Righteousness, the alleged author of other Hodayot compositions, to be the implied speaker. Thus, Esther Eshel suggests that the resemblances between the Teacher of Righteousness and the high priest led to the insertion of the two hymns in the Hodayot; and Michael Wise claims that the self-assertive claims of the speaker, once they were included in the Hodayot, would "call to mind the Teacher" because "the Hodayot were connected to the Teacher as were no other Qumran writings."[24]

Others see the speaker as representing a collective of human beings. Émile Puech briefly compares 4Q491c 1 4–5 to 4Q521 2 ii 7, which says that God will "sanctify the pious ones on a royal throne forever."[25] Hartmut Stegemann claims in a discussion of collective messianism that the speaker of 4Q491c was "the people of Israel, being raised to a quasi 'heavenly' status."[26] Michael Wise agrees, but believes that the idea of a collective speaker is only implicit in 4Q491c. For recension A, on the other hand, Wise offers evidence that the notion of a collective speaker was intentionally made explicit.[27] The purpose of infusing the Self-Glorification Hymn and the Hymn of the Righteous into 1QHodayot[a] was to let ordinary members experience that the words of the Teacher of Righteousness—since only he could have been expected to utter such words—could become true for themselves as they took part through recitation in "the

---

23. Fletcher-Louis, *All the Glory of Adam*, 204–16.

24. Eshel, "4QSelf-Glorification Hymn (= 4QH[e] frg. 1)" (DJD XXIX), 426–27; Wise, "מי כמוני באלים," 218.

25. Puech, "Une apocalypse messianique (4Q521)," 489–90.

26. Stegemann, "Some Remarks to 1QSa, to 1QSb, and to Qumran Messianism," 502. His evaluation is connected with his argument against the expectation of an individual messiah in the War Scroll, the book of Daniel, and other mid-second-century literature. He also finds this phenomenon, a collective speaker expressing himself as if an individual, in Isaiah's texts about the Suffering Servant (Isa 42:1–9; 49:16; 50:4–11; 52:13–53:12). See also Steudel, "The Eternal Reign of the People of God," with analyses of 4Q246 and 1QM in support.

27. Wise, "מי כמוני באלים," 216–17. For instance, the speaker in 4Q427 7 i 13 addresses the congregation as "friends" (ידידים) instead of "righteous ones" (צדיקים), as does recension B. This way he consciously equates the righteous ones with the boasting speaker who in the Self-Glorification Hymn designates himself as "friend of the king (ידיד המלך)" (ibid., 217).

charisma of the Teacher."[28] More recently, Joseph Angel has basically confirmed Wise's interpretation that recension A fuses the two hymns so as to boost the ability of worshipers to identify with the exalted, boasting speaker of the Self-Glorification Hymn. According to Angel, however, we have no way of knowing that the Teacher of Righteousness was the object of identification. Instead, he advocates the idea that the speaker's characteristics point to "a priestly or quasi-priestly figure," and concludes that a priestly identity "appears to extend to all members of the community … who share a special affinity with the speaker."[29] Angel sees the role of the priestly speaker as eschatological; not in the sense that it displays something that was to take place in the future, but in the sense of a realized eschatology taking place within the contemporary Dead Sea community. The speaker "should be considered eschatological only inasmuch as the liturgical experience allowed him to escape linear historical time and take a seat among the angels."[30]

With regard to 4Q491c, I believe that García Martínez is correct to connect its origin to the War Scroll literature rather than to the Hodayot. He brings attention to the uncertainty of several readings that are typically used to argue for the human identity of the speaker: "The only element asserted strongly and clearly is the exalted status of the protagonist, among and above all the angels, and his being endowed with a 'glory' to which no one compares."[31] This content, García Martínez asserts, fits with descriptions not of a priest, teacher, or human messiah, but of the archangel Michael as he is depicted in 1QM XVII 5–9 and with the "Prince of Light" as described in 1QM XIII 10.[32] These are central, superhuman

---

28. Ibid., 218.

29. Angel, *Otherworldly and Eschatological Priesthood*, 143–46, esp. 146.

30. Ibid., 142.

31. García Martínez, "Old Texts and Modern Mirages," 335. This content is seen in phrases like "my glory is in{comparable} and besides me no-one is exalted'" (4Q491c 1 6); "I am counted among the gods and my dwelling is in the holy congregation" (4Q491c 1 7); "my glory is with the sons of the king" (4Q491c 1 11). The difference of the Self-Glorification Hymn and the Hymn of the Righteous from other Hodayot compositions would be another argument in favor of García Martínez's position. According to Björn Frennesson, communion with angels in the Hodayot generally has only "'earthly' and present implications," whereas in 4Q427 "there is an almost tangible atmosphere of immediacy and openness in relation to the heavenly world" (*"In a Common Rejoicing": Liturgical Communion with Angels at Qumran*, 114).

32. García Martínez ("Old Texts and Modern Mirages," 336) highlights the pas-

figures in eschatological warfare. García Martínez's observation that the Self-Glorification Hymn would make sense as a "hymn of victory" in such a context of eschatological battle seems feasible.[33]

In any case, his insistence that 4Q491c (recension B) was created in literary and social contexts different from those of the Hodayot recension is important, and it bears on our readings of each text: terminology shared by the two recensions may have had very different implications in their respective contexts. "Priestly" language may have been used in one context to describe angels, whereas in another context it may have been used of priests or community members fulfilling priestly functions. Priestly and angelic functions are often analogous in the Dead Sea Scrolls, and therefore it can be difficult to define the exact identity of the protagonist.[34]

I side with those who reckon with a corporate speaker in recension A. Insofar as recension B is earlier and in this sense more original than recension A, the composers of recension A may not even have imagined the protagonist narrowly as being either priestly, angelic, or messianic, but may have drawn on various types and figures when expressing their own self-understanding. The following analysis will confirm that efforts were made in 4Q427 7 ii to fuse the righteous ones with the exalted individual boasting of himself in the Self-Glorification Hymn. There is no simple way of outlining how the mechanism of *suture* may have worked for the people reciting or listening to the Self-Glorification Hymn and the Hymn of the Righteous in a Hodayot context. Priestly language and connotations may have contributed to the worshipers' self-understanding, and we shall see that the shape of the text (4Q427) could evoke a sense of being with angels. Another possibility, which does not exclude any of the others, is that the

---

sage: "He will exalt the authority of Michael above all the gods" (1QM XVII 7). Cf. the preceding note. He also brings attention to the fact that "Michael" and the "Prince of Light" appear to be alternating designations for one and the same figure, which by implication in *4QVisions of Amram* may also go by the name Melchizedek. And he concludes that the protagonist of 4Q491c might even be the "heavenly messiah" that "appears as the eschatological savior Melchizedek in 11Q13, and as the 'son of God' who in 4Q242 restores peace after the final battle" (ibid., 337).

33. Ibid., 332.

34. Dimant provides an overview of textual witnesses showing that angels and men fulfill the same functions: e.g., offering bloodless sacrifices, existing in perfect purity, expiating, and teaching (see, e.g., 11Q17 I–III; 4Q400 1 i 14–17; 1QS III 4–10, 13; VIII 5–10; IX 3–5). These tasks are connected to the priestly role ("Men as Angels," 100–101).

boasting speaker of the Self-Glorification Hymn could be used for negative identification. The righteous ones are not quite like him. They have no
reason to be megalomanic because they are exalted by God. I am implying
that the text, as met in 4Q427 7 i–ii, contained a whole range of source
domains available for the identity work of its audience.

Translation of 4Q427 7 i 5–23

5.	[	holy...[35]
6.	[is despised like me ...	like me. And forsake] evil
7.	[is likened to me	is likened to] my [teac]hing
8.	[And who can be compared to me	who is like me][36] among the angels?
9.	[I	that which streams from my lips, who can contain (it)?] Wh[o] can give witness about me with the tongue?[37]
10.	[	friend of the ki]ng, companion of the holy ones. And will not come[38]
11.	[	and with] my g[lory] does not compare; f[o]r I, [my] position is with the angels,
12.	[and the glory	][39]r not with gold 'k ... for me, and neither an orna- ment of Ophir[40]

---

35. The bulk of the reconstructed text in lines 5–10 is based on parallel material
in 4Q431 1 1–6.

36. מי כמוני באלים is reconstructed on the basis of 4Q431 1 4 (= 4Q471b 1a 4).

37. According to Schuller ("A Hymn from a Cave Four Hodayot Manuscript,"
612), the verb יעודני corresponds with יועדני in 4Q491c 1 10 (= 4Q491 11 i 17). She
suggests that they are two alternative spellings of the verb עוד. Several translations are
possible; Schuller suggests "wh[o] by speech is similar to me." The translation given
here, however, prioritizes the common connection between שפתים ("lips") and לשון
("tongue," "language"), which also suggests a correspondence between יעודני and יכיל;
the lack of ability to give witness about the speaker is caused by the inability to "contain" that which streams from his lips.

38. There is no visible subject of this verb in the masculine singular.

39. The reconstructed text in lines 12 and 13 is based on the parallel in 1QH^a
XXVI 8–9.

40. In the following comments on 4Q427 7 i–ii, all references to Schuller,
"Hodayot" (DJD XXIX), are found on pp. 96–108. In this place, Schuller ("Hodayot"
[DJD XXIX], 103) and DSSSE (2:897) both read או ביורים, whereas Eshel reads a
contracted אוביירים ("A Self-Glorification Hymn," 186). Apparently, they all see the
expression as a scribal error for אופירים, which occurs in 4Q491c 1 11 (= 4Q491 11 i
18). Schuller also refers to Isa 13:12; Ps 45:10; Job 28:16.

13. [on me *wh*   ] they do not consider me. Chant, friends, sing to the king

14. [of glory. Rejoice in the congre]gation[41] of God. Shout from joy in the tents of salvation, give praise to the abode

15. [of holiness.[42] R]ise up together with the eternal army.[43] Give greatness to our God and glory to our king.

16. [Sancti]fy his name with strong lips and a mighty tongue. Lift in unison[44] your voice.

17. [At a]ll times, let music of joy sound [45] and increase happiness forever. And with no

18. [ce]ssation, bow down in the unified congregation. Bless the one who brings about wonderful majesty and makes known the strength of his hand

19. [by] sealing up mysteries and revealing secrets, by lifting up those who stumble and those of them who fall,

20. [by tur]ning the course of those who hope for knowledge and by bringing down the lofty assemblies of the eternally proud,[46]

21. [by perfect]ing mysteries of splen[dor] and establish[ing the won]ders of glory. (He is) the one who judges with destructive wrath

22. [*l*   ] with mercy, righteousness, and with plentiful compassion, grace

---

41. "Rejoice" is restored on the basis of 1QHᵃ XXVI 10. בע[עו]דת אל is suggested by Schuller ("Hodayot" [DJD XXIX], 103) with reference to Ps 82:1, quoted in 1QM IV 9; 4Q427 8 i 10; 4Q457a 4; 11Q13 II 10.

42. במעון [קודש: Compare 1QHᵃ XX 5 (XX 2) and 4Q491c 1 13 (= 4Q491 11 i 20). Schuller prefers this reconstruction because it allows a good alignment of the margin ("Hodayot" [DJD XXIX], 104).

43. בצבא עולם. This phrase is probably equivalent to צבא עד in 1QHᵃ XIX 16 (XIX 13), described by Holm-Nielsen as "angels before the throne of God"; i.e., celestial beings (*Hodayot*, 187 n. 26).

44. לבד. I follow Schuller ("Hodayot" [DJD XXIX], 104) in her understanding of the word in this context.

45. השמיעו הגידנה: The feminine imperative form does not fit in this context. The translation reflects Schuller's reading הגי רנה השמיעו, which she bases especially on the occurrence of this phrase in 4Q491c 1 14 (= 4Q491 11 i 21) ("Hodayot" [DJD XXIX], 99, 104). Qimron underscores that הגי has two meanings: "meditation" (which is the one most frequently seen in the Dead Sea Scrolls) and "resounding music" (*The Hebrew of the Dead Sea Scrolls*, 20).

46. גאים עולם: I follow Schuller who, in spite of the form, interprets גאים as a construct ("Hodayot" [DJD XXIX], 105).

23.   [   ] compassion on those who bear the fruit[47] of
his great goodness, and a source

Translation of 4Q427 7 ii 2–23

2.   [and wickedness perishes…[48]

3.   [and opp]ression [ceases; the tyrant ceases with anger[49]

4.   (when) deception [has ceas]ed and there is no witless perversity.
Light will shine forth and j[oy will burst through.

5.   (When) mourning has perished and sorrow has fled, peace will
come forth. When fear has ceased a source to [eternal bless]ing will
open,

6.   and there will be healing for all times. When perversity has perished
and affliction is over, so that there is no disord[er, (when) wickedness has vanished]

7.   [then gui]lt [will be] no more. [So de]clare s[a]y: *vacat* Great is God
who per[forms wonderfully,]

8.   for he has brought down haughtiness[50] until nothing is left, but
raises the poor one from the dust to [eternal height].

9.   To the clouds he elevates[51] him and with the angels in the unity of
the congregation *wrp*[…[52]

10.   wrath to eternal destruction *vacat* But those who stumble on earth
he raises up for free so that [perpetual stren]gth [is with]

---

47. רחמים למפרי טוב גודלו. I take מפרי in a positive sense, seeing it as a *hiphil*
participle of פרה/פרא. Schuller prefers a different solution, seeing מפרי as a form
of פרר: "[God withholds] mercy for/from those who *frustrate* his great goodness"
("Hodayot" [DJD XXIX], 99, 105). The preposition ל renders this solution less likely.

48. The reconstructions of lines 2–7 are based on the parallel material in 4Q431
2 1–9.

49. The reconstructions are based on Isa 14:4. See Schuller, "Hodayot" (DJD
XXIX), 105.

50. גבהות רוח: lit., "haughtiness of spirit."

51. יגבירהו בקומה. The translation deviates from the usual rendering of גבר in
the *hiphil*: "strengthen," "consolidate," and the like. The parallel texts in 1QH[a] XXVI 28
(XXVI 3/*Sukenik frg. 7 ii 3*) and 4Q431 2 8 have יגביה בקומה. See also Ezek 31:10 and
11QPs[a] XXVIII 9 for this phrase.

52. *DSSSE* has the reconstruction ורפא[הו], "and cures[him." Schuller suggests
that a description of miseries that will strike the evil ones begins here ("Hodayot"
[DJD XXIX], 1:106).

11.   their steps and eternal joy in their foundations; perfect glory end-lessly [forever and ever]

12.   Let them say: Blessed be God who works wonders of splendor, and who makes strong in order to bring forth power [and who brings justice]

13.   by knowledge to all his creatures and (spreads) goodness over their faces because of their knowing[53] his great mercy and his plentiful

14.   compassion for all the sons of his truth. We know you, God of jus-tice, and we have insight [in your truth, king]

15.   of glory. For we have seen your zeal in your powerful strength, and we are familiar with [your judgmen]ts in your [plentiful]

16.   compassion and wonderful forgiveness. What is flesh (compared) to these things? And how [are dust and ashes[54] reckoned]

17.   (to be able) to tell of these things from one period to another and to take a stand [before you and come in community with][55]

18.   sons of heaven? For there is no mediator to res[pond to your com-mand

19.   for you. For you have established us for [your plea]sure [b   and we retain]

20.   strength[56] {to respond to you} <to perceive {your} wonders> like[these...

---

53. בדעתמה. Schuller ("Hodayot" [DJD XXIX], 100) as well as *DSSSE* (2:899) and *DSSR* (5:83) translate the phrase as a final clause, "so they might know." But this is an unusual understanding of ב + suffixed infinitive both in the Hebrew Bible and the Dead Sea Scrolls. See Qimron, *The Hebrew of the Dead Sea Scrolls*, 72–73; Waltke and O'Connor, *Biblical Hebrew Syntax*, 604; Weingreen, *A Practical Grammar*, 132–33. In my reading, this phrase denotes the instrumental value of knowing for the spreading of goodness "over their faces," as does "knowledge" for the bringing about of justice in the preceding passage. Compare this type of construction in 1QH[a] XIX 23 (XIX 20/ *XI 20*) and see בדעת אמתכה in 1QH[a] XVIII 31 (XVIII 29/ *X 29*) for this instrumental usage of "knowing" in connection with God's dealings with human beings.

54. עפר ואפר: See 1QH[a] XVIII 7; VII 34; XXI 17.

55. The translation relates to Schuller's restoration, which is based on similar phrases in 1QH[a] XI 22–23 (XI 21–22/*III 21–22*) and XIX 16 (XIX 13/*XI 13*). See Schuller and Stegemann, *1QHodayot[a]* (DJD XL), 307; Schuller, "Hodayot" (DJD XXIX), 107.

56. ונעצור [כוח. In the Hebrew Bible, this expression is restricted to late writings. Its usage here is similar to that of Dan 10:8, 16, where the retaining of strength denotes a human's ability to communicate with heavenly beings.

21.   We have spoken to you and not to an interme[diary   and
      you have inclined]

22.   the ea[r] to that which issues from our lips. Decl[are and say *vacat*[57]
      Blessed be the God of knowledge who stretches out]

23.   heaven with his power, es[tablishes] all of its devices [with] his
      strength, [makes] the earth with [his m]ight

Paraphrase of 4Q427 7 i 5–ii 23

i 7–13: Self-Glorification Hymn
   The speaker prides himself on his teachings and his elevated position, comparing himself to angels.

i 13–ii 23: Hymn of the Righteous
   i 13–18: Exhortation to praise God
   i 18–21: Exhortation to bless God, motivated by God's handling of
   mysteries and men
   ii 3–7: Eschatological scenario
   ii 7–12: Exhortation to acknowledge God's greatness and his deeds
   toward men, to lift some of them up and bring others down
   ii 12–14: Declaration that those who have been lifted up will
   bless God
   ii 14–22: Cognitive section: embedded collective acknowledgement of God's deeds
   ii 22–23: Repeated exhortation to acknowledge (because the text
   is damaged and broken, it is difficult to say anything about the
   motivation)

It is only the latter part of the Self-Glorification Hymn that is contained in col. i 7–13. As to the connection between the Self-Glorification
Hymn and the Hymn of the Righteous, there are no doxologies or other
signs of a formal transition from one to the other. However, the latter starts
with a summons to sing to "the king of glory," a beginning not quite unlike
that of biblical hymns such as Pss 33:1–3 and 113:1. There are no introductory formulas of the kind known from other Hodayot compositions.

---

57. The double imperative followed by a *vacat* has been reconstructed by Schuller with reference to the construction in 4Q427 7 ii 7, 12, which also continues with
doxological passages ("Hodayot" [DJD XXIX], 108).

Both in form and content, i 13–23 is coherent with col. ii, and in spite of the missing lines at the bottom of the first column, there is good reason to believe that the Hymn of the Righteous continues through col. ii. The formal resemblance is significant because this text deviates from other Hodayot compositions, particularly with regard to form. It is not recommendable, therefore, to ignore col. ii as some interpreters do.[58]

By a brief look at the paraphrase, one glimpses the significant structural difference between the Self-Glorification Hymn and the Hymn of the Righteous. In the Self-Glorification Hymn, the speaker addresses neither God nor men, and this makes the hymn extraordinary in comparison with other Qumranic, biblical, or apocryphal hymns and prayers.

The Hymn of the Righteous is more dynamic. It conveys the voices of more than one speaker. An anonymous speaker in part summons a plurality of people to praise God, in part speaks of it in the third person. His series of exhortations includes accounts of how God has dealt with "the poor one" and "those who stumble." He rounds off the exhortation with the words, "Let them say" (ii 12), followed by a lengthy section in which a plural "we" praises God for his workings (ii 12–22). This praise to God is embedded in the series of exhortations, which is taken up again in ii 22. The arrangement of the text implies that the praising "we" is identical to the aforementioned poor and stumbling people. At the same time, readers and listeners would probably see themselves as included in this "we," not least if the text was used in a liturgical setting.[59]

I shall now focus on this collective addressee, which is exhorted by the speaker but also gets to speak for itself during the praise in 4Q427 7 ii 12–22, and reserve only a few comments for the individualistic speaker of the Self-Glorification Hymn. The Hymn of the Righteous has some significant links to the theme of "exaltation" that is so prominent in the Self-Glorification Hymn: God will bring down haughtiness and "the lofty assemblies of the eternally proud," but lift up the poor. Several verbs refer to these opposite, vertical motions: ירים, וירים, השפיל, להשפיל, להרים. These elements contribute to the coherence of the text (including both hymns), but simultaneously they create contrasts and tension between the two compositions and their protagonists. Since so little of the hymn fol-

---

58. See Eshel, "The Identification of the 'Speaker,'" 619–35; Wise, "מי כמוני באלים," 172–219.

59. The alternating speakers could point to a liturgical *Sitz im Leben*, but there is nothing to suggest the same for the Self-Glorification Hymn.

lowing the Self-Glorification Hymn is extant in 4Q491c, it is difficult to
know if those elements were already included in recension B of the Hymn
of the Righteous, or if they are the inventions of recension A. Nevertheless,
we shall see an example of how, in 4Q427 7 i–ii, a deliberate effort has been
made to create or highlight coherence and tension between the compositions in a way that has social as well as theological consequences.

6.2. Approximations

In 4Q491c, the line preceding the beginning of the Hymn of the Righteous
has a very long *vacat* and no visible writing except for the remains of a
huge *lāmed* at the very left end of the line. Wise takes this huge *lāmed*
as a transitional marker of a new composition: "the inseparable preposition separated, properly attaching to the first word of the Hymn of the
Righteous."[60] This implies that the Self-Glorification Hymn and the Hymn
of the Righteous are undoubtedly separate compositions of recension B. In
recension A there are no such transition markers.[61]

Wise and Angel have both pointed out how lexical choices in 4Q427
7 ii create a closer affinity between the righteous of the Hymn of the Righteous and the speaker of the Self-Glorification Hymn. For instance, by
addressing his audience as ידידים rather than צדיקים as in recension B, the
speaker of the Hymn of the Righteous creates a link to the speaker of the
Self-Glorification Hymn, who refers to himself as ידיד המלך. According
to Wise, this effect was not coincidental, but rather "an intentional element of the melding process that was the Hodayot redaction."[62] This way,
the boundary between the two compositions is blotted out in recension
A, and the exalted speaker of the Self-Glorification Hymn steps out of his
complete isolation and is more easily seen as participating in the earthly
community's communication and praise in the ensuing composition.

---

60. Wise, "מי כמוני באלים," 193. He sees this phenomenon as analogous to the use
of large *wāws* to separate compositions in 4QpaleoExod^m (4Q22). In most instances,
these *wāws* also served as the *wāw*-consecutive.

61. In 4Q427 the transition takes place in the middle of a line, clearly without
any space between the compositions. The transition is not extant in 1QHodayot^a, but
clearly it must have taken place in the middle of a line (XXVI 9); there was hardly
room for lengthy *vacat*s. There may have been a small *vacat* before the beginning of
the Hymn of the Righteous in 4Q431 1, but this is not certain. See Schuller, "Hodayot"
(DJD XXIX), 204–5.

62. Wise, "מי כמוני באלים," 216–17.

In the following analysis of 4Q427, I will show not only that the two hymns have become amalgamated in recension A, but also that the human and angelic worlds through this process of amalgamation have been integrated. In the logic of this version of the text, the angelic status is not only conferred on an individual, like the high priest or a teacher, but also on ordinary community members. I shall focus on the beginning of the exhortation to praise God in the text of 4Q427 7 i 13–15, which is a lengthier version of what is contained in the single line of 4Q491c 1 13. In the Hodayot version, this line has in fact been rephrased so as to form a chiastic, meaning-making structure.

4Q491c 1 12–14[63]

[...]   *Vacat*   [...]   *Vacat*   [...] 12
[...צדיקים באלוהי]ן[...] במעון הקודש זמרוה]ו...[ ] 13
[...] ...] בשמחת עולמים ואין כ. [...] ו[שמיעו בהגיא רנה [...] 14

13   [...exult,][64] just ones in the God of [...] in the holy dwelling, sing for h[im...
14 [...p]roclaim during the meditation jubilation [...] in eternal happiness; and there is no ...[...][65]

4Q427 7 i 13–16[66]

[לוא יחשב בי זמרו ידידים שירו למלכ   ] 13
[הכבוד שמחו בע]דת אל הרנינו באהלי ישועה הללו במעון 14
[קודש ר]וממו יחד בצבא עולם הבו גדול לאלנו וכבוד למלכנו 15
[הקדי]שו שמו בשפתי עוז ולשון נצח הרימו לבד קולכמה 16
[בכ]ול קצים השמיעו הגידנה הביעו בשמחות עולמים ואין 17

In the representation of the texts above, I have included not only 4Q427 7 i 13–15 and 4Q491c 1 13 but also the ensuing lines in order to illustrate the justification for my delimitation of the material. It appears

---

63. Baillet, *Qumrân grotte 4.III* (DJD VII), 27.
64. The translation reflects Baillet's suggestion that the verb רננו might be expected here as it precedes צדיקים in Ps 33:1 and occurs with the verb זמר in Pss 71:23; 98:4.
65. Translation from *DSSSE*, 2:981.
66. See section 6.1 for a translation.

that 4Q427 7 i 16–17, which follows the chiastic structure, draws its material from line 14 in 4Q491c 1.[67]

Since both texts are fragmentary, and since we have no way of knowing if the composer of 4Q427 included other sources, it is impossible to show in full detail and with certainty how the author of 4Q427 used elements from the text of 4Q491c. Nevertheless, it is reasonable to assume that no more than a couple of verbs and a few other elements were lost in the lacunae of 4Q491c 1 13. Wise's reconstruction of the line, made on the basis of a comparison with the Hodayot recension, is a reasonable suggestion of what it may have looked like: "(TO) [sic!] the glorious king, sing out] you righteous among the angels [of deliverance. Give praise] in the holy habitation. Hymn h[im...]."[68] Even if the lexical choices of Wise may be incorrect, we can infer that the missing words were pretty much synonymous, and the proposed sentence structures are plausible. The reconstructed phrase [מלך כבוד שירו] at the beginning of the line is based on the corresponding portion of text in 4Q427 7 i 13–14, [הכבוד] שירו למלך.[69] Wise leaves the reconstructed ישועה הללו] באלוהי uncommented, but in all likelihood באהל ("in the tent of") in 4Q427 7 i 14 is a reflection of באלוהי ("among the angels") in 4Q491c. For this reason the suggested reading ישועה is also accepted.[70] The implication of this reading is that באלוהי ישועה in 4Q491c has become באהלי ישועה in 4Q427 by way of (intended) metathesis. The consonants of אלוהים have

---

67. The phrase, "proclaim in an utterance of jubilation" ([...]ו שמיעו בהגיא רנה), in the first half of 4Q491c 1 14 appears to be the basis of 4Q427 7 i 16–17a: "[Sanctify] his name with strong lips and a mighty tongue. Lift in unison your voice. [At a]ll times, let music of joy sound (השמיעו)." The only direct lexical link is the verb שמע, but the same idea is basically being conferred. In the second half of 4Q491c 1 14, a verb is lacking before the phrase בשמחת עולמים ("in happiness forever"). The phrase may have been identical to הביעו בשמחות עולמים ("gush forth with happiness forever") in 4Q427 7 i 17b.

68. Wise, "מי כמוני באלים," 183.

69. Ibid., 193. The word order and syntax of Wise's suggested reading are a consequence of his interpretation of the big *lāmed* at the end of line 12. Wise takes it not only as a separator, but also as a preposition, which must be included in a grammatical analysis and be followed by a noun. Regardless of whether the interpretation of the *lāmed* as a preposition is correct, Wise is justified in assuming that a differing word order between the manuscripts is expectable.

70. The similar phrase א]לוהי ישע occurring in 4Q510 2 2 supports this reading. The alternative reconstruction באלוהי פלא is also likely, however, on the basis of 4Q403 1 i 36; 4Q510 1 8; 4Q511 10 7.

been joined in a different order to produce the word אהל ("tent") instead of "God," or "angels" as Wise has it. The word "tent" is not picked at random, of course, but as a parallel concept to מעון ("dwelling") found in 4Q491c 1 13 and recurring in 4Q427 7 i 14.

It is not certain that the ancient readers of 4Q491c unequivocally read the phrase באלוהי ישועה as meaning "among the angels of salvation." Perhaps they read these words as an exhortation to exult "in the God of salvation."[71] However, this will not have prevented someone reusing the text from applying other interpretations. Just as much as באלוהי may have been the exegetical basis for the introduction of tents into the later recension A, it may also have been the source of the introduction of heavenly beings with the concept of צבא עולם ("the eternal army") in 4Q427 7 i 15.

Now to the organizing of the text in 4Q427 7 i 13–15. In these lines, the lexical elements have been distributed so that they constitute a chiastic structure, which appears *not* to have existed in 4Q491c 1 13.

A1: Chant, friends (ידידים), sing to the king of glory (למלך [הכבוד)!
   B1: Rejoice in the congregation of God (בע[דת אל)!
      C1: Shout from joy in the tents of salvation (באהלי ישועה),
      C2: give praise in the abode of holiness (במעון [קודש)!
   B2: Rise up together with the eternal army (בצבא עולם)!
A2: Give greatness to our God (לאלנו), and glory to our king (למלכנו)!

The text is not divided into poetic verse lines, and therefore the chiastic structure does not immediately catch the eye. Some formal features are helpful: the fact that both A lines (unlike the B and C lines) consist of two clauses (the last of these by ellipsis); and the fact that the B and C lines all begin with a verb phrase and continue with a prepositional phrase. As we look at the content, the distinctions become clearer.

The chiastic structure suggests an approximation of the angelic sphere to the human sphere.[72] In all of the propositions, a collective audience is

---

71. Cf. *DSSSE*, 2:981.

72. Esther Chazon ("Human and Angelic Prayer," 39–43) compares human and angelic prayer as reflected in 4Q503 (Daily Prayers), 4QShirShabbath[a–e] (Songs of the Sabbath Sacrifice), and 4QBer[a–e] (Berakhot). She shows that human worshipers actually perceived themselves as worshiping together with angels. Yet, at the same time she

exhorted to praise God. The first and last pairs of propositions, the A lines, each refer to both *God* and a *praising collective*. That "king of glory" means God is indicated by the juxtaposition in A2 of "God" and "king." In A1 the audience is addressed with the vocative "friends," whereas in A2 the audience is contained in the suffixed pronouns "our." Here, the speaker clearly includes himself in the praising collective.

On the intermediary level B, the *social contexts* of the praising are mentioned. The addressee is exhorted to give praise "in the congregation of God" and "together with the eternal army."[73] Taken together, B1 and B2 imply a vertical movement upward. B1 is ambiguous as to whether the setting is a purely human one or not, but in B2 there is no doubt about the heavenly character of the praising community. Whether the text speaks of praise as something taking place simultaneously on earth and in heaven, or if an ecstatic experience of heavenly ascension is implied, is difficult to say. In any case, other Dead Sea texts employ "the congregation of God" in eschatological contexts where human beings appear in connection with heavenly beings.[74] In light of that, the expression of a present-day communion between earthly and heavenly beings is probably also a way to envision an eschatological phenomenon, apparently an eschatology already being realized in the community.[75]

Finally, level C mentions locations for the praising of God. It is to take place "in the tents of salvation" and "in the abode of holiness." This is a vision of an absolute approximation of the earthly to the heavenly world— whether experiences of ascension are implied or not.

---

detects differences in content and quality between purely angelic prayer and prayer with human participation. See also Devorah Dimant, "Men as Angels," 100–103.

73. Frennesson (*"In a Common Rejoicing,"* 61) notes that יחד in this context probably "refers to the 'togetherness' of men and angels in praise."

74. In the War Scroll, the "congregation of God" is the designation of an ensign to be brought by the eschatological congregation into their fight against the "children of darkness," represented in the text by foreign peoples (1QM IV 9). 11QMelchizedek II 10–11, citing Ps 82:1, equates "the congregation of God" with the company of "sons of God"; i.e., angelic beings. Seemingly, human beings are to receive the judgment of God in company with "sons of God" in "the congregation of God."

75. See Joseph Angel, *Otherworldly and Eschatological Priesthood*, 141–46. According to Martha Himmelfarb (*Ascent to Heaven*, 49), the members of the Dead Sea community saw themselves as righteous due to their community membership, and because of this they "claimed to live in the presence of angels."

The idea of a united human and angelic congregation is also contained in 4Q491c 1 4, in the hymn preceding the Self-Glorification Hymn.[76] Here an earthly congregation is envisioned to step out of its misery and into a heavenly existence: ועצת אביונים לעדת עולמים ("and the council of the poor ones [will be transformed] into an everlasting congregation").[77] The expression עדת עולמים does not occur elsewhere, but is in fact echoed in 4Q427 in the two central B phrases of the chiasm, בעדת אל and בצבא עולם. The idea of communion and joint worship between humans and angels is expressed clearly elsewhere in the Dead Sea Scrolls,[78] and it occurs in the Hodayot as an element that appears to be closely connected to the pessimistic anthropology of the so-called Community Hymns.[79] In other words, it is not so surprising that those responsible for recension A of the Self-Glorification Hymn and the Hymn of the Righteous wanted to highlight this particular idea. The result of their effort is an approximation of human worshipers to angels, an approximation that is also the democratization of a privilege that was usually reserved for priests.

---

76. This text belongs to the hymn preceding the Self-Glorification Hymn in 4Q491c, which is not included in any of the recension A texts.

77. In the Dead Sea Scrolls, אביונים is typically used to depict community members as a suppressed group that after a time of humiliation will "inherit the earth" or pass judgment on their opponents. This way, attention is paid both to the contemporary, miserable conditions of the group and to its eschatological redemption. 1QpHab XII 3, 6, 10 focus on the contemporary and historical conditions under which "the poor ones" live, whereas in other texts the eschatological aspects of belonging in this group are more prominent. Cf. 4QpPs[a] II 10; III 10; 1QH[a] XIII 20 (XIII 22); 1QM XI 9.

78. 4QAges of Creation pictures rather clearly the unification of human and heavenly beings in such a congregation: "In accordance with God's compassion and in accordance with his goodness and the wonder of his glory he approaches some from among the sons of the world *vacat* so that they can be considered with him in the com[munity of the g]ods to be a holy congregation in the position of eternal life and in the lot with his holy ones" (4Q181 [4QAgesCreat B] 1 3–4). The translation is taken from *DSSSE*, 1:373.

79. See, e.g., 1QH[a] XI 22–24; XII 25–26; XIV 16. Regarding these examples, see Harkins, "A New Proposal for Thinking about 1QH[a]," 115–18. For reflections on the anthropology of the so-called Community Hymns, see Berg, "Religious Epistemologies," 153–99.

6.3. A Multifaceted Identity for the Community

With a couple of exceptions, interpretations of the Self-Glorification Hymn and discussions of the speaker's identity have been conducted with little regard to the following Hymn of the Righteous. My brief analysis of the transition between the two compositions demonstrates the significance of the Hymn of the Righteous to an understanding of the Self-Glorification Hymn (and vice versa) in the context of recension A. Its authors must have felt that the compositions belonged together and interpreted them and their protagonists in light of each other. We have seen that the theme of praising with angels in the heavenly abode has been underscored through the exegetical construction of a chiastic structure with use of building blocks from 4Q491c 1 13. We have also seen that this phenomenon is displayed not as the exclusive experience of a priestly or other leadership, but as something experienced by a worshiping community. All of this suggests that some very complex processes of identification, or *suture*, may have taken place in the social context(s) where recension A was used.

Wise, who also underscores the tight connection between the two hymns in recension A, contends that the Teacher of Righteousness was the implied self-glorifying speaker. According to him, community members using the text of recension A could identify as heirs to his status.

> At the center of 1QH[a] stand at least nine hymns written by the Teacher in the first person. Once other hymns were joined to his words, whatever their source, by continuing in the first person they continued the Teacher's instruction. That, I think, was the point: To claim for later disciples the authority of the master. This move is a commonplace in charismatic religious movements. On one level, by inserting the Canticle of Michael in the 1QH[a] form of the Hodayot, the redactor meant for the reader, listener, user to think of the Teacher. The Canticle's assertions were literally true of the Teacher in a way they could not be for anyone else. But on another level, each individual believer could make them true for himself or herself by partaking in the charisma of the Teacher.[80]

Wise's argument hinges on the fact that the Self-Glorification Hymn and the Hymn of the Righteous are included in 1QHodayot[a], and in connec-

---

tion with this argumentation he ignores the occurrences outside of this particular collection. To our knowledge, 4Q427 did not include any hymns "by the Teacher," and we have seen that candidates other than the Teacher of Righteousness were available for identification.

If the shaping and consolidation of a corporate identity was a major motivation for the composition of the Hodayot collections, one should not think it was imperative for the users of the texts to acknowledge *only one figure* among others that came to their mind as suitable for identification. On the contrary: just like modern scholars, the ancient readers of the Self-Glorification Hymn must have been able to suggest several candidates suitable (or unavoidable) for identification as the speaker simply on the basis of their knowledge of the community's oral and literary traditions. This applies also to the composers, and even if they had intended one, particular identification, we know that authors cannot control readers' interpretations of their works once they have left their hands. We have to accept that the intended audience may not have had to pick one candidate; they may have had a "multiple choice."

In order to illustrate the complexity of the question, I am going to argue that even a negative identification of the speaker may have affected the identity of the audience positively. The Self-Glorification Hymn brings associations to an unpopular type like the Babylonian king derided in Isa 14:12–15:

> How you are fallen from heaven,
>   O Day Star, son of Dawn!
> How you are cut down to the ground,
>   you who laid the nations low!
> You said in your heart,
>   "I will ascend to heaven;
> I will raise my throne
>   above the stars of God;
> I will sit on the mount of assembly
>   on the heights of Zaphon;
> I will ascend to the tops of the clouds,
>   I will make myself like the Most High."
> But you are brought down to Sheol,
>   to the depths of the Pit.

This text speaks ironically of the king's self-glorification. The deep fall from the self-proclaimed elevation is not pitied but seen as the outcome of recklessness. Because of this negative outcome of the Babylonian king's self-glorification, Esther Eshel has mentioned the possibility that this or a similar individual could be alluded to in the Self-Glorification Hymn, but she instantly dismisses the idea because of the negative outcome of the self-glorification.[81]

Although the Self-Glorification Hymn brings to mind positive figures like the Teacher of Righteousness, Michael, the Prince of Light, Melchizedek, and the eschatological high priest, it is hard to disregard the hidden sting in it. Particularly when read in the light of the Hymn of the Righteous, it seems to invite multifaceted readings, involving both negative and positive aspects of the speaker. When the Self-Glorification Hymn was read in connection with the Hymn of the Righteous, its allusive potential must ultimately have been subservient to the task of defining a positive corporate identity suited to the congregation—the Dead Sea community.

The Hymn of the Righteous establishes recklessness and downfall as themes. The assertion that God has "brought down haughtiness of spirit (גבהות רוח)" (4Q427 7 ii 8) clearly formulates the opinion that pride goes before a fall. This is also the message of the only biblical text using the noun גבהות (Isa 2:11, 17). The Hymn of the Righteous displays vividly how the congregation will be lifted up, whereas the haughty will be brought down (4Q427 7 i 19–20; ii 8–10). In Ezek 31:10–14 such upward and downward movements are clearly connected with recklessness and the downfall resulting from it: recklessness is unjustified self-glorification (Ezek 31:10–11).[82]

The members of the congregation are also called "the poor ones," a designation used in other Dead Sea texts of oppressed people who, after a time of humiliation, will be lifted up and saved from destruction. In some texts, these people will even be involved in the eschatological judgment of their lofty enemies.[83] The War Scroll gives a very clear expression of this idea: "For into the hand of the oppressed [ביד אביונים] You will deliver the [ene]mies of all the lands; into the hands of those who are prostrate in the dust, in order to bring down all mighty men of the peoples, to return the

---

81. For the same reasons, Eshel ("The Identification of the 'Speaker,'" 627–28) mentions and then dismisses the possibility that Antiochus Epiphanes could be the one alluded to (see 2 Macc 9:8–10).

82. See also Job 12:15–25; 20:4–7.

83. See 4QpPs[a] II 10; 1QH[a] XII 23 (XII 22).

recompense of the wicked" (1QM XI 13–14).[84] Even if 4Q427 does not say that reckless persons are to fall by the hand of the poor ones, the designation of the congregation as "poor" in this context is an allusion to the theme of recklessness and the fact that justice will be done. This complex of ideas is also expressed in the Hebrew Bible in similar words, only not with the eschatological twist that can be found in the Dead Sea Scrolls.[85]

Thus, the Self-Glorification Hymn and the Hymn of the Righteous each in their way thematize recklessness and downfall in connection with the issue of how God sees to justice. The two compositions are complementary. By knitting them closely together, recension A emphasizes the significance of recklessness and downfall, themes that were probably present already in recension B.[86]

Taking a look at how divine knowledge is handled in the Hymn of the Righteous, we can say a little more about how the congregation of the poor ones, or the Dead Sea community, is perceived here. They clearly have access to understanding.[87] There is "no mediator" (מליץ, 4Q427 7 ii 18) and the speakers have spoken to God "and not to an interme[diary" (4Q427 7 ii 21). In the Hodayot, מליץ is used mostly by the speaker of the so-called Leader Hymns, either as a positive self-designation or as a negative characterization of opponents. Here and in other texts dealing with communion between humans and angels, it apparently functions to underscore the direct access to the divine sphere, in this case not of a single person like the Teacher of Righteousness, but of a congregation of poor ones. In 4Q427 7 i 18–20, God is blessed among other things for his marvelous "sealing up mysteries and revealing secrets" and for "tur]ning the course of those who hope for knowledge." This kind of terminology is used in 1QpHab to give the Teacher of Righteousness a special, mediating role in the management of divine knowledge, and this applies also to the speaker of some of the so-called Leader Hymns. In the Hymn of the Righteous, however, there is no such mediator, divine or human, above the

---

84. The translation is taken from *DSSSR*, 1:229. See also 1QM XI 9–10; XIV 7.

85. E.g., Hannah's song in 1 Sam 2:1–11, esp. vv. 7–8; and Ps 113:7.

86. Not enough of recension B of the Hymn of the Righteous is left to give us certainty. The reference to "the might of his hand" (להודיע ידו בכוח) in 4Q491c 1 16, however, suggests that God's lifting the poor ones and bringing down the haughty ones is also a theme in this text. Compare 4Q427 7 ii 18 (ומדיע עוז ידו) and the following couple of lines.

87. See lines ii 14–15: "we know you"; "we have insight"; "for we have seen."

congregation, which worships in communion with angels and has access to divine knowledge. The members of the congregation know God and have insight into his truth (4Q427 7 ii 13–15). The reference to God lifting up the congregation of poor ones and its access to divine knowledge suggest that the community's elevated status is mirrored in the Self-Glorification Hymn. If we disregard any touch of irony, the speaker of the Self-Glorification Hymn seems to embody the congregation as having a legitimate position in the company of angels. Any identification of the speaker with individual, literary figures known from other Dead Sea scrolls must be subservient to the identification of the congregation as the *lawfully* elevated "friend of the king."

In the Hodayot recension, the speaker of the Self-Glorification Hymn clearly represents a corporate identity. A literary figure such as the Teacher of Righteousness is an unnecessary element when we want to explain how a collective of worshipers could identify with this speaker of the Self-Glorification Hymn in a meaningful way. On the contrary, the fact that he appears to be at least as self-centered and exceptionalistic as the speaker of some of the so-called Leader Hymns encourages us to ask if the speaker of those hymns must indeed have been perceived by the worshipers as an individual positioned above them. Perhaps the speaker of the so-called Leader Hymns also represented the collective, elite ethos that we have detected in some of the so-called Community Hymns. I shall leave the question, but we should remember that the merging, or entextualization, of features originating in different contexts certainly renders it likely that such a collective, elite ethos lies behind not only individual compositions, but also the collection as a whole.

As for the collective, elite ethos, it can be recognized in both the Hymn of the Righteous and the Self-Glorification Hymn. Stegemann and, more recently, Israel Knohl have argued that the speaker in the Self-Glorification Hymn is modeled on the Suffering Servant of Second Isaiah. This has led Stegemann to see the speaker as a representative of Israel, whereas Knohl still perceives him as an individual.[88] Like this writer,

---

88. According to Knohl ("The Suffering Servant," 96), the Self-Glorification Hymn reflects Isa 53:3 on the Servant: "He was despised and rejected by others." See 4Q431 1 1–2 for partial reproductions of this place in recension A. Recension B expresses the same idea in somewhat different words, but does not seem to allude to Isaiah (see 4Q491c 1 8). Knohl (ibid., 98–99) sees Isa 52:13 as the prototype for the statement that God "raises the poor one from the dust to [the eternal height]" and elevates him "to

Knohl stresses the need to interpret the Self-Glorification Hymn and the Hymn of the Righteous as a whole, but he does not attach much importance to the collective focus of the latter. Therefore, he does not consider the possibility that the speaker might represent a plurality of members rather than an individual person. This is peculiar since he claims both that Deutero-Isaiah saw the Suffering Servant as a corporate social entity (namely, Israel) and that Daniel's depiction of the group of *maśkilim* is another corporate realization of the Suffering Servant motif. Nevertheless, when recalling how the congregation in recension A is addressed with the appellative "friends," and, thus, likened to or even identified with the speaker of the Self-Glorification Hymn, it becomes obvious that a corporate understanding of the Suffering Servant is held also by those responsible for recension A.[89]

In other words, the compositions analyzed in this chapter are also spoken on behalf of a community that sees itself as responsible for the maintenance of the covenantal people. It is remarkable that the seemingly individualistic and somewhat egocentric voice of the self-glorifying speaker could represent a collective that saw itself as a worshiping elite, but this finding is nevertheless in line with the results of the previous chapters. Furthermore, our analysis of this complex of compositions demonstrates how entextualization—the merging of existing traditions—was used creatively in order to express an adequate identity for the community. The entextualization of disparate literary units resulted in a hybrid Hodayot composition and enabled its users to vividly imagine a hybrid mode of existence in communion with angels. As regards the issue of agency, the speaker was depicted as potent and able to act in the ways of the priestly angels. In this composition, however, agency entails not so much the ability to mediate knowledge on behalf of God for the benefit of a community as it entails having access to God and being independent of mediators.

---

the clouds" (4Q427 7 ii 8–9). When Knohl avoids interpreting the "poor one" with a collective meaning, he fails to account for the speaker becoming part of the community with the angels "in the unity of the congregation" or (as he translates this passage) "in the assembly of the community."

89. See the previous footnote for further argumentation.

7

RECAPITULATION AND RECONTEXTUALIZATION:
SOCIAL AND MENTAL CONTEXTS FOR THE HODAYOT

Up to this point I have sought to disconnect some of the 1QH^a compositions from their commonly presumed social contexts. Elements from Systemic Functional Linguistics, especially transitivity analysis, have aided
me in this process. In this chapter, I shall attempt to recontextualize the
Hodayot compositions analyzed in the preceding chapters and suggest
how 1QHodayot^a may have initially functioned in its social context.

The heterogeneous character of the collection must be explained. The
prevailing idea that some compositions basically expressed leadership
issues whereas others expressed the sentiments of ordinary community
members has not been very helpful. On the contrary, this explanatory
model is weakened by the occurrence of hybrid compositions. It exagger-
ates the significance of the various compositions' original contexts to the
detriment of the originating context of the collected work. It is advisable
instead to see the various compositions as integrated through a process of
entextualization and focus upon the meaning of this process. The composers of 1QHodayot^a must have felt that the compositions included in their
work expressed *various aspects* of a shared self-understanding in the community. Among these various aspects was the sense of being endowed with
divine knowledge in spite of one's lowliness, along with having a special
assignment in the agency of God. In order to account for this process of
entextualization, I will employ Teun van Dijk's sociocognitive theory. It
seeks to explain how mental context models held by speakers and writers
contribute to the formation of discourse that actually makes sense, regardless of the fact that not every aspect of its meaning has been explicitly
expressed, but remains uninscribed.

The next step will be to concretize the social function of 1QHodayot^a,
and I argue that the owners of this collection may have seen themselves

as constituting a religious elite with special functions within the larger community. More than other people belonging to "Israel," this religious elite may have perceived itself as having a special assignment and as acting on God's behalf. This proposal, which deviates somewhat from previous attempts to explain the meaning of 1QHodayot^a, is compatible with aspects of the Dead Sea community's self-understanding as it appears in other major compositions.

Before the attempt to recontextualize the Hodayot, I shall recapitulate the findings of the preceding chapters and offer some reflections on the meaning of agency hierarchies and their relevance to the recontextualization of the compositions.

7.1. Recapitulation

In the preceding chapters I have argued that the hybrid character of the Hodayot refutes the division of texts into two main categories—one spoken by community leadership and the other spoken by rank and file members. By analyzing hybrid compositions, I have demonstrated that they, each in their own way, betray the speaker as someone who has more than one role and that he may simultaneously embody Goal and mediator of the salvific agency of God.

Hybridity results from redactional activity in the "classic" hybrids identified first by Tanzer, including 1QH^a XII 6–XIII 6. The identification between the speakers of the Self-Glorification Hymn and the Hymn of the Righteous in recension A of these compositions also exemplifies a redactionally achieved hybridity. But we have analyzed hybridity also on other levels. The text of 1QH^a VI 19–33 is a hybrid only on the level of "expectancy"; it is generally seen as a community hymn, and in light of this the speaker plays a surprisingly active role in God's agency hierarchy. Finally, on the intertextual level, the strikingly similar texts of 1QH^a XX 7–XXII 39 and 1QS IX 12–XI both designate their speaker as a *maśkîl*, and both display him as an object for God's agency (that is, as Goal in processes analyzed for transitivity). However, 1QS IX 12–XI also makes the *maśkîl* speaker an agent in the divine agency hierarchy (namely, as Actor in processes analyzed for transitivity), and this is probably the reason why the speakers of the two compositions are perceived as representing ordinary members and community leadership, respectively.

As we have seen, the so-called Leader Hymns and Community Hymns do not originate in the exact same setting, and they reflect various perspectives on divine agency. If we were to maintain not only their differing origins but were also to insist that they belonged in and mirrored different social groups (or persons) within the Dead Sea community, their juxtaposition within 1QHodayot^a should be seen primarily as some sort of authorization device. I suppose it also would be possible within this explanatory framework to search for some kind of rhetorical logic in the juxtaposing of the different groups of compositions, but this would require a relatively detailed knowledge of the rhetorical situation and staging, which we do not possess. We certainly do not know that a leader recited so-called leader hymns liturgically or otherwise in the company of "ordinary" community members. If indeed we had had that knowledge, we ought to have asked if the leader(ship)'s performance could by any chance have worked effectively. As we saw in the performance analysis of 1QH^a VI 19–33, the answer may be negative. In any case, although we must be cautious not to infer very detailed information about a rhetorical situation from a text alone, we need to assess the staging of the text and wonder if a given, imagined act of performance would have been worth the effort.

Current theories about the origins and social backgrounds of the so-called Leader and Community Hymns are difficult to sustain and do not adequately explain why these texts were grouped together so meticulously. Therefore, it is with good reason that we suggest another possibility based on new readings informed by linguistic perspectives on the relationship between text and context. The most important observations made in the previous chapters are the following:

1. Origin and use. Generally, the division of 1QHodayot^a into two main categories of compositions can be maintained, but in light of the hybridity in some of the texts, the nature of their relationship needs to be questioned. The difference between them has been correctly interpreted as resulting from difference in origin. Because of similarities between the Hodayot and wisdom texts, not least 4QInstruction and the book of Daniel, there is reason to believe that these hymns were influenced by the same or like-minded social milieus, and that they may even have originated in such a pre-Dead Sea community milieu. This finding poses a problem for the notion that the so-called Community Hymns, in the context of the Dead Sea community, belonged with the so-called "ordinary" members, defined as *other than leadership*. This is so particularly since the texts from outside the community with which they share language show a more or less distinct elite ethos. If the so-called Community Hymns

originated among a religious elite, why do they hardly show any signs of elite identity?

2. Speaker. Strategically, it makes good sense to see the speaker as *one*. Apart from (and because of) general formal, ideological, and terminological differences between the main groups of texts, the speaker also appears different in them. Throughout the history of scholarship, the speaker of the one group has been perceived as a leader or a representation of leadership, whereas the speaker of the other has not. By implication, the latter has been identified as a representative of the ordinary community members. By analyzing some of the hybrid texts for transitivity, we have seen 1) that they are permeated by the agency of God, and 2) that the speaker can hold more than one position in the divine agency hierarchy. The latter point is perhaps the most revealing, since this means, not that different speakers have their own functions in the divine agency hierarchy, but, on the contrary, that a single speaker may have a variety of functions within the agency hierarchy and thus may fill several roles at one and the same time. This change of perspective is in accord with the hybrid character of single compositions and the collection as a whole. If the heterogeneous character of 1QHodayot^a has been an obstacle to understanding its meaning *as a collection*, hybridity now seems to be a part of the solution to this problem.

It is not only the mingling of literary features from compositions not originally belonging together that brings about hybridity. Because of the way that this mingling affects the speaking "I" of the compositions, he too becomes a hybrid speaker. This has implications for how we perceive the logic behind the collection as a whole. Regardless of how individual compositions may have been used earlier in other literary and social contexts, they must have taken on new meanings when incorporated into 1QHodayot^a.

7.2. Multiple Roles in the Divine Agency

It is doubtful whether the speaker of the so-called Leader Hymns, when conducting himself as a mediating Actor in the agency of God, would represent something completely unique in the community. In all likelihood, the properties embodied in this speaker were considered typical or ideal also among the intended users of the Hodayot, so that in the course of singing or praying they would be inclined to identify themselves with the speaker. In this way, the Hodayot could function to create and maintain a corporate elite ethos, such as the one identified in the Hodayot texts that I analyzed in previous chapters.

Admittedly, it is conceivable that a single speaker, a leading figure in the community, spoke or wrote the prayers usually labelled Teacher Hymns or Leader Hymns, with his personal and perhaps even extraordinary experiences in mind. It is questionable, however, whether those compositions continued to be regarded as such by those who owned and used the written collections of Hodayot. The unique would probably be less interesting to reproduce and arrange within a large literary corpus; at least it would not continue to be perceived as unique by the users of the collection. The fact that no attempt was made to demarcate differing liturgical roles throughout 1QHodayot^a makes it likely that the patterns of agency unfolding throughout it—including the varying roles of the speaker—were not perceived as differently as one might think.

Rather than giving too much weight to the differences, therefore, we choose to focus on those elements that unify the compositions of 1QHodayot^a. In addition to the formal communicative situation (an "I" addressing God), the element of blessing and thanksgiving is a constant element that, with few exceptions, runs through the whole collection.

Considering the contents of the compositions, we can observe that the agency of God is another constant factor. Blessing and thanksgiving are offered for the marvelous agency of God. This fact is densely expressed in the introductory lines of many compositions: for example, "Be blessed, Lord, great [in pla]ns and mi[ghty] in acts, everything is your work" (1QH^a VIII 26); "I give you thanks, Lord, because you put me in the bundle of the living and have protected me from all the traps of the pit" (1QH^a X 22); "I give [you] thanks, [Lord], because you have set me at the source of streams in a dry land, at the spring of water in a parched land, in a garden watered by channels [...]" (1QH^a XVI 5–6); and further down in the text, "By my hand you have opened their spring with channels [of water...]" (1QH^a XVI 22).[1]

These three examples show different aspects of divine agency. First, God's agency affects the whole world. Second, it affects the speaker as an object of it. Third, it affects the speaker as an instrument or lower-ranking

---

1. These translations are taken from *DSSSE*, 1:181. More examples are found in 1QH^a IV 29, 38 (IV 17, 26); VI 19, 34 (VI 8, 23); X 33 (X 31); XI 20 (XI 19); XIII 22 (XIII 20); XIX 6, 18–19, 30–31 (XIX 3, 15–16, 27–28).

agent in the divine agency.[2] Nevertheless, the genre itself and the persistent blessing and thanksgiving provide a coherent acknowledgement of divine agency in its many forms. In spite of the varying perspectives and accentuations of its representations, there can be only one divine agency (in a monotheistic religion).

Someone who participated in the reading or singing of these hymns with the sentiment that he was represented by the speaking "I" would probably be capable of seeing himself in more than one role in the divine agency hierarchy. By way of suture, he could identify himself simultaneously as an agent and as an object of God's will. Thus, with the help of SFL transitivity analysis we have seen how the speaker on clause level can be described as Actor and Goal, respectively. This is strongly suggested by the occurrence of hybrid compositions such as 1QH[a] XII 6–XIII 6 and VI 19–33, where the speaker possesses different positions in the divine agency within the same composition. If my assumption is correct, how should we interpret the varying expressions of divine agency, and of human beings' participation in it?

There are different ways in which the Hodayot display the speaker in an active, mediating position in the divine agency hierarchy. The mediating function of the speaker in 1QH[a] VI 19–33 is perhaps low-key compared to the function found in some of the compositions traditionally labelled Leader Hymns (for example, cols. X and XIII). The apocalyptically flavored self-representation of the speaker in these latter texts is often taken as an expression of the special status and quality of the speaker as compared with the ordinary community members allegedly speaking the so-called Community Hymns. That is, the apocalyptic epistemology is taken as an indication of a special quality of the speaker (and of anyone in the audience who, by way of suture, would be inclined to see themselves as represented by this speaker), and as a token of the essential difference between him and the speaker(s) of the nonapocalyptic compositions. This analysis, however, is not self-evident.

Shane Berg is among those scholars who maintain that the occurrence of both an apocalyptic and a sapiential epistemology reflects a social dichotomy between leadership and ordinary members in the Dead Sea community. Yet, one of his central findings is that the sapiential epis-

---

2. For a description of agency hierarchies involving supernatural agents, see McCauley and Lawson, *Bringing Ritual to Mind*, 1–37, esp. 13–37; Lawson, "Cognition," 310–12.

temology of the so-called Community Hymns (as well as 4QInstruction and the Discourse on the Two Spirits in 1QS) is of a special kind because its wisdom is not universally acknowledgeable but is reserved for the few.[3] In this respect, then, it is similar to apocalyptic epistemology. When we see the collection of 1QHodayot[a] as an instance of entextualization, the similarity between the epistemologies becomes (at least) as significant as the differences. The exclusive access to knowledge is a common denominator and a central element in the composers' and owners' self-understandings that, in the course of the production of this composite document, was inscribed in more than just one way. At this point I would like to recall the methodological point made by Rodney Werline regarding apocalypticism in the book of Daniel, and make the claim that apocalyptic epistemology added to sapiential motifs in a given text may have served to *signal* a delimited access to the wisdom held within it.[4] George Nickelsburg has suggested this kind of function for apocalyptic features in pseudepigraphical literature, and to some extent it may explain the variety of agent types acting on behalf of God in early Jewish and Christian literature.[5] In other words, the wish to *communicate* exclusive access

---

3. Berg, "Religious Epistemologies," 154–99. The mediation of knowledge through a spirit is central to this sapiential epistemology in the so-called Community Hymns as a way to be aided to divine knowledge. "'Spirit' is presented in these hymns as the means by which this ignorance is overcome—right hearing and knowing are established by God through the holy spirit and through the granting of spirits, which may in fact be two ways of talking about the same phenomenon. The central idea here is that the human is incapable of unaided knowing, and that the initiative and effective agency that results in human knowing lies with God alone" (ibid, 182). Berg contrasts his finding of two distinct epistemologies in the Hodayot with that of Alex Jassen, who argues that the epistemology in the Hodayot at large can be classified as "sapiential revelation," and that the hymnist accordingly "is presented as a participant in a sapiential experience that identifies its practitioners as recipients of divine revelation" (*Mediating the Divine*, 367). The sapiential revelation met in the so-called Community Hymns represents a democratized form of revelation. When the so-called Leader Hymns seem to underscore the exclusive character of the revelation to the Teacher of Righteousness (who according to Jassen is the probable speaker of those compositions), this is because of the need to underscore his correct understanding of the Torah in a polemic with opponents. In other words, Jassen also interprets the differences in epistemology as resulting from the compositions' different social and situational origins within the Dead Sea community (ibid., 374, 369–71).

4. Werline, "Prayer, Politics, and Social Vision in Daniel 9," 31. See section 5.8.

5. Nickelsburg, "The Nature and Function of Revelation," 116–17.

to knowledge, rather than a general commitment to apocalyptic ideas in a group of people, may in some cases have motivated the choice of apocalyptic rather than sapiential modes of expression. This may very well have been the case in 1QHodayot[a].

Thus, the difference in epistemological strategies used within 1QHodayot[a] does not prove that the collection in the eyes of its composers reflected leadership and membership issues, respectively. The same goes for the different ways in which divine agency was represented. In the wisdom-inspired so-called Community Hymns, the idea of being elected by God for salvation occurs side by side with the idea of being responsible for maintaining the elect. These two notions are met in a seemingly balanced and unproblematic coexistence and are probably two sides of the same coin. The mediating function is not emphasized. In the so-called Leader Hymns, on the other hand, the speaker clearly expresses himself as if he has a special responsibility and sees himself as a mediator between God and people. Furthermore, he hints at situations of crisis and conflict, thus indicating that he is carrying out his duties under difficult conditions. Because of this focus on the obstacles, the speaker's special role as a mediator in God's agency has been inscribed in a more distinct manner than in the so-called Community Hymns.

Regardless of their different ways of inscribing the speaker's role, it is likely that both groups of compositions would nourish one particular self-understanding for the owners of 1QHodayot[a]. They would be encouraged to perceive themselves as having a special function in the agency of God; namely, to maintain "Israel" in a proper, covenantal relationship with him. This self-understanding is similar to the *maśkîl* identity as expressed, for example, in the book of Daniel, and is expressed in a similar language, especially in the so-called Community Hymns. The speaking "I," the most faithfully recurring element throughout the collection, can be regarded as an embodiment of such a *maśkîl* ethos. Because the Hodayot were composed and compiled under specific sociohistorical circumstances, experiential and ideational meaning specific to the owners of the Hodayot was also expressed alongside the more traditional expressions of a *maśkîl* identity. This is seen in the so-called Leader Hymns in particular. Their special emphases reflect the ongoing shaping of an identity that was specific to the Dead Sea community.

We can conceptualize this situation with use of the terms *idem* and *ipse* identity, which have been applied by Jutta Jokiranta in a discussion of whether variations between the Rule of the Community and the Damascus

Document allow us to ascribe these documents to the same social movement.[6] *Idem* identity implies a sense of sharing in a fundamental identity, or sameness, over time. *Ipse* identities take shape in people's efforts to differentiate between themselves and other people of the same *idem* identity. On the social level, this differentiation can take place as an "accentuation of in-group similarities and exaggeration of differences from out-groups."[7] Considering the community behind 1QHodayot[a] from an *emic* perspective, we may suggest that it considered itself *idem* with the wisdom circles whose ideational and literary heritage it had integrated into its own prayers. However, it created its own *ipse* identities in order to manage its own special strains and circumstances.

In sum, the literary hybridity of the speaker is rooted in one, elite, *idem* self-understanding. The mechanism of suture could have worked roughly the same way throughout the collection. An audience consisting of people who saw themselves as collectively responsible for maintaining Israel in the covenant would be inclined to see themselves as represented by the speaker. For the mechanism of suture to take place in this way, the different appearances of the speaker must not have been felt as an obstacle. At all times, the audience must have been able to see the speaker as an appropriate representation of itself. It must have been able to detect sameness across and despite variegated linguistic expressions. This is a question about how cognitive processes are involved in interpretive activity.

7.3. MENTAL MODELS AND CONTEXT MODELS

The composers of 1QHodayot[a] incorporated prayers of seemingly different origins, with diverse epistemological approaches, and varied expressions of the praying individual's relationship with God. I believe they did this in service of just one group of people and its need to build and maintain a particular, relatively uniform self-image. The question is how they could achieve this with the use of such motley components.

Teun van Dijk's theory of mental contexts and context models provides a useful framework for interpreting the hybrid character of 1QHodayot[a] and of the Hodayot in general. It is a theory about the missing link between discourse and context—or about how aspects of the social con-

---

6. Jokiranta, "An Experiment on *Idem* Identity," 309–29. For a theoretical basis she refers her readers to Paul Ricoeur, *Oneself as Another*.

7. Jokiranta, "An Experiment on *Idem* Identity," 313.

texts of texts leave their marks on the texts. According to van Dijk, it is problematic to assume that social contexts influence texts directly. Rather, we communicate our *cognitive concept* of the context. This concept is what governs our engagement in discourse. He sees contexts as "subjective participant representations of communicative situations, and not as the communicative situations themselves."[8] In what follows, I outline some of this theory's main points of relevance and then proceed to discuss its implications for the reading of 1QHodayot[a].

A basic component of the theory is that of *mental models*. People create mental models for all of their experiences (for this reason van Dijk earlier called it "situation models"). A person perceives a discourse as meaningful only if that person is able to create a mental model on the basis of it. Our daily life experiences are stored in our long-term memory with the help of mental models that structure and interpret experiences. In addition to personal experiences, we have a shared social knowledge.

We organize experience in a hierarchy of mental models. We produce mental models for small and trivial activities in our daily lives, and we join them together in larger mental models of sequences of such experiences. The mental modeling activity goes on as we produce and interpret discourse. In order to comprehend and be able to participate in communicative situations, we use a special kind of mental model that not only stores semantic knowledge but also incorporates pragmatic aspects of the communicative situation. Van Dijk calls this a *context model*. Because mental modeling in a communicative situation is a very complex task that has to take place at a rapid pace, there are a limited number of categories involved in this mental process. The categories provide a schema or script for a given situation and restrain our participation in discourse. The categories of the schema are based on general knowledge of how mental modeling works:[9]

1. Setting: time/period, space/place/environment
2. Participants (self, others)
    — Communicative roles (participation structures)
    — Social role types, membership, or identities

---

8. Van Dijk, *Discourse and Context*, 22.
9. Ibid., 76.

— Relations between participants (for example: power, friendship)
— Shared and social knowledge and beliefs
— Intentions and goals
3. Communicative and other actions

The elements of this schema are those that will typically be relevant to participants' discourse in a communicative situation. By analyzing the situation in accordance with these categories, speakers and writers are able to produce appropriate discourse.

7.3.1. K-device and the Handling of Knowledge

One aspect of this theory particularly important for the purpose of explaining the redactional logic of the Hodayot is its attention to how contextual knowledge is managed in language and discourse. Van Dijk introduces the technical term "K-device" for this activity. The K-device is about how and why humans represent or leave out different kinds of knowledge in discourse based on a "calculation" of how much coparticipants know:

> The overall epistemic strategy in discourse production is that shared knowledge need not be expressed, and hence may remain implicit—either because the recipient is believed to have such knowledge already, or because the recipient is assumed to be able to infer such knowledge from already existing knowledge.[10]

I shall reproduce van Dijk's thoughts about knowledge types and K-devices in order to concretize what this means.[11]

Van Dijk operates with three different types of knowledge. Two of these, *personal knowledge* and *specific social knowledge*, deal with specific events and their mental models. A person may have experienced something (for example, a conflict at work), which he recounts to his wife at home. His personal knowledge now becomes a shared or interpersonal knowledge, a common ground. A few weeks later, he experiences something related to the first situation. He knows that he has told his wife (he does this by remembering his context model for that situation), but he

---

10. Ibid., 83.
11. Ibid., 84–88.

cannot be certain that she remembers. He can handle this problem by assuming that his recipient knows what he told her before (K-device 1). He can either be silent about it or remind her: "You remember I told you…" Next, he will assume she does *not* know about the personal knowledge that he has acquired since his last communication with her (K-device 2).

Specific social knowledge also deals with knowledge of specific events, but it is shared by people who do not know each other. Van Dijk uses the news reporter as an example. When he writes about new turns in a pending case, he cannot know if his readers have read the previous articles or if they have their knowledge of the case from other media. Here, too, hypothesizing is necessary. He can assume that recipients know what he (that is, the newspaper) told them before (K-device 3). Management of personal and specific social knowledge involves the use of dynamic context models where "'previous discourse' (propositions, acts, style etc.) becomes a condition for the current state of the context."[12]

The situation is different for *general sociocultural knowledge* because it does not deal with specific events, but "general world knowledge" that is needed in order to understand events. If a journalist reports on casualties in the Iraq war, he must presuppose that his audience knows about the war, what an army is, and so forth. The strategy needed is to assume that recipients have the same sociocultural knowledge as him (K-device 4). This strategy is adequate if the speaker or writer communicates in a so-called *epistemic community*, namely, a group of people sharing background, qualifications, or premises because they belong to the same nation, social class, profession, and so forth.[13]

The point of all this is that "speakers/writers are (mentally) able to represent the knowledge of their recipients in their context models of discourse production."[14] This ability affects their participation in written and spoken discourse and therefore should be taken into account by interpreters of discourse. This means that the human ability to "represent the

---

12. Ibid., 85.

13. Finally, a meta-strategy, K-device 5, can be formulated for overlapping groups of epistemic communities; e.g., two different Western nationalities, the members of which will have much common knowledge on Western culture. Here one can assume that "recipients share the knowledge of all the more inclusive epistemic communities of which they are members" (ibid., 88).

14. Ibid., 87.

knowledge of the recipients" in context models also has implications for how we interpret 1QHodayot[a] and the redactional logic behind it.

7.3.2. A First Attempt at Recontextualization

Context models and K-devices can be of great value in our understanding of the redactional logic behind 1QHodayot[a]. On the basis of what I have concluded above from the textual analyses, I can demonstrate how context models, as interface between text and communicative situation, open up a space where we can hypothesize about the meaning of juxtaposing the so-called Community and Leader Hymns. Doing this, I attempt to keep the promise I made in the introduction to recontextualize compositions that I previously sought to decontextualize by using the methods of Systemic Functional Linguistics. The following two observations constitute the starting point of this endeavor.

First, each composition and the collection as a whole express acknowledgement of divine agency. Insofar as the speaker has a position in this hierarchy, this position is acknowledged as well. This applies regardless that the speaker may hold more than one position, both in the collection as a whole and within individual compositions.

Second, the so-called Community Hymns represent wisdom traditions and a *maśkîl* ethos that do not belong strictly to the Dead Sea community, but originate in wider circles of the Jewish community. For this reason, we can assume that these compositions were either *adopted* from such wisdom traditions or they were *adaptations* of them. In either case, they were representations of wider wisdom circles and probably preceded original productions by the Dead Sea community members, such as the so-called Leader Hymns. This basic notion has a bearing on how I am going to discuss 1QHodayot[a] as a product of context models and K-devices.

The so-called Community Hymns represent what van Dijk labels an "epistemic community," and I dare say that this is a community of wise people, probably educated people with an awareness of belonging to a spiritual elite. The integration of this kind of literature in the Dead Sea Scrolls implies that the owners of the scrolls identified to some extent with such an elite community. As indicated in 4QInstruction, 1QS IX 12–XI, and 1QH[a] VI 19–33, to belong to such a community involved the perception of oneself as represented on more than one level in the divine agency hierarchy. There was a pronounced sense of sharing a special responsibility in the agency. At the same time, however, nothing hindered community members from seeing themselves simultaneously as the objects of this agency.

These two positions, or identities, needed not be visually present in every composition. We have seen that the speaker of 1QHᵃ XX 7–XXII 39 is solely represented as an object (Goal in SFL terminology). By way of comparison with 1QS IX 12–XI, we can assume that a mediator identity is also implied in the Hodayot text. If we apply elements from the context schema, we can say that the communicative role of the speaker is that of a subordinate addressing God, but with regard to social roles he conceptualizes himself not only as someone who has been chosen by God (Goal), but also as someone who has a special responsibility to sustain the people of God (Actor). It is in this dual role that he addresses God, because a dual (potentially multiple) identity is included in his context model. The speaker has of course become a literary figure, so perhaps we should rather say that members of the ideal audience who saw themselves as represented by the speaker would take on the *idem* identity of the religious elite contained in the context model, which included the social roles of both object and agent in the agency of God.

As for the omission of knowledge that is included in the mental model of the text, it is the result of a K-device. The author assumes that recipients of the speaker's communication (including God as formal addressee and the ideal human audience) share the omitted sociocultural knowledge with him. In this particular case, the knowledge of the speaker's elevated, mediating position in the divine agency hierarchy has been omitted because it was assumed to be known. It is reasonable to infer that when using the text in a familiar way, suture would work in such a way that community members saw themselves in the same elevated position as the speaker.

At this point, I would like to propose that this shared knowledge of the context model informed and governed the juxtaposition of the so-called Community Hymns to the so-called Leader Hymns. In all likelihood, the latter group of compositions was even composed under the impression of the former. The composers or compilers of 1QHodayotᵃ, who may also have been the composers of the so-called Leader Hymns, saw themselves as included in the elite ethos of the so-called Community Hymns. They were members of a rather limited community that was at odds with religious authorities in Jerusalem, and both the so-called Leader Hymns and other texts produced by the Dead Sea community reveal a sense of conflict and distress. It seems safe to say that this community was different from the wider wisdom circles from which it had inherited its wisdom compositions. Yet, the community that authored the collection seems to have identified itself as such an elite *maśkîl* community. Furthermore, it seems to have emphasized the aspects of this *maśkîl* identity that they found particularly important or relevant; namely, their identity as mediators or actors in the divine agency.

On the practical level of discourse, the authors' management of the ideal recipients' knowledge may have left its mark in various ways. Leaving out knowledge is one such device; retrieving knowledge is another. We have considered the possibility that the omission of one agency role in some but not all of the wisdom-influenced compositions is the result of such a K-device.

Retrieval of knowledge in 1QH^a XII 6–XIII 6 betrays a context model in which the speaker has an elevated mediator position in the agency of God. Toward the end of the dramatic first section, which is the reason for defining the whole composition as a leader hymn, the author uses main clauses to present the fact that the agency of God works *through* the speaker. We should pay particular attention to the use of the verb גבר in the *hiphil*, which is relatively rare in the Dead Sea Scrolls and hardly seen in the Hebrew Bible;[15] it expresses how the agency of God works through the speaker.

> Through me you have enlightened the face of the many and you have shown endless strength (ותגבר עד לאין מספר). For you have let me know your wonderful secrets and in your wonderful council you have *shown strength in me* (הגברתה עמדי) and you have worked wonders in the presence of the many for the sake of your glory and to make known your mighty deeds (גבורותיכה) to all of the living. (1QH^a XII 28–30)

This is the first time that the speaker of this composition presents his elevated position in the divine agency as main (new) information in a main clause. However, he has already indicated this knowledge through a couple of prepositional phrases with *hiphil* infinitives of גבר: "They do not appreciate me *when you show your strength through me*" (בהגבירכה בי).[16] This kind of presentation of circumstantial information is a typical way of retrieving knowledge assumed by the speaker to be known by his recipients.

---

15. See Ps 12:5; Dan 9:27. The latter also shares the combination of this form of גבר with the noun רבים. The thematic link is not strong, however.
16. 1QH^a XII 9. There is a very similar formulation in line 24.

The recipients may possess this retrieved knowledge beforehand either because they have been presented to it earlier in the discourse or because it is part of the social knowledge of their epistemic community. In this particular case, both eventualities apply.

The fact that God shows his strength through the speaker has not been stated earlier in this composition. However, it has been indicated as circumstantial information earlier in 1QHodayot[a]. Prepositional phrases with *hiphil* infinitives of גבר occur several times within the so-called Leader Hymns to recollect how God shows his strength through the speaker (1QH[a] IX 36/4QpapH[f] 2 1; 1QH[a] X 26; XIII 17, 27). In the text of col. X, the speaker persistently displays himself as part of the divine agency, only in other words.[17] In fact, the speaker's elevated position in the divine agency hierarchy seems to be the main concern of that composition. In that sense, the knowledge of it has been presented before it is retrieved in 1QH[a] XII 9 and 24.

However, we do not find a clear and unequivocal presentation of the speaker's elevated position in the divine agency hierarchy until the very first retrieval of it in 1QH[a] IX 36—unless we acknowledge that 1QH[a] VI 19–33 represents this very opinion in its own way, as argued in chapter 3. The composition of 1QH[a] IX 2–X 4 (IX 3–X 2/ *I 1–39*) generally has the wisdom language so typical of the so-called Community Hymns and is usually designated as such.[18] It is placed just before the group of (for the most part) Leader Hymns, and some scholars see it as a transitional hymn, introducing the collection of so-called Leader or Teacher Hymns.[19] To Michael Douglas, its particular use of גבר in 1QH[a] IX 36 is a central

---

17. The column consists of two compositions with a similar focus, 1QH[a] X 5–21 and X 22–XI 5.

18. See Tanzer, "The Sages at Qumran," 32–36.

19. See Douglas, "The Teacher Hymn Hypothesis Revisited," 256–57; Kim, "Authorizing Interpretation," 35; Schuller, "The Cave 4 Hodayot Manuscripts," 145. Tanzer remarks that, form-critically, a shift occurs toward the end of the composition, and it seems to puzzle her: "While the Hodayot share some of the formal characteristics of thanksgiving psalms and hymns, their use in the Qumran community is not completely clear. Certainly, the movement of this composition from the God who has created and ordered this world by His Wisdom and foreknowledge of absolutely everything—to the exhortations to the wise to make an end of wickedness and lead upright lives, suggests that this composition is intended as much for instruction to the wise as it is for the praise of God" ("The Sages at Qumran," 35). Perhaps this change is indeed a signal of the transition to the so-called Leader Hymns collection.

argument in favor of this opinion, exactly because it is a feature generally occurring in the so-called Leader Hymns. In fact, Douglas sees in
בהגבירכה בי and its equivalent expressions the idiom of the same author
and a signature phrase of the collection of so-called Leader Hymns.

The very first instance of retrieved knowledge of the speaker's elevated
position in the agency hierarchy by way of גבר occurs at the front edge
of the so-called Leader Hymns collection *before* the knowledge of this
position has been elaborated in a significant way that any scholar would
agree on. It is conceivable that such poignant expressions of the speaker's
elevated position, like those of col. X, occurred in parts of the first nine
columns now lost, but the style of the compositions in question does not
render this very likely. A much more compelling explanation is that the
authors of the Community Hymns and the redactors of 1QHodayot[a] made
use of K-device 4 and assumed that their ideal audience would find expressions about the speaker's elevated position appropriate simply because it
was in agreement with their sociocultural knowledge.

The details of this argument need to be examined. I shall see to this
by sketching a tentative scenario for the editorial process. First, the Dead
Sea community possessed the so-called Community Hymns and cognate
wisdom literature, and its members shared the sociocultural knowledge
that this literature expressed a collective, elite (*maśkîl*) ethos involving a
responsibility to maintain the covenant of Israel.

Second, the members identified with this ethos, and, seeing the
speaker of the hymns as a representative of this ethos, they also saw him
as a representative of themselves. This is how suture works. The speaker
mostly represented the community members as the objects of God's
agency. However, the identification also involved an awareness of responsibility for the covenant, both within the community and on behalf of the
covenantal people at large. It is especially with regard to the responsibility for the community at large that this elite attitude surfaces in the texts.
However, it remains mostly implicit.

Third, because the community found itself in a situation of tension and
conflict with outsiders (or former fellow members), community members
felt an urge to distinguish themselves and to win the exclusive right to the
elite ethos with which they identified. This resulted in new compositions
that were juxtaposed to the former—in some instances compositions were
merged and became hybrids.

Because of the ongoing rhetorical situation, of which we know very
little, two major changes occurred in these compositions as compared with

the former. As a device to show a restricted access to divine knowledge, apocalyptic epistemology was added to the well-known wisdom episte-mology. In this way, the community sought to authorize its own claim for the elite *maśkîl* ethos.[20] The other major change was the accentuation of an aspect that was clearly present but mostly implicit in the so-called Community Hymns: the speaker's and thus the community members' ele-vated status in the divine agency hierarchy. I suggest that the main reason for putting so much stress on this aspect was that the community indeed struggled for the right to fulfil its obligations toward the covenant—obli-gations embedded in its elite ethos and therefore deeply rooted in the members' sense of identity.

In conclusion, those who edited 1QHodayot[a] on behalf of the Dead Sea community retrieved and emphasized the speaker's elevated position in the divine agency hierarchy out of the need to create an object of identi-fication that would help the community maintain a sense of authority and legitimacy as the rightful keeper of the one covenant. This could be done by retrieving and attaching weight to knowledge that was assumed to be known by the ideal audience of community members.

At this point, I have accomplished the first and major step in my effort to recontextualize 1QHodayot[a]. Using the concepts of context model and K-device I have provided an explanation for the heterogeneous and hybrid nature of this collection of prayers. However, I still have to assess the compatibility of this model with ideas expressed in other parts of the Dead Sea community's literature. We may want to ask, for instance, if the members of the community saw themselves as *maśkîlîm*, and who, then, were the *rabbîm*?

7.4. MORE RECONTEXTUALIZATION

I have now attempted to recontextualize 1QHodayot[a] with the help of the ideas of mental models and context models. I would like to end this endeavor by taking a brief look at some other Dead Sea texts and iden-tity markers appearing in them—as they have recently been interpreted by some scholars. I shall do this with an eye to the reinterpreted *maśkîl* ethos that has been found embedded in the collection. It was inherited from

---

20. See Nickelsburg ("The Nature and Function of Revelation," 116–17) on this function of apocalyptic motives.

the wider Jewish community and concerned itself with the maintenance of Israel. How could this *maśkîl* ethos continue to work within the confines of the Dead Sea community? Do we find traces of the *maśkîl* ethos and mediating function in other major Dead Sea texts? Did the agency of God only work within the confines of the community or did it have wider implications? It is beyond the scope of this book to provide a full discussion of these questions. A brief outline of some recently presented options will have to suffice.

It is commonplace to talk about the exclusivist tendencies of the Dead Sea literature, and about the unwillingness of its members to associate with outsiders.[21] The conventional division of Hodayot compositions into so-called Leader Hymns and Community Hymns fits well into this framework because it sees the Hodayot as a collection that concerns purely internal issues such as the members' relationship to God and to their communal leadership. However, since we have seen that the compositions from both main groups are more or less explicitly preoccupied with issues pertaining to the speaker's mediating function, we need to ask who the object of the mediating activity is; in other words, who the object of the divine agency is. If the ordinary member is not only an object of God's salvific agency but also a mediator of it, who is meant to benefit from his mediating activity—community members only or outsiders as well?

To a large extent, our answer to this question depends on whether and how we define the Dead Sea community. There is a tendency among scholars to soften the Weberian Church-sect dichotomy and ask, for instance, *to what degree* the Dead Sea community can be defined as sectarian, or to what degree it may or must have associated with outsiders.[22]

---

21. For instance, Schiffman writes: "The Qumran Zadokites gradually developed the sectarian mentality of the despised, rejected, and abandoned outcast. Accordingly, they began to look upon themselves as the true Israel, condemning and despising all others" (*Reclaiming the Dead Sea Scrolls*, 88–89). See also Vermes (*The Dead Sea Scrolls: Qumran in Perspective*, 99), who equates the "men of the pit," with whom no friendly relations were to be found, with "everyone outside the sect."

22. See Wassen and Jokiranta, "Groups in Tension," 205–45; Schofield, "Between Center and Periphery," 330–50. Schofield argues that dialogue and cultural exchange with the surrounding community was vital: "Certainly the communities [sic] behind the Scrolls diverged from the powers that were in the Temple precinct, but an unequal emphasis has been placed on the 'diverging' or 'isolating' aspects of the *Yaḥad* movement. One needs to read relatively few of their texts to see that they established their own identity in two primary ways: both by identifying with their greater Jewish heri-

Stegemann has argued that the Teacher of Righteousness was concerned to reach not only community members, but also all Israel. In fact,
he believes that the Teacher of Righteousness saw the Yaḥad as "a con-
federation of all existing Jewish groups," and that although he sought to
include all Israel, "it was granted that Israel should be represented by a
religious body conforming to God's will as revealed by Moses on Mount
Sinai. Therefore the Yaḥad could be regarded not only as an adequate form
of organization, but also as the unique representative of the *berit El* on
earth."[23] Although I find Stegemann's argument rather speculative, I am
inclined to think he may be right in these conclusions and in his critique of
theories that see the Dead Sea community as a self-contained, geographi-
cally and demographically limited phenomenon.[24]

Recently, Gudrun Holtz has argued that inclusivist tendencies exist
alongside exclusivist tendencies in several of the major Dead Sea scrolls.
By inclusivist tendencies she means an "attempt on the part of the community to reach out beyond its own confines and to open up to the outside
world."[25] Of special interest is her point that the Damascus Document tradition has a "pan-Israelite" perspective. This implies both an eschatological hope for the salvation of all Israel and the idea that all Israel is obliged
to keep the law according to the Dead Sea community's interpretation
of it.[26] Another major point is that the Serekh Hayaḥad tradition, which

---

tage and by simultaneously setting up boundary markers against it, markers which
established themselves as foils to the Jewish 'other' … [B]ut embedded in their renun-
ciation of the Jerusalem elite, the conversation, whether real or imagined, persisted"
(ibid., 335). See also Elgvin, "The Yaḥad Is More than Qumran," 273–79. Based on
a survey of paleographical, literary, and archaeological data, Elgvin argues that the
owners of the Dead Sea Scrolls, the Yaḥad, constituted a historically and geographi-
cally widespread movement, influenced by contemporary literature produced in other
milieus and probably exerting some influence on later, non-Yaḥad literature.

23. Stegemann, "The Qumran Essenes," 155–56.

24. Stegemann speculates that the Teacher of Righteousness must be the unnamed
high priest in office from 159 BCE to the rise of the Maccabean high priest Jonathan in
152 BCE. He connects this idea and his conviction that the author of the Hodayot's so-
called Leader Hymns "must have been a high priest because of his self-consciousness
and because of the special authority claimed by him." See ibid., 148–54, esp. 149 n. 140.

25. Holtz, "Inclusivism at Qumran," 25.

26. Ibid., 37–42. See in particular CD XV 5–XVI 6, talking about the covenant
that applies to "all Israel." Here, the oath to be taken upon admission into the community is equated with "the oath of the covenant which Moses established with Israel"
(CD XV 8–9). And thus, according to Holtz, the mention of the oath establishes not

according to Holtz is the only tradition within the Dead Sea literature that is decidedly community centered, does not seek isolation from other Jews in general, but from groups that may have posed a direct threat to the existence of the Dead Sea community: apostates, former members that have for some reason been expelled, and people who represent competing viewpoints and movements. This picture, argues Holtz, is confirmed within the legal material.[27]

Furthermore, several eschatological texts hold a universalistic perspective and anticipate that humanity as such or all creation will acknowledge God's greatness and righteousness.[28] Holtz reckons 1QH[a] XIV 13–16, XIX 18–30 (esp. XIX 27), and VII 30–34 among these texts. I am not convinced that these texts display a distinct soteriological interest on behalf of creation and humanity as Holtz seems to think, but it is possible. The texts mentioned here are all among the so-called Community Hymns and may have been produced outside of the Dead Sea community. All the same, they were incorporated into the collection 1QHodayot[a], and their viewpoints must, at least to some degree, have appeared appealing, relevant, and representative of community opinions.[29]

All of Holtz's findings point to the need to qualify the exclusivist tendencies that we see in the Dead Sea Scrolls. The community's resistance

---

only "the continuity between the two covenants," but also "the pan-Israelite character of the present covenant" (38–39). This is confirmed by the quotation of Exod 34:27 in 4QD[f] 4 ii 1–3//CD XVI 1, substituting כול ישראל for ישראל as if to underscore inclusivist aspects. Saying that the covenant in CD represents a change from an ethnic to a priestly covenant "which ultimately creates a boundary within Israel," Ellen Christiansen apparently attaches importance to its exclusivist aspects ("The Consciousness of Belonging to God's Covenant," 85). However, she demonstrates that law obedience is the primary condition of belonging to the covenant. This interpretation also seems to cover the potential inclusion of newcomers from "ethnic Israel" (ibid., 76–85).

27. E.g., 1QS V 10–12; VII 23–35; CD XX 3–8. In 1QSa and the early strata of the Serekh Hayaḥad, salvation seems to be for outsiders as well (Holtz, "Inclusivism at Qumran," 44–52). See also Hempel, "Maskil(im) and Rabbim," 152–55.

28. Holtz ("Inclusivism at Qumran," 33) sees inclusivist eschatological tendencies in the following texts covering several literary genres: 4QpNah; 4QFlor; 1QS; 1QSa; 1QM (esp. XI 13–15); 4QMMT; 1QSb; 1QH[a]; 4QSM 8 1–11. Based on legal material and rules regulating the conduct of community members, she furthermore thinks that the Damascus Document tradition held a pan-Israelite, inclusivist perspective.

29. Ibid., 34. A universalistic perspective is also apparent in the so-called leader hymn 1QH[a] XII 30 in the remark that God makes known his "mighty deeds to all of the living."

seems to be directed primarily against people in direct opposition to or in competition with the community, as well as apostates and expelled members. This tendency is also apparent in the Hodayot. I would like to recall the four-party structure of the dramatic section running through most of 1QH^a XII. Here, the people of God ("your people") clearly consists of those taught by the speaker's opponents, but the speaker displays no animosity between this people and himself. On the contrary, the people of God is presented as victimized by the speaker's opponents who flatter and misguide its members, seeking to change the law that God has engraved into the speaker's heart "in order to watch their mistake: Acting foolishly at their festivals and getting caught in their nets" (1QH^a XII 10–13).[30] There is no direct and unequivocal evidence that the redactors or authors of the Hodayot hoped for admission of new members from "the people of God" in contemporary or eschatological times, as in some other Dead Sea texts.[31] However, the drama in 1QH^a XII 7–30 with its outline of true and false teachings, does imply a potential recruitment from the outside. It is doubtful that such recruitment was imagined to include ordinary, illiterate people from the "masses." It is rather to be imagined that the community hoped to include other people from the elite, informed adherents to adversaries of the community.

In conclusion, it seems fair to say that God's agency, as represented in the Hodayot, was intended not only for current members of the Dead Sea community. Rather, there was an interest in expansion, which would come

---

30. 1QH^a XII 7–30 is the Hodayot section most preoccupied with the people of God: "And those who interpret deceitfully [have led] them astray, so that they perish unknowingly" (XII 8). "And [at] a st[ammering] language and an alien tongue they speak to your people to belie all their deeds by way of fraud" (XII 17–18). Besides col. XII, see X 20–21 for the same idea. In XIV 9–11, survivors among the people of God (line 11), in principle at least, have the opportunity to repent and eventually become part of the council of God (line 13). It is hard to tell whether only present members of the community are included in this group of survivors or potential repenters are counted as well. The damaged text of XXIV 15 could also contain a not so negative evaluation of the people of God, but this is very uncertain. This instance of עמכה should definitely be translated "your people" and not "with you," as suggested in Schuller and Stegemann (*1QHodayot^a* [DJD XL], 288), because this reading implies that the preceding *hiphil* infinitive be read as a *niphal*.

31. Holtz correctly suggests that the following texts do: 4QMMT^e 11–13 4–5; 1QSa 1:1; 4QpNah 3–4 iii 3–5; 4QFlor 1:10–13. For details and arguments, see Holtz, "Inclusivism at Qumran," 26–27.

about through the agency of community members. God's agency, mediated by community members, thus had both fellow members and prospective members as its goal.

8
Conclusions

This book is basically a study of how we can, or cannot, access the contexts of ancient texts—in this case 1QHodayot[a]. Textual interpretation is in part a question of understanding the meaning of a text in light of its sociohistorical circumstances. More specifically, I have attempted to reach a meaningful explanation for the heterogeneous character of 1QHodayot[a]. So far, explanations have been based on the notion that differences between the so-called Leader Hymns and the so-called Community Hymns mirror a social dichotomy, and that the one group of hymns was spoken by the community leadership, whereas the other was spoken by ordinary community members. This viewpoint is difficult to sustain, however, in light of the fact that some of the compositions are hybrids that mix significant properties of the two main compositional categories. I have presented close textual analyses of four Hodayot compositions which, in one way or another, show signs of hybridity. This approach has been based on the idea that hybridity betrays how the composers or compilers merged texts of different origins and appearances, because in their eyes they had common denominators that rendered such activity and its outcome—the particular compilation of texts in 1QHodayot[a]—meaningful.

The collection as such has been treated as the result of a process of entextualization. From this theoretical starting point, the natural way of explanation is that texts of different origins had been juxtaposed simply because they were felt to express the self-understanding and situation of just one group of people. Whichever original context the individual compositions had, they were now brought into a (more or less) different literary and sociohistorical context. It is this context that provides the true original context of the collection as such, and the better hypothetical context for interpretations of it. It was not only the inscribed and emphasized information of the individual compositions that mattered to the people responsible for the collection. In the process of entextualization, they must have activated their knowledge and ideas of the compositions' significance—of their typical users and of their common usages. In other words, the various compositions' mute, evocative meanings, which are mostly inaccessible to modern scholars, must have mattered as well.

At the level of inscribed meaning, common denominators were provisionally sought in formal features running throughout the composition, the superscriptions containing formulas of blessing and thanksgiving as well as the recurring "I" of the speaker. From this point of view the speaker, who on the surface appears to be different in the two main categories of compositions, is in fact made into a hybrid speaker through the merging of the categories.

In the introduction, I noted that the speaker in some of the so-called Leader Hymns appears to have the role of a mediator in the agency of God. This is a feature that distinguishes the Hodayot from biblical psalms, where the speaker consistently appears to be the object of God's agency. I suggested that this feature is also present, more subtly however, in compositions not normally designated as leader hymns. This is then a recurring feature that has not always been emphasized, but is still inscribed, or indexed, outside of the so-called Leader Hymns. As a recurring feature, it can also be seen as a common denominator.

Methodologically, a number of approaches have been employed in the textual analyses. SFL transitivity analysis is the method most consistently used in this study. It has the advantage that it can help in retrieving more information from individual clauses than ordinary, grammatical analysis. This is beneficial especially in damaged or fragmentary texts, where analysis of information structures and rhetorical arguments is difficult to undertake. More importantly, however, the use of this method has enabled descriptions of what goes on in the texts without too much recourse to terminology stemming from our preconceptions of their historical and social background. Thus, in some of the compositions I found that the speaker, in fact, expresses himself as someone who is at the bottom of the agency hierarchy, the object of God's agency (that is, a Goal in material processes analyzed for transitivity according to SFL analysis) and at the same time as someone slightly elevated, a mediating actor (that is, an Actor in SFL terminology). In other words, within the framework of this agency hierarchy the speaker can be perceived as having multiple roles in the divine agency. Insofar as members of the ideal audience identified themselves with the speaker, they could accordingly see themselves, too, as having multiple roles in the agency of God.

By the same token, the whole compilation of texts could express multiple roles within the divine agency and therefore encompass several simultaneous identities that the members of the Dead Sea community may have assumed. The use of transitivity analysis and the recognition of a divine agency hierarchy, coupled with an awareness of the genre of prayer, have provided an opportunity for a "reality check." When embedded in prayers of thanksgiving and blessing, the divine agency is acknowledged by anyone speaking them in the act of prayer, and so are the different roles allotted to the praying person within this agency. Seen from this perspective, there is no need for sociohistorical categories like "leaders" and "ordinary members" to explain the juxtaposition of the different categories of compositions in 1QHodayot^a. Furthermore, since the dichotomy of leadership vis-à-vis ordinary membership has been found not to explain adequately the *merging* of different compositions and their speaking voices, there is good reason to leave those well-known categories behind.

As genres are conventional ways of achieving goals in specific social situations, awareness of genre is more important to the way we relate text to context than one might think when looking back on previous interpretations of the Hodayot. For instance, when Hodayot compositions are judged to be acts of leadership, their rhetorical potential is usually prioritized over their edificatory potential, but this approach is overly instrumental. By way of performance analysis of 1QH^a VI 19–33, I have attended to the problem of how we can reasonably infer sociohistorical and rhetorical situations from the texts. The Dead Sea community's general knowledge of the use of hymns and prayers in a ritual context will have rendered some meanings more appropriate in the eyes of performance participants. This applies not least to the performer, who to some extent controlled the means and goals of the performance. Given that he felt his thanksgiving was an act of communion with God, could he simultaneously perform it to display the legitimacy of his leadership—and still be a man of integrity? Aided by performativity analysis, I have shown that this may have been difficult, and is less likely.

Transitivity analysis shows that the agency of God is a major interest in three of the texts studied. The texts of 1QH^a VI 19–33 and XII 6–XIII 6, traditionally considered a community hymn and leader hymn respectively, each in their own way communicate that the agency of God works *through* *the speaker*. However, in both texts the speaker is also made into an object,

a Goal for the agency of God. No such mixing of roles can be detected
by transitivity analysis in the so-called community hymn of 1QH[a] XX 7–
XXII 39; the speaker is solely made a Goal for the agency of God. This does
not mean that no other role performance is in sight. The speaker in this
text identifies himself as a *maśkîl*, a concept having various meanings in
the literature of the Second Temple period, including the Dead Sea Scrolls.
Because of its considerable resemblances with the concluding hymn of the
maśkîl in 1QS X–XI, it is argued that a similarly transitive concept of a
maśkîl as someone through whom the agency of God works also underlies
the text of 1QH[a] XX 7–XXII 39. As regards these three texts analyzed for
transitivity, then, it has been argued that they are all spoken by someone
who simultaneously identifies himself as an object of God's salvific agency
and as someone playing a part in the unfolding of this agency.
    The fourth Hodayot text analyzed consists of two rather anomalous
compositions that in fact originated in a different literary setting. The singular speaker of the Self-Glorification Hymn boasts and equates himself
with angels, thus giving the impression that he is of high rank, comparable
in status to (for example) the high priest as met in other Dead Sea literature. The following Hymn of the Righteous is spoken in part *to*, in part *by*,
a collective of worshipers. By the use of different literary devices the two
texts are knitted closely together, and here, too, the end result is the blend-
ing of the two apparently very different speakers and their properties. In
this composition, however, agency entails not so much the ability to mediate knowledge on behalf of God for the benefit of a community as it entails
having access to God and being independent of mediators.
    Detached readings of the texts have not been ends in themselves, as
they have been meant to suggest a recontextualization. In various ways
a *maśkîl* ethos met elsewhere in texts originating inside and outside the
Dead Sea literature has displayed itself in the analyzed texts: in 1QH[a] XX
7–XXII 39 in the form of the speaker's self-designation as a *maśkîl* and in
the similarities with another Dead Sea text that clearly thematizes the role
and duties of a *maśkîl*; and in 1QH[a] XII 6–XIII 6 in the form of language
and structures shared with Dan 11 on the *maśkîlîm*. This elite ethos is not
one of institutional leadership, but rather an ethos of a corporate identity
involving a responsibility to maintain the people of God in a proper covenantal relationship. In this way, both leadership and membership issues
pertain to any person seeing himself as a *maśkîl*, and they are not in conflict with one another when met in a prayer spoken by and representing
someone identifying as such.

In order to explain the heterogeneous character of the Hodayot from this perspective, I have applied the sociocognitive concept of context models (chapter 7). It entails that texts are not products of social contexts. Rather, they are products of writers' mental conceptions of their contexts, and these mental conceptions include the pragmatic aspects of the communication. The so-called Community Hymns, with their wisdom language and sapiential epistemology, are generally closer to the origin of the *maśkîl* ethos than the apocalyptically flavored, so-called Leader Hymns. In the minds of their owners, these compositions probably entailed aspects of leadership and responsibility for the covenantal people, even if this was not stated explicitly in all of them. This was part of the uninscribed, evocative meaning that these texts had in the Dead Sea community. Because of how leadership issues are inscribed and even stressed in the so-called Leader Hymns, we can surmise that they were composed and juxtaposed to the Community Hymns in an effort to attach weight to these implicit aspects of corporate leadership and responsibility—perhaps in a situation where this identity was under pressure. Their apocalyptically flavored and exclusivist epistemology may result from a need to tie the highly regarded *maśkîl* ethos strictly to the Dead Sea community and render this group of people the only legitimate guardian of the covenant.

It was necessary to investigate how the sociocultural knowledge of the *maśkîl* and the covenant could be managed at the level of the text. I exemplified this by demonstrating how some of the typical terminology of the so-called Leader Hymns may in effect have been accentuations of knowledge that was implied in the preceding so-called Community Hymns, at least in the eyes of community members. This may have worked out because the composers of 1QHodayot[a] were able to use K-devices—namely, the leaving out of knowledge that they presumed to be known by the ideal audience, and the retrieving of shared knowledge when this was deemed beneficial. Because of this cognitive activity, heterogeneity was not a problem to the users of 1QHodayot[a].

As for the range of the *maśkîl*'s responsibility in the divine agency, this is debatable. The Hodayot texts are usually seen as products of the Dead Sea community and are thought to have a narrow, "sectarian" outlook in which it constitutes the true people of God. However, if the community at large saw itself as actors in the salvific agency of God, who, then, were the target groups of the community? It was noted that other major Dead Sea documents show inclusivist tendencies, and this study of 1QHodayot[a] points in the same direction. Surely, 1QHodayot[a] would have served edificatory purposes within the community, but the emphasis on a corporate elite ethos and the corresponding leadership responsibilities also suggest an interest in reaching out beyond its confines to other potential members of the true covenantal people.

In conclusion, regardless of whether the Dead Sea community had an institutionalized leadership in every phase of its existence, whether in the form of a Teacher of Righteousness or a leadership group, 1QHodayot^a is hardly the right place for studying this leadership and its relationship to other members of the community. Rather, it is a document that shows more general aspects of the community's identity at large. It shows a community that saw itself as an instrument of God's will and as keepers, not only exclusive owners, of his covenant.

BIBLIOGRAPHY

TEXT EDITIONS AND REFERENCE WORKS

Abegg, Martin G., James E. Bowley, and Edward M. Cook. *The Dead Sea Scrolls Concordance. Volume One. The Non-biblical Texts from Qumran.* Vols 1–2. Leiden: Brill, 2003.

Alexander, Philip S., and Géza Vermès. *Qumran Cave 4.XIX: Serekh Ha-Yaḥad and Two Related Texts.* DJD XXVI. Oxford: Clarendon, 1998.

Baillet, Maurice. *Qumrân grotte 4.III (4Q482–4Q520).* DJD VII. Oxford: Clarendon, 1982.

Charlesworth, James H. *The Odes of Solomon.* Chico, CA: Scholars Press 1977.

———. *The Old Testament Pseudepigrapha.* 2 vols. New York: Doubleday, 1983–1985.

Clines, David J. A., ed. *The Dictionary of Classical Hebrew.* 5 vols. Sheffield: Sheffield Academic Press, 1993–2001.

Elliger, Karl, and Wilhelm Rudolph, eds. *Biblia Hebraica Stuttgartensia.* Editio quinta emendata. Stuttgart: Deutsche Bibelgesellschaft, 1997.

Eshel, Esther. "4QSelf-Glorification Hymn (=4QHᵉ frg. 1?)." Pages 421–32 in *Qumran Cave 4.XX: Poetical and Liturgical Texts. Part 2.* DJD XXIX. Edited by Esther Chazon et al. Oxford: Clarendon, 1999.

Funk, Franz X., ed. *Didascalia et Constitutiones.* Paederborne: Libraria Ferdinandi Schoeningh, 1905.

García Martínez, Florentino, and Eibert J. C. Tigchelaar, eds. *The Dead Sea Scrolls Study Edition.* 2 vols. Leiden: Brill, 1997–1998.

Gesenius, H. W. F. *Gesenius' Hebrew-Chaldee Lexicon to the Old Testament.* Translated by Samuel Prideaux Tregelles. Grand Rapids: Baker Book House, 1979.

———. *Gesenius' Hebrew Grammar*. Edited and enlarged by E. Kautzsch. Translated and revised by A. E. Cowley. 2nd ed. Oxford: Clarendon, 1910.

Hallbäck, Geert, and Hans Jørgen Lundager Jensen. *Gads Bibel Leksikon*. 2nd ed. 2 vols. København: Gads Forlag, 1998.

Joüon, Paul. *A Grammar of Biblical Hebrew*. Translated and revised by T. Muraoka. 2 vols. Roma: Entrice Pontificio Instituto Biblico, 1991.

Koehler, Ludwig, and Walter Baumgartner. *The Hebrew and Aramaic Lexicon of the Old Testament*. Revised by W. Baumgartner and J. J. Stamm. 5 vols. Leiden: Brill, 1994–2000.

Lim, Timothy H., and Philip S. Alexander, eds. *The Dead Sea Scrolls Electronic Reference Library*. Oxford: Oxford University Press, 1997.

Lisowsky, Gerhard. *Konkordanz zum Hebräischen Alten Testament*. Dritte verbesserte Auflage. Stuttgart: Deutsche Bibelgesellschaft, 1993.

Merwe, Christo H. J. van der, Jackie A. Naudé and Jan H. Kroeze. *A Biblical Hebrew Reference Grammar*. Sheffield: Sheffield Academic Press, 1999. Repr. 2004.

Newsom, Carol A. *Songs of the Sabbath Sacrifice: A Critical Edition*. Atlanta: Scholars Press, 1985.

Parry, Donald W., and Emanuel Tov, eds. *The Dead Sea Scrolls Reader*. 6 vols. Leiden: Brill, 2004–2005.

Qimron, Elisha. *A Grammar of the Hebrew Language of the Dead Sea Scrolls* [Hebrew]. Jerusalem: Hebrew University, 1976.

———. *The Hebrew of the Dead Sea Scrolls*. Atlanta: Scholars Press, 1986.

Qimron, Elisha, and James H. Charlesworth. "Rule of the Community (1QS)." Pages 1–51 in *Rule of the Community and Related Documents*. Vol. 1 of *The Dead Sea Scrolls: Hebrew, Aramaic, and Greek Texts with English Translations*. Edited by James H. Charlesworth with F. M. Cross, J. Milgrom, E. Qimron, L. H. Schiffman, L. T. Stuckenbruck, and R. E. Whitaker. Louisville: Westminster John Knox, 1994.

Schiffman, Lawrence H., and James C. VanderKam. *Encyclopedia of the Dead Sea Scrolls*. Oxford: Oxford University Press, 2000.

Schuller, Eileen. "Hodayot." Pages 69–254 in *Qumran Cave 4.XX: Poetical and Liturgical Texts. Part 2*. DJD XXIX. Edited by Esther Chazon et al. Oxford: Clarendon, 1999.

Schuller, Eileen, and Hartmut Stegemann. *Qumran Cave 1.III: 1QHodayot[a] with Incorporation of 1QHodayot[b] and 4QHodayot[a–f]*. DJD XL. Oxford: Clarendon, 2009.

Strugnell, John, and Daniel K. Harrington. *Qumran Cave 4.XXIV: Sapiential Texts. Part 2. 4QInstruction (Mûsār Le Mēvîn): 4Q415 ff.* DJD XXXIV. Oxford: Clarendon, 1999.

Sukenik, Eleazar L. אוצר המגילות הגנוזות שבידי האוניברסיטה העברית. Jerusalem: Magnes, 1954.

———. *The Dead Sea Scrolls of the Hebrew University.* Jerusalem: Magnes, 1955.

———. מגילות גנוזות. מתוך גניזה קדומה שנמצאה במדבר יהודה. Rev. and enl. ed. Jerusalem: Bialik Institute, 1950.

———. מגילות גנוזות. מתוך גניזה קדומה שנמצאה במדבר יהודה. Jerusalem: Bialik Institute, 1948.

Tov, Emanuel, Stephen J. Pfann, Stephen A. Reed, and Marilyn J. Lundberg, eds. *The Dead Sea Scrolls on Microfiche: A Comprehensive Facsimile Edition of the Texts from the Judean Desert.* Leiden: IDC, 1993.

Waltke, Bruce, and Michael O'Connor. *An Introduction to Biblical Hebrew Syntax.* Winona Lake, IN: Eisenbrauns, 1990.

Weingreen, Jacob. *A Practical Grammar for Classical Hebrew.* Oxford: Clarendon, 1959.

Wright, Robert B. *The Psalms of Solomon: A Critical Edition of the Greek Text.* New York: T&T Clark, 2007.

Secondary Literature

Abegg, Martin G. "4Q471: A Case of Mistaken Identity?" Pages 136–47 in *Pursuing the Text: Studies in Honor of Ben Zion Wacholder on the Occasion of his Seventieth Birthday.* Edited by J. Reeves and J. Kampen. Sheffield: Sheffield Academic Press, 1994.

———. "Who Ascends to Heaven? 4Q491, 4Q427, and the Teacher of Righteousness." Pages 61–73 in *Eschatology, Messianism, and the Dead Sea Scrolls.* Edited by Craig A. Evans and Peter W. Flint. Grand Rapids: Eerdmans, 1997.

Alexander, Jeffrey. "Cultural Pragmatics: social performance between ritual and strategy." Pages 29–90 in *Social Performance: Symbolic Action, Cultural Pragmatics, and Ritual.* Edited by Jeffrey C. Alexander, Bernhard Giesen, and Jason L. Mast. Cambridge: Cambridge University Press, 2006.

Angel, Joseph L. *Otherworldly and Eschatological Priesthood in the Dead Sea Scrolls.* Leiden: Brill, 2010.

Arnold, Russell. "Repentance and the Qumran Covenant Ceremony." Pages 159–75 in *The Development of Penitential Prayer in Second Temple Judaism*. Vol. 2 of *Seeking the Favor of God*. Edited by Mark J. Boda, Daniel K. Falk, and Rodney A. Werline. Atlanta: Society of Biblical Literature, 2007.

———. *The Social Role of Liturgy in the Religion of the Qumran Community*. Leiden: Brill, 2006.

Austin, John L. *How to Do Things with Words*. Oxford: Clarendon, 1962.

Baasten, Martin F. J. "Existential Clauses in Qumran Hebrew." Pages 1–11 in *Diggers at the Well: Proceedings of a Third International Symposium on the Hebrew of the Dead Sea Scrolls and Ben Sira*. Edited by T. Muraoka and J. F. Elwolde. Leiden: Brill, 2000.

———. "Nominal Clauses with Locative and Possessive Predicates in Qumran Hebrew." Pages 25–52 in *Sirach, Scrolls, and Sages. Proceedings of a Second International Symposium on the Hebrew of the Dead Sea Scrolls, Ben Sira, and the Mishnah, held at Leiden University, 15–17 December 1997*. Edited by T. Muraoka and J. F. Elwolde. Leiden: Brill, 1999.

Baumgarten, Joseph M. "Sacrifice and Worship among the Jewish Sectarians of the Dead Sea (Qumran) Scrolls." *HTR* 46 (1953): 141–59.

Bell, Catherine. *Ritual: Perspectives and Dimensions*. New York: Oxford University Press, 1997.

Bendavid, Abba. *Biblical Hebrew and Mishnaic Hebrew* [Hebrew]. 2 vols. Tel Aviv: Dvir, 1967.

Benveniste, Émile. *Problems in General Linguistics*. Translated by Mary Elizabeth Meek. Coral Gables, FL: University of Miami, 1971.

Berg, Shane A. "Religious Epistemologies in the Dead Sea Scrolls: The Heritage and Transformation of the Wisdom Tradition." Ph.D. diss., Yale University, 2008.

Berlin, Adele. *The Dynamics of Biblical Parallelism*. Bloomington: Indiana University Press, 1985.

Bernstein, Moshe. "Introductory Formulas for Citation and Re-Citation of Biblical Verses in the Qumran Pesharim: Observations on a Pesher Technique." *DSD* 1 (1994): 30–70.

Bitzer, Lloyd F. "The Rhetorical Situation." *Philosophy & Rhetoric* 1 (1968): 1–14.

Blenkinsopp, Joseph. *Opening the Sealed Book: Interpretations of the Book of Isaiah in Late Antiquity*. Cambridge: Eerdmans, 2006.

Blommaert, Jan. "Text and Context." Pages 182–200 in *Applied Linguistics Methods: A Reader*. Edited by Caroline Coffin, Theresa Lillis, and Kieran O'Halloran. London: Routledge, 2010.

Boda, Mark J., Daniel K. Falk, and Rodney A. Werline, eds. *Seeking the Favor of God*. 2 vols. Atlanta: Society of Biblical Literature, 2006-2007.

Brin, Gershon. *The Concept of Time in the Bible and the Dead Sea Scrolls*. Leiden: Brill, 2001.

Brooke, George J. "Aspects of the Theological Significance of Prayer and Worship in the Qumran Scrolls." Pages 35–54 in *Prayer and Poetry in the Dead Sea Scrolls and Related Literature: Essays in Honour of Eileen Schuller on the Occasion of her 65th Birthday*. Edited by Jeremy Penner, Ken M. Penner, and Cecilia Wassen. Leiden: Brill, 2011.

———. *Reading the Dead Sea Scrolls: Essays in Method*. Atlanta: Society of Biblical Literature, 2013.

Brownlee, William H. *The Dead Sea Manual of Discipline*. New Haven: ASOR, 1951.

———. "The Servant of the Lord in the Qumran Scrolls I." *BASOR* 132 (1953): 8–15.

———. "The Servant of the Lord in the Qumran Scrolls II." *BASOR* 135 (1954): 33–38.

Burke, Kenneth. *A Rhetoric of Motives*. Los Angeles: University of California Press, 1969.

Burns, Joshua E. "Practical Wisdom in 4QInstruction." *DSD* 11 (2004): 12–42.

Callaway, Philip R. *The History of the Qumran Community: An Investigation*. Sheffield: Sheffield University Press, 1988.

Carmignac, Jean. "Les citations de l'Ancien Testament, et spécialement des Poèmes du Serviteur, dans les Hymnes de Qumrân." *RevQ* 2 (1959–60): 357–94.

———. "Compléments au texte des Hymnes de Qumrân." *RevQ* 2 (1959–60): 267–76, 549–58.

———. *Les textes de Qumrân traduits et annotés*. Paris: Letouzey et Ané, 1961.

Cartledge, Tony W. *Vows in the Hebrew Bible and the Ancient Near East*. Sheffield: JSOT Press, 1992.

Chamberlain, John V. "Toward a Qumran Soteriology." *NovT* 3 (1959): 305–13.

Charlesworth, James H. "Jewish Hymns, Odes, and Prayers (ca. 167 B.C.E.–135 C.E.)." Pages 411–36 in *Early Judaism and its Modern*

Interpreters. Edited by Robert A. Kraft and George W. E. Nickelsburg. Philadelphia: Fortress Press, 1986.

———. "Odes of Solomon." Pages 725–34 in *The Old Testament Pseudepigrapha*. 2nd ed. Edited by James H. Charlesworth. New York: Doubleday, 1985.

Chazon, Esther. "Human and Angelic Prayer in Light of the Dead Sea Scrolls." Pages 35–47 in *Liturgical Perspectives: Prayer and Poetry in Light of the Dead Sea Scrolls. Proceedings of the Fifth International Symposium of the Orion Center for the Study of the Dead Sea Scrolls and Associated Literature, 19–23 January, 2000*. Edited by Esther G. Chazon. Leiden: Brill, 2003.

———. "Prayers from Qumran and their Historical Implications." *DSD* 1 (1994): 265–84.

———. "Tradition and Innovation in Sectarian Religious Poetry." Pages 55–67 in *Prayer and Poetry in the Dead Sea Scrolls and Related Literature: Essays in Honour of Eileen Schuller on the Occasion of Her Sixty-Fifth Birthday*. Edited by Jeremy Penner, Ken M. Penner, and Cecilia Wassen. Leiden: Brill, 2011.

Christiansen, Ellen J. "The Consciousness of Belonging to God's Covenant and What It Entails according to the Damascus Document and the Community Rule." Pages 69–97 in *Qumran between the Old and New Testaments*. Edited by Frederick H. Cryer and Thomas L. Thompson. Sheffield: Sheffield Academic Press, 1998.

Collins, John J. *The Apocalyptic Imagination: An Introduction to Jewish Apocalyptic Literature*. 2nd ed. Cambridge: Eerdmans, 1998.

———. "Prayer and the Meaning of Ritual in the Dead Sea Scrolls." Pages 69–85 in *Prayer and Poetry in the Dead Sea Scrolls and Related Literature: Essays in Honour of Eileen Schuller on the Occasion of her 65th Birthday*. Edited by Jeremy Penner, Ken M. Penner, and Cecilia Wassen. Leiden: Brill, 2011.

———. *The Scepter and the Star: The Messiahs of the Dead Sea Scrolls and Other Ancient Literature*. New York: Doubleday, 1995.

Collins, John J., and Devorah Dimant. "A Thrice-Told Hymn: A Response to Eileen Schuller." *JQR* 85 (1994): 151–55.

Dalgaard, Kasper. "A Priest for All Generations: An Investigation into the Use of the Melchizedek Figure from Genesis to the Cave of Treasures." Ph.D. diss., University of Copenhagen, 2013.

Davies, Philip. *Behind the Essenes: History and Ideology in the Dead Sea Scrolls*. Atlanta: Scholars Press, 1987.

Delcor, Mathias. *Les Hymnes de Qumrân (Hodayot): Texte hébreu, introduction, traduction, commentaire*. Paris: Letouzey et Ané, 1962.

Derrida, Jacques. *Writing and Difference*. London: Routledge & Kegan Paul, 1978.

Dijk, Teun A. van. *Discourse and Context: A Sociocognitive Approach*. Cambridge: Cambridge University Press, 2008.

———. *Macrostructures: An Interdisciplinary Study of Global Structures in Discourse, Interaction, and Cognition*. Hillsdale, NJ: Lawrence Earlbaum Associates, 1980.

———. *Society and Discourse: How Social Contexts Influence Text and Talk*. Cambridge: Cambridge University Press, 2008.

Dimant, Devorah. "Men as Angels: The Self-Image of the Qumran Community." Pages 93–103 in *Religion and Politics in the Ancient Near East*. Edited by Adele Berlin. Bethesda, MD: University of Maryland Press, 1996.

———. "The Qumran Manuscripts: Contents and Significance." Pages 23–58 in *Time to Prepare the Way in the Wilderness: Papers on the Qumran Scrolls by Fellows of the Institute for Advanced Studies of the Hebrew University, Jerusalem, 1989–1990*. Edited by Devorah Dimant and Lawrence H. Schiffman. Leiden: Brill, 1995.

Douglas, Michael C. "Power and Praise in the Hodayot: A Literary Critical Study of 1QH 9–18:14." Ph.D. diss., University of Chicago, 1998.

———. "The Teacher Hymn Hypothesis Revisited: New Data for an Old Crux." *DSD* 6 (1999): 239–66.

Dowty, David R. *Word Meaning and Montague Grammar*. Dordrecht: D. Reidel, 1979.

Driver, Samuel R. *A Treatise on the Use of the Tenses in Hebrew and Some Other Syntactical Questions*. 2nd ed. Oxford: Clarendon, 1881.

Dupont-Sommer, André. *Les écrits esséniens découverts près de la mer Morte*. Deuxième édition revue et augmentée. Paris: Payot, 1960.

———. *Le Livre des Hymnes découvert près de la mer Morte (1QH): Traduction intégrale avec introduction et notes*. Paris: Libraire d'Amérique et d'Orient Adrien-maisonneuve, 1957.

Duranti, Alessandro. *Linguistic Anthropology*. Cambridge: Cambridge University Press, 1997.

Eggins, Suzanne. *An Introduction to Systemic Functional Linguistics*. 2nd ed. London: Continuum, 2007.

Eissfeldt, Otto. *Einleitung in das Alte Testament*. 2nd ed. Tübingen: Mohr (Paul Siebeck), 1976.

Elgvin, Torleif. "The Mystery to Come: Early Essene Theology of Revelation." Pages 113–50 in *Qumran between the Old and New Testaments*. Edited by Frederick H. Cryer and Thomas L. Thompson. Sheffield: Sheffield Academic Press, 1998.

———. "The Yaḥad Is More Than Qumran." Pages 273–79 in *Enoch and Qumran Origins: New Light on a Forgotten Connection*. Edited by Gabriele Boccaccini. Grand Rapids: Eerdmans, 2005.

Elwolde, John. "The Hodayot's Use of the Psalter: Text-Critical Contributions (Book 1)." Pages 79–108 in *Psalms and Prayers: Papers Read at the Joint Meeting of the Society of Old Testament Study and Het Oudtestamentische Werkgezelschap in Nederland en België, Apeldoorn August 2006*. Edited by Bob Becking and Eric Peels. Leiden: Brill, 2007.

Eshel, Esther. "4Q471b: A Self-Glorification Hymn." *RevQ* 17 (1996): 175–203.

———. "The Identification of the 'Speaker' of the Self-Glorification Hymn." Pages 619–35 in *The Provo International Conference on the Dead Sea Scrolls: Technological Innovations, New Texts, and Reformulated Issues*. Edited by Donald W. Parry and Eugene Ulrich. Leiden: Brill, 1999.

Fairclough, Norman. *Analysing Discourse: Textual Analysis for Social Research*. New York: Routledge, 2003.

Falk, Daniel K. "The Contribution of the Qumran Scrolls to the Study of Ancient Jewish Liturgy." In *The Oxford Handbook of the Dead Sea Scrolls*. Edited by Timothy H. Lim and John J. Collins. Oxford: Oxford University Press, 2010. DOI: 10.1093/oxfordhb/9780199207237.003.0027.

———. *Daily, Sabbath, and Festival Prayers in the Dead Sea Scrolls*. Leiden: Brill, 1998.

———. "Qumran Prayer Texts and the Temple." Pages 106–26 in *Sapiential, Liturgical and Poetical Texts from Qumran. Proceedings of the Third Meeting of the International Organization for Qumran Studies Oslo 1998. Published in Memory of Maurice Baillet*. Edited by Daniel K. Falk, Florentino García Martínez, and Eileen M. Schuller. Leiden: Brill, 2000.

Fernández, James W. "Persuasions and Performances." *Daedalus* 101 (1972): 39–60.

Firth, John R. *Papers in Linguistics 1934–1951*. London: Oxford University Press, 1957.

Flesher, Paul. "Palestinian Synagogues before 70 C.E.: A Review of the Evidence." Pages 27–39 in vol. 1 of *Ancient Synagogues: Historical Analysis and Archaeological Discovery*. Edited by Dan Urman and Paul V. M. Flesher. 2 vols. Leiden: Brill, 1995.

Fletcher-Louis, Crispin H. T. *All the Glory of Adam: Liturgical Anthropology in the Dead Sea Scrolls*. Leiden: Brill, 2002.

Franzmann, Majella. *The Odes of Solomon: An Analysis of Poetical Structure and Form*. Freiburg: Universitätsverlag Freiburg, 1991.

French, Brigittine M. "The Semiotics of Collective Memories." *The Annual Review of Anthropology* 41 (2012): 337–53.

Frennesson, Björn. *"In a Common Rejoicing": Liturgical Communion with Angels at Qumran*. Uppsala: Acta Universitatis Upsaliensis, 1999.

García Martínez, Florentino. "Old Texts and Modern Mirages: The 'I' of Two Qumran Hymns." *ETL* 78 (2002): 321–39.

Genette, Gérard. *Paratexts: Tresholds of Interpretation*. Translated by Jane E. Lewin. Cambridge: Cambridge University Press, 1997.

Gerstenberger, Erhard S. *Psalms: Part 1: With an Introduction to Cultic Poetry*. Grand Rapids: Eerdmans, 1988.

Goff, Matthew J. "Reading Wisdom at Qumran: 4QInstruction and the Hodayot." *DSD* 11 (2004): 263–88.

Goody, Jack. *The Logic of Writing and the Organization of Society*. Cambridge: Cambridge University Press, 1986.

Gordley, Matthew E. *The Colossian Hymn in Context: An Exegesis in Light of Jewish and Greco-Roman Hymnic and Epistolary Conventions*. Tübingen: Mohr Siebeck, 2007.

Grabbe, Lester L. "Synagogues in Pre-70 Palestine: A Re-assessment." Pages 17–26 in vol. 1 of *Ancient Synagogues: Historical Analysis and Archaeological Discovery*. Edited by Dan Urman and Paul V. M. Flesher. 2 vols. Leiden: Brill, 1995.

Grossman, Maxine. "Priesthood as Authority." Pages 117–31 in *The Dead Sea Scrolls as Background to Postbiblical Judaism and Early Christianity*. Edited by James Davila. Leiden: Brill, 2001.

Halliday, Michael A. K. *An Introduction to Functional Grammar*. 3rd ed. Revised by Christian M. I. M. Matthiessen. London: Hodder Education, 2004.

———. *Halliday: System and Function in Language*. Edited by G. R. Kress. London: Oxford University Press, 1976.

Harkins, Angela Kim. "The Community Hymns Classification: A Proposal for Further Differentiation." *DSD* 15 (2008): 121–54.

———. "A New Proposal for Thinking about 1QHᵃ Sixty Years after its Discovery." Pages 101–34 in *Qumran Cave 1 Revisited: Texts from Cave 1*

Sixty Years after Their Discovery. Proceedings of the Sixth Meeting of the IOQS in Ljubljana. Edited by Sarianna Metso, Donald W. Parry, and Daniel K. Falk. Boston: Brill, 2010.

———. "Observations on the Editorial Shaping of the So-Called Community Hymns from 1QH[a] and 4QH[a] (4Q427)." *DSD* 12 (2005): 233–56.

Harrington, Daniel J. "Two Early Jewish Approaches to Wisdom: Sirach and Qumran Sapiential Work A." *JSP* 16 (1997): 25–38.

———. "Wisdom and Apocalyptic in 4QInstruction and 4 Ezra." Pages 343–55 in *Wisdom and Apocalypticism in the Dead Sea Scrolls and in Biblical Tradition.* Edited by F. García Martínez. Leuven: Leuven University Press, 2003.

Hasselbalch, Trine B. "En retorisk analyse af en Hodayot-salme fra Qumran: Hvorfor er der to salmister I 1QH[a] 12,5–13,4?" *DTT* 3 (2007): 240–59.

———. "Skriftbrug i Habakkukkommentaren: Den litterære konstruktion af Retfærdighedens Lærers autoritet." Pages 51–66 in *Skriftbrug, autoritet og pseudepigrafi.* Edited by Bodil Ejrnæs and Lone Fatum. København: Museum Tusculanum, 2010.

Hatav, Galia. *The Semantics of Aspect and Modality: Evidence from English and Biblical Hebrew.* Amsterdam: John Benjamins Publishing Company, 1997.

Hempel, Charlotte. *The Laws of the Damascus Document: Sources, Tradition and Redaction.* Leiden: Brill, 1998.

———. "Maskil(im) and Rabbim: From Daniel to Qumran." Pages 133–56 in *Biblical Traditions in Transmission: Essays in Honour of Michael A. Knibb.* Edited by Charlotte Hempel and Judith M. Lieu. Leiden: Brill, 2006.

Herzfeld, Michael. "National Spirit or the Breath of Nature? The Expropriation of Folk Positivism in the Discourse of Greek Nationalism." Pages 277–98 in *Natural Histories of Discourse.* Edited by Michael Silverstein and Greg Urban. Chicago: University of Chicago Press, 1996.

Himmelfarb, Martha. *Ascent to Heaven in Jewish and Christian Apocalypses.* Oxford: Oxford University Press, 1993.

Hodder, Ian. "The Interpretation of Documents and Material Culture." Pages 155–75 in *Collecting and Interpreting Qualitative Materials.* Edited by Norman K. Denzin and Yvonna S. Lincoln. 2nd ed. London: Sage Publications, 2003.

Holm-Nielsen, Svend. *Hodayot: Psalms from Qumran.* Århus: Universitetsforlaget i Aarhus, 1960.

———. "'Ich' in den Hodajoth und die Qumrangemeinde." Pages 217–29 in *Qumran-Probleme: Vorträge des Leipziger Symposions über Qumran-Probleme vom 9. bis 14. Oktober 1961.* Edited by Hans Bardtke. Berlin: Akademie-Verlag Berlin, 1963.

Holst, Søren. *Verbs and War Scroll. Studies in the Hebrew Verbal System and the Qumran War Scroll.* Uppsala: Uppsala Universitet, 2008.

Holtz, Gudrun. "Inclusivism at Qumran." *DSD* 16 (2009): 22–54.

Hopkins, Denise Dombrowski. "The Qumran Community and 1QHodayot: A Reassessment." *RevQ* 39 (1981): 323–64.

Hughes, Julie A. *Scriptural Allusions and Exegesis in the Hodayot.* Leiden: Brill, 2006.

Hunzinger, Claus-Hunno. "Fragmente einer älteren Fassung des Buches Milḥamā aus Höhle 4 von Qumrān." *ZAW* 69 (1957): 131–51.

Jassen, Alex P. *Mediating the Divine: Prophecy and Revelation in the Dead Sea Scrolls and Second Temple Judaism.* Leiden: Brill, 2007.

Jeremias, Gert. *Der Lehrer der Gerechtigkeit.* Göttingen: Vandenhoeck & Ruprecht, 1963.

Jokiranta, Jutta. "An Experiment on *Idem* Identity in the Qumran Movement." *DSD* 16 (2009): 309–29.

Kim, Angela Y. "Authorizing Interpretation in Poetic Compositions in the Dead Sea Scrolls and Later Jewish and Christian Traditions." *DSD* 10 (2003): 26–58.

———. "Signs of Editorial Shaping of the Hodayot Collection: A Redactional Analysis of 1QH^{a-b} and 4QH^{a-f}." Ph.D. diss., University of Notre Dame, 2003.

Kittel, Bonnie P. *The Hymns of Qumran.* Chico, CA: Scholars Press, 1981.

Klutz, Todd. *The Exorcism Stories in Luke-Acts: A Sociostylistic Reading.* Cambridge: Cambridge University Press, 2004.

Knibb, Michael. *The Qumran Community.* Cambridge: Cambridge University Press, 1987.

Knohl, Israel. "Between Voice and Silence: The Relationship between Prayer and Temple Cult." *JBL* 115 (1996): 17–30.

———. "The Suffering Servant: From Isaiah to the Dead Sea Scrolls." Pages 89–104 in *Scriptural Exegesis, the Shape of Cultures and the Religious Imagination: Essays in Honour of Michael Fishbane.* Edited by Deborah A. Greene and Laura S. Lieber. Oxford: Oxford University Press, 2009.

Kosmala, Hans. "Maśkîl." Pages 149–55 in *Studies, Essays and Reviews. Volume One: Old Testament.* Leiden: Brill, 1978.

Kress, G. R. Introduction to *Halliday: System and Function in Language*, by M. A. K. Halliday. Edited by G. R. Kress. London: Oxford University Press, 1976.

Kuhn, Heinz-Wolfgang. *Enderwartung und Gegenwärtiges Heil: Untersuchungen zu den Gemeindeliedern von Qumran mit einem Anhang über die Eschatologie und Gegenwart in der Verkündigung Jesu*. Göttingen: Vandenhoeck & Ruprecht, 1966.

Kutscher, Edward Y. *A History of the Hebrew Language*. Edited by Raphael Kutscher. Jerusalem: Magnes, 1982.

Lange, Armin. *Weisheit und Prädestination: Weisheitliche Urordnung und Prädestination in den Textfunden von Qumran*. Leiden: Brill, 1995.

Lawson, Thomas. "Cognition." Pages 307–19 in *Theorizing Rituals: Classical Topics, Theoretical Approaches, Analytical Concepts*. Edited by Jens Kreinath, Jan Snoek and Michael Stausberg. Leiden: Brill, 2006.

Leaney, Robert. *The Rule of Qumran and Its Meaning*. London: SCM Press, 1966.

Licht, Jacob. *The Thanksgiving Scroll* [Hebrew]. Jerusalem: Bialik Institute, 1957.

Lunn, Nicholas P. *Word-Order Variation in Biblical Hebrew Poetry: Differentiating Pragmatics and Poetics*. Milton Keynes: Paternoster, 2006.

MacDonald, Peter J. "Discourse Analysis and Biblical Interpretation." Pages 152–75 in *Linguistics and Biblical Hebrew*. Edited by Walter R. Bodine. Winona Lake, IN: Eisenbrauns, 1992.

Malinowski, Branislaw. "The Problem of Meaning in Primitive Languages." Pages 296–336 (Supplement I) in C. K. Ogden and I. A. Richards, *The Meaning of Meaning*. 8th ed. New York: Hartcourt Brace & World, 1946 (1923).

———. *The Language of Magic and Gardening*. Vol. 2 of *Coral Gardens and Their Magic: A Study of the Methods of Tilling the Soil and of Agricultural Rites in the Trobriand Islands*. London: Allen and Unwin, 1935.

Mansoor, Menahem. *The Thanksgiving Hymns: Translated and Annotated with an Introduction*. Leiden: Brill, 1961.

Martin, Jim. "Language, Register and Genre." Pages 12–32 in *Applied Linguistics Methods: A Reader*. Edited by Caroline Coffin, Theresa Lilis, and Kieran O'Halloran. London: Routledge, 2010.

———. "Process and Text: Two Aspects of Semiosis." Pages 248–74 in *Selected Theoretical Papers from the 9th International Systemic Workshop*. Vol. 1 of *Systemic Perspectives on Discourse*. Edited by James D. Benson and William S. Greaves. Norwood, NJ: Ablex, 1985.

Martin, Malachi. *The Scribal Character of the Dead Sea Scrolls*. 2 vols. Louvain: Publications Universitaires Institute Orientaliste, 1958.

Mauss, Marcel. *On Prayer*. Translated by S. Leslie and edited by W. S. F. Pickering. New York: Durkheim Press, 2003.

McCauley, Robert N., and Thomas Lawson. *Bringing Ritual to Mind: Psychological Foundations of Cultural Forms*. Cambridge: Cambridge University Press, 2002.

McCawley, James. *Everything that Linguists Have Always Wanted to Know about Logic but Were Ashamed to Ask*. Chicago: University of Chicago Press, 1981.

Merwe, Christo H. J. van der. "Some Recent Trends in Biblical Hebrew Linguistics: A Few Pointers Towards a More Comprehensive Model of Language Use." *HS* 44 (2003): 7–24.

Metso, Sarianna. *The Textual Development of the Qumran Community Rule*. Leiden: Brill, 1997.

Miller, Patrick D. *They Cried to the Lord: The Form and Theology of Biblical Prayer*. Minneapolis: Fortress Press, 1994.

Morawe, Günter. *Aufbau und Abgrenzung der Loblieder von Qumran*. Berlin: Evangelische Verlagsanstalt, 1961.

Muraoka, Takamitsu. "An Approach to the Morphosyntax and Syntax of Qumran Hebrew." Pages 193–214 in *Diggers at the Well: Proceedings of a Third International Symposium on the Hebrew of the Dead Sea Scrolls and Ben Sira*. Edited by T. Muraoka and J. F. Elwolde. Leiden: Brill, 2000.

Murphy-O'Connor, Jerome. "La genèse littéraire de la Règle de la Communauté." *RB* 76 (1969): 528–49.

Newman, Judith H. *Praying by the Book: The Scripturalization of Prayer in Second Temple Judaism*. Atlanta: Scholars Press, 1999.

Newsom, Carol A. "Kenneth Burke Meets the Teacher of Righteousness: Rhetorical Strategies in the Hodayot and the Serek Ha-Yahad." Pages 121–32 in *Of Scribes and Scrolls: Studies on the Hebrew Bible, Intertestamental Judaism, and Christian Origins Presented to John Strugnell on the Occasion of his Sixtieth Birthday*. Edited by Harold W. Attridge, John Collins and Thomas H. Tobin. London: The College Theology Society University Press of America, 1990.

———. "The Sage in the Literature of Qumran: The Functions of the Maśkîl." Pages 373–82 in *The Sage in Israel and the Ancient Near East*. Edited by John G. Gammie and Leo G. Perdue. Winona Lake, IN: Eisenbrauns, 1990.

———. *The Self as Symbolic Space: Constructing Identity and Community at Qumran*. Atlanta: Society of Biblical Literature, 2004.

Niccacci, Alviero. "Analysing Biblical Hebrew Poetry." *JSOT* 74 (1997): 77–93.

———. "A Neglected Point of Hebrew Syntax: Yiqtol and Position in the Sentence." *SBFLA* 37 (1987): 7–19.

Nickelsburg, George W. E. "The Nature and Function of Revelation in 1 Enoch, Jubilees, and some Qumranic Documents." Pages 91–119 in *Pseudepigraphic Perspectives: The Apocrypha and Pseudepigrapha in Light of the Dead Sea Scrolls; Proceedings of the International Symposium of the Orion Center for the Study of the Dead Sea Scrolls and Associated Literature, 12-14 January, 1997*. Edited by Esther G. Chazon and Michael Stone. Leiden: Brill, 1999.

Nielsen, Inge. "Synagogue (synagogé) and Prayerhouse (proseuché): The Relationship between Jewish Religious Architecture in Palestine and the Diaspora." *Hephaistos* 23 (2005): 63–111.

Nissen, Johannes. "Fadervor—håbet og bønnen om en ny verden." Pages 79–93 in *Teologiske studier og brugstekster: Festsskrift til Anne Marie Aagaard 14. januar 1985*. Edited by Hans Raun Iversen. Frederiksberg: Anis, 1985.

Nitzan, Bilhah. "The Idea of Holiness in Qumran Poetry and Liturgy." Pages 127–45 in *Sapiential, Liturgical and Poetical Texts from Qumran. Proceedings of the Third Meeting of the International Organization for Qumran Studies Oslo 1998. Published in Memory of Maurice Baillet*. Edited by Daniel K. Falk, Florentino García Martínez, and Eileen M. Schuller. Leiden: Brill, 2000.

———. *Qumran Prayer and Religious Poetry*. Translated from the Hebrew by Jonathan Chipman. Leiden: Brill, 1994.

O'Halloran, Kieran. *Critical Discourse Analysis and Language Cognition*. Edinburgh: Edinburgh University Press, 2003.

O'Neill, J. C. "'Who is Comparable to Me in My Glory?' 4Q491 Fragment 11 (4Q491c) and the New Testament." *NovT* 42 (2000): 24–38.

Palmer, F. R. *Mood and Modality*. 2nd ed. Cambridge: Cambridge University Press, 2001.

———. *Mood and Modality*. Cambridge: Cambridge University Press, 1998.

Patrick, Dale, and Kenneth Diable. "Persuading the One and Only God to Intervene." Pages 19–32 in *My Words are Lovely: Studies in the Rhetoric of the Psalms*. Edited by Robert L. Foster and David M. Howard. New York: T&T Clark, 2008.

Penner, Ken. "Verb Form Semantics in Qumran Hebrew Texts: Tense, Aspect, and Modality between the Bible and the Mishnah." Ph.D. diss., McMaster University, 2006.

Peursen, W. T. van. "Negation in the Hebrew of Ben Sira." Pages 223–43 in *Sirach, Scrolls, and Sages: Proceedings of a Second International Symposium on the Hebrew of the Dead Sea Scrolls, Ben Sira, and the Mishnah, held at Leiden University, 15–17 December, 1997*. Edited by T. Muraoka and J. F. Elwolde. Leiden: Brill, 1999.

Puech, Émile. "Une apocalypse messianique (4Q521)." *RevQ* 15 (1992): 475–522.

———. *Les données qumraniennes et classiques*. Vol. 2 of *La croyance des Esséniens en la vie future: Immortalité, resurrection, vie éternelle? Histoire d'une croyance dans le Judaïsme ancien*. Paris: Gabalda, 1993.

———. "Hodayot." Pages 365–69 in *Encyclopedia of the Dead Sea Scrolls*. Edited by Lawrence H. Schiffman and James C. VanderKam. 2 vols. Oxford: Oxford University Press, 2000.

———. "Quelques aspects de la restauration du rouleau des hymnes (1QH)." *JJS* 39 (1988): 38–55.

Rampton, Ben. "Linguistic Ethnography, Interactional Sociolinguistics and the Study of Identities." Pages 234–50 in *Applied Linguistics Methods: A Reader*. Edited by Caroline Coffin, Theresa Lilis, and Kieran O'Halloran. London: Routledge, 2010.

Reichenbach, Hans. *Elements of Symbolic Logic*. New York: Collier-Macmillan, 1947.

Reike, Bo. "Remarques sur l'histoire de la forme (Formgeschichte) des textes de Qumran." Pages 38–44 in *Les manuscrits de la mer Morte: Colloque de Strasbourg 25–27 Mai 1955*. Edited by Jean Daniélou. Paris: Paris University Press, 1955.

Richardson, Peter. "Early Synagogues as Collegia in the Diaspora and Palestine." Pages 90–109 in *Voluntary Associations in the Graeco-Roman World*. Edited by John S. Kloppenborg and Stephen G. Wilson. London: Routledge, 1996.

Ricoeur, Paul. "The Model of the Text: Meaningful Action Considered as Text." *Social Research* 38 (1971): 529–562.

———. *Oneself as Another*. Chicago: University of Chicago Press, 1992.

Rietz, Henry W. Morisada. "Identifying Compositions and Traditions of the Qumran Community: The Songs of the Sabbath Sacrifice as a Test

Case." Pages 29–52 in *Qumran Studies: New Approaches, New Questions*. Edited by Michael Thomas Davis and Brent A. Strawn. Cambridge: Eerdmans, 2007.

Schechner, Richard. Introduction to *The Anthropology of Performance*, by Victor Turner. New York: PAJ Publications, 1987.

Schiffman, Lawrence H. *Reclaiming the Dead Sea Scrolls: Their True Meaning for Judaism and Christianity*. New York: Doubleday, 1994.

Schofield, Alison. "Between Center and Periphery: The Yaḥad in Context." *DSD* 16 (2009): 330–50.

Schuller, Eileen. "The Cave 4 Hodayot Manuscripts: A Preliminary Description." *JQR* 85 (1994): 137–50.

———. "The Classification *Hodayot* and *Hodayot*-Like (with Particular Attention to 4Q433, 4Q433a and 4Q440). Pages 182–93 in *Sapiential, Liturgical and Poetical Texts from Qumran. Proceedings of the Third Meeting of the International Organization for Qumran Studies Oslo 1998. Published in Memory of Maurice Baillet*. Edited by Daniel K. Falk, Florentino García Martínez, and Eileen M. Schuller. Leiden: Brill, 2000.

———. "A Hymn from a Cave Four *Hodayot* Manuscript: 4Q427 7 i + ii." *JBL* 112 (1993): 605–28.

———. "Petitionary Prayer and the Religion of Qumran." Pages 29–45 in *Religion in the Dead Sea Scrolls*. Edited by John J. Collins and Robert A. Kugler. Grand Rapids: Eerdmans, 2000.

———. "Prayer, Hymnic, and Liturgical Texts from Qumran." Pages 153–71 in *The Community of the Renewed Covenant: The Notre Dame Symposium on the Dead Sea Scrolls*. Edited by Eugene Ulrich and James VanderKam. Notre Dame: University of Notre Dame Press, 1994.

Silverman, Kaja. *The Subject of Semiotics*. New York: Oxford University Press, 1983.

Silverstein, Michael, and Greg Urban, eds. *Natural Histories of Discourse*. Chicago: University of Chicago Press, 1996.

Slembrouck, Stef. "Discourse, Critique and Ethnography." Pages 251–66 in *Applied Linguistics Methods: A Reader*. Edited by Caroline Coffin, Theresa Lilis, and Kieran O'Halloran. London: Routledge, 2010.

Smith, Morton. "Ascent to the Heavens and Deification in 4QM^a." Pages 181–88 in *Archaeology and History in the Dead Sea Scrolls: The New York University Conference in Memory of Yigael Yadin*. Edited by Lawrence H. Schiffman. Sheffield: JSOT Press, 1990.

———. "Two Ascended to Heaven—Jesus and the Author of 4Q491." Pages 290–301 in *Jesus and the Dead Sea Scrolls.* Edited by James H. Charlesworth. New York: Doubleday, 1992.

Stegemann, Hartmut. *Die Entstehung der Qumrangemeinde.* Bonn, 1971.

———. "The Material Reconstruction of 1QHodayot." Pages 272–84 in *The Dead Sea Scrolls Fifty Years after Their Discovery: Proceedings of the Jerusalem Congress, July 20–25, 1997.* Edited by Lawrence H. Schiffman, Emanuel Tov, and James C. VanderKam. Jerusalem: Israel Exploration Society in cooperation with The Shrine of the Book, Israel Museum, 2000.

———. "The Number of Psalms in the 1QHodayot[a] and Some of Their Sections." Pages 191–234 in *Liturgical Perspectives: Prayer and Poetry in Light of the Dead Sea Scrolls; Proceedings of the Fifth International Symposium of the Orion Center for the Study of the Dead Sea Scrolls and Associated Literature, 19–23 January, 2000.* Edited by Esther G. Chazon. Leiden: Brill, 2003.

———. "The Qumran Essenes: Local Members of the Main Jewish Union in Late Second Temple Times." Pages 83–166 in vol. 1 of *The Madrid Qumran Congress: Proceedings of the International Congress on the Dead Sea Scrolls, Madrid, 18–21 March, 1991.* Edited by Julio Trebolle Barrera and Luis Vegas Montaner. Leiden: Brill, 1997.

———. "Some Remarks to 1QSa, to 1QSb, and to Qumran Messianism." *RevQ* 17 (1996): 479–505.

Steudel, Annette. "The Eternal Reign of the People of God—Collective Expectations in Qumran Texts (4Q246 and 1QM)." *RevQ* 17 (1996): 507–25.

Stroumsa, Guy G. *The End of Sacrifice: Religious Transformations in Late Antiquity.* Translated by Susan Emanuel. Chicago: University of Chicago Press, 2009.

Svendsen, Stefan Nordgaard. *Allegory Transformed.* Tübingen: Mohr Siebeck, 2009.

Talstra, Eep, and Carl J. Bosma. "Psalm 67: Blessing, Harvest and History; A Proposal for Exegetical Methodology." *CTJ* 36 (2001): 290–313.

Tanzer, Sarah. "The Sages at Qumran." Ph.D. diss., Harvard University, 1987.

Tatu, Silviu. *The Qatal//Yiqtol (Yiqtol//Qatal) Verbal Sequence in Semitic Couplets: A Case Study in Systemic Functional Grammar with Applications in the Hebrew Psalter and Ugaritic Poetry.* Piscataway, NJ: Gorgias Press, 2008.

Thomason, Richmond H. "Indeterminist Time and Truth-Value Gaps." *Theoria* 18 (1970): 264–81.

Tigchelaar, Eibert J. C. "The Addressees of 4QInstruction." Pages 62–75 in *Sapiential, Liturgical and Poetical Texts from Qumran: Proceedings of the Third Meeting of the International Organization for Qumran Studies, Oslo, 1998; Published in Memory of Maurice Baillet.* Edited by Daniel K. Falk, Florentino García Martínez, and Eileen M. Schuller. Leiden: Brill, 2000.

———. *To Increase Learning for the Understanding Ones: Reading and Reconstructing the Fragmentary Early Jewish Sapiential Text 4QInstruction.* Leiden: Brill, 2001.

Tukasi, Emmanuel O. *Determinism and Petitionary Prayer in John and the Rule of the Community: An Ideological Reading of John and the Rule of the Community (1QS).* London: T&T Clark International, 2008.

Vegas Montaner, Luis. "Some Features of the Hebrew Verbal Syntax in the Qumran Hodayot." Pages 273–86 in vol. 1 of *The Madrid Qumran Congress: Proceedings of the International Congress on the Dead Sea Scrolls, Madrid, 18–21 March, 1991.* Edited by Julio Trebolle Barrera and Luis Vegas Montaner. Leiden: Brill, 1997.

Vermes, Geza. *The Dead Sea Scrolls in English.* 4th ed. London: Penguin, 1995.

———. *The Dead Sea Scrolls: Qumran in Perspective.* London: Collins, 1977.

Wacholder, Ben Zion. *The New Damascus Document: The Midrash on the Eschatological Torah of the Dead Sea Scrolls; Reconstruction, Translation and Commentary.* Leiden: Brill, 2007.

Wassen, Cecilia, and Jutta Jokiranta. "Groups in Tension: Sectarianism in the Damascus Document and the Community Rule." Pages 205–45 in *Sectarianism in Early Judaism: Sociological Advances.* Edited by David J. Chalcraft. London: Equinox, 2007.

Weise, Manfred. *Kultzeiten und kultischer Bundesschluss in der "Ordensregel" vom Toten Meer.* Leiden: Brill, 1961.

Werline, Rodney A. "Defining Penitential Prayer." Pages xiii–xvii in *The Origins of Penitential Prayer in Second Temple Judaism.* Vol. 1 of *Seeking the Favor of God.* Edited by Mark J. Boda, Daniel K. Falk, and Rodney A. Werline. Atlanta: Society of Biblical Literature, 2006.

———. "Prayer, Politics, and Social Vision in Daniel 9." Pages 17–32 in *The Development of Penitential Prayer in Second Temple Judaism.* Vol. 2 of *Seeking the Favor of God.* Edited by Mark J. Boda, Daniel K. Falk, and Rodney A. Werline. Atlanta: Society of Biblical Literature, 2007.

Wernberg-Møller, P. *The Manual of Discipline: Translated and Annotated with an Introduction.* Leiden: Brill, 1957.

Whorf, Benjamin L. *Language, Thought and Reality: Selected Papers of Benjamin Lee Whorf.* Cambridge: Cambridge University Press, 1965.

Wieder, Naftali. *The Judaean Scrolls and Karaism.* London: Horowitz Publishing Co., 1962.

Wise, Michael O. "מי כמוני באלים: A Study of 4Q491c, 4Q471b, 4Q427 7 and 1QHᵃ 25:35–26:10." *DSD* 7 (2000): 173–219.

Wise, Michael O., Martin Abegg, and Edward Cook. *The Dead Sea Scrolls: A New Translation.* London: HarperCollins, 1996.

Ancient Sources Index

Modern Authors Index

Subject Index

CPSIA information can be obtained at www.ICGtesting.com
Printed in the USA
BVOW04s0645200315

392495BV00001B/4/P